5 —

The
Eclectic
Gourmet
Guide to
Chicago

Also available from MENASHA RIDGE PRESS

The Eclectic Gourmet Guide to Los Angeles,
   by Colleen Dunn Bates

The Eclectic Gourmet Guide to New Orleans,
   by Tom Fitzmorris

The Eclectic Gourmet Guide to San Francisco & the Bay Area,
   by Richard Sterling

The Eclectic Gourmet Guide to San Diego,
   by Stephen Silverman

The Eclectic Gourmet Guide to Washington, D.C.,
   by Eve Zibart

The Eclectic Gourmet Guide to Atlanta,
   by Jane Garvey

The Eclectic Gourmet Guide to Chicago

Camille Stagg

MENASHA
RIDGE
PRESS

Every effort has been made to ensure the accuracy of information throughout this book. Bear in mind, however, that prices, schedules, etc., are constantly changing. Readers should always verify information before making final plans.

Menasha Ridge Press, Inc.
P.O. Box 43059
Birmingham, Alabama 35243

Cover and text design by Suzanne Holt

Cover art by Michele Natale

ISBN 0-89732-247-9

Library of Congress Catalog Card Number: 98-5854

Manufactured in the United States of America

10 9 8 7 6 5 4 3 2 1

First Edition

CONTENTS

acknowledgments

A special thank you to the many people who assisted with the research and compilation of this book, including those who shared their restaurant experiences. Special thanks to the crack team of Medill School of Journalism students and recent graduates who assisted with gathering the current restaurant data for the first book edition: Meg McGinity, American and seafood restaurants; Greg Henkin, steak and German restaurants; Andrea Sachs, French and vegetarian restaurants; and Sarah Stirland, from Hong Kong, Asian cuisine and many others. Many thanks to Rummana Hussain, whose Indian heritage, knowledge of Middle Eastern cuisines, and journalistic skills were invaluable as she worked with me to the final deadline on both editions. Ritu Upadhyay also deserves thanks for her contribution to the book and for sharing information on Indian culture. A special note of gratitude to Lyle Sinrod Walter (M.S., Medill School of Journalism; certificate, L'Academie de Cuisine, Bethesda, Maryland), whose knowledge of cuisines, languages, and journalism helped immensely. Thanks also to Maya Norris of Hawaii, who put in long hours to help complete this second edition while earning her master's. And thanks to sophomore Jennifer Wielgus, who assisted with the final phase of this book.

Thanks to several for their help with the initial book: Joan Hersh, owner of A Matter of Course catering; Robert Rohden, president of Laser List Chicago, wine consultant, and computer consultant; John Davis, owner and president of several companies, including A Taste of California, the largest wine mail-order business in the United States; Lucia de la Cruz, a bilingual friend who lived in Spain, for Spanish vocabulary advice; Lowell B. Komie, for his counsel and dining reports;

Kay Komie and Ann Lee, for their Hyde Park restaurant recommendations; Mel Markon, former restaurateur, for his restaurant suggestions; Toshihiko Sawada, former director of the Japan National Tourist Organization, for sharing his expertise on his native cuisine; and Yong-Ku Hwang, director of the Korea National Tourist Organization, for his Korean restaurant suggestions.

And a very special thank you to my dining companions for both editions, including my mother, Jeanette Stagg, who instilled in me a love of food and cooking; Jim White, Dallas broadcaster and food lover, whose articulate critiques breathed life into the original project; Ed Jarratt, who is without food prejudices and is willing to try anything once—even czarnina; to B. C. Kent, whose knowledge of fish (and penchant for catfish) and fondness for desserts helped immeasurably; to Lyle Sinrod Walter, who assisted with communicating in Thai for that cuisine category; to Rummana Hussain and Maya Norris, for opinions of several places we tried; to Phyllis Magida, who accompanied me in sampling vegetarian food; and to Julie Youngs, a frequent diner-about-town who assisted in many ways, including sharing her various restaurant experiences; and to journalist Gary Moore, for sharing his Hispanic expertise regarding Mexican cuisine.

And gratitude to publisher Bob Sehlinger and his cheerful staff at Menasha Ridge Press, especially Associate Publisher Molly Burns, Editor Holly Brown, and Production Editor Caroline Carr, for their continuing support and teamwork.

About the Author

Camille Stagg is a food and travel writer and editor with more than 25 years of experience in the journalism and consulting profession. Her work for over 12 years as food editor for the *Chicago Sun-Times* won awards for excellence in food journalism. She was also food editor of *Cuisine* magazine, has appeared regularly on television and radio, and is the author of several books, including *The Unofficial Guide to Dining in Chicago* (Macmillan Travel) and the culinary troubleshooting reference, *The Best of The Cook's Advisor.* Her latest cookbook, *Cooking with Wine* (Time-Life), was released in August 1997. She appeared on leading television and radio shows during national media tours with her first best-selling book, *The Cook's Advisor.*

Ms. Stagg has directed a cooking school and continues teaching numerous seminars and classes. She develops recipes for "A Taste of California," a wine-of-the-month club (50,000 members), and conducts food and wine tastings with that organization. Her recipes appear in the second edition of *A Taste of California: Tenth Anniversary Cookbook,* which pairs dishes with varietal wines. Ms. Stagg has served as dining critic for the *Chicago Sun-Times, Pulitzer-Lerner Newspapers, Inside Chicago* magazine, *Talking to the Boss, Chicago Social,* and currently for *Copley Chicago Newspapers' Fox Valley Villages 60504.* Her travel assignments focusing on cuisine and culture have included Europe, Australia, North Africa, Hong Kong, Canada, the Caribbean, Mexico, and most of the United States. She holds a B.S. in food science and journalism from the University of Illinois and has studied cooking with experts in the United States and abroad.

GETTING IT RIGHT

A lot of thought went into this guide. While producing a dining guide may appear to be a straightforward endeavor, I can assure you that it is fraught with peril. I have read dining guides by authors who turn up their noses at anything except four-star French restaurants (of which there are a whole lot fewer than people think). Likewise, I have seen a guide that totally omits Thai and Indian restaurants—among others—because the author did not understand those cuisines. I have read guides absolutely devoid of criticism, written by "experts" unwilling to risk offending the source of their free meals. Finally, I've seen those books that are based on surveys and write-ins from diners whose credentials for evaluating fine dining are mysterious at best and questionable at least.

How, then, do you go about developing a truly excellent dining guide? What is the best way to get it right?

If dining guides are among the most idiosyncratic of reference books, it is primarily because the background, taste, integrity, and personal agenda of each author are problematical. The authors of most dining guides are vocational or avocational restaurant or food critics. Some of these critics are schooled professionals, with palates refined by years of practical experience and culinary study; others are journalists, often with no background in food criticism or cooking, who are arbitrarily assigned the job of reviewing restaurants by their newspaper or magazine publisher (although it *is* occasionally possible to find journalists who are also culinary professionals). The worst cases are the legions of self-proclaimed food critics who mooch their way from restaurant to restaurant, growing fat on free meals in exchange for writing glowing reviews.

Ignorance of ethnic cuisine or old assumptions about what makes for haute cuisine particularly plague authors in cities without much ethnic variety in restaurants, or authors who have been writing for years about the same old, white linen, expense-account tourist traps. Many years ago in Lexington, Kentucky, for example, there was only one Chinese restaurant in town and it was wildly successful—in spite of the fact that it was Chinese in name only. Its specialty dishes, which were essentially American vegetable casseroles smothered in corn starch, were happily gobbled up by loyal patrons who had never been exposed to real Chinese cooking. The food was not bad, but it was not Chinese either. Visitors from out of town, inquiring about a good local Chinese restaurant, were invariably directed to this place. As you would expect, they were routinely horrified by the fare.

And, while you might argue that American diners are more sophisticated and knowledgeable nowadays than at the time of the Lexington pavilion, the evidence suggests otherwise. In Las Vegas, for instance, a good restaurant town with a number of excellent Italian eateries, the local Olive Garden (a chain restaurant) is consistently voted the city's best Italian restaurant in a yearly newspaper poll. There is absolutely nothing wrong with the Las Vegas Olive Garden, but to suggest that it is the best Italian restaurant in the city is ludicrous. In point of fact, the annual survey says much more about the relative sophistication of Las Vegas diners than it does about the quality of local Italian restaurants.

But if you pick up a guide that reflects the views of many survey respondents, a *vox populi* or reader's choice compendium, that is exactly the problem. You are dependent on the average restaurant-goer's capacity to make sound, qualitative judgments—judgments almost always impaired by extraneous variables. How many times have you had a wonderful experience at a restaurant, only to be disappointed on a subsequent visit? Trying to reconcile the inconsistency, you recall that on your previous visit, you were in the company of someone particularly stimulating, and that perhaps you had enjoyed a couple of drinks before eating. What I am getting at is that our reflections on restaurant experiences are often colored by variables having little or nothing to do with the restaurant itself. And while I am given to the democratic process in theory, I have my doubts about depending entirely on survey forms that reflect such experiences.

There are more pragmatic arguments to be made about such eaters' guides as well. If you cannot control or properly qualify your survey respondents, you cannot ensure their independence, knowledge, or critical sensitivity. And, since literally anyone can participate in such surveys, the ratings can be easily slanted by those with vested interests. How many bogus responses would it take to dramatically upgrade a restaurant's rating in a survey-based, big-city dining guide? Forty or even fewer. Why? Because the publisher receives patron reports (survey responses, readers' calls) covering more restaurants than can be listed in the book. Thus the "voting" is distributed over such a large number of candidate restaurants that the median number of reports for the vast majority of establishments is 120 or fewer. A cunning restaurant proprietor who is willing to stuff the ballot box, therefore, could easily improve his own rating—or lower that of a competitor.

So my mission in the *Eclectic Gourmet Guides* is to provide you with the most meaningful, useful, and accessible restaurant evaluations possible. Weighing the alternatives, I have elected to work with culinary experts, augmenting their opinions with a carefully qualified survey population of totally independent local diners of demonstrated culinary sophistication. The experts I have sought to author the *Eclectic Gourmet Guides* are knowledgeable, seasoned professionals; they have studied around the world and written cookbooks or columns, and they closely follow the development of restaurants in their cities. They are well versed in ethnic dining, many having studied cuisines in their native lands. And they have no prejudice about high or low cuisine. They are as at home in a Tupelo, Mississippi, catfish shack as in an exclusive French restaurant on New York's Upper East Side. Thus the name *Eclectic Gourmet*.

Equally important, I have sought experts who make every effort to conduct their reviews anonymously, and who always pay full menu prices for their meals. We are credible not only because we are knowledgeable, but also because we are independent.

You, the reader of this *Eclectic Gourmet Guide,* are the inspiration for and, we hope, the beneficiary of our diligence and methodology. Though we cannot evaluate your credentials as a restaurant critic, your opinion as a consumer—of this guide and the restaurants within—is very important to us. Please tell us about your dining experiences and let us know whether you agree with our reviews.

Eat well. Be happy.

Bob Sehlinger

dining in chicago

Chicago, in my opinion, is the dining mecca of the United States—certainly in terms of ethnic diversity. It's no longer the "Second City." Even a well-known New York critic wrote several years ago that Chicago was the most exciting city for dining. Most experts agree that it is one of the best places for cuisine quality and variety. New York, still deemed number one by many, excels in many ethnic cuisines as well. However, dining in Chicago is less of a hassle—not as crowded and certainly less costly. This heartland city has not only caught up, but has surpassed most other key cities in the dining arena.

O'Hare International Airport, the busiest airport in the world, provides a port of entry for the best fresh seafood and other products to be flown in regularly from around the globe. In fact, Chicago has a wider assortment of fresh seafood than many coastal cities, although it's in the Midwest. And because Chicago is a key convention town, it features many restaurants and hotels for diners demanding the best quality.

At last count, Chicago had just under 6,000 restaurants in the city, and about 2,000 of those hold liquor licenses. Including Chicago, Cook County boasts approximately 9,000 food service establishments, according to the Illinois Restaurant Association. No one can give an exact count of restaurants in this vast suburbia. To select just 215 or so of the best of these was no easy task. The restaurants profiled reflect a balance of cuisines, styles, geographic locations, price, and the popular as well as the hidden gems. Numerous fine restaurants are not included here, but that doesn't mean they are unworthy. Some are quite new and need a chance to settle in; others were in the process of change at press time; some will be covered in subsequent editions of this book.

4

bURGEONING NEIGHboRHOODS

Particularly hot neighborhoods for new restaurants include the following:

River North, with its art galleries and antique shops, is home to **Michael Jordan's Restaurant, Brasserie Jo,** and **Wildfire.**

The gentrified diagonal Near North Clybourn Corridor: **Goose Island Brewing** (1800 North Clybourn Avenue; (312) 915-0071) makes great seasonal beers and serves appropriate fare.

The booming United Center neighborhood—Madison from the stadium to Halsted Street: the new **Madison's,** an Italian steakhouse (1330 West Madison Street; (312) 455-0099), has good seafood and a comprehensive wine list. **Flat Top Grill** (American stir-fry, (312) 829-4800) allows diners to create their own stir-fry meals.

Navy Pier's grand opening was July 1995; **Riva's** (Seafood/Steak/Pasta, (312) 644-RIVA) and **Widow Newton's Tavern** (American, (312) 595-5500) are two anchor restaurants there, and several others offer a variety of food choices. **Joe's Be-Bop Cafe & Jazz Emporium** (Barbecue, (312) 595-5299), operated by Wayne Segal (who operates Jazz Showcase), has a bandstand and a menu featuring barbecue-style foods.

Randolph Market: **Vivo** (Italian, (312) 733-3379), **Marché** (French/American brasserie, (312) 226-8399), and the latest by same owners, **Red Light** (Pan-Asian—especially Chinese and Thai with Malaysian and Vietnamese elements, (312) 733-8880), provide a good dining mix. Newcomers include **Bluepoint** (oysters, seafood, and sushi, (312) 207-1222); **Millenium** (steak house, (312) 455-1400); and **Blackbird** (seasonal American with French inspiration, (312) 715-0708).

Wicker Park/Bucktown, one of the top three artist communities in the United States: One newcomer is **ConFusion** (1620 North Damen Avenue; (773) 772-7100), serving fusion cuisine; lovely outdoor garden. One of the co-owner chefs at ConFusion opened **Feast** (1835 West North Avenue; (773) 235-6361), a neighborhood restaurant with a lush garden, serving global cuisine. And the latest addition is **Cafe Matou** (1846–48 North Milwaukee Avenue; (773) 384-8911), serving traditional French cuisine in a casual setting.

Halsted Street, which was called First Street in earlier times, continues to be "restaurant row," with many good dining spots on the same block, especially north from North Avenue. Printer's Row in the south downtown area developed several years ago and seems well anchored with some stable restaurants. Some restaurants recently opened in Chinatown, and several years ago Greektown got a few new faces. The "Little Saigon" or

"New Asia" area at North Argyle Street and Sheridan Road is home to a few good storefront restaurants and ethnic shops. And West Devon Avenue has several special street signs designating its diverse ethnicity. Some of the best Indian restaurants are found from 2300–2600 West Devon Avenue, and new ones keep popping up.

There are great Italian shops and restaurants along the middle section of North Harlem Avenue, in the Norridge area.

The southwest suburban area has developed so much in the past several years that it is called a "boom town." New additions duplicating city restaurants in Naperville in that area are **La Sorella de Francesca, Rosebud,** and **Mongolian Barbecue.** The southwest area is considered to be the fastest-growing community in the United States.

Except for the bastions of old Italian neighborhoods such as the Heart of Italy (near Midway Airport—see profiles of **Bruna's** and **Alfo's**) and Taylor Street (see profiles of **Tuscany** and **Tufano's**), and several fine restaurants here and there, the South Side is sparse as a dining zone (Zone 7). **Chesden's,** 4465 South Archer, dates back to the mid-1940s and serves good, straightforward Italian fare. The Hyde Park area around the University of Chicago, however, is an enclave of some nice restaurants, including **Piccolo Mondo,** 1642 East 56th Street (phone (773) 643-1106); **Lulu's** (offshoot of Lulu's in Evanston; see profile), 1333 East 57th Street (phone (773) 288-2988); **Pizza Capri** (a branch of the one in Lincoln Park) 1501 East 53rd Street (phone (773) 324-7777); **Thai 55th,** 1607 East 55th Street (phone (773) 363-7119); **Medici's on 57th** (famous coffeehouse), 1327 East 57th Street (phone (773) 667-7394); and **Valois Restaurant,** a popular cafeteria at 1518 East 53rd Street (phone (773) 667-0647).

Much new restaurant activity has recently occurred in the north and northwest suburbs, too. Highwood (in the North Shore), anchored by generations-old Italian establishments, has diversified (**Carlos'** in adjacent Highland Park, **Gabriel's, Froggy's, Del Rio,** and **Pappagallo's**) and now supposedly boasts more restaurants per capita than almost any other suburb in the country.

The Rosemont area near O'Hare offers a good assortment of restaurants because many conventions and business meetings are held there. The Westin Hotel O'Hare (6100 North River Road; (847) 698-6000) has two good restaurants: **The Benchmark** (bistro-style atmosphere with French influence in dishes) and **The Bakery Cafe** (American cuisine, casual). The Hotel Sofitel (5550 North River Road; (847) 678-4488) also has two restaurants: **Chez Colette** (charming French brasserie with a fireplace) and the fine dining **Le Cafe de Paris** (which offers a unique très-French menu with waiter and maître d' speaking only French on Thursday and Friday evenings; reservations requested, (847) 928-6950). For other noteworthy restaurants in this area, see profiles of **Carlucci** (Rosemont) and **Pazzo's Cucina Italiana.**

Connoisseurs with cars seeking unusual places with exceptional wine lists will not mind the 30- or 45-minute trips to **1776** in Crystal Lake (take Northwest Tollway to Randall Exchange; (815) 356-1776) for unusual regional American food, including midwestern (plenty of game). Also worth the drive are **Courtwright's** in Willow Springs, **302 West** in Geneva, and **Bistro Banlieue** in Lombard (see profiles). **D & J Bistro** (phone (847) 438-8001) in Lake Zurich serves mostly French fare. And certainly the well-established **Le Vichyssois** in Lakemoor, **Montparnasse** in Naperville, **Carlos'** in Highland Park, and **Le Titi de Paris** in Arlington Heights are four of the best suburban French restaurants (see profiles). **Tallgrass** in Lockport is a great destination for New French cuisine (two prix fixe menus; see profile).

Downtown Chicago amazingly continues to build and develop areas such as Cityfront, Navy Pier, the River East Plaza, and the planned East River area. The relocated **The Palm,** now in the Swissôtel Chicago hotel, has one of the best views of the new golf course (to the east) and of Navy Pier.

hotel dining

Hotel dining is better than ever; executive chefs allot large budgets for the best ingredients and can concentrate on their kitchens, unlike the owner-chefs running independent places. Also, since hotels must attract a local clientele to survive and competition is fierce, they've really improved their dining act in the past several years. Hotel dining has become a destination, and it's often complemented by live music in a nearby lounge. Many hotels have made their restaurants more casual and lower priced.

Examples of luxury hotels with top-notch dining options are The Ritz-Carlton (see profiles of **The Dining Room** and **The Cafe**), Four Seasons Hotel (see profile of **Seasons**), The Drake Hotel (see profile of **Cape Cod Room**), The Fairmont Hotel at Grant Park (see profile of **Entre Nous**), and Westin Hotel River North (formerly Nikko) on the Chicago River (**Celebrity Cafe** has a nice Sunday brunch, and there's a

7

new **Hana Lounge Sushi Hut**). Swissôtel Chicago (phone (312) 565-0565) has a charming **Konditorei** (bakery), **Cafe Suisse** (serving daily buffet breakfasts and lunches), and **Palm Restaurant** (see profile). I also recommend cuisine at the Omni Ambassador East (see profile of **Pump Room**) and the Hyatt on Printer's Row (see profile of **Prairie**). The Hotel Inter-Continental (phone (312) 944-4100) features the award-winning **Boulevard Restaurant** and the casual **Cafe 525**. The Westin Hotel recently underwent a $6.5 million renovation and enlarged and combined the previous restaurant and bar into **The Chelsea Restaurant and Bar,** an American bistro with innovative American cuisine.

Other noteworthy hotel dining: The Regal Knickerbocker Hotel's new **Nix** (a restaurant serving fusion cuisine—here Asian/American with some southwestern influences); Sutton Place Hotel (see profile of **Brasserie Bellevue**); Midland Hotel (the **Exchange Restaurant,** fine dining; the **Ticker Tape Bar & Bistro**); the Palmer House Hilton (**French Quarter** and **Big Downtown Chicago**); Chicago Hilton and Towers (see profile of **Kitty O'Shea's**); Chicago Marriott Downtown (**Allie's Bakery** and JW's are being merged into a new bistro interior); Sheraton Chicago Hotel and Towers (**Streeterville**); The Tremont Hotel (**Iron Mike's Grille**), and across the street, the Whitehall Hotel (**Whitehall Place Restaurant**—a bistro with multicultural cuisine and a nice Sunday brunch). And this list is not comprehensive!

cElEbRiTy RESTAURANTS

This is a big sports city, so naturally a few athletes, coaches, and announcers own restaurants. Some, like Ditka's (which was overpriced) and Red Kerr's (which was good), have closed. Others, such as **Harry Caray's** and **Michael Jordan's,** offer good food and service (see profiles). Former Bears Coach Mike Ditka (now in New Orleans) just combined forces with restaurateur Joe Carlucci and opened **Iron Mike's Grille** in The Tremont Hotel (see profile). There are numerous restaurant hangouts around the ballparks, and some of the food service within the parks is noteworthy. Food service at both Comiskey Park, home of the Chicago White Sox, and Wrigley Field, home of the Chicago Cubs, is managed by Levy Restaurants and is excellent. Entertainment celebrities, political figures, and other VIPs have their favored haunts as well, and many are included in this guide. **The Pump Room, Cape Cod Room,** and **Spiaggia** are just three examples. A longtime standby is **Eli's, the Place for Steak** (see profiles).

NEW-AGE CUISINE

Food is more enlightened today—lighter, with flavoring coming from fresh herbs, spices, infused oils, vinaigrettes, and wines, and from healthful cooking methods like grilling, flat-top grilling, and roasting in wood-burning ovens. Sure, restaurant icons still offer some old-guard, flour-thickened sauces with cream and butter, but they are usually enjoyed only occasionally. Most day-to-day eating is geared to feeling fine, and that means lower fat (less meat and fried fare), higher carbohydrates (grains, veggies, and fruit), and less sodium and sugar. New-age cuisine leans in the direction of natural and organically grown foods, chemical-free ingredients, line-caught fish, and vegetarian fare. Chefs proudly promote vegetarian specialties and menus, and more businesspeople are ordering these items for lunch with mineral water instead of the steaks and martinis they downed years ago. However, history repeats itself, and we're seeing a comeback of steak places and martini bars, touting their special flavors and concoctions that sell for a whopping $6–9 a drink!

NEW-AGE DINING STYLE

There is a tendency for restaurant interiors to be casual and more homey these days, bringing some comfort and a nurturing environment to our dining-out experiences—much needed in our fast-paced, high-stress lives. Food at such places is appropriately simple and home-style.

Smoking recently has become a more important health and social issue, and in Chicago all restaurants must set aside a minimum of 30 percent of their active dining room for nonsmokers. Restaurants that wish to establish larger nonsmoking sections have the option of certifying a minimum of 50 percent of their space as nonsmoking. Once a minimum is decided upon, it must be maintained until the next license renewal. Establishments may also select to be 100 percent smoke-free, and several enlightened owners have banned smoke from their places. The designated nonsmoking area must be contiguous. Bars and meeting rooms for private functions are exempt. Sign postings with specific wording designated by the city are required.

The cigar craze was launched by a cigar magazine and backed by the tobacco industry, and many restaurants, seeking to please all customers, have beckoned to gimmicky "cigar dinners" and cigar lounges.

Stir-fry and flat-top grill places are a rage spreading quickly in both the city and suburbs. The magical formula tends to be as follows: First, the customer selects preferences from a vast raw buffet of vegetables, meats, poultry, seafood, and sauces, and combines them in a bowl. Second, the contents of the coded bowl are cooked by the staff for all to watch, and within minutes the dish is ready to eat. Some aspects of the process may vary with the restaurant (the combination of self-serve and service, the number of helpings, etc.), but the concept is the same. The food is fresh, tends to be healthful, and is served quickly.

Cuisines that are hot:

Spanish cuisine made a splash here in the years following 1992, the year commemorating the 500th anniversary of the discovery of America, the Barcelona Summer Olympics, and Expo '92 in Seville. Spain's tapas and the sampling or "tasting" style has spread from the host cuisine to others, so we now see American and eclectic tapas.

Pan-Asian restaurants, especially noodle shops, are growing. Fusion cuisine, often East-West of some sort, is adopted by many chefs today, and restaurants like **Nix** in the Regal Knickerbocker Hotel and **ConFusion** in Wicker Park are devoted to it.

Mediterranean and Italian cuisines continue to be popular. Recently more French bistros and brasseries and Louisiana and South American places have appeared. Two completely new cuisines just opened on North Sheridan Road, just south of L'Olive. One is **Tibet Cafe,** and next to that is a Nigerian place called **Suya African Grill.**

We've seen a glut of bagel shops, and it undoubtedly will come down to the survival of the fittest. And after all our new coffee houses, some predict that soon we will see more tea cafés and houses.

In the heartland, chefs take pride in seeking out small, quality purveyors and changing their menus to utilize the freshest of seasonal ingredients. Wine lists have improved dramatically, and many have become user friendly. Restaurants are giving customers more options, and many offer half-portions when possible. Some places even offer half-glasses of wine so people can do more tastings. More wine bars have sprung up and more restaurants are adding "wine bar" to their name. One example is **Cyrano's Bistrot & Wine Bar** (see profile).

TOURIST plACES

There are many places that tourists, for one reason or another, have heard about and want to try. Some, like The Pump Room, Michael Jordan's Restaurant, and Iron Mike's Grille are excellent or very good. Others are less so, and many are overpriced. Some of the following may offer good food and unique atmosphere, but overall they do not merit full profiles:

Dick's Last Resort
435 East Illinois Street

This River East Plaza spot attracts tourists who shop in the building and see the riverfront. It's fine for simple American fare and music (especially for young groups), but not as a dining destination.

Ed Debevic's Short Order Deluxe
640 North Wells Street

Typical American diner food in a fun atmosphere.

Gene & Georgetti
500 North Franklin Street

Considered by many steak-lovers to be a great place, but inconsistent food and service, crowded conditions, and dated decor prevent a recommendation.

Greek Islands Restaurant
200 South Halsted Street

A popular, large Greektown favorite that is attractive and serves decent Greek food. Unfortunately, much of it is kept on a steam table. Several other nearby restaurants are profiled in this guide.

The Hard Rock Cafe
63 West Ontario Street

Good American/ethnic food and glitzy presentations; decibel level has been lowered to a comfortable level.

Planet Hollywood
633 North Wells Street

Flashy decor and mediocre American fare.

Three Happiness
2130 South Wentworth Avenue, Chinatown

Bustling, popular Cantonese and dim sum place; good, authentic food, if you don't mind crowds. Reservations accepted weekdays.

NEW ANd CHANGING PLACES

Here are just a few of the new places that opened or changed in the past 18 months or so. They show great promise for future editions:

Restaurant	Cuisine
A La Turka	Turkish
Bistrot Zinc/Café Zinc	French
Blackbird	Seasonal American with French inspiration
Bluepoint	Oyster bar/seafood/sushi bar
Bricks	Pizza and beer
Brown Dog Tavern	Contemporary American, global touches
Buca Di Beppo	Italian, family style
Cafe Matou	Traditional French
The Capital Grille	New York–style steak house
Carpaccio (Palatine)	Italian
Cheesecake Factory (John Hancock Building)	Eclectic American
Churrasco's	South American
The Clubhouse (Oak Brook)	Contemporary American classics
CoCo Pazzo Cafe	Italian
ConFusion	Fusion
Crofton on Wells	Seasonal American
Cy's Steak & Chop House	Steak house
Foreign Affairs (Claridge Hotel)	French-Japanese
Grapes	Mediterranean
Hacienda Tecalitlan	Mexican
Harvest on Huron	New American
Havana	Cuban
Hudson Club	Eclectic; extraordinary wine bar
Jaipur Palace	Authentic Royal Indian
Julie Mai's Le Bistro	French/Vietnamese
Madam B	Pacific Rim
M-Cafe (Museum of Contemporary Art)	Eclectic
Meritage	Pacific Northwest, Asian influences

12

Restaurant	Cuisine *(Continued)*
Millennium	Steak and seafood
Nick & Tony's	Home-style Italian (two locations)
Nix (Regal Knickerbocker Hotel)	Fusion
Palette's	American
Patrick and James' (Glencoe)	American with a French twist
Phoenix (Chinatown)	Chinese
Plentywood Restaurant (Bensenville)	American/midwestern
Pollo Rey (in Wrigleyville)	Mexican; quick, full-service
Provençe (in Winnetka)	Southern French
Quincy Grille on the River	Regional American
Red Rock Grill	Texan
Red Light (Randolph Market)	Pan-Asian
Rhapsody	Regional American with European influences
Rhumba	Brazilian
Rocco's Ristorante	Italian
The Shark Bar Restaurant	Southern
Southern Roots	Southern
Taza's	Marinated, grilled Amish chicken
Texas Star Fajita Bar	Texan
Tibet Cafe	Tibetan
Tomboy	Eclectic
Trattoria No. 10	Contemporary Italian classics
Triple Crown Seafood (Chinatown)	Cantonese/seafood
Vegetarian Garden (Chinatown)	Vegetarian Chinese
Voila!	Creative French brasserie
Wonton Club	Asian with sushi bar
Zealous (Elmhurst)	New American
Zinfandel	Contemporary regional American

◆ Best Bagels

Arnie's
1315 West Diversey Parkway   (773) 296-0745
1001 West North Avenue   (312) 944-0745

Bruegger's Bagel Bakery
711 Church Street, Evanston   (847) 475-1056
Bruegger's also has outlets in Chicago, Naperville, and Elmhurst.

Jacob Bros. Bagels
953 West Armitage Avenue   (773) 248-9606
50 East Chicago Avenue   (312) 664-0026
Call for other locations.

Einstein Bros. Bagels
44 East Walton (Gold Coast)   (312) 943-9888
949 West Diversey Parkway   (773) 935-9888
About 30 locations; bagels made on premises. Favorites include
    cinnamon-raisin, blueberry, spinach-herb, and sundried tomato.

The Great American Bagel Co.
(Various locations; for information call (630) 963-3393.)
617 Meachem Road, Elk Grove Village   (847) 539-0959
This fast-growing chain is a bagel-deli that serves sandwiches on 14
    different types of bagels with 15 different spreads.

Kaufman's Bagel and Delicatessen
4905 Dempster Street, Skokie   (847) 677-9880
Old-fashioned Jewish deli–style bagels.

Upper Crust Bagels
835 Waukegan Road (just north of Deerfield Road), Deerfield
    (847) 405-0805
Kettle-boiled, New York–style, hand-rolled bialys; specialty sand-
    wiches; flavored cream cheese; lox; smoked fish; and deli fare.

◆ Best Bakeries

Ambrosia Euro-American Patisserie
710 West Northwest Highway, Barrington   (847) 304-8278

Blind Faith Cafe and Bakery
525 Dempster Street, Evanston   (847) 328-6875
3300 North Lincoln Avenue   (773) 871-3820

Bread with Appeal

1009 West Armitage Avenue   (773) 244-2700

Excellent breads and baked items; also sandwiches, salads, soups, and
box lunches. Dine in or carry out; catering.

The Corner Bakery

516 North Clark Street   (312) 644-8100

Union Station, Adams Street Concourse, 210 South Canal Street
    (312) 441-0821

Water Tower Place, Mezzanine, 835 North Michigan Avenue
    (312) 335-3663

Sante Fe Building, 224 South Michigan Avenue (at Jackson Boulevard)
    (630) 431-7600

Oakbrook Center, Route 83 at 22nd Street, Oak Brook
    (630) 368-0505

1901 East Woodfield Road, Schaumburg   (847) 240-1111

Foodstuffs

2106 Central Avenue, Evanston   (847) 328-7704

338 Park Avenue, Glencoe   (847) 835-5105

Great Harvest Bread Co.

2120 Central Street, Evanston   (847) 866-8609

846 West Armitage Avenue   (773) 528-6211

Konditorei

Swissôtel Chicago, 323 East Wacker Drive   (312) 565-0565

St. Germain Restaurant/Bakery Cafe

1210 North State Parkway   (312) 266-9900

Swedish Bakery

5348 North Clark Street, Andersonville   (773) 561-8919

Swedish coffee cakes and other European pastries, cakes, and breads.

◆ Best Barbecue and Ribs

Bones

7110 North Lincoln Avenue, Lincolnwood   (847) 677-3350

Brother Jimmy's BBQ

2909 North Sheffield   (773) 528-0888

Northern- and southern-style and dry-rubbed. Live music in lounge.

Gayle Street Inn

4914 North Milwaukee Avenue   (773) 725-1300

Baby-back ribs.

Hecky's BBQ
1902 Green Bay Road, Evanston   (847) 492-1182
Rib tips and chicken wings.

Leon's Bar-B-Q
8259 South Cottage Grove Avenue   (773) 488-4556
1158 West 59th Street   (773) 778-7828
1640 East 79th Street   (773) 731-1454

Miller's Pub
134 South Wabash Avenue   (312) 645-5377

N. N. Smokehouse
1465–67 West Irving Park Road   (773) TNT-4700

Robinson's No. 1 Ribs
655 West Armitage Avenue   (312) 337-1399
Ribs and chicken.

Smoke Daddy
1804 West Division Street   (773) 772-MOJO
Specialties: Three kinds of ribs; ribs sampler and smoked sweet potato.
Live blues, jazz Monday–Saturday; live mambo Wednesday.

Twin Anchors Restaurant and Tavern
1655 North Sedgwick Street   (312) 266-1616
In business for over 60 years.

◆ Best Beer Lists

Big Bar
Hyatt Regency, 151 East Wacker Drive   (312) 565-1234

Cork & Carry
10614 South Western Avenue   (773) 445-2675
Seventy varieties, twelve on tap.

Goose Island Brewing Company
1800 North Clybourn Avenue   (312) 915-0071

Jameson's Tavern
118 South Clinton Street   (312) 876-0016

Joe Bailly's
10854 South Western Avenue   (773) 238-1313

Millrose Brewing Company
45 South Barrington Road, South Barrington   (847) 382-7673

Ranalli's
1925 North Lincoln Avenue   (312) 642-4700

Red Lion Pub

2446 North Lincoln Avenue   (773) 348-2695

One of the best selections of English beers.

Resi's Bierstube

2034 West Irving Park Road   (773) 472-1749

Perhaps the oldest beer garden in the city; 60 imports—6 on tap.

◆ Best Breakfasts

Ann Sather

929 West Belmont Avenue   (773) 348-2378

5207 North Clark Street, Andersonville   (773) 271-6677

2665 North Clark Street, Lincoln Park   (773) 327-9522

Army & Lou's

422 East 75th Street   (773) 483-3100

The Corner Bakery

516 North Clark Street   (312) 644-8100

Union Station, Adams Street Concourse, 210 South Canal Street
   (312) 441-0821

Water Tower Place, Mezzanine, 835 North Michigan Avenue
   (312) 335-3663

Sante Fe Building, 224 South Michigan Avenue (at Jackson Boulevard)
   (630) 431-7600

Oakbrook Center, Route 83 at 22nd Street, Oak Brook   (630) 368-0505

1901 East Woodfield Road, Schaumburg   (847) 240-1111

Egg Harbor Cafe

512 North Western Avenue, Lake Forest   (847) 295-3449

Elaine & Ina's

Ontario Center Building, 448 East Ontario Street   (312) 337-6700

Formerly Ina's Kitchen.

Heaven on Seven

111 North Wabash Avenue   (312) 263-6443

Iron Mike's Grille

100 East Chestnut   (312) 587-8989

Lou Mitchell's

565 West Jackson Boulevard   (312) 939-3111

Mrs. Park's Tavern

198 East Delaware Place   (312) 280-8882

The Pump Room

Omni Ambassador East Hotel, 1301 North State Parkway (312) 266-0360

Seasons Restaurant
Four Seasons Hotel, 120 East Delaware Place at Michigan Avenue
   (312) 280-8800, ext. 2134
3rd Coast
29 East Delaware Place   (312) 664-7225
1260 North Dearborn Street   (312) 649-0730
The Dearborn location is the original; open 24 hours.

◆ Best Brunches

Bistro 110
110 East Pearson Street   (312) 266-3110
New Orleans–style jazz brunch on Sunday.
Blue Mesa
1729 North Halsted Street   (312) 944-5990
New Mexican cuisine and Sunday brunch.
Celebrity Cafe
Westin Hotel River North, 320 North Dearborn Street
   (312) 744-1900
Sunday brunch.
Cité
Top of Lake Point Tower (world's tallest residential building),
70th floor, 505 North Lake Shore Drive   (312) 644-4050
Sunday champagne brunch.
The Dining Room
The Ritz-Carlton Chicago, 160 East Pearson Street   (312) 266-1000
Exquisite and extensive Sunday brunch.
Four Farthings Tavern & Grill
2060 North Cleveland Avenue   (773) 935-2060
Newly expanded Sunday buffet brunch.
Hong Min
221 West Cermak Road, Chinatown   (312) 842-5026
Saturday and Sunday brunch.
House of Blues
329 North Dearborn Street   (312) 527-2583
Sunday gospel brunch; seatings at 10 A.M., 12:15 P.M., and 2:30 P.M.
The Pump Room
Omni Ambassador East Hotel, 1301 North State Parkway
   (312) 266-0360
Sunday brunch.

Seasons Restaurant

Four Seasons Hotel, 120 East Delaware Place at Michigan Avenue
   (312) 280-8800

Sunday brunch.

The Signature Room at the Ninety-Fifth

John Hancock Center, 95th floor, 875 North Michigan Avenue
   (312) 787-9596

Elegant Sunday buffet champagne brunch with live music and an
   excellent panoramic city view.

◆ Best Burgers and Sandwiches

Bigsby's Bar & Grill

1750 North Clark Street   (312) 642-5200

Home of the Raging Bull Burger (blackened beef, Cajun spices,
   guacamole, Monterey Jack). A place to watch Bulls games.

Hackney's

1514 East Lake Avenue, Glenview   (847) 724-7171

1241 Harms Road, Glenview   (847) 724-5577

Known for burgers and fried onion loaf. Other suburban locations.
   Wheeling, LaGrange, and Lake Zurich.

John Barleycorn Memorial Pub, Inc.

658 West Belden Avenue   (773) 348-8899

Bar food, good burgers and sandwiches, salads; classical music and
   art slides. Nice garden.

Moody's

5910 North Broadway   (773) 275-2696

Muskie's

2870 North Lincoln Avenue   (773) 883-1633

963 West Belmont Avenue   (773) 477-1880

This place has a 50s theme and turns out good charburgers, charbroiled chicken, and vegetarian sandwiches.

◆ Best Coffees and Desserts

The Buzz Cup Coffee Shop

5750 Rogers Street   (773) 205-6196

Wide variety of coffees, smoothies and shakes, pastries, muffins,
   bagels, sandwiches, soups, and pizza; hot entree special daily.

Cafe Express

615 Dempster Street, Evanston   (847) 864-1868

Cafe Express South

500 Main Street, Evanston   (847) 328-7940

Jazz and Java

3428 South King Drive   (312) 791-1300

Live jazz Friday and Saturday; offers soups, sandwiches, and salads.

Jillian's Coffe House & Bistro

674 West Diversey Parkway   (773) 529-7012

Soups, quiches, salads, sandwiches, desserts, wine, beer, and coffee drinks.

Lutz's Continental Cafe and Pastry Shop

2458 West Montrose Avenue   (773) 478-7785

St. Germain Restaurant/Bakery Cafe

1210 North State Parkway   (312) 266-9900

The Vanilla Bean Bakery

301 South Happ Road, Northfield   (847) 446-5444

Pastry chef Gale Gand started this quaint, cozy bakery next to
    Brasserie T, which she and her husband, chef Rick Tramonto,
    own. The Vanilla Bean Bakery produces breads and desserts for
    their restaurant and has a retail shop with a variety of pastries.
    They also offer specialty coffee drinks and their own root beer.

◆ Best Cornbread

Bazzell's French Quarter Bistro

215 West North Avenue   (312) 787-1131

Moist, slightly crusty; cornbread mix is sold at the restaurant and
    Treasure Island food stores throughout Chicago.

Bandera

535 North Michigan Avenue   (312) 644-FLAG

Made in an iron skillet.

Pollo Rey

3545 North Clark Street   (773) 325-2500

Slightly sweet cornbread muffin.

Redfish and The Voodoo Lounge

400 North State Street   (312) 467-1600

Moist inside, crusty outside.

◆ Best Delis

Bagel Restaurant and Deli
3107 North Broadway   (773) 477-0300
50 Old Orchard Shopping Center, Skokie   (847) 677-0100
Manny's Coffee Shop and Deli
1141 South Jefferson   (312) 939-2855
Since 1942. Great corned beef and pastrami sandwiches.

◆ Best Hot Dogs

Gold Coast Dogs
418 North State Street   (312) 527-1222
25 South Franklin Street   (312) 939-2624
Vienna beef dogs; friendly service; also great burgers. Other locations include Northwestern Atrium, (312) 879-0447, or Union
Station, (312) 258-8585.
Wiener Circle
2622 North Clark   (773) 477-7444
Tasty Dawg
1041 Rohlwing Road, Elk Grove   (847) 593-3294

◆ Best Picnic Meals

Ann Sather
929 West Belmont Avenue   (773) 348-2378
5207 North Clark Street, Andersonville   (773) 271-6677
2665 North Clark Street, Lincoln Park   (773) 327-9522
Open daily; 24-hour advance notice required.
Convito Italiano
1515 Sheridan Road, Plaza Del Lago, Wilmette   (847) 251-3654
(original location)
Several picnics include salad duo, freshly baked bread, and fruit;
24-hour notice required.
Mitchell Cobey Cuisine
100 East Walton   (312) 944-3411
Mostly French cuisine with international influences; numbered box
lunches can be customized; 24-hour advance notice for large orders.
Rocco's Ristorante
21 West Goethe   (312) 944-0199
Will pack anything from the menu to go for picnics.

Sopraffina
10 North Dearborn Street   (312) 984-0044
Italian. Create your own menu; 24-hour notice required.
Tutto Pronto
401 East Ontario Street   (312) 587-7700
Italian food and wine shop with deli.

◆ Best Pizza

Bacino's (several locations)
Bacino's of Lincoln Park, 2204 North Lincoln Avenue
   (773) 472-7400
Good stuffed and heart-healthy pizza.
Bertucci's Brick Oven Pizza
675 North LaSalle Street   (312) 266-3400
Three other new locations in suburbs. More thick-crust pizza pie.
California Pizza Kitchen
414 North Orleans Street   (312) 222-9030
Call about other locations. Thin-crust/gourmet.
Edwardo's Natural Pizza Restaurant
1212 North Dearborn Street   (312) 337-4490
521 South Dearborn Street   (312) 939-3366
Call for other locations.
Giovanni's Pizza
6823 West Roosevelt Road, Berwyn   (708) 795-7171
Lou Malnati's
439 North Wells Street   (312) 828-9800
6649 North Lincoln Avenue, Lincolnwood   (847) 673-0800
Gourmet deep-dish and thin-crust pizza.
O Famé
750 West Webster Avenue   (773) 929-5111
Good thin-crust, pan, or Chicago-style pizzas; they also have a full menu.
The Original Gino's East
1321 West Golf Road, Rolling Meadows   (847) 364-6644
Rated number one in the nation by *People* magazine editors.
Pat's Pizzeria & Ristorante
3114 North Sheffield Avenue   (773) 248-0168
211 North Stetson   (312) 946-0732
Named the number one thin crust pizza by the *Chicago Tribune* and
   the *Chicago Sun-Times*.

Pizzeria Uno
29 East Ohio Street   (312) 321-1000
Pizzeria Due
619 North Wabash Avenue   (312) 943-2400
Both Uno and Due serve Chicago-style, deep-dish pizza.
Suparossa
7309 West Lawrence Avenue, Harwood Heights   (847) 867-4611
Newest locations at press time: 210 East Ohio Street and another in
    Woodridge. Call for other locations. Original stuffed pizza—the
    award-winning lasagna pizza stuffed with ricotta and spinach is a
    favorite. The new wood-fired oven pizzas are great appetizers.

◆ Best Wine Bars

Espial Bistro & Bar
948 West Armitage Avenue   (773) 871-8123
French/Italian food; international wines.

Geja's Cafe
340 West Armitage Avenue   (773) 281-9101
This fondue cafe was the city's first wine bar. It's very romantic
    with live guitar.

Hudson Club
5504 North Wells Street   (312) 467-1947
Large list of wines by the glass—over 100. A wine-oriented restaurant.

Madison's (Italian Steakhouse)
1330 West Madison Street, United Center area   (312) 455-0099
More than 20 wines by the glass. Good wine list.

Meritage Cafe and Wine Bar
2118 North Damen Avenue   (773) 235-6434

Narcisse Champagne Salon & Caviar Bar
710 North Clark Street   (312) 787-2675
New champagne and caviar bar with light fare.

Pops for Champagne
2934 North Sheffield Avenue   (773) 472-1000
Adjacent Star Bar does monthly tastings. Call (312) 472-7272.

Webster's Wine Bar
1480 West Webster Avenue   (773) 868-0608
Long list of wines by the glass or two-ounce tastes; complementary,
    healthful, simple foods.

uNdERSTANdiNq tHE RATiNqs

We have developed detailed profiles for what we consider the best restaurants in town. Each profile features an easy-to-scan heading that allows you to check out the restaurant's name, cuisine, star rating, cost, quality rating, and value rating quickly.

Star Rating. The star rating is an overall rating that encompasses the entire dining experience, including style, service, and ambiance in addition to the taste, presentation, and quality of the food. Five stars is the highest rating possible and connotes the best of everything. Four-star restaurants are exceptional, and three-star restaurants are well above average. Two-star restaurants are good. One star is used to connote an average restaurant that demonstrates an unusual capability in some area of specialization, for example, an otherwise unmemorable place that has great barbecued chicken.

Cost. Beneath the star rating is an expense description that provides a comparative sense of how much a complete meal will cost. A complete meal for our purposes consists of an entree with vegetable or side dish, and choice of soup or salad. Appetizers, desserts, drinks, and tips are excluded.

Inexpensive	$16 and less per person
Moderate	$17–29 per person
Expensive	$30–40 per person
Very Expensive	$40 or more per person

Quality Rating. Below the cost rating appear a number and a letter. The number is a quality rating based on a scale of 0–100, with 100 being the highest (best) rating attainable. The quality rating is based expressly on the taste, freshness of ingredients, preparation, presentation, and creativity of food served. There is no consideration of price. If you are a person who wants the best food available and cost is not an issue, you need look no further than the quality ratings.

Value Rating. If, on the other hand, you are looking for both quality and value, then you should check the value rating, expressed in letters. The value ratings are defined as follows:

A   Exceptional value, a real bargain
B   Good value
C   Fair value, you get exactly what you pay for
D   Somewhat overpriced
F   Significantly overpriced

Locating the restaurant

Just below the restaurant name is a designation for geographic zone. This zone description will give you a general idea of where the restaurant described is located. For ease of use, we divide Chicago into 11 geographic zones.

Zone 1.   North Side
Zone 2.   North Central/O'Hare
Zone 3.   Near North
Zone 4.   The Loop
Zone 5.   South Loop
Zone 6.   South Central/Midway
Zone 7.   South Side
Zone 8.   Southern Suburbs
Zone 9.   Western Suburbs
Zone 10.   Northwest Suburbs
Zone 11.   Northern Suburbs

If you're on Michigan Avenue and intend to walk or take a cab to dinner, you may want to choose a restaurant from among those located in Zone 4. If you have a car, you might include restaurants from contiguous zones in your consideration.

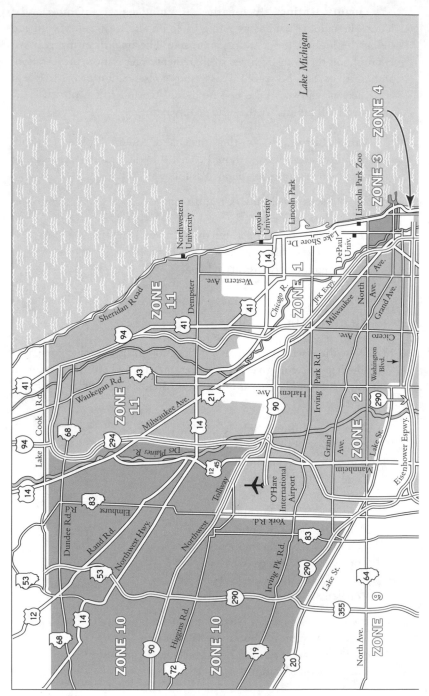

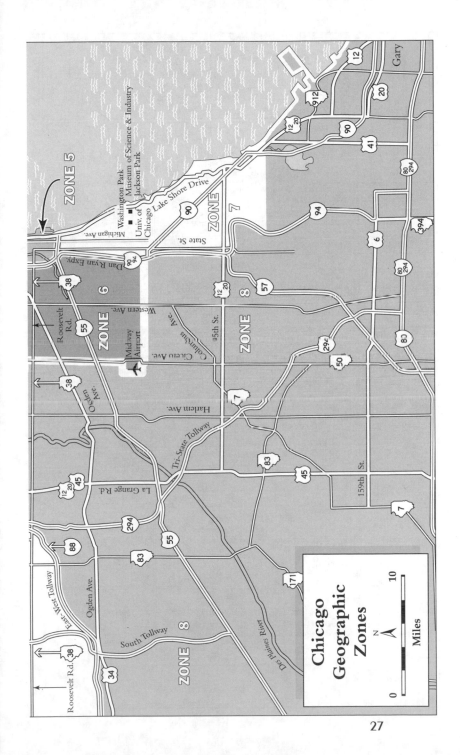

Chicago Geographic Zones

N

Miles

0   10

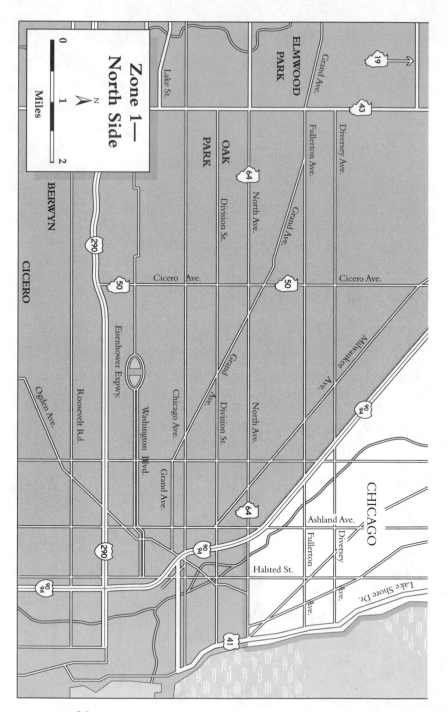

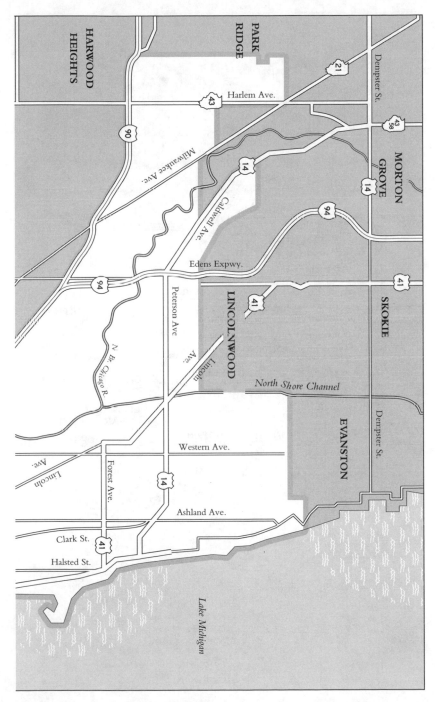

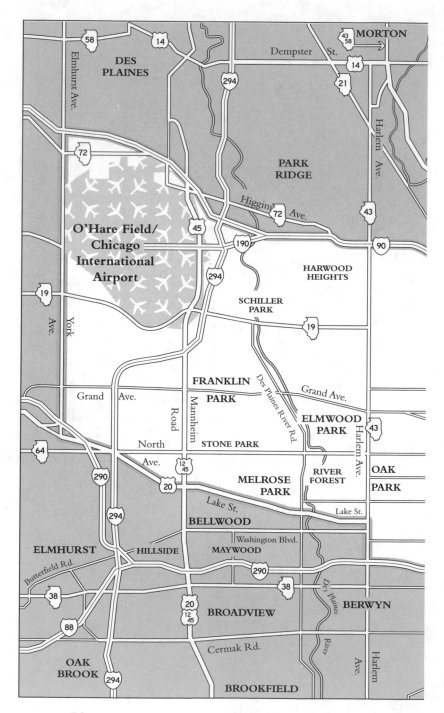

Zone 2—
North Central/
O'Hare

N

| 0 | 1 | 2 |

Miles

GROVE

SKOKIE

Dempster St.

EVANSTON

Edens Expwy.

Shore Channel

North

Western Ave.

Ashland Ave.

LINCOLNWOOD

Caldwell Ave.

Lincoln

Peterson Ave.

Lake
Michigan

Ave.

North Br.

Chicago River

Foster

Ave.

Ashland Ave.

Clark St.

Milwaukee

Lincoln Ave.

CHICAGO

Ave.

Halsted St.

Diversey

Ave.

Diversey Ave.

Fullerton

Ave.

Milwaukee Ave.

Fullerton Ave.

Halsted St.

North Ave.

Grand

Division St.

Ave.

Ave.

Cicero

Chicago Ave.

Grand Ave.

Washington

Ave.

Ashland

Michigan

Eisenhower

Blvd.

Expwy.

Roosevelt Rd.

CICERO

Ogden Ave.

Cermak Rd.

Archer Ave.

Halsted Ave.

Ave.

MLK, Jr. Dr.

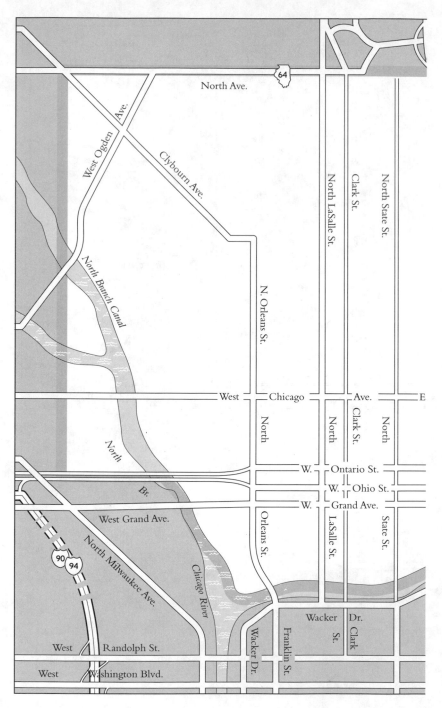

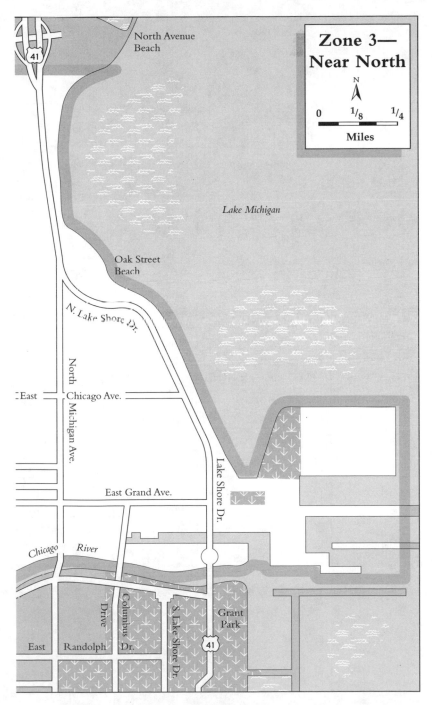

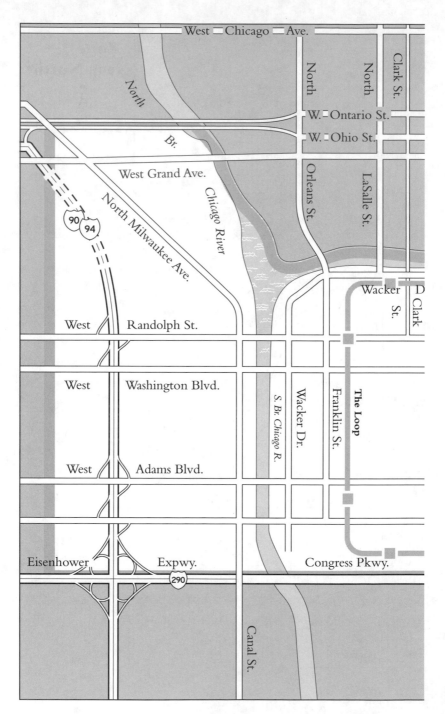

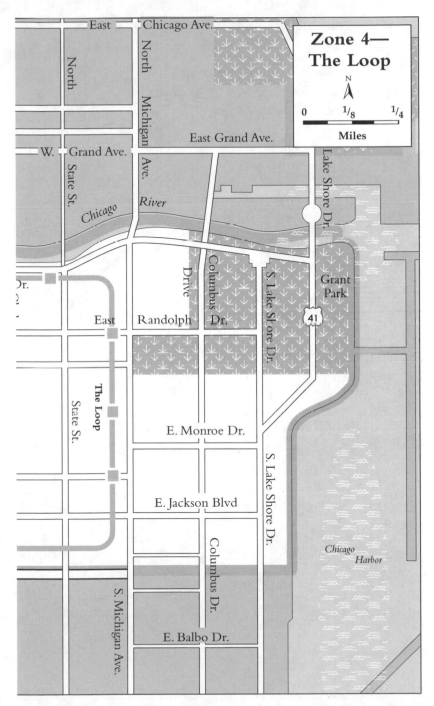

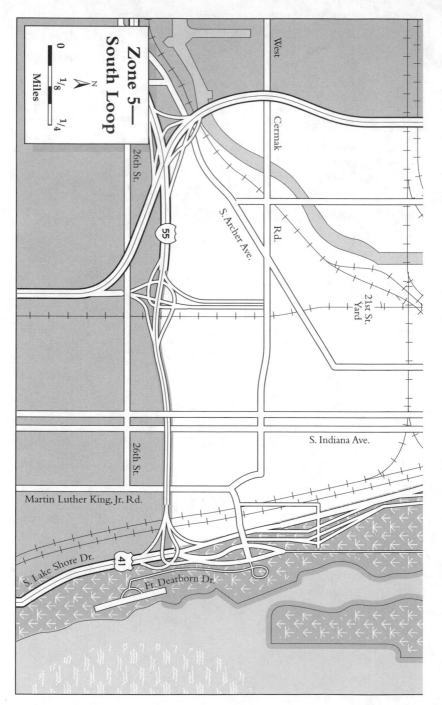

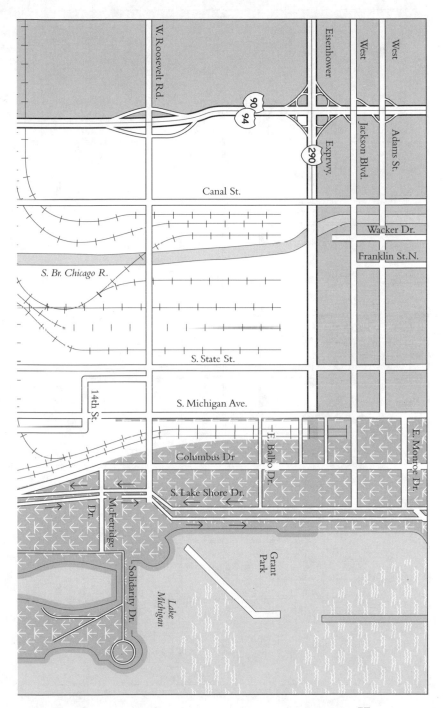

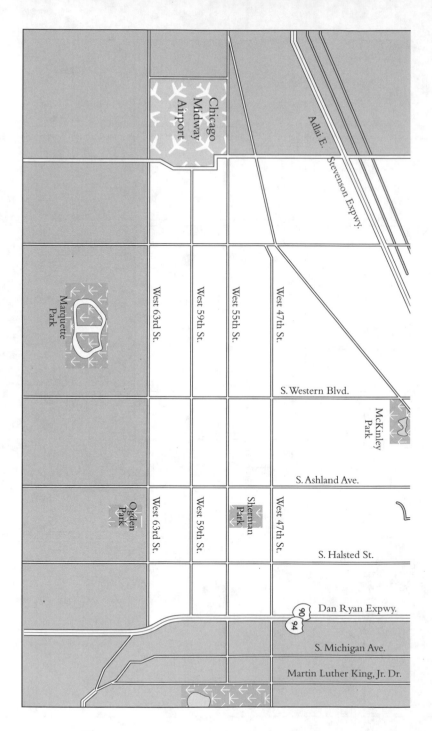

Chicago Midway Airport

Adlai E. Stevenson Expwy.

Marquette Park

West 63rd St.

West 59th St.

West 55th St.

West 47th St.

S. Western Blvd.

McKinley Park

S. Ashland Ave.

Ogden Park

West 63rd St.

West 59th St.

Sherman Park

West 47th St.

S. Halsted St.

90 94 Dan Ryan Expwy.

S. Michigan Ave.

Martin Luther King, Jr. Dr.

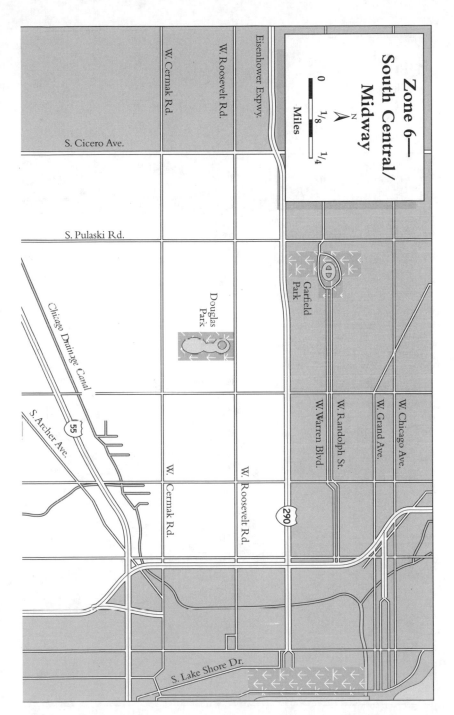

Zone 6—
South Central/
Midway

N

0   1/8   1/4
Miles

Eisenhower Expwy.
W. Roosevelt Rd.
W. Cermak Rd.
S. Cicero Ave.
S. Pulaski Rd.
Douglas Park
Garfield Park
Chicago Drainage Canal
S. Archer Ave.
55
W. Cermak Rd.
W. Roosevelt Rd.
290
W. Warren Blvd.
W. Randolph St.
W. Grand Ave.
W. Chicago Ave.
S. Lake Shore Dr.

39

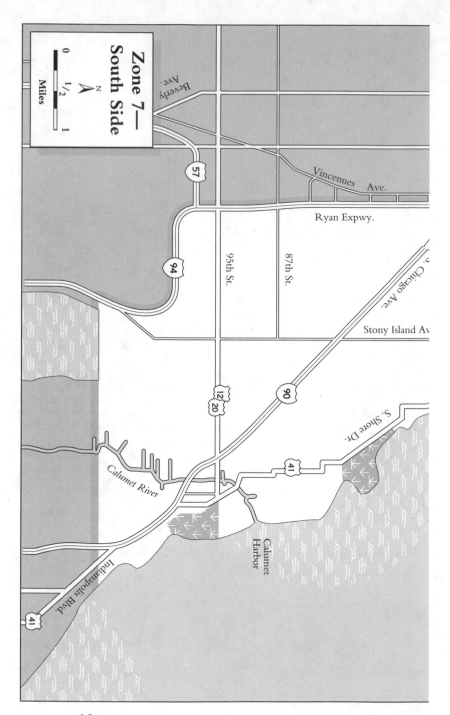

Zone 7—
South Side

0   ½   1
Miles

N

Beverly Ave.

57

Vincennes Ave.

Ryan Expwy.

95th St.

87th St.

94

Chicago Ave.

Stony Island Av

12
20

90

S. Shore Dr.

41

Calumet River

41

Calumet
Harbor

Indianapolis Blvd.

40

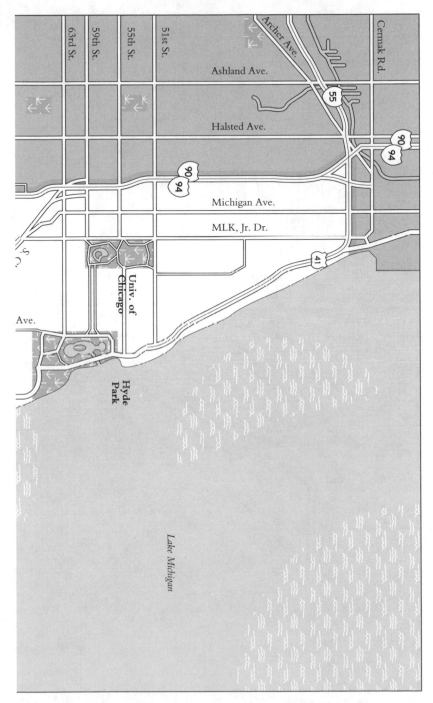

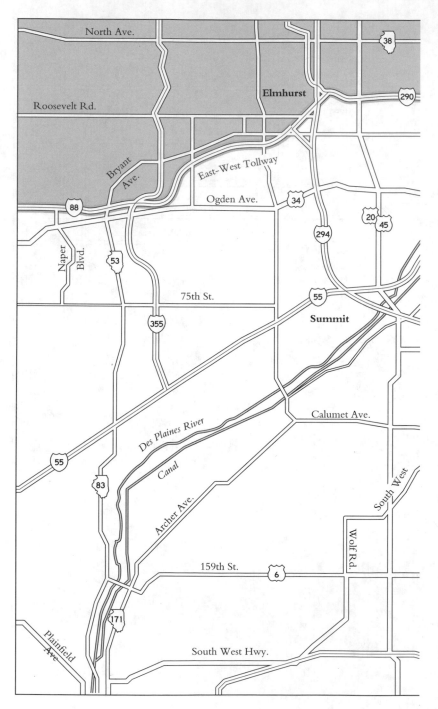

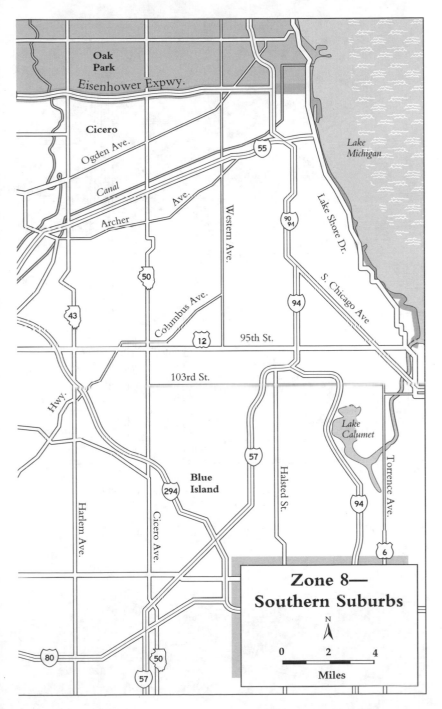

Oak
Park

Eisenhower Expwy.

Cicero

Ogden Ave.

Canal

55

Lake
Michigan

Archer

Ave.

Western Ave.

90
91

Lake Shore Dr.

50

94

S. Chicago Ave.

43

Columbus Ave.

12

95th St.

103rd St.

Lake
Calumet

94

Torrence Ave.

Hwy.

57

Blue
Island

294

Halsted St.

94

Harlem Ave.

Cicero Ave.

6

80

50

57

Zone 8—
Southern Suburbs

N

| 0 | 2 | 4 |

Miles

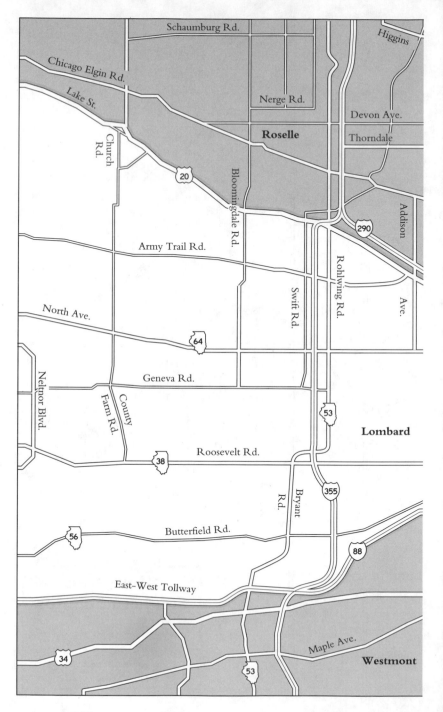

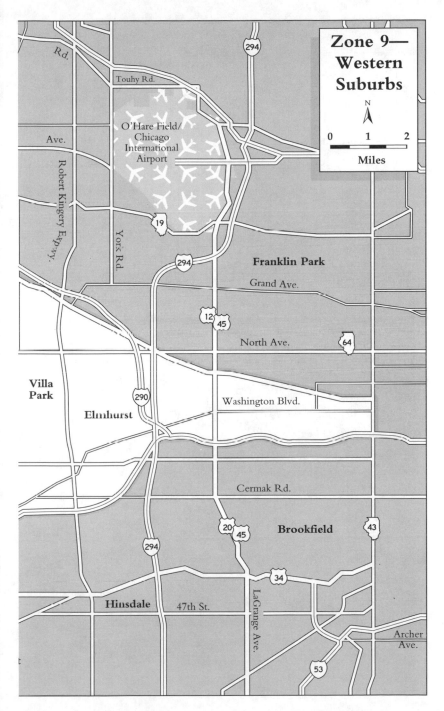

Zone 9—
Western
Suburbs

O'Hare Field/
Chicago
International
Airport

Rd.

Touhy Rd.

Ave.

Robert Kingery Expwy.

York Rd.

19

294

Franklin Park

Grand Ave.

12
45

North Ave.

64

Villa
Park

290

Elmhurst

Washington Blvd.

Cermak Rd.

20
45

Brookfield

43

294

34

Hinsdale

47th St.

LaGrange Ave.

Archer
Ave.

53

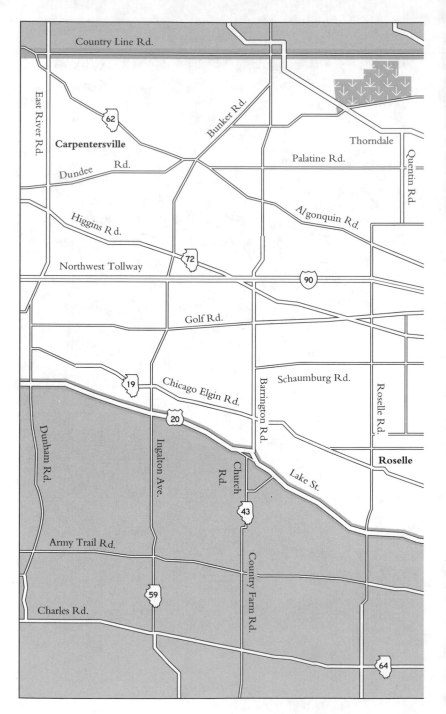

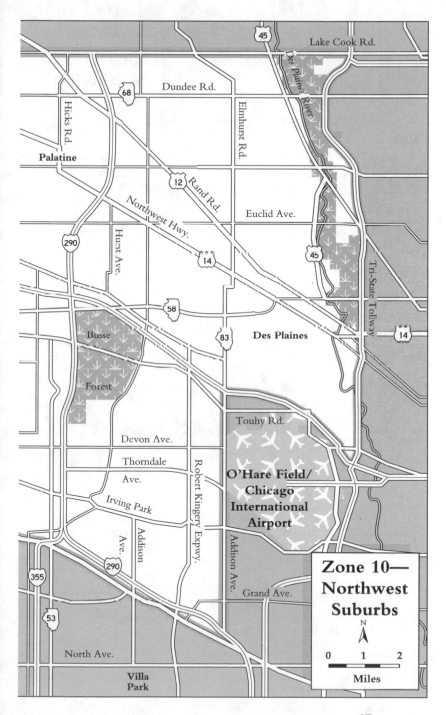

Lake Cook Rd.

Des Plaines River

68 Dundee Rd.

Hicks Rd.

Elmhurst Rd.

Palatine

12 Rand Rd.

Northwest Hwy.

Euclid Ave.

290

14

45

Hurst Ave.

Tri-State Tollway

58

14

83 **Des Plaines**

Busse

Forest

Touhy Rd.

Devon Ave.

Thorndale Ave.

O'Hare Field/ Chicago International Airport

Robert Kingery Expwy.

Irving Park

Addison Ave.

Addison Ave.

355

290

Grand Ave.

53

North Ave.

Villa Park

Zone 10— Northwest Suburbs

N

0   1   2

Miles

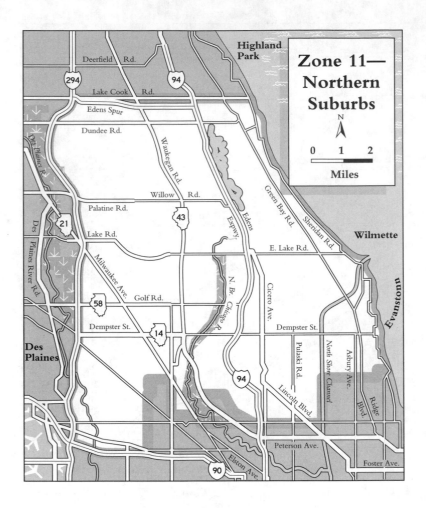

Zone 11—
Northern
Suburbs

N

0   1   2

Miles

Highland
Park

Deerfield Rd.

294

94

Lake Cook Rd.

Edens Spur

Dundee Rd.

Des Plaines R.

Des Plaines River Rd.

21

Palatine Rd.

Lake Rd.

Willow Rd.

43

Waukegan Rd.

Edens Expwy.

Green Bay Rd.

Sheridan Rd.

Wilmette

E. Lake Rd.

Milwaukee Ave.

Golf Rd.

58

N. Br. Chicago R.

Cicero Ave.

Dempster St.

14

Dempster St.

94

Pulaski Rd.

North Shore Channel

Asbury Ave.

Ridge Blvd.

Evanston

Des
Plaines

Lincoln Blvd.

Peterson Ave.

Foster Ave.

Elston Ave.

90

ǂ OUR pick of THE bEST
ǂ chicAɢo RESTAURANTS

B ecause restaurants open and close all the time in Chicago, we have confined our list to establishments with a proven track record over a fairly long period of time. Newer restaurants (and older restaurants under new management) are listed but not profiled. Those newer or changed establishments that demonstrate staying power and consistency will be profiled in subsequent editions.

The list is highly selective. Noninclusion of a particular place does not necessarily indicate that the restaurant is not good, but only that it was not ranked among the best in its genre. Note that some restaurants appear in more than one category. Detailed profiles of each restaurant follow in alphabetical order at the end of this chapter. Also, we've listed the types of payment accepted at each restaurant using the following codes:

AMEX	American Express
CB	Carte Blanche
D	Discover
DC	Diners Club
MC	MasterCard
VISA	VISA

A NOTE AboUT SpEllING

Most diners who enjoy ethnic restaurants have noticed subtle variations in the spelling of certain dishes and preparations from one menu to the next. A noodle dish found on almost all Thai menus, for example, appears in one restaurant as *pad thai,* in another as *Phat Thai,* and in a third as *Phad Thai.*

This and similar inconsistencies arise from attempts to derive a phonetic English spelling from the name of a dish as pronounced in its country of origin. While one particular English spelling might be more frequently used than others, there is usually no definitive correct spelling for the names of many dishes. In this guide, we have elected to use the spelling most commonly found in authoritative ethnic cookbooks and other reference works.

We call this to your attention because the spelling we use in this guide could be different from that which you encounter on the menu in a certain restaurant. We might say, for instance, that the *tabbouleh* is good at the Pillars of Lebanon, while at the restaurant itself the dish is listed on the menu as *tabouli.*

Restaurants by Cuisine

Name	Star Rating	Price Rating	Quality Rating	Value Rating	Zone
American					
Seasons Restaurant at the Four Seasons Hotel	★★★★★	Mod/Exp	99	C	3
Prairie	★★★★½	Mod/Exp	95	C	5
Spago	★★★★½	Mod/Exp	94	B	3
Toulouse on the Park	★★★★½	Mod	94	B	1
Spago Grill	★★★★	Mod/Exp	94	B	3
The Pump Room	★★★★	Exp	92	C	3
House of Blues	★★★★	Inexp/Mod	90	B	3
Brasserie T	★★★½	Inexp/Mod	90	B	11
Iron Mike's Grille	★★★½	Mod/Exp	90	C	3
Mango	★★★½	Inexp/Mod	90	B	3
The Greenery	★★★½	Mod/Exp	88	C	10
Harry Caray's	★★★½	Mod/Exp	86	C	4
The Mity Nice Grill	★★★½	Inexp/Mod	86	C	3
Relish	★★★½	Inexp/Mod	86	C	1
Harry Caray's (Wheeling)	★★★½	Mod	85	C	10
Michael Jordan's Restaurant	★★★½	Inexp/Mod	85	C	3
Wild Onion	★★★½	Inexp/Mod	85	B	1
Walker Bros. Original Pancake House	★★★	Inexp	88	B	10, 11
Flat Top Grill	★★★	Inexp	85	B	2, 3, 11
Widow Newton's Tavern	★★★	Mod	85	C	3
Don Roth's in Wheeling	★★★	Mod	84	C	10
Wildfire (Russell Bry's)	★★★	Inexp/Mod	84	C	3
Big Shoulders	★★★	Inexp	82	B	1
foodlife	★★★	Inexp	82	C	3
R. J. Grunts	★★★	Inexp	82	A	1
Argentinian					
Tango Sur	★★½	Inexp/Mod	78	B	1
Armenian					
Sayat Nova	★★★½	Inexp/Mod	88	C	10
Bakery Cafe					
Corner Bakery	★★★½	Inexp/Mod	90	B	4
St. Germain Restaurant/ Bakery Cafe	★★★½	Inexp/Mod	88	C	3

Restaurants by Cuisine (continued)

Name	Star Rating	Price Rating	Quality Rating	Value Rating	Zone
Barbecue					
Gateway Bar & Grill	★★★	Inexp/Mod	85	B	1
N. N. Smokehouse	★★★	Inexp/Mod	82	B	1
Bones	★★½	Inexp/Mod	78	C	11
Cajun/Creole					
House of Blues	★★★★	Inexp/Mod	90	B	3
Bazzell's French Quarter Bistro	★★★½	Inexp/Mod	89	B	3
Carzz Grilleria	★★★½	Inexp/Mod	88	B	8
Maple Tree Inn	★★★½	Inexp/Mod	88	B	8
Heaven on Seven	★★★½	Inexp	86	B	4
Caribbean					
Carzz Grilleria	★★★½	Inexp/Mod	88	B	8
Chez Delphonse	★★★	Inexp/Mod	83	B	1
Julio's Latin Cafe	★★★	Mod	83	C	10
El Dinamico Dallas	★★½	Inexp	79	B	1
Chinese					
Szechwan East	★★★★	Mod	92	C	4
Ben Pao	★★★½	Inexp/Mod	90	B	3
Emperor's Choice	★★★½	Inexp/Mod	88	B	5
Mandar Inn	★★★½	Inexp/Mod	88	C	5
Mei-Shung Restaurant	★★★½	Inexp	87	B	1
Hong Min Chinese Restaurant	★★★	Inexp/Mod	85	B	5, 8
Szechwan Restaurant	★★★	Inexp/Mod	83	C	3
Continental					
The Pump Room	★★★★	Exp	92	C	3
Biggs	★★★★	Mod	90	C	3
Cité	★★★★	Exp/V Exp	89	D	1
Zum Deutschen Eck (The German Corner)	★★★½	Inexp/Mod	88	C	1
Brasserie Bellevue	★★★	Mod	85	C	3
Cuban/Spanish					
Tania's	★★★½	Mod	86	B	2

Restaurants by Cuisine (continued)

Name	Star Rating	Price Rating	Quality Rating	Value Rating	Zone
Eclectic					
Green Dolphin Street	★★★½	Mod/Exp	89	C	1
Pastiche	★★★½	Inexp/Mod	87	B	1
Gateway Bar & Grill	★★★	Inexp/Mod	85	B	1
Ethiopian					
Mama Desta's Red Sea Ethiopian Restaurant	★★★	Inexp	86	B	1
Addis Abeba	★★★	Inexp	84	C	1
Filipino					
Pampanga Restaurant	★★½	Inexp	77	B	1
Fondue					
Geja's Cafe	★★★½	Exp	90	B	1
French					
Everest	★★★★★	Exp	98	C	4
Le Français	★★★★★	Exp	97	C	10
Carlos	★★★★½	Mod/Exp	96	C	11
Le Vichyssois	★★★★½	Mod	95	B	10
Toulouse on the Park	★★★★½	Mod	94	B	1
Entre Nous	★★★★	Mod/Exp	90	C	4
Oceanique	★★★½	Mod/Exp	88	C	11
Wild Onion	★★★½	Inexp/Mod	85	B	1
Amourette	★★★	Inexp/Mod	83	B	10
La Crêperie	★★½	Inexp	80	A	1
French Bistro					
Kiki's Bistro	★★★★	Inexp/Mod	94	C	3
Bistro Banlieue	★★★★	Inexp/Mod	93	B	8
Brasserie Jo	★★★★	Inexp/Mod	92	B	3
Un Grand Cafe	★★★★	Mod	92	C	1
Cyrano's Bistrot & Wine Bar	★★★½	Inexp/Mod	90	B	3
St. Germain Restaurant/ Bakery Cafe	★★★½	Inexp/Mod	88	C	3
Bistro 110	★★★½	Mod	86	C	3

Name	Star Rating	Price Rating	Quality Rating	Value Rating	Zone
French/Italian					
Gabriel's Restaurant	★★★★	Mod/Exp	93	C	11
French/Vietnamese					
Le Colonial	★★★½	Mod	88	C	1
Fusion					
Trio	★★★★★	Exp/V Exp	98	C	11
Jerome's Red Ginger	★★★½	Inexp/Mod	89	B	1
German					
Golden Ox	★★★★	Mod	90	C	1
The Berghoff	★★★½	Inexp	88	B	4
Mirabell Restaurant	★★★½	Inexp/Mod	88	B	2
Zum Deutschen Eck (The German Corner)	★★★½	Inexp/Mod	88	C	1
Hans' Bavarian Lodge	★★★	Inexp/Mod	80	B	10
Greek					
The Parthenon	★★★★	Inexp/Mod	95	B	4
Mykonos	★★★½	Inexp/Mod	92	B	11
Papagus Greek Taverna	★★★½	Mod	90	C	3, 6
Roditys	★★★	Inexp/Mod	89	B	4
Santorini	★★★	Inexp/Mod	89	C	4
Pegasus Restaurant and Taverna	★★★	Inexp/Mod	83	C	4
Indian					
Indian Summer	★★★★	Inexp/Mod	94	C	8
Klay Oven	★★★★	Mod	94	B	4
Bukara	★★★½	Mod	80	C	3
Viceroy of India	★★★	Inexp/Mod	84	B	1, 9
Sher-A-Punjab	★★★	Inexp	82	B	1
Chowpatti Vegetarian Restaurant	★★★	Inexp	80	B	10
Kanval Palace	★★½	Inexp	76	B	1

Name	Star Rating	Price Rating	Quality Rating	Value Rating	Zone
Irish Pub					
Kitty O'Shea's	★★★	Inexp	81	B	5
Italian					
Va Pensiero	★★★★½	Mod	96	C	11
Spiaggia	★★★★½	Mod/Exp	95	C	3
Vivere (Italian Village)	★★★★½	Mod	95	C	4
Campagnola	★★★★	Inexp/Mod	94	B	11
Coco Pazzo	★★★★	Mod	91	C	4
Trattoria Gianni	★★★★	Inexp/Mod	91	C	1
Avanzare	★★★½	Mod	90	C	3
Cafe Spiaggia	★★★½	Mod	89	C	3
Cucina Roma	★★★½	Inexp/Mod	89	B	8
Cuisines	★★★½	Inexp/Mod	89	B	4
Pane Caldo	★★★½	Mod/V Exp	89	D	3
Trattoria Parma	★★★½	Inexp/Mod	89	B	3
Cafe Luciano	★★★½	Inexp/Mod	88	B	3, 11
Carlucci	★★★½	Mod	88	C	2
The Primavera Ristorante	★★★½	Inexp/Mod	88	C	4
Bice Ristorante	★★★½	Mod/Exp	87	D	3
La Strada	★★★½	Mod/Exp	87	C	4
Harry Caray's	★★★½	Mod/Exp	86	C	4
Harry Caray's (Wheeling)	★★★½	Mod	85	C	10
Wild Onion	★★★½	Inexp/Mod	85	B	1
Bacino's Trattoria	★★★	Inexp/Mod	84	B	8
Da Nicola Ristorante	★★★	Inexp/Mod	84	B	1
La Bocca Della Verita	★★★	Inexp/Mod	84	B	1
Pappagallo's	★★★	Inexp/Mod	84	B	11
Red Tomato	★★★	Inexp	84	B	1
Tuscany	★★★	Mod	84	C	5
Del Rio	★★★	Inexp/Mod	83	B	11
Francesco's Hole in the Wall	★★★	Inexp/Mod	83	B	11
Rosebud Cafe	★★★	Inexp/Mod	83	C	5
Filippo's	★★★	Inexp/Mod	82	C	1
Mia Francesca	★★★	Inexp/Mod	82	B	1
Tucci Milan	★★★	Inexp/Mod	82	C	4

Name	Star Rating	Price Rating	Quality Rating	Value Rating	Zone
Italian *(continued)*					
Maggiano's Little Italy	★★★	Mod	81	C	4, 8, 11
Bruna's Ristorante	★★★	Inexp/Mod	80	B	5
Alfo's Ristorante	★★½	Inexp	79	B	5
Cafe Borgia	★★½	Inexp/Mod	78	B	8
Tufano's (Vernon Park Tap)	★★½	Inexp/Mod	76	B	5
Japanese					
Kuni's	★★★★½	Inexp/Mod	96	C	11
Katsu Japanese Restaurant	★★★½	Inexp/Mod	90	B	1
Akai Hana	★★★½	Inexp/Mod	88	C	11
Hatsuhana	★★½	Inexp/Mod	76	C	3
Korean					
Woo Lae Oak	★★★★	Inexp	94	C	3
Korea Garden	★★★½	Inexp/Mod	88	B	8
Shilla	★★★½	Mod	86	C	1
Bando	★★★	Inexp/Mod	83	C	1
Amitabul	★★½	Inexp	80	B	1
Mediterranean					
Mantuano Mediterranean Table	★★★★	Inexp/Mod	91	C	3
L'Olive Cafe	★★★½	Inexp	91	A	1
Cuisines	★★★½	Inexp/Mod	89	B	4
Mexican					
Topolobampo	★★★★½	Mod	95	C	4
Frontera Grill	★★★★	Inexp	93	B	4
¡Salpicón! A Taste of Mexico	★★★½	Inexp/Mod	85	C	3
Don Juan	★★★	Inexp/Mod	84	C	1
El Tipico	★★½	Inexp	79	B	1, 11
Middle Eastern					
Uncle Tutunji's	★★★	Inexp	85	B	3
Uncle Tannous	★★★	Inexp/Mod	84	B	1
Moroccan					
L'Olive Cafe	★★★½	Inexp	91	A	1

Name	Star Rating	Price Rating	Quality Rating	Value Rating	Zone
New American					
Charlie Trotter's	★★★★★	Very Exp	99	C	1
Courtwright's	★★★★½	Mod/Exp	96	B	8
Printer's Row	★★★★½	Mod	95	B	5
Gordon	★★★★½	Exp	94	C	4
Park Avenue Cafe	★★★★½	Mod/Exp	94	C	3
Spruce	★★★★½	Inexp/Mod	94	B	3
erwin	★★★★	Inexp/Mod	94	B	1
302 West	★★★★	Mod	92	C	9
The Signature Room at the 95th	★★★★	Mod/Exp	90	C	3
The Cafe	★★★½	Mod	90	C	3
Elaine and Ina's	★★★½	Inexp/Mod	89	B	3
Mrs. Park's Tavern	★★★½	Inexp/Mod	89	C	3
Jilly's Cafe	★★★½	Inexp/Mod	85	B	11
Blackhawk Lodge	★★★	Mod	82	C	3
Hubbard Street Grill	★★★	Inexp/Mod	81	C	4
New French					
Tallgrass	★★★★★	Very Exp	98	C	8
The Dining Room	★★★★½	Mod/Exp	97	C	3
Le Titi de Paris	★★★★½	Mod/Exp	97	C	10
Ambria	★★★★½	Mod/Exp	96	C	1
Montparnasse	★★★★½	Mod/Exp	95	C	8
Yvette	★★★½	Inexp/Mod	85	C	3
Yvette Wintergarden	★★★½	Inexp/Mod	85	C	4
Froggy's French Cafe	★★★	Mod	84	B	11
New French/Japanese					
Yoshi's Cafe	★★★★	Inexp/Mod	94	B	1
New Italian					
Bella Vista	★★★½	Inexp/Mod	86	C	1
Via Veneto	★★★½	Inexp	85	B	1
Pazzo's Cucina Italiana	★★½	Inexp/Mod	79	B	2, 8

Name	Star Rating	Price Rating	Quality Rating	Value Rating	Zone
Pan-Asian					
Stir Crazy	★★★½	Inexp	88	B	9
Mongolian Barbeque	★★★	Inexp	85	B	1, 8
Big Bowl Cafe	★★★	Inexp	84	B	3
Lulu's	★★½	Inexp	80	B	11
Persian					
Pars Cove	★★★½	Inexp	89	B	1
Reza's	★★★½	Inexp/Mod	89	C	1, 3
Cy's Crab House	★★★	Inexp/Mod	84	B	1
Peruvian					
Machu Picchu	★★	Inexp	74	B	1
Polish					
Lutnia Continental Cafe	★★★½	Inexp/Mod	87	C	2
Pierogi Inn	★★½	Inexp	79	B	2
Home Bakery	★★½	Inexp	77	B	2
Russian					
Russian Tea Time	★★★★	Mod	93	C	4
Seafood					
Shaw's Crab House and Shaw's Blue Crab Lounge & Oyster Bar	★★★★½	Mod	95	C	4
Don's Fishmarket and Tavern	★★★★	Inexp/Exp	95	B	11
Nick's Fishmarket	★★★★	Mod/Exp	95	D	2,4
Catch 35	★★★½	Mod/Exp	93	C	4
Cape Cod Room	★★★½	Mod/Exp	91	C	3
Riva	★★★½	Mod/Exp	90	C	3
Oceanique	★★★½	Mod/Exp	88	C	11
Cy's Crab House	★★★	Inexp/Mod	84	B	1
Bob Chinn's Crab House	★★★	Mod	82	B	10
Shaw's Seafood Grill	★★★	Mod	80	C	11
Serbian/Continental					
Skadarlija	★★★	Mod	84	B	1

Name	Star Rating	Price Rating	Quality Rating	Value Rating	Zone
Southern					
Army & Lou's	★★★★	Inexp/Mod	90	B	7
House of Blues	★★★★	Inexp/Mod	90	B	3
Carzz Grilleria	★★★½	Inexp/Mod	88	B	8
Soul Kitchen	★★★	Inexp/Mod	84	C	2
Stanley's Kitchen & Tap	★★½	Inexp	79	A	1
Southwestern					
Blue Mesa	★★★★	Inexp/Mod	89	B	1
Twisted Lizard	★★★½	Inexp	87	B	1
Spanish					
Emilio's Meson Sabika Tapas Bar Restaurant	★★★★	Mod	93	C	8
Emilio's Tapas Bar Restaurant	★★★★	Mod	91	C	1
Cafe-Ba-Ba-Reeba!	★★★½	Mod	87	C	1
Cafe Iberico Tapas Bar	★★★½	Inexp/Mod	87	B	3
Steak/Prime Rib					
Gibson's Steakhouse	★★★★½	Mod/V Exp	94	C	3
Don's Fishmarket and Tavern	★★★★	Inexp/Exp	95	B	11
Chicago Chop House	★★★★	Mod	94	C	3
Morton's of Chicago	★★★★	Exp	93	C	2, 3, 8
Ruth's Chris Steakhouse	★★★★	Mod/Exp	93	B	4
Kinzie Street Chophouse	★★★★	Mod	91	B	4
Lawry's The Prime Rib	★★★★	Mod	90	B	3
Riva	★★★½	Mod/Exp	90	C	3
The Saloon	★★★½	Mod/Exp	89	C	3
Eli's, The Place for Steak	★★★½	Mod/Exp	88	C	3
Palm Restaurant	★★★½	Mod/Exp	87	C	4
Swedish					
Ann Sather	★★★	Inexp	83	B	1
Thai					
Arun's	★★★★½	Mod/Exp	95	C	1
Thai Borrahn	★★★★	Inexp/Mod	90	B	3

Restaurants by Cuisine (continued)

Name	Star Rating	Price Rating	Quality Rating	Value Rating	Zone
Thai *(continued)*					
P.S. Bangkok	★★★	Inexp	84	A	1
Siam Cafe	★★★	Inexp	84	A	1
Vegetarian					
Reza's	★★★½	Inexp/Mod	89	C	1, 3
Karyn's Fresh Corner	★★★	Inexp	84	C	1
Blind Faith Cafe	★★★	Inexp	82	B	1, 11
Chowpatti Vegetarian Restaurant	★★★	Inexp	80	B	10
Vietnamese					
Pasteur	★★★★	Inexp/Mod	92	B	1
Hoang Mai	★★★½	Inexp	89	A	1
Nhu Hoa Cafe	★★★½	Inexp/Mod	89	B	1

Restaurants by Star Rating

Name	Cuisine	Price Rating	Quality Rating	Value Rating	Zone
Five-Star Restaurants					
Charlie Trotter's	New American	Very Exp	99	C	1
Seasons Restaurant at the Four Seasons Hotel	American	Mod/Exp	99	C	3
Everest	French	Exp	98	C	4
Tallgrass	New French	Very Exp	98	C	8
Trio	Fusion	Exp/V Exp	98	C	11
Le Français	French	Exp	97	C	10
Four-and-a-Half-Star Restaurants					
The Dining Room	New French	Mod/Exp	97	C	3
Le Titi de Paris	New French	Mod/Exp	97	C	10
Ambria	New French	Mod/Exp	96	C	1
Carlos'	French	Mod/Exp	96	C	11
Courtwright's	NewAmerican	Mod/Exp	96	B	8
Kuni's	Japanese	Inexp/Mod	96	C	11
Va Pensiero	Italian	Mod	96	C	11
Arun's	Thai	Mod/Exp	95	C	1
Le Vichyssois	French	Mod	95	B	10
Montparnasse	New French	Mod/Exp	95	C	8
Prairie	American	Mod/Exp	95	C	5
Printer's Row	New American	Mod	95	B	5
Shaw's Crab House and Shaw's Blue Crab Lounge & Oyster Bar	Seafood	Mod	95	C	4
Spiaggia	Italian	Mod/Exp	95	C	3
Topolobampo	Mexican	Mod	95	C	4
Vivere (Italian Village)	Italian	Mod	95	C	4
Gibson's Steakhouse	Steak	Mod/V Exp	94	C	3
Gordon	New American	Exp	94	C	4
Park Avenue Cafe	New American	Mod/Exp	94	C	3
Spago	American	Mod/Exp	94	B	3
Spruce	New American	Inexp/Mod	94	B	3
Toulouse on the Park	French/American	Mod	94	B	1

61

Name	Cuisine	Price Rating	Quality Rating	Value Rating	Zone
Four-Star Restaurants					
Don's Fishmarket and Tavern	Seafood/Steak	Inexp/Exp	95	B	11
Nick's Fishmarket	Seafood	Mod/Exp	95	D	4
The Parthenon	Greek	Inexp/Mod	95	B	4
Campagnola	Italian	Inexp/Mod	94	B	11
Chicago Chop House	Steak	Mod	94	C	3
erwin	New American	Inexp/Mod	94	B	1
Indian Summer	Indian	Inexp/Mod	94	C	8
Kiki's Bistro	French Bistro	Inexp/Mod	94	C	3
Klay Oven	Indian	Mod	94	B	4
Spago Grill	American	Mod/Exp	94	B	3
Woo Lae Oak	Korean	Inexp	94	C	3
Yoshi's Cafe	New French/ Japanese	Inexp/Mod	94	B	1
Bistro Banlieue	French Bistro	Inexp/Mod	93	B	8
Emilio's Meson Sabika Tapas Bar Restaurant	Spanish	Mod	93	C	8
Frontera Grill	Mexican	Inexp	93	B	4
Gabriel's Restaurant	French/Italian	Mod/Exp	93	C	11
Morton's of Chicago	Steak	Exp	93	C	2, 3, 8
Russian Tea Time	Russian	Mod	93	C	4
Ruth's Chris Steakhouse	Steak	Mod/Exp	93	B	4
Brasserie Jo	French Bistro	Inexp/Mod	92	B	3
Pasteur	Vietnamese	Inexp/Mod	92	B	1
The Pump Room	American/ Continental	Exp	92	C	3
Szechwan East	Chinese	Mod	92	C	4
302 West	New American	Mod	92	C	9
Un Grand Cafe	French Bistro	Mod	92	C	1
Coco Pazzo	Italian	Mod	91	C	4
Emilio's Tapas Bar Restaurant	Spanish	Mod	91	C	1
Kinzie Street Chophouse	Steak	Mod	91	B	4

Name	Cuisine	Price Rating	Quality Rating	Value Rating	Zone
Mantuano Mediterranean Table	Mediterranean	Inexp/Mod	91	C	3
Trattoria Gianni	Italian	Inexp/Mod	91	C	1
Army & Lou's	Southern	Inexp/Mod	90	B	7
Biggs	Continental	Mod	90	C	3
Entre Nous	French	Mod/Exp	90	C	4
Golden Ox	German	Mod	90	C	1
House of Blues	American/ Southern	Inexp/Mod	90	B	3
Lawry's The Prime Rib	Steak/Prime Rib	Mod	90	B	3
The Signature Room at the 95th	New American	Mod/Exp	90	C	3
Thai Borrahn	Thai	Inexp/Mod	90	B	3
Blue Mesa	Southwestern	Inexp/Mod	89	B	1
Cité	Continental	Exp/V Exp	89	D	1

Three-and-a-Half-Star Restaurants

Name	Cuisine	Price Rating	Quality Rating	Value Rating	Zone
Catch 35	Seafood	Mod/Exp	93	C	4
Mykonos	Greek	Inexp/Mod	92	B	11
Cape Cod Room	Seafood	Mod/Exp	91	C	3
L'Olive Cafe	Moroccan/ Mediterranean	Inexp	91	A	1
Avanzare	Italian	Mod	90	C	3
Ben Pao	Chinese	Inexp/Mod	90	B	3
Brasserie T	American	Inexp/Mod	90	B	11
The Cafe	New American	Mod	90	C	3
Corner Bakery	Bakery Cafe	Inexp/Mod	90	B	4
Cyrano's Bistrot & Wine Bar	French Bistro	Inexp/Mod	90	B	3
Geja's Cafe	Fondue	Exp	90	B	1
Iron Mike's Grille	American	Mod/Exp	90	C	3
Katsu Japanese Restaurant	Japanese	Inexp/Mod	90	B	1
Mango	American	Inexp/Mod	90	B	3
Papagus Greek Taverna	Greek	Mod	90	C	3, 6

Name	Cuisine	Price Rating	Quality Rating	Value Rating	Zone
Three-and-a-Half-Star Restaurants *(continued)*					
Riva	Seafood/Steak	Mod/Exp	90	C	3
Bazzell's French Quarter Bistro	Cajun/Creole	Inexp/Mod	89	B	3
Cafe Spiaggia	Italian	Mod	89	C	3
Cucina Roma	Italian	Inexp/Mod	89	B	8
Cuisines	Italian/ Mediterranean	Inexp/Mod	89	B	4
Elaine and Ina's	New American	Inexp/Mod	89	B	3
Green Dolphin Street	Eclectic	Mod/Exp	89	C	1
Hoang Mai	Vietnamese	Inexp	89	A	1
Jerome's Red Ginger	Fusion	Inexp/Mod	89	B	1
Mrs. Park's Tavern	New American	Inexp/Mod	89	C	3
Nhu Hoa Cafe	Vietnamese	Inexp/Mod	89	B	1
Pane Caldo	Italian	Mod/VExp	89	D	3
Pars Cove	Persian	Inexp	89	B	1
Reza's	Persian/ Vegetarian	Inexp/Mod	89	C	1, 3
The Saloon	Steak	Mod/Exp	89	C	3
Trattoria Parma	Italian	Inexp/Mod	89	B	3
Akai Hana	Japanese	Inexp/Mod	88	C	11
The Berghoff	German	Inexp	88	B	4
Cafe Luciano	Italian	Inexp/Mod	88	B	3, 11
Carlucci	Italian	Mod	88	C	2
Carzz Grilleria	Southern/ Caribbean	Inexp/Mod	88	B	8
Eli's, The Place for Steak	Steak	Mod/Exp	88	C	3
Emperor's Choice	Chinese	Inexp/Mod	88	B	5
The Greenery	American	Mod/Exp	88	C	10
Korea Garden	Korean	Inexp/Mod	88	B	8
Le Colonial	French/ Vietnamese	Mod	88	C	1
Mandar Inn	Chinese	Inexp/Mod	88	C	5
Maple Tree Inn	Cajun/Creole	Inexp/Mod	88	B	8
Mirabell Restaurant	German	Inexp/Mod	88	B	2

Restaurants by Star Rating (continued)

Name	Cuisine	Price Rating	Quality Rating	Value Rating	Zone
Oceanique	French/Seafood	Mod/Exp	88	C	11
The Primavera Ristorante	Italian	Inexp/Mod	88	C	4
Sayat Nova	Armenian	Inexp/Mod	88	C	10
St. Germain Restaurant/ Bakery Cafe	French Bistro	Inexp/Mod	88	C	3
Stir Crazy	Pan-Asian	Inexp	88	B	9
Zum Deutschen Eck (The German Corner)	Continental/ German	Incxp/Mod	88	C	1
Bice Ristorante	Italian	Mod/Exp	87	D	3
Cafe Ba Ba Reeba!	Spanish	Mod	87	C	1
Cafe Iberico Tapas Bar	Spanish	Inexp/Mod	87	B	3
La Strada	Italian	Mod/Exp	87	C	4
Lutnia Continental Cafe	Polish	Inexp/Mod	87	C	2
Mei-Shung Chinese Restaurant	Chinese	Inexp	87	B	1
Palm Restaurant	Steak	Mod/Exp	87	C	4
Pastiche	Eclectic	Inexp/Mod	87	B	1
Twisted Lizard	Southwestern	Inexp	87	B	1
Bella Vista	New Italian	Inexp/Mod	86	C	1
Bistro 110	French Bistro	Mod	86	C	3
Harry Caray's	American/Italian	Mod/Exp	86	C	4
Heaven on Seven	Cajun/Creole	Inexp	86	B	4
The Mity Nice Grill	American	Inexp/Mod	86	C	3
Relish	American	Inexp/Mod	86	C	1
Shilla	Korean	Mod	86	C	1
Tania's	Cuban/Spanish	Mod	86	B	2
Harry Caray's (Wheeling)	American/ Italian	Mod	85	C	10
Jilly's Cafe	New American	Inexp/Mod	85	B	11
Michael Jordan's Restaurant	American	Inexp/Mod	85	C	3

Name	Cuisine	Price Rating	Quality Rating	Value Rating	Zone

Three-and-a-Half-Star Restaurants *(continued)*

Name	Cuisine	Price Rating	Quality Rating	Value Rating	Zone
¡Salpicón! A Taste of Mexico	Mexican	Inexp/Mod	85	C	3
Via Veneto	New Italian	Inexp	85	B	1
Wild Onion	American/French/ Italian	Inexp/Mod	85	B	1
Yvette	New French	Inexp/Mod	85	C	3
Yvette Wintergarden	New French	Inexp/Mod	85	C	4
Bukara	Indian	Mod	80	C	3

Three-Star Restaurants

Name	Cuisine	Price Rating	Quality Rating	Value Rating	Zone
Roditys	Greek	Inexp/Mod	89	B	4
Santorini	Greek	Inexp/Mod	89	C	4
Walker Bros. Original Pancake House	American	Inexp	88	B	10, 11
Mama Desta's Red Sea Ethiopian Restaurant	Ethiopian	Inexp	86	B	1
Brasserie Bellevue	Continental	Mod	85	C	3
Flat Top Grill	American	Inexp	85	B	2, 3, 11
Gateway Bar & Grill	Eclectic	Inexp/Mod	85	B	1
Hong Min Restaurant	Chinese	Inexp/Mod	85	B	5
Mongolian Barbeque	Pan-Asian	Inexp	85	B	1, 8
Uncle Tutunji's	Middle Eastern	Inexp	85	B	3
Widow Newton's Tavern	American	Mod	85	C	3
Addis Abeba	Ethiopian	Inexp	84	C	1
Bacino's Trattoria	Italian	Inexp/Mod	84	B	8
Big Bowl Cafe	Pan-Asian	Inexp	84	B	3
Cy's Crab House	Persian/Seafood	Inexp/Mod	84	B	1
Da Nicola Ristorante	Italian	Inexp/Mod	84	B	1
Don Juan	Mexican	Inexp/Mod	84	C	1
Don Roth's in Wheeling	American	Mod	84	C	10
Froggy's French Cafe	New French	Mod	84	B	11
Karyn's Fresh Corner	Vegetarian	Inexp	84	C	1
La Bocca Della Verita	Italian	Inexp/Mod	84	B	1
P.S. Bangkok	Thai	Inexp	84	A	1

Restaurants by Star Rating (continued)

Name	Cuisine	Price Rating	Quality Rating	Value Rating	Zone
Pappagallo's	Italian	Inexp/Mod	84	B	11
Red Tomato	Italian	Inexp	84	B	1
Reza's	Persian/ Vegetarian	Inexp/Mod	84	C	1, 3
Siam Cafe	Thai	Inexp	84	A	1
Skadarlija	Serbian/ Continental	Mod	84	B	1
Soul Kitchen	Southern	Inexp/Mod	84	C	2
Tuscany	Italian	Mod	84	C	5
Uncle Tannous	Middle Eastern	Inexp/Mod	84	B	1
Viceroy of India	Indian	Inexp/Mod	84	B	1
Wildfire (Russell Bry's)	American	Inexp/Mod	84	C	3
Amourette	French	Inexp/Mod	83	B	10
Ann Sather	Swedish	Inexp	83	B	1
Bando	Korean	Inexp/Mod	83	C	1
Chez Delphouse	Caribbean	Inexp/Mod	83	B	1
Del Rio	Italian	Inexp/Mod	83	B	11
Francesco's Hole in the Wall	Italian	Inexp/Mod	83	B	11
Julio's Latin Cafe	Latin	Mod	83	C	10
Pegasus Restaurant and Taverna	Greek	Inexp/Mod	83	C	4
Rosebud Cafe	Italian	Inexp/Mod	83	C	5
Szechwan Restaurant	Chinese	Inexp/Mod	83	C	3
Big Shoulders	American	Inexp	82	B	1
Blackhawk Lodge	New American	Mod	82	C	3
Blind Faith Cafe	Vegetarian	Inexp	82	B	1, 11
Bob Chinn's Crab House	Seafood	Mod	82	B	10
Filippo's	Italian	Inexp/Mod	82	C	1
foodlife	American	Inexp	82	C	3
Mia Francesca	Italian	Inexp/Mod	82	B	1
N. N. Smokehouse	Barbecue	Inexp/Mod	82	B	1
R. J. Grunts	American	Inexp	82	A	1
Sher-A-Punjab	Indian	Inexp	82	B	1
Tucci Milan	Italian	Inexp/Mod	82	C	4

Restaurants by Star Rating *(continued)*

Name	Cuisine	Price Rating	Quality Rating	Value Rating	Zone
Three-Star Restaurants *(continued)*					
Hubbard Street Grill	New American	Inexp/Mod	81	C	4
Kitty O'Shea's	Irish Pub	Inexp	81	B	5
Maggiano's Little Italy	Italian	Mod	81	C	4
Bruna's Ristorante	Italian	Inexp/Mod	80	B	5
Chowpatti Vegetarian Restaurant	Indian/ Vegetarian	Inexp	80	B	10
Hans' Bavarian Lodge	German	Inexp/Mod	80	B	10
Shaw's Seafood Grill	Seafood	Mod	80	C	11
Two-and-a-Half-Star Restaurants					
Amitabul	Korean	Inexp	80	B	1
La Crêperie	French	Inexp	80	A	1
Lulu's	Pan-Asian	Inexp	80	B	11
Alfo's Ristorante	Italian	Inexp	79	B	5
El Dinamico Dallas	Caribbean	Inexp	79	B	1
El Tipico	Mexican	Inexp	79	B	1
Pazzo's Cucina Italiana	New Italian	Inexp/Mod	79	B	2, 8
Pierogi Inn	Polish	Inexp	79	B	2
Stanley's Kitchen & Tap	Southern	Inexp	79	A	1
Bones	Barbecue	Inexp/Mod	78	C	11
Cafe Borgia	Italian	Inexp/Mod	78	B	8
Tango Sur	Argentinian	Inexp/Mod	78	B	1
Home Bakery	Polish	Inexp	77	B	2
Pampanga Restaurant	Filipino	Inexp	77	B	1
Hatsuhana	Japanese	Inexp/Mod	76	C	3
Kanval Palace	Indian	Inexp	76	B	1
Tufano's (Vernon Park Tap)	Italian	Inexp/Mod	76	B	5
Two-Star Restaurants					
Machu Picchu	Peruvian	Inexp	74	B	1

Restaurants by Zone

Name	Star Rating	Price Rating	Quality Rating	Value Rating
Zone 1—North Side				
◆ *American*				
Toulouse on the Park	★★★★½	Mod	94	B
Relish	★★★½	Inexp/Mod	86	C
Wild Onion	★★★½	Inexp/Mod	85	B
Big Shoulders	★★★	Inexp	82	B
R. J. Grunts	★★★	Inexp	82	A
◆ *Argentinian*				
Tango Sur	★★½	Inexp/Mod	78	B
◆ *Barbecue*				
N. N. Smokehouse	★★★	Inexp/Mod	82	B
◆ *Caribbean*				
Chez Delphonse	★★★	Inexp/Mod	83	B
El Dinamico Dallas	★★½	Inexp	79	B
◆ *Chinese*				
Mei-Shung Chinese Restaurant	★★★½	Inexp	87	B
◆ *Continental*				
Cité	★★★★	Exp/V Exp	89	D
Zum Deutschen Eck (The German Corner)	★★★½	Inexp/Mod	88	C
◆ *Eclectic*				
Green Dolphin Street	★★★½	Mod/Exp	89	C
Pastiche	★★★½	Inexp/Mod	87	B
Gateway Bar & Grill	★★★	Inexp/Mod	85	B
◆ *Ethiopian*				
Mama Desta's Red Sea Ethiopian Restaurant	★★★	Inexp	86	B
Addis Abeba	★★★	Inexp	84	C
◆ *Filipino*				
Pampanga Restaurant	★★½	Inexp	77	B

Restaurants by Zone (continued)

Name	Star Rating	Price Rating	Quality Rating	Value Rating
Zone 1—North Side (continued)				
◆ *Fondue*				
Geja's Cafe	★★★½	Exp	90	B
◆ *French*				
Toulouse on the Park	★★★★½	Mod	94	B
Wild Onion	★★★½	Inexp/Mod	85	B
La Crêperie	★★½	Inexp	80	A
◆ *French Bistro*				
Un Grand Cafe	★★★★	Mod	92	C
◆ *French/Vietnamese*				
Le Colonial	★★★½	Mod	88	C
◆ *Fusion*				
Jerome's Red Ginger	★★★½	Inexp/Mod	89	B
◆ *German*				
Golden Ox	★★★★	Mod	90	C
Zum Deutschen Eck (The German Corner)	★★★½	Inexp/Mod	88	C
◆ *Indian*				
Viceroy of India	★★★	Inexp/Mod	84	B
Sher-A-Punjab	★★★	Inexp	82	B
Kanval Palace	★★½	Inexp	76	B
◆ *Italian*				
Trattoria Gianni	★★★★	Inexp/Mod	91	C
Wild Onion	★★★½	Inexp/Mod	85	B
Da Nicola Ristorante	★★★	Inexp/Mod	84	B
La Bocca Della Verita	★★★	Inexp/Mod	84	B
Red Tomato	★★★	Inexp	84	B
Filippo's	★★★	Inexp/Mod	82	C
Mia Francesca	★★★	Inexp/Mod	82	B
◆ *Japanese*				
Katsu Japanese Restaurant	★★★½	Inexp/Mod	90	B

Restaurants by Zone (continued)

Name	Star Rating	Price Rating	Quality Rating	Value Rating
◆ **Korean**				
Shilla	★★★½	Mod	86	C
Bando	★★★	Inexp/Mod	83	C
Amitabul	★★½	Inexp	80	B
◆ **Mexican**				
Don Juan	★★★	Inexp/Mod	84	C
El Tipico	★★½	Inexp	79	B
◆ **Middle Eastern**				
Uncle Tannous	★★★	Inexp/Mod	84	B
◆ **Moroccan/Mediterranean**				
L'Olive Cafe	★★★½	Inexp	91	A
◆ **New American**				
Charlie Trotter's	★★★★★	Very Exp	98	C
erwin	★★★★	Incxp/Mod	94	B
◆ **New French**				
Ambria	★★★★½	Mod/Exp	96	C
◆ **New French/Japanese**				
Yoshi's Cafe	★★★★	Inexp/Mod	94	B
◆ **New Italian**				
Bella Vista	★★★½	Inexp/Mod	86	C
Via Veneto	★★★½	Inexp	85	B
◆ **Pan-Asian**				
Mongolian Barbeque	★★★	Inexp	85	B
◆ **Persian**				
Pars Cove	★★★½	Inexp	89	B
Reza's	★★★½	Inexp/Mod	89	C
Cy's Crab House	★★★	Inexp/Mod	84	B
◆ **Peruvian**				
Machu Picchu	★★	Inexp	74	B

Name	Star Rating	Price Rating	Quality Rating	Value Rating
Zone 1—North Side *(continued)*				
◆ *Seafood*				
Cy's Crab House	★★★	Inexp/Mod	84	B
◆ *Serbian/Continental*				
Skadarlija	★★★	Mod	84	B
◆ *Southern*				
Stanley's Kitchen & Tap	★★½	Inexp	79	A
◆ *Southwestern*				
Blue Mesa	★★★★	Inexp/Mod	89	B
Twisted Lizard	★★★½	Inexp	87	B
◆ *Spanish*				
Emilio's Tapas Bar Restaurant	★★★★	Mod	91	C
Cafe-Ba-Ba-Reeba!	★★★½	Mod	87	C
◆ *Swedish*				
Ann Sather	★★★	Inexp	83	B
◆ *Thai*				
Arun's	★★★★½	Mod/Exp	95	C
P.S. Bangkok	★★★	Inexp	84	A
Siam Cafe	★★★	Inexp	84	A
◆ *Vegetarian*				
Reza's	★★★½	Inexp/Mod	89	C
Karyn's Fresh Corner	★★★	Inexp	84	C
Blind Faith Cafe	★★★	Inexp	82	B
◆ *Vietnamese*				
Pasteur	★★★★	Inexp/Mod	92	B
Hoang Mai	★★★½	Inexp	89	A
Nhu Hoa Cafe	★★★½	Inexp/Mod	89	B
Zone 2—North Central/O'Hare				
◆ *Cuban/Spanish*				
Tania's	★★★½	Mod	86	B

Name	Star Rating	Price Rating	Quality Rating	Value Rating
◆ *German*				
Mirabell Restaurant	★★★½	Inexp/Mod	88	B
◆ *Italian*				
Carlucci	★★★½	Mod	88	C
◆ *New Italian*				
Pazzo's Cucina Italiana	★★½	Inexp/Mod	79	B
◆ *Polish*				
Lutnia Continental Cafe	★★★½	Inexp/Mod	87	C
Pierogi Inn	★★½	Inexp	79	B
Home Bakery	★★½	Inexp	77	B
◆ *Seafood*				
Nick's Fishmarket	★★★★	Mod/Exp	95	D
◆ *Southern*				
Soul Kitchen	★★★	Inexp/Mod	84	C
◆ *Steak*				
Morton's of Chicago	★★★★	Exp	93	C
Zone 3—Near North				
◆ *American*				
Seasons Restaurant at the Four Seasons Hotel	★★★★★	Mod/Exp	99	C
Spago	★★★★½	Mod/Exp	94	B
Spago Grill	★★★★	Mod/Exp	94	B
The Pump Room	★★★★	Exp	92	C
House of Blues	★★★★	Inexp/Mod	90	B
Iron Mike's Grille	★★★½	Mod/Exp	90	C
Mango	★★★½	Inexp/Mod	90	B
The Mity Nice Grill	★★★½	Inexp/Mod	86	C
Michael Jordan's Restaurant	★★★½	Inexp/Mod	85	C
Flat Top Grill	★★★	Inexp	85	B
Widow Newton's Tavern	★★★	Mod	85	C
Wildfire (Russell Bry's)	★★★	Inexp/Mod	84	C
foodlife	★★★	Inexp	82	C

Restaurants by Zone (continued)

Name	Star Rating	Price Rating	Quality Rating	Value Rating
Zone 3—Near North (continued)				
◆ *Cajun/Creole*				
Bazzell's French Quarter Bistro	★★★½	Inexp/Mod	89	B
◆ *Chinese*				
Ben Pao	★★★½	Inexp/Mod	90	B
Szechwan Restaurant	★★★	Inexp/Mod	83	C
◆ *Continental*				
The Pump Room	★★★★	Exp	92	C
Biggs	★★★★	Mod	90	C
Brasserie Bellevue	★★★	Mod	85	C
◆ *French Bistro*				
Kiki's Bistro	★★★★	Inexp/Mod	94	C
Brasserie Jo	★★★★	Inexp/Mod	92	B
Cyrano's Bistrot & Wine Bar	★★★½	Inexp/Mod	90	B
St. Germain Restaurant/ Bakery Cafe	★★★½	Inexp/Mod	88	C
Bistro 110	★★★½	Mod	86	C
◆ *Greek*				
Papagus Greek Taverna	★★★½	Mod	90	C
◆ *Indian*				
Bukara	★★★½	Mod	80	C
◆ *Italian*				
Spiaggia	★★★★½	Mod/Exp	95	C
Avanzare	★★★½	Mod	90	C
Cafe Spiaggia	★★★½	Mod	89	C
Pane Caldo	★★★½	Mod/VExp	89	D
Trattoria Parma	★★★½	Inexp/Mod	89	B
Cafe Luciano	★★★½	Inexp/Mod	88	B
Bice Ristorante	★★★½	Mod/Exp	87	D
◆ *Japanese*				
Hatsuhana	★★½	Inexp/Mod	76	C

Name	Star Rating	Price Rating	Quality Rating	Value Rating
◆ *Korean*				
Woo Lae Oak	★★★★	Inexp	94	C
◆ *Mediterranean*				
Mantuano Mediterranean Table	★★★★	Inexp/Mod	91	C
◆ *Mexican*				
¡Salpicón! A Taste of Mexico	★★★½	Inexp/Mod	85	C
◆ *Middle Eastern*				
Uncle Tutunji's	★★★	Inexp	85	B
◆ *New American*				
Park Avenue Cafe	★★★★½	Mod/Exp	94	C
Spruce	★★★★½	Inexp/Mod	94	B
The Signature Room at the 95th	★★★★	Mod/Exp	90	C
The Cafe	★★★½	Mod	90	C
Elaine and Ina's	★★★½	Inexp/Mod	89	B
Mrs. Park's Tavern	★★★½	Inexp/Mod	89	C
Blackhawk Lodge	★★★	Mod	82	C
◆ *New French*				
The Dining Room	★★★★½	Mod/Exp	97	C
Yvette	★★★½	Inexp/Mod	85	C
◆ *Pan-Asian*				
Big Bowl Cafe	★★★	Inexp	84	B
◆ *Persian / Vegetarian*				
Reza's	★★★½	Inexp/Mod	89	C
◆ *Seafood*				
Cape Cod Room	★★★½	Mod/Exp	91	C
Riva	★★★½	Mod/Exp	90	C
◆ *Spanish*				
Cafe Iberico Tapas Bar	★★★½	Inexp/Mod	87	B

Restaurants by Zone (continued)

Name	Star Rating	Price Rating	Quality Rating	Value Rating
Zone 3—Near North *(continued)*				
◆ *Steak*				
Gibson's Steakhouse	★★★★½	Mod/V Exp	94	C
Chicago Chop House	★★★★	Mod	94	C
Morton's of Chicago	★★★★	Exp	93	C
Lawry's The Prime Rib	★★★★	Mod	90	B
Riva	★★★½	Mod/Exp	90	C
The Saloon	★★★½	Mod/Exp	89	C
Eli's, The Place for Steak	★★★½	Mod/Exp	88	C
◆ *Thai*				
Thai Borrahn	★★★★	Inexp/Mod	90	B
Zone 4—The Loop				
◆ *American/Italian*				
Harry Caray's	★★★½	Mod/Exp	86	C
◆ *Bakery Cafe*				
Corner Bakery	★★★½	Inexp/Mod	90	B
◆ *Cajun/Creole*				
Heaven on Seven	★★★½	Inexp	86	B
◆ *Chinese*				
Szechwan East	★★★★	Mod	92	C
◆ *French*				
Everest	★★★★★	Exp	98	C
Entre Nous	★★★★	Mod/Exp	90	C
◆ *German*				
The Berghoff	★★★½	Inexp	88	B
◆ *Greek*				
The Parthenon	★★★★	Inexp/Mod	95	B
Roditys	★★★	Inexp/Mod	89	B
Santorini	★★★	Inexp/Mod	89	C
Pegasus Restaurant and Taverna	★★★	Inexp/Mod	83	C

Name	Star Rating	Price Rating	Quality Rating	Value Rating
◆ *Indian*				
Klay Oven	★★★★	Mod	94	B
◆ *Italian*				
Vivere (Italian Village)	★★★★½	Mod	95	C
Coco Pazzo	★★★★	Mod	91	C
The Primavera Ristorante	★★★½	Inexp/Mod	88	C
La Strada	★★★½	Mod/Exp	87	C
Tucci Milan	★★★	Inexp/Mod	82	C
Maggiano's Little Italy	★★★	Mod	81	C
◆ *Italian/Mediterranean*				
Cuisines	★★★½	Inexp/Mod	89	B
◆ *Mexican*				
Topolobampo	★★★★½	Mod	95	C
Frontera Grill	★★★★	Inexp	93	B
◆ *New American*				
Gordon	★★★★½	Exp	94	C
Hubbard Street Grill	★★★	Inexp/Mod	81	C
◆ *New French*				
Yvette Wintergarden	★★★½	Inexp/Mod	85	C
◆ *Russian*				
Russian Tea Time	★★★★	Mod	93	C
◆ *Seafood*				
Shaw's Crab House and Shaw's Blue Crab Lounge & Oyster Bar	★★★★½	Mod	95	C
Nick's Fishmarket	★★★★	Mod/Exp	95	D
Catch 35	★★★½	Mod/Exp	93	C
◆ *Steak*				
Ruth's Chris Steakhouse	★★★★	Mod/Exp	93	B
Kinzie Street Chophouse	★★★★	Mod	91	B
Palm Restaurant	★★★½	Mod/Exp	87	C

Restaurants by Zone (continued)

Name	Star Rating	Price Rating	Quality Rating	Value Rating
Zone Five—South Loop				
◆ *American*				
Prairie	★★★★½	Mod/Exp	95	C
◆ *Chinese*				
Emperor's Choice	★★★½	Inexp/Mod	88	B
Mandar Inn	★★★½	Inexp/Mod	88	C
Hong Min Restaurant	★★★	Inexp/Mod	85	B
◆ *Irish Pub*				
Kitty O'Shea's	★★★	Inexp	81	B
◆ *Italian*				
Tuscany	★★★	Mod	84	C
Rosebud Cafe	★★★	Inexp/Mod	83	C
Bruna's Ristorante	★★★	Inexp/Mod	80	B
Alfo's Ristorante	★★½	Inexp	79	B
Tufano's (Vernon Park Tap)	★★½	Inexp/Mod	76	B
◆ *New American*				
Printer's Row	★★★★½	Mod	95	B
Zone Six—South Central/Midway				
◆ *Greek*				
Papagus Greek Taverna	★★★½	Mod	90	C
Zone Seven—South Side				
◆ *Southern*				
Army & Lou's	★★★★	Inexp/Mod	90	B
Zone Eight—Southern Suburbs				
◆ *Cajun/Creole*				
Maple Tree Inn	★★★½	Inexp/Mod	88	B
◆ *Chinese*				
Hong Min Chinese Restaurant	★★★	Inexp/Mod	85	B

Restaurants by Zone (continued)

Name	Star Rating	Price Rating	Quality Rating	Value Rating
◆ *French Bistro*				
Bistro Banlieue	★★★★	Inexp/Mod	93	B
◆ *Indian*				
Indian Summer	★★★★	Inexp/Mod	94	C
◆ *Italian*				
Cucina Roma	★★★½	Inexp/Mod	89	B
Bacino's Trattoria	★★★	Inexp/Mod	84	B
Maggiano's Little Italy	★★★	Mod	81	C
Cafe Borgia	★★½	Inexp/Mod	78	B
◆ *Korean*				
Korea Garden	★★★½	Inexp/Mod	88	B
◆ *New American*				
Courtwright's	★★★★½	Mod/Exp	96	B
◆ *New French*				
Tallgrass	★★★★★	Very Exp	98	C
Montparnasse	★★★★½	Mod/Exp	95	C
◆ *New Italian*				
Pazzo's Cucina Italiana	★★½	Inexp/Mod	79	B
◆ *Pan-Asian*				
Mongolian Barbeque	★★★	Inexp	85	B
◆ *Southern/Caribbean*				
Carzz Grilleria	★★★½	Inexp/Mod	88	B
◆ *Spanish*				
Emilio's Meson Sabika Tapas Bar Restaurant	★★★★	Mod	93	C
◆ *Steak*				
Morton's of Chicago	★★★★	Exp	93	C

Name	Star Rating	Price Rating	Quality Rating	Value Rating
Zone Nine—Western Suburbs				
◆ *Indian*				
Viceroy of India	★★★	Inexp/Mod	84	B
◆ *New American*				
302 West	★★★★	Mod	92	C
◆ *Pan-Asian*				
Stir Crazy	★★★½	Inexp	88	B
Zone Ten—Northwest Suburbs				
◆ *American*				
The Greenery	★★★½	Mod/Exp	88	C
Walker Bros. Original Pancake House	★★★	Inexp	88	B
Don Roth's in Wheeling	★★★	Mod	84	C
◆ *American/Italian*				
Harry Caray's (Wheeling)	★★★½	Mod	85	C
◆ *Armenian*				
Sayat Nova	★★★½	Inexp/Mod	88	C
◆ *Caribbean*				
Julio's Latin Cafe	★★★	Mod	83	C
◆ *French*				
Le Français	★★★★★	Exp	97	C
Le Vichyssois	★★★★½	Mod	95	B
Amourette	★★★	Inexp/Mod	83	B
◆ *German*				
Hans' Bavarian Lodge	★★★	Inexp/Mod	80	B
◆ *Indian/Vegetarian*				
Chowpatti Vegetarian Restaurant	★★★	Inexp	80	B
◆ *New French*				
Le Titi de Paris	★★★★½	Mod/Exp	97	C

Name	Star Rating	Price Rating	Quality Rating	Value Rating

◆ *Seafood*

Name	Star Rating	Price Rating	Quality Rating	Value Rating
Bob Chinn's Crab House	★★★	Mod	82	B

Zone Eleven—Northern Suburbs

◆ *American*

Name	Star Rating	Price Rating	Quality Rating	Value Rating
Brasserie T	★★★½	Inexp/Mod	90	B
Walker Bros. Original Pancake House	★★★	Inexp	88	B
Flat Top Grill	★★★	Inexp	85	B

◆ *Barbecue*

Name	Star Rating	Price Rating	Quality Rating	Value Rating
Bones	★★½	Inexp/Mod	78	C

◆ *French*

Name	Star Rating	Price Rating	Quality Rating	Value Rating
Carlos'	★★★★½	Mod/Exp	96	C
Oceanique	★★★½	Mod/Exp	88	C

◆ *French/Italian*

Name	Star Rating	Price Rating	Quality Rating	Value Rating
Gabriel's Restaurant	★★★★	Mod/Exp	93	C

◆ *Fusion*

Name	Star Rating	Price Rating	Quality Rating	Value Rating
Trio	★★★★★	Exp/V Exp	98	C

◆ *Greek*

Name	Star Rating	Price Rating	Quality Rating	Value Rating
Mykonos	★★★½	Inexp/Mod	92	B

◆ *Italian*

Name	Star Rating	Price Rating	Quality Rating	Value Rating
Va Pensiero	★★★★½	Mod	96	C
Campagnola	★★★★	Inexp/Mod	94	B
Cafe Luciano	★★★½	Inexp/Mod	88	B
Pappagallo's	★★★	Inexp/Mod	84	B
Del Rio	★★★	Inexp/Mod	83	B
Francesco's Hole in the Wall	★★★	Inexp/Mod	83	B
Maggiano's Little Italy	★★★	Mod	81	C

◆ *Japanese*

Name	Star Rating	Price Rating	Quality Rating	Value Rating
Kuni's	★★★★½	Inexp/Mod	96	C
Akai Hana	★★★½	Inexp/Mod	88	C

Restaurants by Zone (continued)

Name	Star Rating	Price Rating	Quality Rating	Value Rating
Zone Eleven—Northern Suburbs (continued)				
◆ *Mexican*				
El Tipico	★★½	Inexp	79	B
◆ *New American*				
Jilly's Cafe	★★★½	Inexp/Mod	85	B
◆ *New French*				
Froggy's French Cafe	★★★	Mod	84	B
◆ *Pan-Asian*				
Lulu's	★★½	Inexp	80	B
◆ *Seafood*				
Oceanique	★★★½	Mod/Exp	88	C
Shaw's Seafood Grill	★★★	Mod	80	C
◆ *Seafood/Steak*				
Don's Fishmarket and Tavern	★★★★	Inexp/Exp	95	B
◆ *Vegetarian*				
Blind Faith Cafe	★★★	Inexp	82	B

Addis Abeba

Zone 1   North Side
3521 North Clark Street
(773) 929-9383

Ethiopian	
★★★	
Inexpensive	
Quality 84	Value C

Reservations:	Recommended on weekends
When to go:	Weekdays are less crowded
Entree range:	$8.50–10
Payment:	All major credit cards
Service rating:	★★★
Friendliness rating:	★★★
Parking:	Street, three garages nearby
Bar:	Full service
Wine selection:	Italian, American, and Ethiopian
Dress:	Casual
Disabled access:	Yes, including rest rooms
Customers:	Mostly locals, ethnics; a few tourists
Dinner:	Monday–Thursday, 5–10 P.M.; Friday and Saturday, 5–11 P.M.; Sunday, 4–10 P.M.

Atmosphere/setting: Clean, well-lit setting filled with exotic artifacts of Ethiopia, including paintings and handwoven straw baskets. African tablecloths with ivory and black batik prints add to the ethnic aura.

House specialties: Fosolia (string beans, onions, and carrots cooked in tomato sauce) is exceptional; other vegetarian dishes of lentils, chickpeas, and mushrooms, seasoned with exotic spices, are equally zesty; savory doro tibs (breast of chicken stir-fried in Ethiopian herb butter and garlic) comes mild or spicy, as do many other entrees.

Other recommendations: Spicy appetizers such as the sambussa, jalapeño, and lentil "egg roll" will tingle your taste buds; katenya (spinach and cheese blended with spiced butter and cardamom, rolled up in injera, the spongy, sour bread) is another superb, tangy treat.

Summary & comments: Ethiopian dishes, most of which are saucy, are served on communal platters, from which customers dip them with injera. If you're eating with friends, it is a great idea to order the vegetarian, meat, veg-meat, or seafood and meat combinations so you can sample the wide array of succulent dishes available at Addis Abeba.

Akai Hana

Zone 11 Northern Suburbs	Japanese
3217 West Lake Avenue, Wilmette	★★★½
(847) 251-0384; fax (847) 251-0384	Inexpensive/Moderate
	Quality 88 Value C

Reservations: Accepted for 6 or more
When to go: Before 6 P.M.
Entree range: $10–14. Sushi combination boxes: lunch,
                    $7.75–16; dinner, $15–16
Payment: All major credit cards
Service rating: ★★★½
Friendliness rating: ★★★★
Parking: Free
Bar: Wine and beer
Wine selection: Average for Japanese restaurant: limited—sake,
                    some American
Dress: Casual
Disabled access: Yes
Customers: Locals, including Japanese businesspeople who
                    settled in the area
Lunch: Every day, 11:30 A.M.–2 P.M.
Dinner: Monday–Thursday, 5–10 P.M.; Friday and Saturday,
                    5–10:20 P.M.; Sunday, 4:30–9:20 P.M.

Atmosphere/setting: Bright and bustling; white tablecloths with wooden accents. Recently added 50 more seats.

House specialties: Sushi combination boxes; sautéed giant clam. Salmon teriyaki is one of the best dishes. Extensive appetizer list includes some very native Japanese items, such as fried shrimp heads.

Other recommendations: Teriyaki preparations; combo plates. Green tea ice cream is a refreshing finish.

Summary & comments: This restaurant grew from a grocery and became an instant success, and it recently expanded again. The North Shore was lacking a good Japanese restaurant, and this place filled the niche. The success of Akai Hana is a good start toward expanding suburban culinary horizons beyond French, Italian, and American.

Alfo's Ristorante

Zone 5 South Loop	Italian
2512 South Oakley Avenue,	★★½
Heart of Italy neighborhood	Inexpensive
(773) 523-6994	Quality 79 Value B

Reservations:	Recommended
When to go:	Any time
Entree range:	$8.50–15.95
Payment:	VISA, MC, AMEX, DC
Service rating:	★★★½
Friendliness rating:	★★★★½
Parking:	Adjacent lot
Bar:	Full service
Wine selection:	Italian, some Californian
Dress:	Casual
Disabled access:	Yes
Customers:	Diverse
Lunch:	Tuesday–Friday, 11 A.M.–3 P.M.
Dinner:	Tuesday–Friday, 3–10 P.M.; Saturday, 4:30–11 P.M.; Sunday, 2–9 P.M., bar open until 2 A.M.

Atmosphere/setting: Cozy, intimate setting; homey and dimly lit. Large, private booths.

House specialties: Fried calamari (some of the best); veal saltimbocca; beef braggiole (flattened, rolled steak filled with prosciutto, sausage, cheese, and seasonings and topped with tomato sauce; served with pasta).

Other recommendations: Chicken Vesuvio; homemade ravioli; lasagna; linguine with clam sauce.

Summary & comments: This longtime establishment is one of the anchors in this Heart of Italy neighborhood brimming with Italian eateries. Owner Josette Pieroni is motherly and nurturing. Service takes a cue from her direction and is caring and friendly. Food may be a bit old-fashioned in style, but it's prepared well and served with love. Very Italian and comforting.

Ambria

Zone 1 North Side	New French
Beldon Stratford Hotel,	★★★★½
2300 North Lincoln Park West	Moderate/Expensive
(773) 472-0076	Quality 96 Value C

Reservations:	Required
When to go:	Early on weeknights; late on weekends
Entree range:	$19.50–29.95; 5-course degustation menus, $48 and $64 (larger)
Payment:	All major credit cards
Service rating:	★★★★
Friendliness rating:	★★★★
Parking:	Valet, $4
Bar:	Full-service, dining bar for customers only
Wine selection:	Award-winning; 570 international, $15–1,500; 5 by the glass, $8–12; sommelier Robert Bansberg shows exceptional skill at matching wines with food and personal tastes
Dress:	Dressy; jacket required, tie optional
Disabled access:	Wheelchair accessible; call ahead
Customers:	Sophisticated, selective, international, locals
Dinner:	Monday–Thursday, 6–9:30 P.M.; Friday and Saturday, 6–10:30 P.M.

Atmosphere/setting: Deep-toned woods, ultrasuede banquettes, and crystalline etched glass; tiny shaded lamps on each table; massive flower-filled urns. Resembles an old mansion or turn-of-the-century club; murals and elegant fixtures; fashionable decor.

House specialties: Roasted New York state foie gras with caramelized apples; loin of lamb; fillet of Casco Bay cod; mango parfait with berries.

Other recommendations: Baby pheasant with foie gras, wild mushrooms, and thyme broth; a symphony of market vegetables and grains; venison medallions with blackberry sauce; soufflé du jour.

Summary & comments: Well-established (17-plus years) and the crème de la crème of French restaurants. Longtime chef-owner Gabino Sotelino maintains fine quality here. Lovely presentations. Some minor flaws occasionally in food and service, but overall, a very reliable place.

Honors/awards: Four-star rating from *Chicago* magazine, *Chicago Tribune,* and *Mobil Travel Guide;* five diamonds from AAA; *Wine Spectator* Award of Excellence.

Amitabul

Zone 1   North Side
3418 North Southport
(773) 472-4060

Korean Buddhist Vegetarian	
★★½	
Inexpensive	
Quality 80	Value B

Reservations:	Accepted only for 6 or more
When to go:	Weekdays after 3 P.M. are less crowded
Entree range:	$5.50–7.99
Payment:	AMEX, VISA, MC, DC
Service rating:	★★★
Friendliness rating:	★★★★
Parking:	Street
Bar:	Wine and beer; serves only microbrewery gourmet beer
Wine selection:	A small selection, including sake and Zinfandel
Dress:	Casual
Disabled access:	Yes
Customers:	Young urbans, older couples, singles, vegetarians, enlightened diners
Lunch/Dinner:	Every day, 11 A.M.–9:30 P.M.

Atmosphere / setting: Contemporary, simple decor; beamed ceilings; clean design lines; attractive service bar; Buddhist meditative music.

House specialties: Mandoo can do (12 Korean-style egg rolls, served as an appetizer); entrees of Amitabul bi–bim–bop (various steamed vegetables and roots over steamed brown rice); Buddha bop (steamed brown rice with chestnuts, dates, and red beans); Amitabul original, a vegan item (whole-wheat pancakes with vegetables); very attractive jade maki (rice rolls with avocado, cucumber, and spinach); and a potent ginger tea.

Other recommendations: Real vegan egg roll (egg and dairy free); Buddha's three luck dish (steamed zucchini, green beans, wild sesame leaves, and lotus roots); heavenly nirvana (flavorful salad); vegan energy cakes; nine ways to nirvana (whole-wheat noodle soup made with nine-grain miso beans aged for 12 years); vegan tofu young (crushed tofu and vegetable dish); and barley tea.

Summary & comments: Amitabul in Korean Buddhist terms means "awakening," which is appropriate for this spiritual, healthful food. Some dishes are spicy, and others are a bit too bland, but they can be enlivened with the sauces on the table—hot or sweet, or a blend. This menu is large—as are the portions—and quite whimsically written with a spiritual and health slant.

Amourette

Zone 10 Northwest Suburbs	French
2275 Rand Road, Palatine	★★★
(847) 359-6220	Inexpensive/Moderate
	Quality 83 Value B

Reservations:	Recommended; necessary on Friday and Saturday
When to go:	Weekdays
Entree range:	$9.95–22
Payment:	All major credit cards
Service rating:	★★★★
Friendliness rating:	★★★★½
Parking:	Lot around restaurant
Bar:	Full service ·
Wine selection:	International by bottle and glass
Dress:	Casual
Disabled access:	Yes
Customers:	Diverse, businesspeople, couples, locals
Lunch:	Tuesday–Friday, 11:30 A.M.–2 P.M.
Dinner:	Tuesday–Sunday, 5–10:30 P.M.

Atmosphere/setting: Romantic French cafe; cozy with Gallic decorative touches; welcoming.

House specialties: Fromage de chevre sur son lit vert (Caesar salad with romaine lettuce, Parmesan cheese, Dijon mustard, Worcestershire sauce, minced anchovy, olive oil, and croutons topped with sautéed, herb-encrusted goat cheese); assortment of pâtés and fine cheeses; rack of lamb; roast duck.

Other recommendations: Sautéed Dover sole meunière or amandine, filleted tableside; snapper fillets and herbal Boursin cheese in phyllo, atop fresh spinach; monthly prix-fixe, four-course dinner, $19.50, Sunday–Friday.

Summary & comments: This charming suburban place serves well-prepared French cuisine that doesn't deviate much from the classics. Chef Michel Coatrieux keeps his cooking simple, and the finished dishes are not fussy in presentation. Happily, Amourette offers excellent French fare at reasonable prices. Restaurant is available for parties.

Ann Sather

Zone 1   North Side
929 West Belmont Avenue, Lakeview
(773) 348-2378; fax (773) 348-1713

Zone 1   North Side
5207 North Clark Street, Andersonville
(312) 271-6677

Zone 1   North Side
2665 North Clark Street, Lincoln Park
(773) 327-9522

Swedish/American (diner-style)	
★★★	
Inexpensive	
Quality 83	Value B

Reservations:	Accepted for 6 or more
When to go:	Monday, Tuesday, and Wednesday
Entree range:	$7.95–11.95
Payment:	VISA, MC, AMEX
Service rating:	★★★★
Friendliness rating:	★★★★½
Parking:	Lot (Belmont); street (Linclon Park); call for details (Andersonville)
Bar:	Full service, including Swedish beer and cocktails, such as glögg and Simply Swedish (Absolut on the rocks)
Wine selection:	6 American choices at the reasonable price of $3 a glass or $12 a bottle
Dress:	Casual
Disabled access:	Yes (Lakeview and Lincoln Park); no (Andersonville)
Customers:	Neighborhood regulars, families, singles, seniors
Open:	Every day, 7 A.M.–10 P.M.; breakfast served all day; lunch/dinner starts at 11 A.M.; Lincoln Park location does not serve dinner

Atmosphere / setting: Hand-painted Scandinavian murals grace the walls. The original Lakeview location has six rooms on two levels. The third and newest Lincoln Park cafe is the tiniest. All the locations are homey and welcoming—you'd be secure in taking your mother or children there. Andersonville designates the downstairs a nonsmoking area on weekends, 9:30 A.M.–2 P.M.

House specialties: For dinner, Swedish sampler (roast duck with lingonberry glaze, meatball, potato sausage, sauerkraut, and brown beans); broiled salmon with mustard dill sauce; Swedish meatballs. Lunch items include grilled chicken breast sandwich; burgers of several styles (avocado Swiss, blue cheese);

(continued)

veggie burger; and cold sandwich: chef's market ham, roast turkey, or roasted beef tenderloin served on choice of bread (Swedish limpa, rye) with trimmings. A variety of enticing salads include shrimp and seafood, stuffed tomato, and citrus chicken. For breakfast, don't miss the signature large cinnamon rolls or the Swedish pancakes with lingonberries.

Other recommendations: For dinner, Swedish sirloin steak with onions; roast loin of pork with celery dressing and gravy; Swedish potato sausage; Lake Superior whitefish broiled with lemon and tartar sauce; hot peach cobbler with ice cream; Swedish spritzer. Lunch: vegetarian chili and daily homemade soup. Breakfast: Swedish waffles with option of ice cream and strawberries.

Summary & comments: The only restaurant serving Swedish specialties at meals other than breakfast, and dinner items come in two sizes and prices, diner-style. Complete meals include a starter, an entree, two sides, and a dessert; light meals include a light portion entree and two sides. The menu prices appear to be yesterday's, so dining here is a great value today. This Swedish diner founded by Ann Sather in 1945 was bought by current owner Tom Tunney. Very comfortable for dining alone. Friendly, nurturing staffers welcome customers of any age—kids get complimentary kiddy cocktails and rainbow sherbet.

Honors/awards: Voted best breakfast in the Midwest, January 1994, by *CBS This Morning.*

ARMY & LOU'S

Zone 7   South Side
422 East 75th Street
(773) 483-3100; fax (773) 483-1304

Southern	★★★★
Inexpensive/Moderate	
Quality 90 Value B	

Reservations:	Accepted any time for any size group
When to go:	Weekdays after lunch rush
Entree range:	$6.95–22.95
Payment:	VISA, MC, AMEX; no checks
Service rating:	★★★★
Friendliness rating:	★★★★
Parking:	Lot next door
Bar:	Full service
Wine selection:	About 12 selections by the glass only; reasonably priced; mostly Californian
Dress:	Casual
Disabled access:	Yes
Customers:	From all over the area; many out-of-state visitors
Open:	Wednesday–Monday, 9 A.M.–10 P.M.

Atmosphere/setting: Bright, cheerful, and comfortable with light-colored sponged walls and a rotating art exhibit from the gallery across the street featuring African and Haitian art. Tablecloths and flowers. Nonsmoking dining room.

House specialties: Fresh farm-raised catfish steaks and catfish fillet; half a fried chicken (juicy, not greasy); award-winning seafood gumbo; U.S. prime kosher short ribs of beef jardinière; meaty baby-back ribs with zesty barbecue sauce.

Other recommendations: Chicken gumbo; New England clam chowder; fried jumbo oysters; fried jumbo shrimp; cornbread stuffing; peach cobbler; sweet potato pie.

Summary & comments: This popular South Side restaurant celebrated its 52nd anniversary in 1997. Original recipes are used but have been adjusted to be lower in sodium and fat. The food is excellent, the servers charming and friendly, and the place comfortable, so it's no wonder that the regulars keep returning. The place swells on Sunday after church, and politicians and community groups keep the private room busy. Children's menu available.

ARUN'S

Zone 1   North Side
4156 North Kedzie Avenue
(773) 539-1909

Thai	
★★★★½	
Moderate/Expensive	
Quality 95	Value C

Reservations:	Recommended
When to go:	Dinner
Entree range:	$13.95–23.95
Payment:	Major credit cards
Service rating:	★★★★★
Friendliness rating:	★★★★½
Parking:	Street
Bar:	Full service, including Thai and Japanese beers
Wine selection:	International—about two dozen Austrian, French, Italian, and Californian, $18–46; about 5 by the glass (often pinot grigio, chardonnay, Beaujolais, and sparkling)
Dress:	Casual; mostly chic and business attire
Disabled access:	Yes
Customers:	Locals and visitors, businesspeople, couples, groups
Dinner:	Tuesday–Saturday, 5–10 P.M.; Sunday, 5–9 P.M.

Atmosphere / setting: Colorful exterior is quite simple, which makes entering this place a surprise. Beautifully appointed, multilevel interior of simple overall design contrasted by rich textures and colors. Small, museum-like front alcove is a gallery devoted to antiques and exquisite art. Colorful authentic art and other Thai artifacts adorn the intimate rooms, which project an ancient aesthetic tradition. Kitchen has been enlarged; the owner's youngest brother, an artist/architect, did much of the design and art work, and the talented owner, Arun Sampanthavivat, modestly hung his own paintings in the rest rooms.

House specialties: Khao kriab (steamed rice dumplings filled with Dungeness crab meat, shrimp, chicken, peanuts, garlic, and a tangy sweet-sour vinaigrette); picturesque golden baskets (flower-shaped, bite-sized pastries filled with a mixture of shrimp, chicken, sweet corn, and shiitake mushrooms, garnished with intricately carved vegetable baskets); pad thai with chicken; three-flavored red snapper (crisply fried whole fish with traditional Bangkok-style three-flavored tamarind sauce: spicy, sweet, and sour); three-combination curry (country-style yellow curry with shrimp quenelle, chicken, squash, and fuzzy melon in a sauce

(continued)

that's hot, spicy, and peppery). Lemongrass ice cream with coconut milk and a sweet rice flower with palm nuts; sliced summer mango served with a ball of sticky rice enhanced with a coconut glaze (take a bite of each together)—a very Thai dessert.

Other recommendations: Hoy tord (crusty golden mussel pancake topped with bean sprouts, garlic chive, and hot chile and sweet chile-garlic sauces); Siamese dumplings (delicate rice dumplings with minced shrimp, chicken, sweet daikon turnips, peanuts, fragrant fried garlic) served on lettuce (as a wrap); crab spring roll; fish dumpling (snapper or market catch); chicken coconut soup with cilantro and lime; summer salad (seasonal) with mint, sprouts, and fish cake slices; gingery veal with lemongrass and miso (no veal in Thai history—the owner created this); meefun delight (soft-fried noodles with shrimp, chicken, and scallions). Desserts are delightful: seven-layer rice custard (alternating colors of white, pink, and pale green) steamed from a mixture of rice flour and coconut milk. And while poetic license was employed with the next, it's great nonetheless: poached pear in red wine with bite-sized chocolate cakes and strawberry-ginger sauce. End with a wonderful elixir of sweet lemongrass soup with tiny fruit balls, which is purifying and serves as a digestive.

Summary & comments: This magnificently decorated restaurant serves appropriately exquisite food; plate presentations are stunning. Executive chef-owner Arun Sampanthavivat has refined traditional Thai cuisine, blended it with creative touches, and elevated Thai cooking to a new fine-dining plateau. His menu reveals the use of chiles, but the food doesn't cause burns and tears if you're cautious about not eating the peppers. The nuances here are more herbal, delicately spicy, sweet, and sour. Arun loves to carve the intricate vegetable baskets that garnish plates, and he spends about two hours daily on this task. His brother, Akanit Sampanthavivat, is the chef, and their mother also works in the kitchen. In late 1994, a party room was built and the kitchen was enlarged. The higher prices at this Thai restaurant are understandable once you see and taste the results of this labor-intensive cuisine. I'd prefer several more wines by the glass on the list. Arun's is by far one of the top Thai restaurants in the country.

Honors/awards: Four stars from *Mobil Travel Guide,* 1997; chef was named Best Chef in the Midwest by the James Beard Foundation, 1997.

Avanzare

Zone 3 Near North	Northern Italian
161 East Huron Street	★★★½
(312) 337-8056	Moderate
	Quality 90 Value C

Reservations:	Strongly recommended
When to go:	Lunch; dinner, 5–6:30 P.M.
Entree range:	Lunch, $11–17; dinner, $13–26.25
Payment:	All major credit cards
Service rating:	★★★★½
Friendliness rating:	★★★★½
Parking:	Valet
Bar:	Full service, but no beer on tap
Wine selection:	Italian, some American; $25–220 a bottle; $5.25–8.75 a glass; champagnes, $28–30 a half bottle, or $7–13 a glass
Dress:	Upscale casual to dressy
Disabled access:	Yes; call first
Customers:	Locals, professionals, businesspeople, travelers
Open:	Monday–Thursday, 5:30–10 P.M.; Friday and Saturday, 5–11 P.M.; Sunday, 5–9:30 P.M.

Atmosphere/setting: Large and stately with high ceilings and beautiful wood. Second level has more seating. Lovely sidewalk cafe.

House specialties: Cuscusu di tonno Sardegnese (seared tuna); insalata di Gorgonzola e pere (grilled pear with watercress); Agnolotti di spinaci e ricotta con brodo di funghi porcini (pasta pillows stuffed with spinach, aged ricotta, and mushrooms); torre di verdure (grilled vegetable tower); salmone in padella (pan-seared salmon); and budino di cioccolato (chocolate-banana pudding cake).

Other recommendations: Polenta con mascarpone e funghi di bosco (soft polenta, truffled mascarpone cheese, wild mushrooms); pappardelle con verdure e pancetta (fresh pappardelle pasta, baby artichokes, broccoli rabe, pancetta); tagliarini all'erbe con asparagi e due pomodori (fresh herb pasta ribbons with asparagus, tomatoes, arugula); risotto del giorno; stinco di agnello con pure di cannellini (braised lamb shank); and warm peach strudel with blueberry gelato and fresh blueberry compote (a summer special).

Summary & comments: Chef Geoff Felsanthal and pastry chef Salvadore Gomez have greatly improved the menu recently. Selections sampled were expertly prepared, and desserts were the best they've ever been here. Our attentive waiter was very informed. Dining here is a delight.

BACINO'S TRATTORIA

Italian and American
★★★
Inexpensive/Moderate

Quality 84   Value B

Zone 8   Southern Suburbs
1504 North Naper Boulevard,
    Tower Crossing Shopping Center,
    Naperville
(630) 505-0600

Reservations:	Friday and Saturday for parties of 6 or more
When to go:	Weekends and evenings
Entree range:	$7.50–14.95 or market prices
Payment:	Major credit cards
Service rating:	★★★½
Friendliness rating:	★★★★
Parking:	Mall parking lot
Bar:	Full service
Wine selection:	Extensive; from $4.25 a glass and $14 a bottle
Dress:	Casual
Disabled access:	Yes, except for upper level and roof deck
Customers:	Professionals and families; mostly local
Lunch:	Monday–Friday, 11 A.M.–4 P.M., pasta bar ($7.95) 11 A.M.–2 P.M.; Saturday, noon–4 P.M.
Dinner:	Monday–Thursday, 4–10 P.M.; Friday and Saturday, 4 P.M.–midnight; Sunday, 3–10 P.M.

Atmosphere/setting: Painted pillars; whimsical geometric shapes; unique fireplace with painted marble tiles; hand-painted walls.

House specialties: Gorgonzola salad with watercress; bruschetta; cavatappi con pollo e spinaci (corkscrew pasta with chicken and spinach Alfredo); Heart Healthy spinach pizza; tiramisu; semifreddo (light almond semifrozen cream).

Other recommendations: Artichoke hearts baked with mascarpone; grilled portobellos; grilled calamari; pollo e verdure gourmet pizza (grilled chicken, mushrooms, etc.); pasta trio of angel hair with marinara, fettuccine with Parmesan cream sauce, and cavatappi with pesto; garganelli al granchio e'rucola (tube-shaped egg pasta, crab meat, shrimp); profiteroles filled with vanilla ice cream.

Entertainment & amenities: Various bands play Thursday; jazz on Saturday.

Summary & comments: Owners Linda and Dan Bacin created this trattoria in Naperville to offer diners a greater variety of chef's selections, as well as America's First Heart Healthy pizza. The Roof Top Cafe is open during warmer months with its own menu and bar; it features an herb garden and a huge mural of classic buildings and scenes of Italy. A popular all-you-can-eat lunch pasta bar features 4 pastas, 3–4 sauces, and about 20 different ingredients cooked to order.

Bando

Reservations:	Accepted
When to go:	Any time
Entree range:	$9.95–12.95
Payment:	VISA, MC, AMEX
Service rating:	★★★
Friendliness rating:	★★½
Parking:	Free indoor parking
Bar:	Full service
Wine selection:	American; affordable
Dress:	Dressy
Disabled access:	Yes
Customers:	Local ethnic and American
Open:	Every day, 11 A.M.–11 P.M.

Atmosphere/setting: Spacious, splashy, split-level dining room with bottom-vented, built-in grills at the tables.

House specialties: Bulgoki (barbecued beef), gahl-bee (barbecued beef short ribs), dahk bulgoki (sliced, boneless barbecue chicken), and spicy barbecued pork, all marinated, with grilled onions and mushrooms; kim chee; pan-fried, egg-battered oysters and butterfly shrimp.

Other recommendations: Spicy seafood casserole with noodles; catfish and red snapper, each prepared two ways; buckwheat noodles with sliced beef, cucumber, and a mild sauce.

Entertainment & amenities: Grilling your own dinner at your table.

Summary & comments: This Korean restaurant with large banquet facilities is popular with the Korean community. At times there seems to be a language problem; some staffers speak and understand minimal English. The food is mainly authentic, although certain dishes are milder for American tastes. Japanese tempura and some Chinese-influenced dishes are on the menu, too. Included with dinners are soup, rice, and numerous sides, Korean-style. Fresh fruit and ginseng tea make a nice finish.

BAZZELL'S FRENCH QUARTER BISTRO

Zone 3   Near North
215 West North Avenue
(312) 787-1131

Cajun/Creole	
★★★½	
Inexpensive/Moderate	
Quality 89	Value B

Reservations: Accepted
When to go: Any time
Entree range: $9.95–17.95
Payment: All major credit cards
Service rating: ★★★½
Friendliness rating: ★★★★½
Parking: Valet, Wednesday–Sunday
Bar: Full service
Wine selection: International; unique vintages; from $4 a glass
                     and $20 a bottle
Dress: Casual
Disabled access: Yes
Customers: Locals, tourists, suburbanites, couples
Dinner: Monday–Wednesday, 5–10 P.M.; Thursday, 5–11 P.M.;
                     Friday and Saturday, 5 P.M.–midnight; Sunday,
                     4–9 P.M.

Atmosphere/setting: Three contemporary, romantic dining areas: One is casual; another is for private parties; and an outdoor courtyard with a waterfall.

House specialties: Shrimp Bazzell's (sautéed with garlic, tomatoes, and green onions); Bazzell's crab cakes; seafood gumbo; house salad, house dressing; Bazzell's jambalaya; sautéed shrimp and blackened catfish Acadienne; lobster and shrimp d'Orleans (blackened and served over rice); and Bazzell's bread pudding.

Other recommendations: Acadienne crawfish sautéed; fried oysters; Cajun-style blackened chicken; Bazzell's shrimp or crawfish étouffée; French Quarter cheesecake; and pecan caramel cheesecake.

Entertainment & amenities: Jazz pianist Ken Chaney entertains Friday and Saturday, 7 P.M.–12:30 A.M. Courtyard for cigar and pipe smoking.

Summary & comments: Owner and chef John Moultrie is a Chicago native whose great-grandparents opened the original Bazzell's in St. Augustine, Florida, in 1910. Moultrie looks to his familial past to create his signature Cajun and Creole cooking, which is ideal for those who don't like spicy food. A vegetarian menu is available. Moultrie's line of seasonings and cornbread mix are sold both in Bazzell's and Chicagoland Treasure Island food stores.

Bella Vista

Zone 1   North Side
1001 West Belmont Avenue
(773) 404-0111

New Italian
★★★½
Inexpensive/Moderate

Quality 86   Value C

Reservations:	Recommended
When to go:	Weeknights
Entree range:	$8–18
Payment:	All major credit cards
Service rating:	★★★★
Friendliness rating:	★★★★
Parking:	Valet, $5
Bar:	Full service
Wine selection:	300 international, $19–150; substantial Italian; $4.50–6.50 a glass; reserve list on main list
Dress:	Casual
Disabled access:	Yes
Customers:	Professionals, couples, families with children
Lunch:	Monday–Saturday, 11:30 A.M.–5 P.M.; pasta bar ($7.95), 11:30 A.M.–2:30 P.M.
Dinner:	Monday–Thursday, 5–11 P.M.; Friday and Saturday, 5 P.M.–2 A.M.; Sunday, 5–10 P.M.

Atmosphere/setting: The name "beautiful view" says it well—a stunning multilevel, colorful interior and elegant, award-winning architecture in the former Belmont Trust and Savings Bank (1929). Exquisite hand-painted walls, walk-through wine cellar, 30-foot ceiling.

House specialties: Antipasto del giorno with seasonal oak-roasted vegetables, seafood salad, oak-roasted potato salad, and two other selections; gourmet wood-fire pizzas; black-pepper linguine with shiitakes and portobellos; free-form lamb and potato torta (grilled loin layered with potato "sheets").

Other recommendations: Oak-roasted calamari with plum tomatoes and wilted arugula; Gorgonzola salad with endive, watercress, and red wine vinaigrette.

Entertainment & amenities: Architectural tours of the restaurant. Special dinners held around winemakers and menus from films such as *Big Night.*

Summary & comments: The architecture and interior design are a feast for the eyes, and the dishes are colorful and intricately presented. The Bella Vista Cafe, a more casual bar room, serves the same menu as the dining room. Owners Dan and Linda Bacin added the pasta bar at lunch, based on its success at their Bacino Trattoria (see Summary & comments, page 95).

BEN PAO, CHINESE
RESTAURANT & SATAY BAR

Zone 3   Near North
52 West Illinois
(312) 222-1888

<table>
<tr><td>Chinese
★★★½
Inexpensive/Moderate</td></tr>
<tr><td>Quality 90   Value B</td></tr>
</table>

Reservations:	Recommended, especially 7:30–9 P.M.
When to go:	Any time; before 7 P.M. for dinner
Entree range:	$7.95–14.95
Payment:	Major credit cards
Service rating:	★★★★½
Friendliness rating:	★★★★½
Parking:	Valet, $5
Bar:	Full service; microbrewed and Asian beers
Wine selection:	About 25 selections; 15 by the glass; affordable; Japanese Kinsen plum wine; two chilled sakes
Dress:	Casual
Disabled access:	Yes
Customers:	Businesspeople, tourists, suburbanites, locals
Lunch:	Monday–Friday, 11 A.M.–2 P.M.
Dinner:	Monday–Thursday, 5–10 P.M.; Friday and Saturday, 5–11 P.M.; Sunday, 4–9 P.M.

Atmosphere/setting: Ben Pao's exquisite interior was designed with harmony and balance in accordance with traditional Feng Shui philosophy. The stunning entryway is flanked by two granite columns with water rippling down.

House specialties: Satays, including tamarind chicken, five-spice shrimp, ginger portobello, lamb, vegetable, and Mongolian beef. Black-peppered scallops; good luck shrimp dumplings; Hong Kong spicy eggplant; Teh's curried noodles; soongs (wok-seared fillings such as chicken or vegetables); tea-smoked half duck; Tony's amazing chicken; pan-fried wrinkled string beans. Mango-vanilla swirl cheesecake; triple chocolate treasure; coconut tapioca custard.

Other recommendations: Orange-peel beef; Shanghai peanut noodles; "fiery" Szechuan noodles; "crispy garlic tofu." Pineapple-ginger float; chocolate spring rolls.

Entertainment & amenities: Outdoor cafe; Autumn Moon Festival; Chinese New Year celebration.

Summary & comments: Lettuce Entertain You Enterprises' first venture into Chinese restaurants, Ben Pao is unique in Chicago for its harmonious mix of the traditional and the adventurous. It features Chicago's first satay bar; these grilled-to-order skewers are great as an appetizer or a light bite. Carryout and delivery available.

The Berghoff

Zone 4 The Loop	German/American
17 West Adams Street	★★★½
(312) 427-3170	Inexpensive
	Quality 88 Value B

Reservations:	Recommended for 5 or more
When to go:	Avoid lunch and early dinner if you're in a rush
Entree range:	Lunch, $8–12; dinner, $9–17
Payment:	VISA, MC, AMEX, DC
Service rating:	★★★½
Friendliness rating:	★★★★
Parking:	Discount in nearby garages after 4 P.M.
Bar:	Full service; The Berghoff's own regular and dark beer
Wine selection:	Extensive; inexpensive house wines
Dress:	Summer, casual; winter, dressier
Disabled access:	Yes, including rest rooms
Customers:	Locals, including a loyal German clientele; some tourists
Lunch/Dinner:	Monday–Thursday, 11 A.M.–9 P.M.; Friday, 11 A.M.–9:30 P.M.; Saturday, 11 A.M.–10 P.M.

Atmosphere/setting: Turn-of-the-century building; old paintings; lots of wood in the spacious dining room. Rathskeller downstairs serves lunch.

House specialties: Good traditional German specialties: sauerbraten and Wiener Schnitzel; seafood such as fillet of sole. Daily specials include some German items, such as Schlachtplatte (bratwurst, "Kasseler Rippchen," and smoked Thuringer with kraut). Creamed herring and chilled smoked salmon are two nice appetizers.

Other recommendations: Seafood de Jonghe; veal medallions; chicken schnitzel; broiled swordfish steak; Black Forest torte.

Summary & comments: The menu proudly states, "family operated since 1898," when Herman Joseph Berghoff opened his cafe as a showcase for his celebrated Dortmunder-style beer. The Berghoff, which will turn 100 in April 1998, is a Chicago landmark because of the good-quality food, fine Berghoff beer and bourbon, low prices, old-world atmosphere, and efficient service. The management has modernized the menu to satisfy current desires for lighter fare. The delicious, textured bread is made from the brewery side products (hops, etc.), and loaves are sold to carry home. This place is a great success story, serving 2,000 a day in the street-level dining room and downstairs for lunch. Private parties and catering are available.

BICE RISTORANTE

Zone 3   Near North
158 East Ontario Street
(312) 664-1474; fax (312) 664-9008

Italian
★★★½
Moderate/Expensive
Quality 87   Value D

Reservations:	Recommended
When to go:	Wednesday, Thursday, and Sunday
Entree range:	$14–26
Payment:	All major credit cards except D
Service rating:	★★★½
Friendliness rating:	★★★
Parking:	Valet
Bar:	Full service
Wine selection:	On the costly end; 110 selections; $25–300 a bottle; 8 by the glass, exclusively Italian and Californian cabernet sauvignon, $10
Dress:	Moderately casual to dressy; shorts discouraged
Disabled access:	Wheelchair; no rest room access
Customers:	Businesspeople, Italians; diverse and sophisticated
Lunch:	Monday–Saturday, 11:30 A.M.–5:30 P.M.
Dinner:	Monday–Thursday, 5:30–10:30 P.M.; Friday and Saturday, 5:30–11:30 P.M.; Sunday, 5:30–10 P.M.

Atmosphere/setting: Upscale, contemporary Italian; well-lit, fun, and lively. Bar area in front opens onto sidewalk. At press time, the Bice Grill opened adjacent to Bice. It's more casual.

House specialties: Menu changes daily. Fresh pastas; tuna carpaccio (appetizer); risotto fruitti di mare; panesotti stuffed with wild game; orange cake glazed with bittersweet chocolate.

Other recommendations: Veal Milanese; tiramisu; ice creams and sorbets. In the Bice Grill, pizza bianca (Parma ham and arugula); lasagna giardiniera (fresh vegetables); Toscano sandwich (on focaccia with grilled sausages); grilled Italian sausage.

Summary & comments: A chic place with prices to match, but the steady crowds here don't seem to care. It's a gathering spot for many of the Italian foodies. Excellent, very Italian food and comprehensive menu, but pricey, even for a pasta dish. Bice Grill is a welcome addition, since it offers an alternative: casual dining with lighter fare at lower prices. Service is professional and attentive at both places.

Big Bowl Cafe

Zone 3   Near North
159-½ West Erie Street
(312) 787-8297
Zone 3 Near North
6 East Cedar
(312) 640-8888

Pan-Asian	
★★★	
Inexpensive	
Quality 84	Value B

Reservations:	Not accepted
When to go:	Avoid peak lunch and dinner hours
Entree range:	$7.25–9.95
Payment:	All major credit cards
Service rating:	★★★½
Friendliness rating:	★★★★
Parking:	Valet; street; nearby lots
Bar:	*Erie:* beer, wine, and selected mixed drinks; *Cedar:* full service, good selection
Wine selection:	Changes seasonally; mostly Californian; by glass or bottle; modestly priced
Dress:	Casual
Disabled access:	Yes
Customers:	Locals, businesspeople, professionals, couples
Lunch/Dinner:	*Erie:* Monday–Thursday, 11:30 A.M.–10 P.M.; Friday and Saturday, 11:30 A.M.–11 P.M.; Sunday, 5–9 P.M.; *Cedar:* Sunday–Thursday, 11:30 A.M.–10 P.M.; Friday and Saturday, 11:30 A.M.–11 P.M.

Atmosphere/setting: Original, expanded Erie location has a casual interior and a sidewalk cafe (weather permitting). Cedar location features soft green and yellow accents, a modern bar , an open kitchen, an enclosed sidewalk cafe.

House specialties: Pan-Asian creations in bowls; pot stickers; Thai-herb calamari; eight-vegetable stir-fry; Burmese curry shrimp; Asian wraps; Vietnamese noodle soup (pho); Chinese chicken salad with plum dressing and wontons; macadamia tart with coconut ice cream; ginger spice cake with crème fraîche.

Other recommendations: Indonesian satay with Thai cucumber salad; Mindful Vegetable spring roll (baked); noodle dishes; Indochine combo (chicken satay, Mindful spring roll, chicken pot stickers); ice creams and sorbets; iced tea.

Summary & comments: Big Bowl's food is lively in Asian flavors and textures, and much of it is soothing and comforting. Leftovers can be carried out in "porta-bowls." One of the best restaurants of this genre and a top value.

Big Shoulders

Zone 1 North Side	American
Chicago Historical Society,	★★★
1601 North Clark Street	Inexpensive
(312) 587-7766 or 587-7342	Quality 82 Value B

Reservations:	Recommended (especially for Sunday brunch)
When to go:	Lunch or Sunday brunch
Entree range:	Lunch, $5–10; no dinner
Payment:	VISA, MC, AMEX, DC
Service rating:	★★★½
Friendliness rating:	★★★½
Parking:	Street or metered lot in park nearby
Bar:	Full service
Wine selection:	American
Dress:	Casual
Disabled access:	Yes
Customers:	Locals and visitors to the Chicago Historical Society
Brunch:	Sunday, 10.30 A.M.–3 P.M.
Lunch:	Every day, 11 A.M.–3 P.M.

Atmosphere / setting: The restaurant is a semicircle enclosed in glass and resembles a greenhouse. It features murals, a magnificent terra-cotta arch (from the bank at the Union Exchange), and high ceilings. Windows overlook a lovely garden.

House specialties: Grilled chicken Caesar salad; daily soups; Sheboygan-style bratwurst. Signature whole-wheat millet bread and jalapeño cornbread come with selections.

Other recommendations: Wild rice cakes with wild mushroom sauce; sirloin salad with asparagus, pistachios, chèvre, and sherry-mustard vinaigrette; apple-streusel pie à la mode.

Summary & comments: Named for Carl Sandburg's description of the city in his poem, "Chicago," this lovely restaurant has a special intellectual style befitting the Chicago Historical Society and what it represents. Owner Jerome F. Kliejunas has long been a proponent of additive-free, fresh, natural ingredients and smoke-free dining and states on his menus, "If the selection seems limited, it's because I believe one of the keys to maintaining my standard is to try to do a few things well." Dishes are attractively presented and freshly prepared with harmonious flavors. The short menu is appropriate for a place that no longer serves dinner. Catering is available for business meetings of 30 to weddings of 300.

Biggs

<table>
<tr><td></td><td>Classic and Contemporary
Continental
★★★★
Moderate</td></tr>
</table>

Zone 3   Near North
1150 North Dearborn Street
(312) 787-0900

Quality 90   Value C

Reservations:	Recommended
When to go:	Dinner
Entree range:	$17.95–32.95
Payment:	All major credit cards
Service rating:	★★★½
Friendliness rating:	★★★★
Parking:	Valet, $6; street and nearby lot parking
Bar:	Full service
Wine selection:	Extensive; 250 international; American, European, New Zealand, Australian, and Chilean, $19–120; 15 by the glass; reserve list of famous and first-growth Bordeaux
Dress:	Casual elegance
Disabled access:	No ramp; stairs to restaurant and rest room
Customers:	Businesspeople (lunch), couples (weekends)
Dinner:	Sunday–Thursday, 5–11 P.M.; Friday and Saturday, 5 P.M.–1 A.M. Bars: every day, 5 P.M.–2 A.M.

Atmosphere/setting: Exquisite, romantic setting in a Victorian mansion (built in 1874). Caviar and Martini Bar, Cigar and Cognac Bar, and outdoor cafe.

House specialties: Scottish smoked salmon; escargot bourguignonne; beef Wellington; rack of lamb; center cut, 16-ounce veal chop; Biggs cigar dessert.

Other recommendations: Oysters Bienville; lobster bisque; confit of duck; red snapper meunière or Provençal; Dover sole meunière or amandine. White chocolate pyramid; tower of chocolate power; Bavarian cheesecake; trifle; and fresh berries sabayon. Caviar and Martini Bar serves caviar, smoked salmon, and foie gras. Cigar and Cognac Bar and the outdoor cafe also serve a lighter menu.

Entertainment & amenities: Fine cigars and live swing music.

Summary & comments: The second owner of this landmark mansion was Joseph Biggs, who managed his catering business from the coach house and catered the most social parties of the day. Today, Biggs carries on the tradition and caters parties for up to 175 people. The food has maintained a high quality over the years, evolving from modern continental to classic/creative French, to a blend of the two through executive chef Robert Walsh's creative culinary touches.

Honors/awards: Five-Diamond Award, AAA.

Bistro 110

Zone 3 Near North	French Bistro
110 East Pearson Street	★★★½
(312) 266-3110	Moderate
	Quality 86 Value C

Reservations:	Recommended for 5 or more
When to go:	Any time
Entree range:	$10–17
Payment:	All major credit cards
Service rating:	★★★½
Friendliness rating:	★★★★½
Parking:	Valet
Bar:	Full service
Wine selection:	Extensive French and domestic list with some worthy selections by the glass
Dress:	Casual
Disabled access:	Yes
Customers:	Neighborhood, businesspeople, tourists
Brunch:	Sunday, 11 A.M.–3 P.M.
Lunch/Dinner:	Monday–Thursday, 11:30 A.M.–11 P.M.; Friday and Saturday, 11:30 A.M.–midnight; Sunday, 11:30 A.M.–10 P.M.

Atmosphere/setting: Sidewalk cafe in summer; attractive bar area with tables near the window for a great view of the Water Tower; colorful murals.

House specialties: Oven-roasted whole garlic served with fresh, crusty French bread; wood-roasted chicken, snapper, and fish specials; onion soup; creative pastas (e.g., linguine with rock shrimp).

Other recommendations: Cassoulet Toulousain; bouillabaise; clafouti "tutti frutti" berries; chocolate mousse; crème brûlée; for smallfry, see the kids' menu; giant pecan pancake with pecan-maple syrup and sausages (brunch).

Entertainment & amenities: Sunday New Orleans–style à la carte jazz brunch. Occasional French promotions with exchange chefs from France.

Summary & comments: Energetic bistro. New chef, Dominique Tougne, changed the menu slightly with a re-emphasis on bistro classics. The food is well prepared and especially flavorful and healthful. Pastries for savory and sweet tarts are flaky and very French. This place can reach high decibel levels on a bustling night, but it's always uplifting. Bistro 110 celebrated its tenth anniversary in 1997. As part of its celebration it launched a kids' menu. Items designed to tickle *petit palates* include chicken tenders and pommes frites, Bistro grilled-cheese sandwich, spaghetti à la France, and a cheese pizzette ($5.95 each).

BISTRO BANLIEUE

Zone 8 Southern Suburbs	French Bistro
44 Yorktown Convenience Center,	★★★★
Lombard	Inexpensive/Moderate
(630) 629-6560	Quality 93 Value B

Reservations: Recommended, especially on weekends
When to go: Any time
Entree range: $10.95–20.95
Payment: AMEX, D, DC, MC, VISA
Service rating: ★★★★
Friendliness rating: ★★★★
Parking: Mall lot
Bar: Full-service
Wine selection: Mostly French and American; from $18 a bottle
Dress: Chic casual
Disabled access: Partial accessibility; call first
Customers: Local suburbanites, businesspeople, couples
Lunch: Monday–Friday, 11:30 A.M.–4:30 P.M.; dinner
                      specials at 4:30 P.M.
Dinner: Monday–Thursday, last seating, 9 P.M., and Friday,
                      10 P.M.; Saturday, 5–10 P.M.; Sunday, 4–9 P.M.

Atmosphere/setting: Charming lace curtains, floral wall border murals, and light-hearted Parisian posters. A black-and-white tile floor and white butcher paper covering tablecloths give an appropriate bistro-casual feel.

House specialties: Smoked salmon, goat cheese, and leek tart served warm, with two colorful sauces: an excellent tomato-basil blend and a tart lemon beurre blanc. Soupe a l'Oignon gratinée (the quintessential French onion soup). Steak pommes frites and ragôut of lamb. There is also a "selection du jour" menu at both lunch and dinner. Desserts: crème brûlée, apple tarte Tatin, and bittersweet chocolate mousse with pistachio crème anglaise.

Other recommendations: Roasted duck breast and braised leg; ratatouille with fresh cheese in a puff pastry; duck liver pâté with onion marmalade; pear and Roquefort with mixed greens; white chocolate mousse with raspberry sauce.

Summary & comments: When Bistro Banlieue opened in 1989, it was rare to find good French food in a suburban strip mall. But one visit to this charming place in Lombard convinced the skeptical gourmets. The split-level dining room is smoke-free. Thoughtfully, the menu offers both "entrees et petites entrees." This is an excellent, affordable French dining experience.

Blackhawk Lodge

Zone 3 Near North	New American
41 East Superior Street	★★★
(312) 280-4080	Moderate
	Quality 82 Value C

Reservations: Recommended
When to go: Any time
Entree range: Lunch, $8.95–14.95; dinner, $8.95–25.95
Payment: All major credit cards
Service rating: ★★★★
Friendliness rating: ★★★½
Parking: Valet in the evenings; self-park garage nearby on
                       Wabash south of Superior, $5 with validation
Bar: Full service
Wine selection: Nice American selection; $18–65 a bottle; several
                       by the glass
Dress: Casual; some business and dressy
Disabled access: Yes
Customers: Locals, businesspeople, tourists, shoppers, families
Brunch: Sunday, 11:30 A.M.–3 P.M.
Lunch/Dinner: Monday–Thursday, 11:30 A.M.–10 P.M.; Friday,
                       11:30 A.M.–11 P.M.; Saturday, 5–11 P.M. (out-
                       door seating available)

Atmosphere/setting: Rustic, gracious setting resembles a family vacation home: oak floors, knotty pine paneling, timber walls, wicker furniture, tapestries.

House specialties: Award-winning ribs such as the hickory-smoked Wichita baby-back ribs with Blackhawk barbecue sauce; fabulous signature cheddar cheese grits with tasso ham; puréed vegetable soup; house-smoked trout Caesar salad with salmon caviar; oak-fired Arkansas half-chicken. Desserts: banana pudding with caramel sauce; chocolate walnut tart with Wild Turkey Bourbon crème anglaise.

Other recommendations: Crab cakes; goat cheese soufflé; roasted rack of lamb; organic vegetable platter (grilled, braised, and roasted); cappuccino ice-cream pie.

Entertainment & amenities: Bluegrass band at Sunday brunch.

Summary & comments: This place suggests an era when life was easygoing and basic values centered around family and honesty. The back-to-basics cuisine with regional influences focuses on simple preparations with creative touches. New executive chef is Corky O'Conner, who carries on the tradition here.

Honors/awards: Ribs voted second best in Chicago by the *Chicago Tribune.*

Blind Faith Cafe

Zone 11   Northern Suburbs
525 Dempster Street, Evanston
(847) 328-6875; fax (847) 864-6177

Zone 1   North Side
3300 North Lincoln Avenue
(773) 871-3820; fax (773) 871-3890

Vegetarian	
★★★	
Inexpensive	
Quality 82	Value B

Reservations: Accepted weekdays only for 4 or more
When to go: Avoid peak mealtimes
Entree range: $6.50–8.95
Payment: VISA, MC, AMEX
Service rating: ★★★
Friendliness rating: ★★★★
Parking: Street (metered)
Bar: Wine and beer; juice bar
Wine selection: Organic house wines, $17 average a bottle, $4 a
                       glass
Dress: Casual
Disabled access: Yes
Customers: Students and professors; the health-conscious
Bakery: Monday–Friday, 8 A.M.–7 P.M.; Saturday and
                       Sunday, 8 A.M.–8 P.M.
Breakfast: Monday–Friday, 10 A.M.–2 P.M.; Saturday and
                       Sunday, 8 A.M.–2 P.M.
Lunch/Dinner: Monday–Saturday, 2–10 P.M.; Sunday, 2–8 P.M.

Atmosphere/setting: This bright, airy restaurant is divided into the casual dining room and the self-serve area. There's also an adjacent bakery. Colorful handmade quilts adorn the walls.

House specialties: Breakfast: chilaquiles, eggs, or tofu sautéed; homemade granola. Lunch/dinner: broccoli-shoyu-soba stir-fry; macrobiotic plate; fruit smoothie. The new Chicago location has more creative, exciting food.

Other recommendations: Breakfast: banana-almond pancakes; cinnamon-raisin French toast. Lunch/dinner: spicy seitan fajitas; black bean burrito; peanut butter–tofu–banana shake.

Summary & comments: This is one of Chicago's best-known and respected vegetarian restaurants. All the dishes are prepared with fresh, unprocessed, and mostly organic ingredients; dairy-free and low-fat alternatives are also available. You can take home baked goods such as potato-dill bread or tofu no-cheesecake, as well as traditional fare such as chunky chocolate cookies.

BLUE MESA

Zone 1   North Side
1729 North Halsted Street
(312) 944-5990

	Southwestern
	★★★★
	Inexpensive/Moderate
	Quality 89 Value B

Reservations:	Accepted
When to go:	Any time
Entree range:	$8–13
Payment:	V, MC, AMEX, D, DC
Service rating:	★★★½
Friendliness rating:	★★★★½
Parking:	Valet, $4
Bar:	Full service
Wine selection:	Limited Spanish and American
Dress:	Casual
Disabled access:	Yes
Customers:	Mixed
Brunch:	Sunday, 11 A.M.–3 P.M.
Lunch:	Monday–Saturday, 11:30 A.M.–2:30 P.M.
Dinner:	Monday–Saturday, 5–10:30 P.M.; Sunday, 4–10 P.M.

Atmosphere/setting: Authentic adobe restaurant with kiva fireplaces and large rounded rooms with dried chiles and native artwork. Outdoor patio.

House specialties: Enchilada del mar, a blend of shrimp, scallops, fish, corn, mushrooms, and leeks in a lobster-chipotle sauce, layered between two blue corn tortillas; blue corn tamales; chicken and steak fajitas; Southwestern Caesar salad; Navajo posole with tomatoes, onions, garlic, and herbs, topped with avocado and pico de gallo. Sopaipillas are served with most entrees. Desserts include white chocolate quesadilla (white chocolate mousse served in a crispy cinnamon tortilla with honey-raspberry sauce) and adobe pie (coffee and chocolate Häagen-Dazs layered with fudge on an Oreo crust).

Other recommendations: Taste of Santa Fe appetizer; the Grande Platter. Crossing the border, there's a Tex-Mex combination with barbecue chicken and blackened shrimp.

Summary & comments: Blue Mesa is devoted to the unique cuisine of New Mexico, with some creative license. The cooking and atmosphere pay tribute to Santa Fe culture, which is an exciting blend of Indian and Spanish traditions. The Marienthal brothers built this gem after researching it carefully. Enjoy a drink at the lovely bar and then move to the dining room for a meal that gives a taste of historical Santa Fe right in Chicago.

Bob Chinn's Crab House

	Seafood
Zone 10 Northwest Suburbs	★★★
393 South Milwaukee Avenue,	Moderate
Wheeling	
(847) 520-3633; fax (847) 520-3633	Quality 82 Value B

Reservations:	Only for 6 or more; number system used
When to go:	Any day before 6 P.M. or after 9 P.M.
Entree range:	$9.95–34.95
Payment:	All major credit cards
Service rating:	★★★
Friendliness rating:	★★★
Parking:	Free valet
Bar:	Full service
Wine selection:	Wide range of Californian; approximately 40
Dress:	Casual
Disabled access:	Yes
Customers:	International, couples, families, businesspeople
Lunch:	Monday–Friday, 11 A.M.–2:30 P.M.; Saturday, noon–3 P.M.
Dinner:	Monday–Thursday, 4:30–10:30 P.M.; Friday, 4:30–11:30 P.M.; Saturday, 3–11:30 P.M.; Sunday, 3–10 P.M.

Atmosphere/setting: Similar to an old-fashioned crab house, except more vast and bustling. Very casual, no-frills, 650-seat eatery. Walls are adorned with memorabilia, kudos, and air-freight receipts as proof of the freshness of the supplies. Sinks are available for rinsing your hands.

House specialties: Alaskan Dungeness crab; raw bar; Kona crab steamed with garlic; variety of fresh fish.

Other recommendations: Beer-batter fried-fish sampler with dipping sauces; six-way fish special; aged steak dishes (e.g., choice center-cut strip steak).

Summary & comments: Early raw bar special offered daily is a great value and a nice appetizer while you wait for a table. Helpful, efficient staff offers quick service and instruction on how to tackle a Dungeness crab. This amazingly high-volume place (serving an average of 2,500 people a day!) maintains its high quality and fair pricing. Owner Bob Chinn and his wife, Marilyn, run this establishment with marketing savvy. Although not a relaxed environment, it's worth it for the good selection of simply prepared seafood.

Honors/awards: Silver Platter Award; Restaurant and Institutions 1993 Top Ten Independents award (served 1,200,000 per year).

BONES

Zone 11 Northern Suburbs	Barbecue
7110 North Lincoln Avenue,	★★½
Lincolnwood	Inexpensive/Moderate
(847) 677-3350; fax (847) 677-3403	Quality 78 Value C

Reservations:	Accepted
When to go:	Avoid busy weekends
Entree range:	$9.95–17.95
Payment:	All major credit cards
Service rating:	★★★½
Friendliness rating:	★★★★
Parking:	Lot
Bar:	Full service
Wine selection:	Medium-sized list; mostly domestic, house wines
Dress:	Casual
Disabled access:	Yes
Customers:	Mixed locals; more families, couples weekends
Lunch/Dinner:	Sunday–Thursday, 11:30 A.M.–10:30 P.M.; Friday and Saturday, 11:30 A.M.–midnight. *Carryout Store:* Monday–Saturday, opens at 4 P.M.; Sunday, opens at 3 P.M.

Atmosphere/setting: Decorated with logos of theaters, hotels, radio stations, and the late Riverview Park, as well as sports memorabilia and caricatures.

House specialties: Hickory slow-smoked barbecue baby-back ribs and chicken; Sima's whole garlic chicken; roasted brisket with potato pancakes; center-cut skirt steak; Lake Superior whitefish and salmon; shrimp prepared several ways. Regular pasta items: two-sauce rigatoni; shrimp and angel hair with broccoli, tomato; and California chicken rotini. Appetizer of buffalo chicken wings. Shrimp or chicken Caesar salads.

Other recommendations: Combination platters: select two items from barbecue, garlic chicken, brisket, garlic shrimp, and more. Appetizers: spinach fingers, potato skins, garlic chicken fingers. Chilled poached salmon fillet salad; Mediterranean chicken with pasta; blue-cheese burger. Skoog pie (rich with caramel, chocolate, and nuts); Key lime pie.

Summary & comments: In adapting to today's healthful requests, the restaurant has been updating its menu periodically, and it recently added a pasta section; some pastas can be made vegetarian to order. In addition, there are daily specials. Casual, bustling place with a regular local following. Private parties accommodated.

BRASSERIE BELLEVUE

Zone 3   Near North
Sutton Place Hotel,
  21 East Bellevue Place
(312) 266-9212

Continental Bistro
★★★
Moderate
Quality 85   Value C

Reservations:	Recommended and accepted
When to go:	The earlier for each meal the better
Entree range:	$10.50–19.95; 4-course prix fixe, $16.95
Payment:	VISA, MC, AMEX, DC, D
Service rating:	★★★★
Friendliness rating:	★★★★½
Parking:	Valet parking, $3 discount with validation
Bar:	Full selection
Wine selection:	Extensive; few half-bottles; several by the glass
Dress:	Casual to dressy
Disabled access:	Yes
Customers:	Neighborhood, businesspeople, and many local and national celebrities
Breakfast:	Every day, 7–11 A.M.
Brunch:	Sunday and major holidays, 11 A.M.–5 P.M.
Lunch:	Every day, 11 A.M.–5 P.M.
Dinner:	Every day, 5–11 P.M.

Atmosphere/setting: Casual brasserie with a long bar and lovely view. Comfortable banquettes and tables; billowy white ceiling draperies. Sidewalk terrace in summer.

House specialties: Braised escargot in Macon wine cream sauce with puff pastry shell; seared snow crab cakes with citrus aïoli; Brasserie salad (assorted greens with unusual potted gizzard and baguette garlic croutons); grilled fillet of salmon; Louisiana prawns Provençal; grilled meadow lamb chops with garlic and rosemary.

Other recommendations: Spinach salad with roasted peppers, shiitake mushrooms, and pine nuts. Daily lunch special: appetizer or soup with main course ($9.95); daily dinner special: appetizer, soup, main course, and pastry cart ($16.95). Every Saturday from 2:30 to 10 P.M. and every brunch, the Chocolate Lover's Buffet is available, $7.50 per person without dinner, $5.50 with dinner.

Summary & comments: This charming brasserie is pleasant anytime except the peak mealtimes, when it can be busy. The cuisine has a French-American slant. Servers are friendly and helpful.

BRASSERIE JO

Zone 3   Near North
59 West Hubbard Street
(312) 595-0800

Alsatian French
★★★★
Inexpensive/Moderate

Quality 92   Value B

Reservations:	Accepted
When to go:	Avoid peak mealtimes without a reservation
Entree range:	$10–18
Payment:	All major credit cards
Service rating:	★★★★½
Friendliness rating:	★★★½
Parking:	Valet
Bar:	Full service, including Hopla—an Alsatian beer made for the restaurant by Baderbrau Brewery
Wine selection:	Extensive, moderately priced regional French
Dress:	Casual
Disabled access:	Yes
Customers:	Businesspeople, international, tourists, couples
Lunch:	Monday–Friday, 11:30 A.M.–4 P.M.
Dinner:	Monday–Thursday, 5–10:30 P.M.; Friday and Saturday, 5–11:30 P.M.; Sunday, 4–10 P.M.

Atmosphere/setting: Parisian Sam Lopata has created an authentic, comfortable brasserie with a 1940s look. Also a glass-enclosed winter garden with palm trees.

House specialties: Onion soup gratinée in crock; croque monsieur with mesclun; warm pretzel baguette with smoked chicken, Brie, and mesclun; Alsace cheesy sausage salad; crêpes with spinach, baked ham, blue cheese, mushrooms, and cheese; fish du jour; pâté en croûte Strasbourgeoise; house salad; Brasserie steak; onion tart Uncle Hansi; mussels in white wine; steak tartare; escalope of salmon.

Other recommendations: Cod brandade; chicken ravioli; mussels in parchment; Les Plats du Jour de Jo; fruit tarts; ice creams.

Summary & comments: Master chef–owner Jean Joho, well known for his upscale Everest (see profile), injects his Alsatian heritage in this brasserie, which literally translates as "brewery." It's also a place to relax, socialize, dine, and drink into the wee hours. A unique touch that reflects Joho's culinary breadth is Les Plats du Jour. The melt-in-the-mouth onion tart was named after his Uncle Hansi, who gave him the recipe.

Honors/awards: Best New Restaurant in 1995 by the James Beard Foundation; chef Joho won the 1995 Perrier-Jouet Best American Midwest Chef Award.

BRASSERIE T

Zone 11 Northern Suburbs	American Brasserie
305 South Happ Road, Northfield	★★★½
(847) 446-0444	Inexpensive/Moderate
	Quality 90 Value B

Reservations: Accepted
When to go: Any time, but weekend nights are busy
Entree range: $9.95–23.95
Payment: VISA, MC, AMEX, D
Service rating: ★★★★½
Friendliness rating: ★★★★½
Parking: Free shopping mall lot
Bar: Full service; a collection of cognacs, brandies, and ports
Wine selection: Well-balanced selection of international and domestic; several by the glass
Dress: Casual
Disabled access: Yes
Customers: Diverse, locals, young, old, and families
Open: Monday–Thursday, 11:30 A.M.–10 P.M.; Friday, 11:30 A.M.–11 P.M.; Saturday, 11:30 A.M.–10:30 P.M.; Sunday, 4:30–9:30 P.M.

Atmosphere/setting: Elegant mosaic marbles and slate floors, frosted glass and copper chandeliers, and an arched ceiling create a stylish yet timeless decor.

House specialties: Mussels marinière; fish and chips (special); wood-grilled portobellos with roasted sweet corn polenta tart, mixed greens, and shaved Parmesan; Tramonto's escarole of braised white beans, Italian sausage, tomato (seasonal); goat cheese salad with warm, sliced potatoes, celery, roasted onions, smoked bacon vinaigrette; blue cheese and pear salad with French beans, grapes, spiced pecans, apple-walnut vinaigrette; Tuscan-style pizza; caramelized onion pizza (oven-roasted tomatoes, eggplant, black olives, and fontina); farfalle pasta with wild mushrooms, fresh tomatoes, Parmesan; goat cheese ravioli with Parmesan broth; fusilli with grilled chicken, asparagus, and tomato–Alfredo sauce; braised lamb shank with garlicky potato cake, roasted vegetables; wood-grilled salmon with spinach, roasted garlic mashed potatoes; osso buco (braised veal shank, chunky vegetables, saffron risotto). Not-your-usual lemon meringue pie; banana cream pie; and root beer float with Gale's cinnamon-ginger-vanilla root beer.

(continued)

Other recommendations: Wood-grilled shrimp wrapped in pancetta; tuna tartar with arugula salad and herbed flatbread (seasonal); crab cakes; "A Great Caesar Salad"; three-grain risotto with barley, wild mushrooms, and artichokes; wood-grilled pork chop with barley ragôut, sautéed cabbage, bacon, apples; porcini-crusted mahi mahi with barley ragôut and wild mushroom sauce. Profiteroles with a trio of ice creams, warm bittersweet chocolate sauce, and caramel-almond lace; sticky toffee pudding with dates, caramelized apples, butterscotch sauce, and honey ice cream; and assortment of sorbets with seasonal fruits.

Entertainment & amenities: Outdoor cafe.

Summary & comments: Husband-and-wife owner-chefs Rick Tramonto and Gale Gand opened Brasserie T in 1995 after a dozen years of experience at some of the best restaurants in Chicago, New York, and Europe, most recently as chefs and partners of the successful, fine-dining Trio Restaurant in Evanston, Illinois (see profile). Located in the popular, upscale Northfield Village Square, Brasserie T features an affordable menu that will appeal to everyone, offering tried-and-true country dishes from Europe and America that are big on hearty flavor and ample portions.

Honors / awards: In 1994, both Tramonto and Gand were named among the country's Top Ten Best New Chefs by *Food & Wine* magazine. They also received the coveted Michelin Guide's Red "M" after only a year at the Stapleford Park Hotel in Leicestershire, England. Their previous venture, Trio, earned *Chicago Tribune* critic Phil Vettel's first four-star rating to a new restaurant in six years. Tramonto was selected in 1995 as America's Rising Star Chef by Robert Mondavi and was nominated for the James Beard Award that same year. Pastry Chef Gand received the Robert Mondavi Award for Culinary Excellence in 1994, as well as honors for her pastries and desserts.

BRUNA'S RISTORANTE

Zone 5 South Loop	Italian
2424 South Oakley Avenue	★★★
(773) 254-5550	Inexpensive/Moderate
	Quality 80 Value B

Reservations:	Recommended
When to go:	Any time
Entree range:	$8.95–16.95
Payment:	VISA, MC, AMEX, DC, CB, D
Service rating:	★★★½
Friendliness rating:	★★★★½
Parking:	Street; valet on Friday and Saturday evenings
Bar:	Full service
Wine selection:	Mostly Italian, including restaurant's private label imported from Italy (Vino Nobile di Montepulciano and Chianti); $15.50–95 a bottle; some great choices by the glass, $3.50–4.50
Dress:	Casual
Disabled access:	No, but staff will assist those in wheelchairs up the 2 steps
Customers:	Diverse, businesspeople (lunch); mostly couples and families (dinner)
Lunch/Dinner:	Monday–Thursday, 11 A.M.–10 P.M.; Friday and Saturday, 11 A.M.–11 P.M.; Sunday, 1–10 P.M.

Atmosphere/setting: Old-world style with original, oil-painted murals; ceramics; casual, warm look.

House specialties: Pastas (e.g., Luciano's fusilli, various ravioli, tortellini alla Bolognese); Bruna's veal scaloppine; shrimp fra diavolo (spicy shrimp with linguine and piquant tomato sauce); chicken limone.

Other recommendations: Desserts including tiramisu and fruit tart.

Summary & comments: Owner Luciano Silvestri is on hand to direct the operation and has a keen pride in his wine cellar and the recipes he brings back from his biannual trips to Italy. He and his wife, Ilona, bought this restaurant from the original owner in 1981; it has been open since 1933—the oldest restaurant in the Heart of Italy, a close-knit Italian community on the near Southwest Side. The cooking here is full flavored and well prepared, and is served with style.

BUKARA

Zone 3 Near North	Indian
2 East Ontario Street	★★★½
(312) 943-0188	Moderate
	Quality 80 Value C

Reservations: Recommended
When to go: Any time
Entree range: $8–25
Payment: All major credit cards
Service rating: ★★★★
Friendliness rating: ★★★½
Parking: Discount with validation at garage at 10 East
                        Ontario
Bar: Full service, including Taj Mahal beer
Wine selection: Fairly extensive variety
Dress: Moderately casual, business
Disabled access: Yes, including rest rooms
Customers: Diverse, businesspeople
Lunch: Monday–Friday (buffet available for $7.95),
                        11:30 A.M.–2:30 P.M.; Saturday and Sunday,
                        noon–3 P.M.
Dinner: Sunday–Thursday, 5:30–10 P.M.; Friday and
                        Saturday, 5:30–10:30 P.M.

Atmosphere/setting: Handsomely appointed, classy interior with visible
tandoor kitchen. Newly built, comfortable Uncle Phil's Global Bar features 42
beers from 22 nations and international music.

House specialties: Marinated fresh seafood, poultry, and meats roasted in
tandoors; sikandari raan (whole leg of lamb); tiger prawns Bukara; dal Bukara
(black lentils); and roti (whole-wheat bread).

Other recommendations: Spiced cottage cheese–stuffed bread; roomali (plain
wheat bread); shish kebab (skewered, charcoal-grilled, cumin-flavored, minced
lamb). Flavorful kulfi gulabi dessert, an exotic pudding of dates, almonds, and milk.

Summary & comments: The ancient nomad cooking of the Indian sub-
continent was introduced at this restaurant several years ago. To be authentic, no
utensils are used. Eating with your hands as the nomads did is sensuous and fun,
although they weren't seated in such an elegant atmosphere. There's an Indian
saying, "Eating with utensils is like making love through an interpreter." Sauces
are well spiced, and, although some tandoori meats can be on the dry side, most
are delectable. Catering is available.

THE CAFE

Zone 3 Near North	American/International
The Ritz-Carlton, Chicago,	★★★½
160 East Pearson Street	Moderate
(312) 266-1000	Quality 90 Value C

Reservations:	Recommended
When to go:	Weekends are the busiest
Entree range:	$11–28; most lunch entrees $14–19.50
Payment:	All major credit cards
Service rating:	★★★★½
Friendliness rating:	★★★★★
Parking:	Ask about reduced parking fee
Bar:	Beer and wine selections
Wine selection:	Extensive Californian, French, and Italian by bottle or by glass
Dress:	Casual to dressy
Disabled access:	Yes, entrance and main floor seating
Customers:	Businesspeople, locals, and hotel guests, including many celebrities
Open:	Sunday–Thursday, 6:30 A.M.–midnight; Friday and Saturday, 6:30–1 A.M.

Atmosphere/setting: An open alcove of the spectacular 12th-floor hotel lobby. Marble-topped oak cafe tables, botanical Wedgewood china, glistening sterling silver flatware, and fresh flowers; colorful art on walls.

House specialties: Heartland Breakfast, which includes juice, two eggs over easy, homemade chicken or country sausage, Mom's hash browns, toasted bread, and coffee ($15.50). For lunch and dinner, specialties include chilled, grilled vegetable antipasto mozzarella di bufala, French onion soup gratinée, triple-decker turkey club sandwich, and dairy-free vegetarian lasagna. Signature dessert: crème brûlée in various flavors.

Other recommendations: Daily specials: a wonderful corn chowder or grilled salmon entree with vegetables. Caesar salad comes as an appetizer or entree, and with grilled chicken breast. Pumpkin risotto with porcini mushrooms. Hearty side orders: mashed Idaho potatoes and roasted garlic and Parmesan bread. Desserts rotate; the peach cobbler is noteworthy.

Summary & comments: This cafe offers a fine dining experience with china and silver, top-quality food and service, and beautiful surroundings for the price. Special menus occasionally celebrate Chicago Art Institute exhibits.

Honors/awards: See profile of The Dining Room.

Café-Ba-Ba-Reeba!

Zone 1   North Side
2024 North Halsted Street
(773) 935-5000; fax (773) 935-0660

Spanish/Tapas	
★★★½	
Moderate	
Quality 87	Value C

Reservations:	Lunch, accepted; dinner, limited; not accepted for patio
When to go:	Early or late to avoid waits
Entree range:	Tapas, $1.95–5.95; paella, $10.95
Payment:	All major credit cards
Service rating:	★★★½
Friendliness rating:	★★★½
Parking:	Valet, $4
Bar:	2 bars seat 170 people
Wine selection:	120 Spanish, a few American, $8–45; 4 by the glass; sangría, sherries, and Spanish liquors
Dress:	Casual, dressy
Disabled access:	Wheelchair accessible; call ahead
Customers:	Young and lively; students, professionals, tourists
Lunch:	Tuesday–Friday, 11 A.M.–2:30 P.M.; Saturday, 11:30 A.M.–3 P.M.
Dinner:	Monday–Thursday, 5:30–11 P.M.; Friday and Saturday, 5:30 P.M.–midnight; Sunday, noon–10 P.M.

Atmosphere/setting: Upbeat, vibrant interior with vivid Mediterranean colors. Murals of Spain, with a gallery of Spanish artists. Garden patio.

House specialties: Tapas: patatas con allioli (garlic potato salad); terrine of grilled eggplant; bambas a la parrilla (grilled shrimp brochette); paella Valenciana (Spanish saffron-rice, chicken, pork, seafood, green beans, and tomatoes); Fideua de mariscos (cazuela of lobster, shrimp, and monkfish baked with saffron broth and angel hair pasta); sautéed octopus; vieiras a la parrilla (grilled sea scallops).

Other recommendations: Calamares a la plancha (fresh grilled squid); champinones rellenos (mushrooms stuffed with spinach, manchego cheese, and red-pepper sauce); black bean soup with chorizo; flan de la casa; tarta de almen dras y fruta (fresh seasonal fruit and almond pastry cream in an almond-rum crust).

Summary & comments: This was the first Spanish restaurant to introduce the "little plate" concept. This lively, large place with a menu to match has a clientele that seems to continue to grow. Sample several tapas items to create a full meal—it's fun to share—or choose from the traditional Spanish dishes in larger portions.

Café Borgia

Zone 8   Southern Suburbs
17923 Torrence Avenue, Lansing
(708) 474-5515

Italian
★★½
Inexpensive/Moderate
Quality 78   Value B

Reservations:	No
When to go:	Weekday evenings often less busy
Entree range:	$12.95–16.95
Payment:	All major credit cards
Service rating:	★★★
Friendliness rating:	★★★½
Parking:	Free lot or street
Bar:	None
Wine selection:	None, BYOB
Dress:	Casual, but dressier on weekends
Disabled access:	Entrance, no; rest rooms, yes
Customers:	Professionals, students, couples, families
Lunch/Dinner:	Sunday–Thursday, 11 A.M.–11 P.M.; Friday and Saturday, 11 A.M.–midnight; Saturday, closed 3–4:30 P.M.

Atmosphere/setting: Informal; granite tables with wrought-iron bases; expanded back room with bay window. Pastel-colored outdoor patio; new mural of Italian scenes.

House specialties: Cream of eggplant and roasted red pepper soup; linguine pescatore with calamari, bay scallops, and mussels in a red or white sauce; tender steamed baby clams in garlic, lemon, and oil sauce; stuffed eggplant with prosciutto and mozzarella, baked in a tomato-cream sauce; zuccotto (layered sponge cake soaked in Marsala and brandy, filled with whipped cream, hazelnuts, and almonds, and topped with chocolate and raspberry sauces).

Other recommendations: Roasted lamb shank, rosemary jus, with roasted potatoes and onions; veal-spinach cannelloni; four cheese–stuffed chicken breast; tiramisu.

Summary & comments: The simple Roman cooking here is aggressively flavored by innovative chef-owner Mike Jesso. Major triumphs are his favorites: cream of eggplant and roasted red pepper soup and tender baby clams, above. This well-established place is one of the best restaurants on the South Side and has a loyal following.

Café Iberico Tapas Bar

Zone 3   Near North
739 North LaSalle Street
(312) 573-1510

Spanish/Tapas
★★★½
Inexpensive/Moderate

Quality 87   Value B

Reservations:	Recommended for 9 or more
When to go:	Before 6:30 P.M. or after 8:30 P.M.
Entree range:	$7.50–17.95; tapas, $3.50–4
Payment:	VISA, MC, D
Service rating:	★★★½
Friendliness rating:	★★★½
Parking:	Valet
Bar:	Full service
Wine selection:	Spanish; some nice selections, including sangría
Dress:	Casual
Disabled access:	Yes, including rest rooms
Customers:	Diverse, many Latin Americans and Europeans
Lunch/Dinner:	Monday–Friday, 11 A.M.–midnight., Saturday and Sunday, noon–1:30 A.M.

Atmosphere/setting: Authentic touch of Spain: a tapas bar that has recently been expanded with 85 extra seats; a dining room with checkered tablecloths, wall murals, and wine bottles on ceiling racks; the rustic bodega (wine cellar room) downstairs; and a newly built deli and ceramic shop.

House specialties: Paella estilo Iberico; gazpacho Andaluz. Tapas include grilled octopus with potatoes and olive oil; Spanish cured ham, manchego cheese, and toasted tomato bread; tortilla Española. Specials include hard-to-find fish cheeks with baby eels. Poached pears with wine and ice cream.

Other recommendations: Shrimp with wine and garlic sauce; croquetas de pollo (chicken croquettes), a home-style dish; stuffed eggplant with goat cheese; crema Catalana for dessert.

Summary & comments: Just north of downtown, this popular place has expanded by adding a bodega complete with wood-burning oven. Authentic atmosphere, cuisine, and wines make this one of the best tapas places in the city, especially for the prices. Spanish food conveys passionate regionalism and culinary traditions, and it's possible to experience a good sampling of that here.

121

Café Luciano

Zone 3   Near North
871 North Rush Street
(312) 266-1414

Zone 11   Northern Suburbs
2676 Green Bay Road, Evanston
(847) 864-6060

Italian
★★★½
Inexpensive/Moderate
Quality 88   Value B

Reservations:	*Chicago:* recommended; *Evanston:* only for large groups on Friday and Saturday
When to go:	*Chicago:* before 7 P.M.; *Evanston:* before 5 P.M.
Entree range:	*Chicago:* $8.95–18.95; *Evanston:* $6.95–16.95
Payment:	Major credit cards (*Evanston:* AMEX *not* accepted)
Service rating:	★★★★
Friendliness rating:	★★★★½
Parking:	*Chicago:* street, city lots, valet after 5 P.M.; *Evanston:* free valet
Bar:	Full service
Wine selection:	Moderate, mostly Italian
Dress:	Casual
Disabled access:	*Chicago:* no; *Evanston:* yes
Customers:	Mostly local
Lunch/Dinner:	*Chicago:* Monday–Thursday, 11:30 A.M.–10 P.M.; Friday and Saturday, 11:30 A.M.–11 P.M.; Sunday, 4–10 P.M.
Dinner:	*Evanston:* Sunday–Thursday, 5–10 P.M.; Friday and Saturday, 5–11 P.M.

Atmosphere/setting: Home-style Italian bistro setting; rustic walls and wooden floors. Outdoor seating in Chicago; Evanston location is smoke-free.

House specialties: Roasted peppers; polenta con funghi; mussels alla Luciano. Rigatoni country-style; giambotta (hearty mix of chicken and sweet sausage.); eggplant parmigiana.

Other recommendations: Farfalle alla Stefano (with porcini mushrooms and asparagus); seafood pomodoro (marinara, linguine); rotating desserts such as berry tarts.

Entertainment & amenities: *Chicago:* piano, 7 P.M. to closing.

Summary & comments: Classic Italian cooking with bold flavors is presented beautifully here. "Luciano Lite" offerings available. Hearty portions, a good wine selection, a casual atmosphere, and friendly, efficient service spell success.

Cafe Spiaggia

Zone 3   Near North
980 North Michigan Avenue
(312) 280-2755

Italian	
★★★½	
Moderate	
Quality 89	Value C

Reservations:	Accepted for dinner only
When to go:	Any time
Entree range:	$13.50–22.50
Payment:	Major credit cards
Service rating:	★★★★
Friendliness rating:	★★★★½
Parking:	Validated in garage next door; call for directions
Bar:	Full service
Wine selection:	Italian; bottles, $22–49; a few by the glass, $6–10
Dress:	Casual; chic
Disabled access:	Yes
Customers:	Tourists, conventioneers, and local residents
Lunch:	Every day, 11:30 A.M.–2 P.M.
Dinner:	Every day, 5:30 P.M.–9 P.M.

Atmosphere/setting: Decor was inspired by fifteenth-century Italian frescos from a castle in Mantua, Italy. Great view of North Michigan Avenue.

House specialties: Pasticcio di salmone all'erba cipollina (demi-smoked salmon mousse); prosciutto d'anitra (duck prosciutto with zucchini salad); ravioli di ricotta con porcini (ricotta-filled ravioli with imported porcinis); tagliatelle con cappesante e gamberi (handmade ribbon pasta with scallops and shrimp); gnocchi alla crema di pomodoro con speck (potato gnocchi in a creamy sauce with smoked prosciutto); tortellini pasticciati al ragu (classic handmade filled pasta with meat sauce); trancio di salmone con funghi (wood-roasted salmon with wild mushrooms); cotolette di vitello alla Milanese (pan-fried veal cutlet on mixed greens); tiramisu; and bavarese alla noce di cocco (coconut Bavarian cream).

Other recommendations: Prosciutto e melone (imported Italian Parma, San Daniele, and Carpegna prosciutto with melon); pomodoro, cipolla e Gorgonzola (tomato, red onion, and Gorgonzola); and quaglia ripiena con polenta (wood-roasted quail with Italian sausage stuffing on creamy polenta with mushrooms).

Entertainment & amenities: Live piano music in the formal dining room.

Summary & comments: The menu reflects cuisine from all regions of Italy with chef Bartolotta's modern interpretation, as opposed to only regional cuisine.

Honors/awards: Chef has won many awards, including James Beard Foundation Best Midwest Chef in 1994.

CAMPAGNOLA

Zone 11   Northern Suburbs
815 Chicago Avenue, Evanston
(847) 475-6100

Italian
★★★★
Inexpensive/Moderate
Quality 94   Value B

Reservations:	Accepted
When to go:	Early or late dinner
Entree range:	$9.95–21.95
Payment:	VISA, MC
Service rating:	★★★★
Friendliness rating:	★★★★½
Parking:	Street parking available
Bar:	Full service
Wine selection:	Italian; $3.50–5 a glass and $14–36 a bottle
Dress:	Casual
Disabled access:	Yes
Customers:	Largely local; couples, businesspeople, families
Dinner:	Tuesday–Thursday, 5:30–9:30 P.M.; Friday and Saturday, 5:30–10:30 P.M.; Sunday, 5–9 P.M.

Atmosphere/setting: Rustic decor with polished wood tables, chairs, and floor; exposed brick walls; creatively draped ceiling. The outdoor deck is perfect for romantic dining.

House specialties: First courses: Salad of toe crab, pickled baby beets, and grilled wild leeks; grilled organic nectarines with Parma prosciutto and mascarpone; wood-fired radicchio and pancetta with marinated goat cheese. Entrees: linguine with Maine crabmeat; conchiglie (shell pasta) with Gorgonzola; Chianti-glazed duckling; pan-roasted striped bass; Verdura del Giorno, a vegan dish. Desserts: sorbetti and gelato; tiramisu; lemon tart; and chocolate budino, a baked pudding filled with melted chocolate.

Other recommendations: Roasted eggplant salad; grilled calamari; arugula with prawns; piegata folded pizza; pasta dishes; crème brûlée; plum cobbler (special).

Summary & comments: Roughly translated to "person of the countryside," Campagnola offers diners high-quality, organic ingredients, straightforward Italian cooking, and a relaxed atmosphere. Executive chef and partner Michael Altenberg and owner Steven Schwartz opened Campagnola in June 1996; they are both enthusiastic and dedicated, and it shows. Altenberg dubs his fare "clean Italian cuisine" because he uses only free-range, antibiotic-free meats and organic produce, which is virtually unprecedented among Italian restaurants.

Cape Cod Room

Zone 3   Near North
The Drake Hotel, 140 Walton Place
(312) 787-2200

Seafood	
★★★½	
Moderate/Expensive	
Quality 91	Value C

Reservations: Recommended
When to go: Monday, Tuesday, or Wednesday
Entree range: $15–35, served with potato and salad or slaw
Payment: All major credit cards
Service rating: ★★★★
Friendliness rating: ★★★★½
Parking: Valet
Bar: Full service
Wine selection: Good assortment of champagnes; chosen for the
                       seafood menu; house wines by the glass; bottles,
                       $23–100; hotel's reserve list available
Dress: Jackets required
Disabled access: Yes, including rest rooms
Customers: Travelers, regulars, locals, businesspeople, celebrities
Lunch/Dinner: Every day, 11:30 A.M.–11:30 P.M.

Atmosphere/setting: Very authentic-looking rustic Cape Cod setting with nautical decor. Charming and intimate.

House specialties: The Cape Cod's famous Bookbinder red snapper soup with sherry; New England clam chowder; bouillabaisse; raw bar; oysters Rockefeller; halibut papillote (fillet in parchment with lobster, mushrooms); imported Dover sole and turbot; New England scrod.

Other recommendations: Smoked salmon; oyster stew; Drake stew; crabmeat à la Newburg; shrimp à la Drake (casserole with shallots and Newburg sauce); Key lime pie; strawberry rhubarb crumble with vanilla ice cream.

Entertainment & amenities: Viewing initials carved in the bar by visiting celebrities. Longtime manager Patrick Bredin will gladly help interpret them.

Summary & comments: This seaworthy legend has been sailing full tilt since 1933, and at "60-something" is the city's oldest seafood restaurant. Located on the main floor of one of the city's finest hotels, it has long been a premier place. The raw bar continues to be a reliable source for oysters or clams on the shell and is a great socializing spot for single travelers. The menu also offers items from the land—steaks and lamb chops, for instance.

Honors/awards: Holiday Award for 35 years; Fine Dining Hall of Fame by *Nations Restaurant News.*

CARLOS'

Zone 11   Northern Suburbs
429 Temple Avenue, Highland Park
(847) 432-0770; fax (847) 432-2047

French
★★★★½
Moderate/Expensive

Quality 96   Value C

Reservations:	Recommended, especially for weekends
When to go:	Sunday and Monday
Entree range:	$27–37
Payment:	All major credit cards
Service rating:	★★★★½
Friendliness rating:	★★★★★
Parking:	Free valet
Bar:	None
Wine selection:	40-plus-page list; bottles for $28–2,000; $7–12 a glass (most selections)
Dress:	Jacket required, tie optional
Disabled access:	No, but easy entrance; accessible rest rooms
Customers:	North Shore locals, businesspeople, couples, families
Dinner:	*Summer:* Sunday, Monday, Wednesday, and Thursday, 5–8:30 P.M. (last seating); Friday and Saturday, seatings 5–6:30 P.M. and 8:45–9:30 P.M. *Other seasons:* dinner starts at 5:30 P.M. and kitchen closes earlier, but patrons can stay as late as they like

Atmosphere / setting: Elegant, stylized fine-dining ambiance: wood-paneled walls, mirrors, and Art Deco; quiet and intimate; facilities for private parties.

House specialties: Warm oysters with cucumbers; sautéed Hudson Valley foie gras; superb lobster ravioli. Sautéed soft-shell crab and stuffed roasted quail; duck breast and leg confit; loin of rabbit. Desserts (change regularly): fruit tart; chocolate fantasy. Pastries and desserts are as delicious as they look.

Other recommendations: Sautéed scallops; potato-wrapped escargot. Sautéed halibut; vegetable platter; roasted loin of Jamison baby lamb; degustation menu, $70 ($100 with wine); vegetarian degustation available with advance request.

Summary & comments: The ratio of staff members to diners on a busy night is about one to three. Guests are given complimentary hors d'oeuvres to start and mignardises (tiny sweets) at the end. Carlos' continues to be one of the best fine-dining restaurants in the Chicago area.

Honors / awards: Grand Award from *Wine Spectator*; featured on PBS/ WTTW's *Great Chefs of Chicago*.

Carlucci

Zone 2   North Central/O'Hare
6111 North River Road, Rosemont
(847) 518-0990

Tuscan Italian	
★★★½	
Moderate	
Quality 88	Value C

Reservations:	Recommended
When to go:	Any time
Entree range:	$11.95–24.95
Payment:	All major credit cards
Service rating:	★★★★
Friendliness rating:	★★★★
Parking:	Free valet and lot
Bar:	Full service
Wine selection:	Extensive Italian; selected for the rustic food; several by the glass; fairly priced
Dress:	Business attire preferable; chic casual
Disabled access:	Yes
Customers:	Businesspeople, travelers, couples (especially in the evenings)
Lunch:	Monday–Friday, 11 A.M.–2.30 P.M.
Dinner:	Monday–Thursday, 5–10 P.M.; Friday and Saturday, 5–11 P.M.; Sunday, 4:30–9 P.M.

Atmosphere/setting: Open kitchen with rotisserie; handsome bar area; exquisite doorways, frescoes, and tiles.

House specialties: Roasted quail; roasted pork loin; wood-fired pizzas; black olive pasta with sea scallops; Chianti-poached pears.

Other recommendations: Antipasto; Tuscan seafood soup.

Summary & comments: This, the second of the Carlucci restaurants, has served excellent Tuscan cuisine since it opened several years ago and is a great place for dinner before going to or returning from O'Hare International Airport. The space is beautifully designed with a lovely bar area and a welcoming, open kitchen with a rotisserie in the main dining room. There's lots of bustle, especially on weekends, and showmanship with grappa carts displaying the liquor infused with fruits. Well managed by the Carlucci family and partners, who train their staff well, including in the art of proper Italian wine and dish pronunciation. The first Carlucci on Halsted closed in early 1997 to possibly reopen in the House of Blues Hotel.

CARZZ GRILLERIA

Zone 8   Southern Suburbs
216 South Washington Street, Naperville
(630) 778-1944

New Orleans, Southern,
and Caribbean
★★★½
Inexpensive/Moderate

Quality 88   Value B

Reservations:	Accepted
When to go:	Weeknights; weekends 5–6 P.M. or after 8 P.M.
Entree range:	$8.95–20.95
Payment:	Major credit cards
Service rating:	★★★½
Friendliness rating:	★★★★½
Parking:	Free municipal parking lot behind restaurant
Bar:	Full service
Wine selection:	Extensive; African and American; $3.95–5.25 by the glass; $14–36 by the bottle
Dress:	Casual
Disabled access:	Yes, call ahead; one step
Customers:	Locals, suburbanites and city residents, couples
Lunch:	Tuesday–Saturday, 11:30 A.M.–2:30 P.M.
Dinner:	Tuesday–Thursday, 5–9:30 P.M.; Friday and Saturday, 5–10:30 P.M.; Sunday, 4–8:30 P.M.

Atmosphere/setting: Colorful, vibrant interior. Eye-catching high, patterned tin ceiling. Whimsical mural of the grilleria's logo. Lively music.

House specialties: New beginnings combo platter (grilled wild mushrooms, Jamaican jerk wings, baked Gorgonzola bread); Southern blackened amberjack; zesty shrimp salsa with parsley-garlic fettuccine; mushrooms marinated in herbed balsamic vinegar; lobster cakes; crawfish (not crayfish here) torte. Specials such as tomato artichoke soup and Jamaican barbecue chicken.

Other recommendations: Fried Brie with raspberry-jalapeño sauce. Rib Night features barbecue baby-back ribs in seven styles, including Cajun, Jamaican, Hawaiian, mango-rum, and sun-dried cherry tomato sauce. Ultimate peanut butter pie and pumpkin cheescake.

Entertainment & amenities: Fun promotions. On Sunday, children under age seven eat free. Wednesday is rib night; Thursday is Mardi Gras night.

Summary & comments: "Carzz" is derived from chef-owner Tom Burke's wife's name, Carla. "Car" is her nickname, and since they didn't want the name to be Car's Grilleria, the double z's were added; they stand for zest both in life and cooking. The chef has won awards for his soups. This restaurant gains momentum from the enthusiastic owners and their community involvement.

Catch 35

Zone 4 The Loop	Seafood
Leo Burnett Building,	★★★½
35 West Wacker Drive	Moderate/Expensive
(312) 346-3500; fax (312) 346-3534	Quality 93 Value C

Reservations:	Recommended
When to go:	Early weekdays, 5:15–6:30 P.M.
Entree range:	$16–40
Payment:	All major credit cards
Service rating:	★★★★
Friendliness rating:	★★★★½
Parking:	Valet, $5
Bar:	Full service
Wine selection:	Extensive, mostly Californian; several by the glass
Dress:	Chic casual or business; no dress code
Disabled access:	Yes
Customers:	Many from nearby ad agencies, locals, tourists
Lunch:	Monday–Friday, 11 A.M.–1:45 P.M. (after 1:45 bar remains open through dinner)
Dinner:	Monday–Thursday, 5:15–10 P.M.; Friday and Saturday, 5:15–11 P.M.; Sunday, 5–9 P.M.

Atmosphere/setting: Spectacular granite lobby entryway of Leo Burnett Building; revolving piano bar with a display of enlarged award-winning ads; stunning step interior with marble walls; colorful, elegant setting.

House specialties: Menu changes daily. Typical items are grilled grouper; grilled swordfish with light cognac-avocado salsa. Appetizers include Catch's crab cake (not fried) with rémoulade sauce; Szechuan scallops; Martha's Vineyard salad; Black Island swordfish.

Other recommendations: From the wok section: stir-fried crab claws, shrimp, and scallops with a hint of tomato sauce; nice variety of oysters on the half shell. Chocolate Kahlúa mousse (served in a caramel basket); pecan tart; white chocolate cheesecake; Key lime pie; handmade cannoli.

Entertainment & amenities: Piano player and vocalists perform evenings.

Summary & comments: Nicely prepared, showy food, some with Thai influences reflecting the chef's background. Daily menu lists categories, and main-course seafood is grouped by preparation methods (baked, grilled, wok, pan-seared). Nothing is fried. Popular with the advertising agency crowd, this is an impressive restaurant for entertaining clients.

Honors/awards: Silver Platter Award.

CHARLIE TROTTER'S

Zone 1　North Side
816 West Armitage Avenue
(773) 248-6228

New American
★★★★★
Very Expensive

Quality 99　Value C

Reservations:	Required
When to go:	Wednesday seems to be the least crowded
Entree range:	Prix-fixe menu: $70, vegetarian; $90, regular
Payment:	VISA, MC, AMEX, CB, DC
Service rating:	★★★★★
Friendliness rating:	★★★★½
Parking:	Valet
Bar:	Full service
Wine selection:	Extensive, award-winning, international list with 1,000 wines; Burgundies and Bordeaux, $40–1,000 per bottle; by the glass, $9–16
Dress:	Business; jackets requested, not required
Disabled access:	Yes
Customers:	Locals, tourists, businesspeople
Dinner:	Tuesday–Thursday, 6 P.M.–?; Friday and Saturday, 5:15 P.M.–?; (closing depends on business)

Atmosphere/setting: Upscale, understated elegance in a renovated 1880s townhouse. Quietly elegant, contemporary dining rooms on two floors.

House specialties: Menu changes daily according to season and market availability. Examples: smoked Atlantic salmon, Maine lobster, and Oestra caviar; toe crab and black striped bass; California pigeon breast; Iowa lamb loin. Vegetarian menus include dishes such as warm goat cheese package with bleeding heart radishes, artichokes, roasted hickory nuts; ragôut of early spring morels, fava beans, haricots verts, baby leeks. Some items flavored with chef's infused oils.

Other recommendations: Vanilla-yogurt, pineapple, and pink guava sorbets with lemongrass broth; desserts vary daily along with the menu.

Summary & comments: Chef-owner Charlie Trotter is extremely gifted (he's been termed a culinary genius) in creating dishes from sometimes disparate ingredients and eclectic foreign influences. His menu reflects market availability and his creative use of seldom-used vegetables. The fixed degustation menu limits diners' choices, however, and is not everyone's favored way of dining. Call ahead to request special food for dietary restrictions. Available for special parties.

Honors/awards: AAA five diamonds; five stars from *Mobil Travel Guide;* Relais Gourmand member; *Wine Spectator* readers voted it Best Restaurant in the U.S. and Charlie Trotter Best Chef in the U.S.

Chez Delphonse

Zone 1   North Side
2201 North Clybourn Avenue
(773) 472-9920

Caribbean
★★★
Inexpensive/Moderate

Quality 83   Value B

Reservations:	Accepted
When to go:	Any time; call ahead Friday and Saturday nights
Entree range:	$7.95–14.95
Payment:	Major credit cards
Service rating:	★★★
Friendliness rating:	★★★★½
Parking:	Street
Bar:	Full service, including rum punch
Wine selection:	Limited; from $16 a bottle and $4.50 a glass
Dress:	Casual
Disabled access:	No, call first; staff can help people up the 2 steps
Customers:	Diverse and ethnic; professionals, couples, business-people
Open:	Tuesday–Thursday, 5–10 P.M.; Friday, 5 11 P.M.; Saturday and Sunday, noon–11 P.M.

Atmosphere/setting: Bentwood chairs, straw hats, and yellow lights hanging from the beamed ceiling create the ambiance of a charming Caribbean shack.

House specialties: Seafood gumbo; shrimp and calamari Provençal; jerk chicken; lambi (conch slow-cooked for four hours); chicken and shrimp sautéed and served with a Caribbean tomato sauce; "gumbolaya" with beef, shrimp, calamari, and mushrooms; Caribbean paella with chicken, sausage, and seafood. Cinnamon iced tea; rum punch; cinnamon flan.

Other recommendations: Samba shrimp sautéed with vegetables; grilled tilapia with shrimp in lobster sauce; jerk steak (skirt steak); barbecued chicken breast or pork chops; bread pudding with raspberry sauce.

Entertainment & amenities: A charming outdoor patio.

Summary & comments: Owners Mark and Theresa Delphonse truly bring the style and unique taste of the Caribbean to Chicago's West Lincoln Park area. Because of his Haitian background and previous stint as head chef of Cafe Bernard, chef Mark Delphonse's Caribbean cuisine incorporates French influences and remains remarkably light and healthy. You can take a minitour of the menu by ordering appetizers, which are also available as entrees. Vegetarian entrees are also available. Carryout service.

Honors/awards: A four-star review from the *Chicago Sun-Times*. Named as one of Chicago's best in the *Quarterly Review of Wines*.

Chicago Chop House

Zone 3   Near North
60 West Ontario Street
(312) 787-7100

Steak	
★★★★	
Moderate	
Quality 94	Value C

Reservations:	Recommended
When to go:	Before 7 P.M. or after 10 P.M.; lunch
Entree range:	$15–29
Payment:	All major credit cards
Service rating:	★★★★½
Friendliness rating:	★★★★½
Parking:	Valet; $4, lunch; $5, dinner
Bar:	Full service
Wine selection:	International, extensive (has own warehouse)
Dress:	Semicasual
Disabled access:	No, but managers are willing to assist
Customers:	Businesspeople, VIPs, lots of celebrities
Lunch/Dinner:	Monday–Friday, 11:30 A.M.–11 P.M.
Dinner:	Saturday, 5–11:30 P.M.; Sunday, 5–11 P.M.

Atmosphere/setting: Century-old brownstone with three floors of dining rooms and more than 1,400 historical Chicago pictures. Every city map is on the wall—not even City Hall has that!

House specialties: Dry-aged, charred, U.S. prime rib; Chop House broiled New York strip steak, either 16- or 24-ounce; T-bone steak, 24-ounce; namesake potato pancake.

Other recommendations: Spring lamb chops; roast loin of pork chops; broiled Lake Superior whitefish with lemon butter; Russ's American fries; sautéed spinach.

Entertainment & amenities: Pianist on Monday–Friday, 5–11 P.M.; Saturday and Sunday, 6–11 P.M.

Summary & comments: One of Chicago's best restaurants for quality steaks and chops, founded by the late well-known restaurateur, Henry Morton. It has a loyal following, especially with certain celebrities. A place to see VIPs. Menu is traditional steak house–style, featuring steaks and chops, a couple of chicken items, several seafood preparations, a handful of appetizers (all seafood), and some sides. Food is kept simple and properly prepared.

Honors/awards: *Knife and Fork* Award 1992–96 for America's Top Ten Steak Houses. In 1994 voted number two steak house in the United States.

Chowpatti Vegetarian Restaurant

	Indian/Vegetarian
	★★★
Zone 10 Northwest Suburbs	Inexpensive
1035 South Arlington Heights Road,	Quality 80 Value B
Arlington Heights	
(847) 640-9554	

Reservations:	Not accepted
When to go:	Any time
Entree range:	$8–18
Payment:	All major credit cards for checks over $10
Service rating:	★★★
Friendliness rating:	★★★★
Parking:	Free lot
Bar:	No liquor; juice bar with 20–25 fruit juice combinations; nonalcoholic beer
Wine selection:	None
Dress:	Casual
Disabled access:	Yes
Customers:	International, out-of-towners, couples, families
Lunch/Dinner:	Tuesday–Thursday, Sunday, 11:30 A.M.–9 P.M.; Friday and Saturday, 11:30 A.M.–10 P.M.

Atmosphere/setting: Upscale casual, spring-looking, quiet.

House specialties: Special bhel puri with dahl; basic bhel puri with whipped homemade yogurt and chopped cucumber and tomatoes; samosa with dahl (samosa topped with whipped yogurt, sweet chutney sauce, onions, and coriander); masala dosa (dosa filled with lightly seasoned onions, potatoes, tomatoes, coriander, cashews, and raisins); aloo mutter (potato chunks and pea curry).

Other recommendations: Special sev batata puri with dahl (loaded Indian nachos); grilled club pav bhaji (grilled sandwich with layers of meatless stew and cheese); aloo paratha (paratha [flaky bread made with whole-wheat flour] stuffed with mildly spiced potatoes); veg biryani (basmati rice with green beans, carrots, green peas, cashew nuts, herbs, and spices). Kulfis (homemade Indian ice cream): malai (plain), mango, kesar-pista (saffron pistachio), and chiku (exotic fruit).

Summary & comments: Building was recently remodeled with a state-of-the-art air-filtration system and lead-free dishes. Meals are low in calories, fat, and cholesterol. Family owned and run. Very health-concerned and quality-oriented owner, and it shows in the results. This 15-year-old restaurant has a following.

Honors/awards: Voted Best Vegetarian Restaurant and third in the Healthy Menu Items category in *North Shore* magazine, 1994.

Cité

Zone 1   North Side
Top of Lake Point Tower,
  505 North Lake Shore Drive
(312) 644-4050

Continental
★★★★
Expensive/Very Expensive
Quality 89   Value D

Reservations:	Required (weekends book up fast; plan ahead)
When to go:	It's easier to get a reservation on weeknights
Entree range:	$19–38
Payment:	Major credit cards
Service rating:	★★★★½
Friendliness rating:	★★★★
Parking:	Valet in building garage
Bar:	Full service
Wine selection:	Extensive; American and European wines, from $40–80 a bottle; 4 by the glass
Dress:	Jackets required for men
Disabled access:	Yes
Customers:	Businesspeople, tourists, couples, guests of special events
Lunch:	Every day, noon–3 P.M.
Dinner:	Every day, 5–11 P.M.

Atmosphere/setting: Cité's panoramic, 70th-floor view of Chicago's skyline and lakefront fosters a heady, romantic atmosphere. The spectacular view is enhanced with fresh flowers. Elegant circular dining room with marble floor.

House specialties: Appetizers: sautéed wild mushrooms in puff pastry; Mediterranean tapas; shrimp coriander. Entrees (include Cité salad): grilled Norwegian salmon fillet; roast rack of spring lamb; fresh seafood (depending on availability): baked red snapper Mediterranean. Grand Marnier soufflé and several desserts prepared tableside; crêpes suzette, bananas Foster, cherries jubilee.

Other recommendations: Pasta primavera; steak Diane; desserts on pastry trolley.

Entertainment & amenities: Piano music nightly. Live music and entertainment at Le Cabaret at Cité, Wednesday–Sunday evenings ($25 cover); dinner and show package available.

Summary & comments: As the restaurant's postcard states: "Let the skyline surround you," and indeed it does here. The restaurant has had its ups and downs over the years, but lately it has been reliable in its commitment to fine dining. Singer and actress Karen Mason opened Le Cabaret at Cité in April 1997. A great restaurant for a special occasion: birthday guests see their name in a frame at the table.

COCO PAZZO

Zone 4   The Loop
300 West Hubbard Street
(312) 836-0900

Italian	
★★★★	
Moderate	
Quality 91	Value C

Reservations:	Highly recommended, especially on weekends
When to go:	During the week
Entree range:	$12.50–26
Payment:	All major credit cards except Discover
Service rating:	★★★★
Friendliness rating:	★★★★
Parking:	Valet; city garages nearby
Bar:	Full service, including grappa selection
Wine selection:	85 Italian, French champagne, sparkling wines from California; $20–225 a bottle
Dress:	Casual to upscale; no jacket required
Disabled access:	Yes
Customers:	Locals, professionals, couples, businesspeople
Lunch:	Monday–Friday, 11:30 A.M.–2:30 P.M.
Dinner:	Monday–Thursday, 5:30–10:30 P.M.; Friday and Saturday, 5:30–11:30 P.M.; Sunday, 5–10 P.M.

Atmosphere/setting: Open kitchen with wood-burning oven and rotisserie produces a warm, inviting interior. Brick walls; wooden floors, beams, and chairs; track lighting; sophisticated blue velvet drapes; elegant bar.

House specialties: Rotisserie special of the day; tagliata alla Fiorentina (grilled rib-eye steak); baked vegetables and roasted butterflied trout; ravioli filled with baby artichokes; sea bass. Signature dessert: cioccolato fondente con gelato cappuccino (flourless chocolate cake with warm mousse center and cappuccino ice cream).

Other recommendations: Risotto del giorno (Arborio rice of the day); coscia di agnello al giarrosto (rotisserie leg of lamb, thinly sliced and served with potatoes); osso buco (veal shank); vegetali al forno (thinly sliced seasonal vegetables baked in a wood-burning oven).

Summary & comments: Star executive chef, Gregorio Stephenson, prepares creative, hearty Tuscan-style dishes; specialties change every day. The pastry chef bakes bread and wonderful, simple, flavorful desserts such as lemon tarts and white chocolate bread pudding. This restaurant and the wonderful CoCo Pazzo Cafe (636 North St. Clair; (312) 664-2777) are restaurateur Pino Luongo's only Chicago entries of his successful group of New York–based dining establishments.

Honors/awards: *Mobil Travel Guide* Award; AAA four diamonds.

CORNER BAKERY

Zone 4   The Loop
516 North Clark Street
(312) 644-8100

Zone 4   The Loop
Sante Fe Building,
  224 South Michigan Avenue (at Jackson Boulevard)
(312) 431-7600
(See More Recommendations, page 15, for other locations throughout
the Chicago area.)

	Bakery Cafe
	★★★½
	Inexpensive/Moderate
	Quality 90 Value B

Reservations:	Not accepted
When to go:	Any time; busiest at peak breakfast and lunch hours
Entree range:	Loaves, $1.50–6; sandwiches and soups, $1.95–5.25.
Payment:	All major credit cards
Service rating:	★★★★ (since self-serve, pertains to clerks)
Friendliness rating:	★★★★½
Parking:	Street or nearby garages or lots
Bar:	None
Wine selection:	None
Dress:	Casual
Disabled access:	Yes; call first
Customers:	Varied, professionals (before and after work and for lunch)
Open:	Monday–Friday, 6:30 A.M.–9 P.M.; Saturday and Sunday, 7:30 A.M.–9 P.M.; call individual locations for hours; some vary

Atmosphere/setting: The original Clark Street location is a small, cozy shop with several tables near windows; hearth bakery; great aromas. The Santa Fe Building is historic, and the 80-seat bakery is probably the largest of the ten locations; the sidewalk cafe on Michigan Avenue is open in the summer. Other locations are slightly different, but the basic concept is the same.

House specialties: A variety of approximately 25 breads baked fresh daily, including baguettes, country loaves, and specialty breads. Lunch items: focaccia and various sandwiches such as chicken pesto or tuna salad; roasted vegetable salad; Oriental pasta salad; rope pasta salad with butternut squash, goat cheese, and spinach.

(continued)

Other recommendations: Raisin-nut bread; kugelhopf (seasonal); mushroom pizza; cheese bread; tomato flatbread; variety of muffins; bars (try lemon and apricot); cookies; mini Bundt cakes; hot chocolate; juices; cappuccino.

Summary & comments: This bakery concept, originated by Lettuce Entertain You Enterprises and chef Jean Joho in 1991, produces some of the finest hearth-cooked, European-style breads and rolls anywhere; therefore, their sandwiches are excellent. The number of locations is growing: bakeries are now in the Water Tower Place, Union Station, Oak Brook, Old Orchard, and Schaumburg, and adjacent to some Maggiano's Little Italy restaurants. The success of this place proves that people have been starving for great bread.

COURTWRIGHT'S

Zone 8 Southern Suburbs	Creative American
8989 Archer Avenue, Willow Springs	★★★★½
(708) 839-8000	Moderate/Expensive
	Quality 96 Value B

Reservations: Necessary Saturday; recommended for large groups
When to go: Any time
Entree range: Lunch, $5.95–10.95; dinner, $14.95–24.95
Payment: AMEX, D, DC, MC, VISA
Service rating: ★★★★★
Friendliness rating: ★★★★★
Parking: Lot
Bar: Full service
Wine selection: More than 500 offerings; 40 by the glass, from $4.50; $18 a bottle; strong on verticals (3 or more vintages of the same wine)
Dress: Chic casual, business or dressy
Disabled access: Yes
Customers: Businesspeople, romantic couples, locals, city people
Lunch: Monday–Saturday, 11:30 A.M.–2:30 P.M.
Dinner: Monday–Friday, 4:30–10 P.M.; Saturday, 4:30–11 P.M.

Atmosphere/setting: Beautiful indoor/outdoor architecture with large windows overlooking a garden sculpted into the woodland hillside. A winding staircase bordered by flowers leads to the charming gazebo outside. Inside, a five-sided curved ceiling, globe chandelier and sconces, white linens, and spectacular floral arrangements. Painted tile inserts in the lounge fireplace symbolically represent the three generations of management here, and the animal carvings in the dining room's fireplace represent William, Rebecca, and their children.

House specialties: Appetizers: the popular lobster purse (medallions of Australian lobster, roasted red peppers, sweet peas, and baby leeks wrapped in crisp phyllo with sauce américaine; spring vegetable terrine (charcoal-grilled portobello, baby artichokes, and asparagus); special soup one night was roasted garlic, garnished with croutons and slivers of bell peppers and carrots; house salad (organic mesclun and seasonal vegetables with herb Balsamic vinaigrette). Entrees: medallions of lobster with sautéed Gulf shrimp and freshwater prawn; medallions of pork tenderloin marinated in lemongrass and truffle oil, sautéed

(continued)

and dressed in a sweet-tart, sun-dried mango wine sauce; rock Cornish hen stuffed with mushroom game mousse served with wild rice pilaf and sun-dried cherries, vegetables, and Riesling reduction; rack of New Zealand lamb (encrusted in fresh herbs, seared and oven-roasted with potato galette); chargrilled 10-oz. prime filet mignon (served with sautéed portobello mushroom and pinot noir reduction). Chef's degustation five-course menu, $44.95 a person.

Desserts are prepared on premises and change: rich Chocolate Fantasy, a trio of white, dark, and milk chocolate mousse with caramelized orange rum sauce. A lighter creation is Rainbow Fruit Mousse, a stunning tricolored wedge of layered raspberry, mango, and kiwi mousses with three fruit purees: blackberry, gooseberry, and raspberry; berries are arranged on the plate and a delicate pastry decorates the top. Homemade ice creams; tropical fruit sorbets in champagne with edible flowers; raspberry pecan tart with passion fruit ice cream.

Other recommendations: Warm Brie and poached pear salad (served with honey-ginger dressing and toasted pistachios). Entrees: sautéed jumbo shrimp and sea scallops on capellini with oyster mushrooms, baby artichoke halves, arugula, and a lemon pesto sauce; vegetarian bouquet (quiche of sautéed shiitake, baby leeks, roasted peppers, asparagus, and Asiago cheese); grilled fillet of fresh Atlantic salmon, ginger couscous, asparagus, and lemon-tarragon beurre blanc. White chocolate mousse cake; espresso crème anglaise; cheeses served with walnuts and grapes.

Entertainment & amenities: Occasional special events, such as wine-tasting dinners and fund-raisers with other southwest suburban chefs cooking along with the chef here.

Summary & comments: There's a family legacy at Courtwright's that goes back more than four decades in the dining business, beginning in 1956, when Ken Courtright, Sr., and his bride, Sally, opened Ken's in Chicago's Beverly area. After expanding, the Courtwright hallmark became known for caring, friendly service as well as for good food. The business grew to include several more restaurants, including Courtwright's in March 1995. William Courtwright, the second son, and his wife, Rebecca, created this beautiful place and now manage it. Three of their four children assist. The creative American cuisine here attests great cooking skills and shows a sensitivity to combining compatible flavors and ingredients. This is definitely a destination fine-dining place that is perfect for special occasions or any time you'd like to have an aesthetic, educational culinary experience.

Honors/awards: Good press, including *Fox Valley Villages 60504.*

Cucina Roma

	Italian Bistro
	★★★½

Zone 8   Southern Suburbs
1163 East Ogden Avenue at Iroquois
    Center, Naperville
(630) 355-4444

Inexpensive/Moderate

Quality 89   Value B

Reservations:	Accepted up to about half-capacity
When to go:	Avoid peak time, 6:30–8:30 P.M.
Entree range:	$9.50–18.95
Payment:	Major credit cards
Service rating:	★★★
Friendliness rating:	★★★½
Parking:	Shopping mall lot
Bar:	Full service; extensive martini list
Wine selection:	Italian; from $16 a bottle and $5 a glass
Dress:	Casual
Disabled access:	Yes
Customers:	Diverse; families, young professionals, and seniors
Lunch:	Monday–Friday, 11 a.m–3 P.M.
Dinner:	Monday–Thursday, 3–10 P.M.; Friday, 3–11 P.M.; Saturday, 4–11 P.M.; Sunday, 4–9 P.M.

Atmosphere / setting: A bit of nature enlivens the split-level space as hand-painted grapevines climb the creamy-hued walls and woodwork. Each of the four nonsmoking dining rooms is intimate yet allows space for privacy.

House specialties: Polenta con funghi (baked polenta with mushroom sauce); marinated sweet roasted peppers; antipasto alla Roma; escarole, white bean, and sausage soup (called "our specialty"—it's worth the trip here); veal osso buco (braised shank); farfalle Stefano; whitefish Milano. Chocolate blackout cake; fat-free cheesecake; frutti de bosco.

Other recommendations: Grilled portobello; stuffed artichoke; chicken and sausage pot pie; veal marsala; veal chop classico; bread pudding served with gelato; Italian lemon ice.

Entertainment & amenities: Outdoor cafe; cigar parlor; executive dining room.

Summary & comments: An impressive, lengthy menu features several categories, including the "Cucina Lite." Most entrees are grilled with bold flavors and seasoned with garlic and herbs. The chef uses vegetables liberally, which balances meals and adds texture and flavor. Cucina Roma opened in Naperville in 1997, fashioned after its successful sibling in Westmont. The caring management, fine food, and pleasant atmosphere make it one of the best Italian bistros in the suburbs.

Cuisines

	Mediterranean/Italian
Zone 4 The Loop	★★★½
Renaissance Chicago Hotel,	Inexpensive/Moderate
One West Wacker Drive	
(312) 372-4459	Quality 89 Value B

Reservations: Requested and suggested
When to go: Weekdays
Entree range: $8.95–29; one item at $32.95
Payment: VISA, MC, AMEX, D, DC, CB, JCB
Service rating: ★★★★½
Friendliness rating: ★★★★★
Parking: Valet
Bar: Full service
Wine selection: Extensive, over 220 bottles; 8-page list and 1-page
                         by-the-glass list
Dress: Tastefully casual; dressier weekend evenings
Disabled access: Yes
Customers: Tourists, hotel guests, locals, theatergoers
Breakfast: Monday–Friday, 6 A.M.–10:30 P.M., Saturday and
                         Sunday, 6–11:30 A.M.
Lunch: Monday–Friday, 11:30 A.M.–2 P.M.
Dinner: Every day, 5:30–10:30 P.M.

Atmosphere/setting: Opulent: plush, romantic, and elegant with comfortable banquettes; wood and marble; open kitchen with wood-burning oven.

House specialties: Grilled octopus with warm Spanish potato salad; snapper Napoleon; lobster bisque; crabmeat and scallop lasagna. Apple phyllo basket; chocolate cigar (Cointreau white chocolate mousse wrapped in dark chocolate).

Other recommendations: Robust, grilled small pizza; appetizer of crab meat and shiitakes in phyllo; grilled swordfish (ordered with accompaniments from red snapper dish); three-layer chocolate torte; papaya compote; ethereal tiramisu.

Summary & comments: Start with the nine-page wine list here, then look at the one-page menu for dishes to match your bottle selection. There's a Mediterranean influence and an element of surprise (e.g., a salad of field greens with quail eggs). A refreshing complimentary fruit plate arrives at the end of the meal—a thoughtful touch. Executive chef Dennis Kolodziejski developed a Summer Chill Menu, featuring chilled soups (minted peach), appetizers (tuna carpaccio), entrees and salads (scallop ceviche), and desserts (frozen zabaglione cream sandwich); his winter menu is just as creative. The value here is excellent considering the creative food and quality of wine and hospitality.

Cyrano's Bistrot & Wine Bar

<table>
<tr><td>French Bistro
★★★½
Inexpensive/Moderate

Quality 90   Value B</td></tr>
</table>

Zone 3   Near North
546 North Wells Street
(312) 467-0546

Reservations:	Accepted
When to go:	Any time
Entree range:	$10.95–15.95
Payment:	Major credit cards
Service rating:	★★★★
Friendliness rating:	★★★★
Parking:	Valet
Bar:	Full service
Wine selection:	Country French selections; fairly priced; some by the glass
Dress:	Casual
Disabled access:	Yes
Customers:	Young professionals, couples, families
Open:	Sunday–Thursday, 11:30 A.M.–10 P.M.; Friday and Saturday, 11:30 A.M.–11 P.M.

Atmosphere/setting: Mustard-yellow walls, burgundy banquettes, wooden beams, mirrors, and a sidewalk cafe with riotous fresh flowers (during fine weather) give the feeling of a cozy cafe in France.

House specialties: Rotisserie duck maison; bouillabaisse; Bergerac-style braised pork and beef tips; Simone's simply steamed artichoke with sauce tartare; house-cured salmon gravlax with cucumber rémoulade; steamed mussels marinière in wine cream; sweet onion and mushroom tart with petite salade; salad of red leaf lettuce, frisée, Belgian endive, blue cheese, and walnuts in garlic vinaigrette; Cyrano's salade maison; warm apple tart with rosemary ice cream.

Other recommendations: Grilled steak; coq au vin bordelaise; cassoulet from Toulouse with duck, lamb, sausage, and white beans; ostrich country pâté; les fromages plate (at least four imported cheeses); chocolate bread pudding.

Summary & comments: Cyrano's, one of Chicago's newest French bistrots, is the husband-and-wife operation of chef Didier Durand, a native of Bergerac, France, and his wife, Jamie Pellar, who directs the front of the house and the wine cellar. Durand prepares variations on the classical French cuisine of his roots, an approach that's proving successful. This is a nonsmoking environment. Many love "Le Grand Lunch Express," a four-course meal on an oversized tray for $10.96.

Honors/awards: Sherman Kaplan's Top 13 Restaurants of 1996.

Cy's Crab House

Zone 1   North Side
3819 North Ashland Avenue
(773) 883-8900; fax (773) 883-1205

Seafood/Persian
★★★
Inexpensive/Moderate

Quality 84   Value B

Reservations:	Recommended for 5 or more
When to go:	Monday–Thursday
Entree range:	$6–22 and market price
Payment:	VISA, MC, AMEX
Service rating:	★★★½
Friendliness rating:	★★★★½
Parking:	Owns 2 adjacent lots
Bar:	Full service
Wine selection:	American; several by the glass, $3–5
Dress:	Casual
Disabled access:	Yes, including rest rooms
Customers:	Locals, diverse, businesspeople, couples, families
Lunch/Dinner:	Monday–Thursday, 11:30 A.M.–11 P.M.; Friday–Sunday, 11:30 A.M.–midnight

Atmosphere/setting: Simple contemporary decor; semiformal, spacious, two-level main dining room; Recently remodeled outdoor/indoor casual cafe with patio. New raw bar with specials for $9.95.

House specialties: Prawns stuffed with crabmeat; Cy's crab cake; joojeh kebab (charcoal-broiled, marinated chicken); prime dry-aged steaks.

Other recommendations: Mussels steamed with garlic; oysters on the half shell; garlic blue crab claw; Key lime pie; turtle cheesecake. Cy's Crab platter with Alaskan, Dungeness, king, and snow crabs.

Entertainment & amenities: Eating all the oysters you can for $9.95 at the raw bar from 4 P.M. until closing.

Summary & comments: Daily ordering ensures that about ten different fish are offered in addition to the shellfish during the week; occasionally the restaurant runs out of a particular fish item—a good sign of turnover. One page of Cy's menu features Persian specialties, including vegetarian dishes and many kebabs—some with mahi mahi, shrimp, and scallops; combination platters include "crabs and slabs" (barbecue baby-back ribs and snow crab legs). Besides this six-year-old restaurant, Cy Sadaka owns King Crab, an affordable, casual seafood restaurant at 1816 North Halsted Street (phone (312) 280-8990); his newest restaurant is Cy's Steak & Chop House at 4138 North Lincoln Avenue (phone (773) 404-5800).

Da Nicola Ristorante

Zone 1 North Side	Italian
3114 North Lincoln Avenue	★★★
(773) 935-8000; fax (773) 935-1664	Inexpensive/Moderate
	Quality 84 Value B

Reservations:	Recommended on weekends
When to go:	Any time
Entree range:	Lunch, $4.95–12.95; dinner, $8.95–18.95
Payment:	All major credit cards
Service rating:	★★★★
Friendliness rating:	★★★★½
Parking:	Lot
Bar:	Full service
Wine selection:	About 50; mostly Italian, $15–125; several by the glass
Dress:	Moderately casual, jackets not required
Disabled access:	Yes
Customers:	Mixed, businesspeople, professionals, families
Lunch:	Monday, Wednesday–Friday, 11 A.M.–3 P.M.
Dinner:	Monday–Thursday, 5–11 P.M.; Friday and Saturday, 5–11:30 P.M.

Atmosphere/setting: Romantic and intimate with an Italian feel; tile roof alcove decor; stucco and stone; beamed ceilings.

House specialties: Ravioli porcini (handmade, filled with porcini mushrooms); rotini napoletani (pasta layered with sautéed spinach, bocconcini di mozzarella, sautéed beef, prosciutto, and Parmigiano-Reggiano); salmone portofino (sautéed salmon fillet); scampi alla Miguel; stuffed artichoke; tomato, red onion, and fresh Gorgonzola salad.

Other recommendations: Vitello Caprese (veal medallions with plum-tomato sauce); vitello Rossini (veal medallions with tomato cream sauce); linguine with littleneck clams; bruschetta; tiramisu served unusually in a tall footed glass— light and brandy-flavored, not so sweet; tortoni; granita lemon ice.

Summary & comments: This charming neighborhood restaurant is a hidden gem offering a substantial menu. Good variety of daily specials, which come with a choice of soup or salad and a side. The couple who own it work hard to make it as good as possible, from getting local farm tomatoes to fine-tuning the wine list; the wife makes the desserts. Very accommodating—they will split pastas and other dishes on request.

Del Rio

Zone 11 Northern Suburbs	Italian
228 Green Bay Road, Highwood	★★★
(847) 432-4608; fax (847) 432-7517	Inexpensive/Moderate
	Quality 83 Value B

Reservations:	Recommended for 6 or more
When to go:	5–6 P.M.
Entree range:	$10.95–24
Payment:	All major credit cards
Service rating:	★★★½
Friendliness rating:	★★★★
Parking:	Lot
Bar:	Full service
Wine selection:	Extensive, international; one of the largest selections in the Midwest
Dress:	Moderately casual to dressy
Disabled access:	Yes
Customers:	Diverse, including loyal locals
Dinner:	Monday–Thursday, 5–10 P.M., Friday and Saturday, 5–11 P.M.

Atmosphere/setting: Home-style "family restaurant look"; linen table-cloths; dimly lit and cozy; nice bar.

House specialties: Veal Del Rio and other veal dishes; homemade bread and pastas (e.g., ravioli al forno); low-fat healthy chicken items; custard grussini.

Other recommendations: Steak; fresh fish (e.g., salmon modenese) and pasta items (ask server for recommendations).

Entertainment & amenities: Reviewing the grand wine list.

Summary & comments: This is one of the oldest Italian family-owned restaurants in Highwood—about 73 years old at press time and approaching the big 75th anniversary—a major milestone in this competitive restaurant field! Family pride in overseeing the operation keeps it running smoothly. Cooking is solid, with the predictable standards, and you can be blown away by the scope and quality of the wines.

The Dining Room

Zone 3 Near North	New French
The Ritz-Carlton Hotel,	★★★★½
160 East Pearson Street	Moderate/Expensive
(312) 266-1000, ext. 4223	Quality 97 Value C

Reservations: Strongly recommended; call 1 week ahead for Sunday and holidays and midweek for weekends

When to go: Weekends are busiest; business depends on conventions and events

Entree range: $24–30

Payment: VISA, MC, AMEX, DC, CB

Service rating: ★★★★★

Friendliness rating: ★★★★★

Parking: Valet at hotel entrance, 3 hours free with validation

Bar: Full service; 2 bars in hotel

Wine selection: Extensive 50-page list; over 470 vintages; 20,000 bottles; $30–1,800 a bottle

Dress: Jacket required, tie optional; brunch, moderately casual

Disabled access: Yes, entrance and rest rooms

Customers: Businesspeople, hotel guests, locals; not touristy

Brunch: Sunday, 2 seatings at 10:30 A.M. and 1 P.M.

Dinner: Monday–Thursday, 6–11 P.M.; Friday and Saturday, 5:30–11 P.M.; Sunday, 6–10 P.M.

Atmosphere/setting: Luxurious Edwardian-style two-level room. Quiet, cozy niches; large tables for families; intimate banquettes. Sunday buffet brunch served on outdoor terrace.

House specialties: Maine lobster with couscous and stuffed zucchini blossom; applewood-smoked salmon; Beluga caviar parfait. ★Chilled terrine of artichokes, baby spinach, and oven-dried tomatoes; veal chop with spring morel mushrooms. Four to five items change daily; verbal special of the day. (★=low in fat, sodium, calories, and cholesterol.)

Other recommendations: Shrimp cake; Colorado rack of lamb; sautéed swordfish; six-course vegetarian degustation menu, $50; set pretheater menu, 6–7 P.M.; six-course degustation menu, $60.

Entertainment & amenities: Pianist during dining hours.

(continued)

Summary & comments: Voted by readers of several magazines to be the best hotel dining room in Chicago, and every visit here proves why. Top-flight, progressive French cuisine, opulent atmosphere, and professionally friendly— never intimidating—service. This is a stellar dining experience at one of the finest hotels anywhere.

Honors/awards: Chef Sarah Stegner won New York's James Beard Award for upcoming chefs; *Gourmet* magazine, Best Restaurant in Chicago, 1996; *Bon Appetit* magazine, One of the Top 13 Hotel Dining Rooms in the United States, 1996; *Wine Spectator* Grand Award for 12 years in succession.

DON JUAN

Zone 1   North Side
6730 North Northwest Highway
(733) 775-6438; fax (773) 775-1052

Mexican	
★★★	
Inexpensive/Moderate	
Quality 84	Value C

Reservations:	Recommended for 5 or more; not accepted on Friday and Saturday
When to go:	Monday–Thursday; Sunday is good for families
Entree range:	$6.95–13.25 on menu; up to $21 on special menu
Payment:	All major credit cards
Service rating:	★★★
Friendliness rating:	★★★★
Parking:	Free lot or street
Bar:	Full service; all Mexican beers
Wine selection:	Spanish, Chilean, and some Mexican wines
Dress:	Very casual
Disabled access:	Yes
Customers:	Families, couples, 20-somethings; mostly local
Lunch/Dinner:	Monday–Thursday, 11 A.M.–10 P.M.; Friday and Saturday, 11 A.M.–11 P.M.; Sunday, noon–9 P.M.

Atmosphere/setting: Mexican feeling in split-level dining room with many artifacts and colorful touches.

House specialties: Seafood dishes on daily special menu; game such as grilled venison chop, barley risotto with wild mushrooms, and dried blueberry pasilla sauce. From the regular menu, traditional items such as classic steak tacos, burrito Don Juan, and enchiladas suizas.

Other recommendations: Nachos de marisco with crab meat and shrimp; stuffed jalapeños; duck tamales; fajitas with chicken, steak, pork, or shrimp—a combo or vegetarian. Flan, good sorbets and ice creams, and plum-almond tart.

Entertainment & amenities: Variety (except in the summer), including flamenco guitar and a harpist.

Summary & comments: Named for the legendary promiscuous lover, Don Juan has a flirtatious menu appeal with a creative departure from the carbon-copy Mexican fare. Allow yourself to be seduced by the chef's creative specials. On busy nights, the restaurant's noise level can be annoying. Private party room available for up to 30 people.

Honors/awards: *Chicago* magazine's Best Fajita.

Don Roth's in Wheeling

Zone 10 Northwest Suburbs	American
61 North Milwaukee Avenue, Wheeling	★★★
(847) 537-5800; fax (847) 537-5828	Moderate
	Quality 84 Value C

Reservations: Recommended
When to go: Any time
Entree range: $15.95–27.95
Payment: VISA, MC, AMEX, D, DC, CB
Service rating: ★★★
Friendliness rating: ★★★★
Parking: Lot
Bar: Full service
Wine selection: Limited—mostly American and French
Dress: Casual but in good taste
Disabled access: Yes
Customers: Families, suburban locals, businesspeople
Lunch: Monday–Friday, 11:30 A.M. 2:30 P.M.
Dinner: Monday–Thursday, 5:30–9:30 P.M., Friday,
                         5–10.30 P.M.; Saturday, 5–11 P.M.; Sunday,
                         4–8:30 P.M.

Atmosphere/setting: Memorabilia dating back to 1920, when owner Don Roth's father Otto started and ran the famed former Blackhawk Restaurant downtown, a popular, big-band supper club; Don Roth operated it for decades afterward. Lovely outdoor garden.

House specialties: Roast prime ribs of beef (three cuts); Boston scrod; the legendary Spinning Salad Bowl and special dressing with blue cheese, egg, and shrimp (included with entree).

Other recommendations: Sirloin strip steak; specials such as broiled Lake Superior whitefish and chicken Blackhawk.

Entertainment & amenities: Tapes of WGN broadcasts from the former Blackhawk Restaurant.

Summary & comments: Owner Don Roth is a veritable encyclopedia of history from the big-band supper club era, and he has wisely displayed his memorabilia collection. Together with prime rib and his famous Spinning Salad Bowl (dressing now sold), he transformed his restaurant from costly big-band entertainment to entertaining customers tableside, where "food is the show." Seniors especially enjoy browsing at this Wheeling location. The menu is simple, the cooking good, and the service consistently accommodating.

Honors/awards: Don Roth has received many awards over the years.

Don's Fishmarket
and Tavern

	Seafood/Steak
	★★★★
Zone 11 Northern Suburbs	Inexpensive/Expensive
9335 Skokie Boulevard, Skokie	Quality 95 Value B
(847) 677-3424; fax (847) 679-5849	

Reservations: Accepted
When to go: Any time
Entree range: *Fishmarket,* $15.95–40; *Tavern,* $8–12
Payment: VISA, MC, DC, CB
Service rating: ★★★½
Friendliness rating: ★★★★
Parking: Lot
Bar: Full service, extensive beer list
Wine selection: Award-winning Californian; fairly priced
Dress: Casual, both places
Disabled access: Yes, both places
Customers: Diverse; some moviegoers; locals; travelers
Lunch: *Fishmarket:* Monday–Friday, 11:30 A.M.–2:30 P.M.
                    Tavern: Monday–Saturday, 11:30 A.M.–4 P.M.
Dinner: *Fishmarket:* Monday–Thursday, 5–10 P.M.; Friday
                    and Saturday, 5–11 P.M.; Sunday, 4–9 P.M. *Tavern:*
                    Monday–Saturday, 5–10 P.M.; Sunday, 4–9 P.M.

Atmosphere/setting: The fishmarket has a homey atmosphere and slight nautical decor. The tavern is more casual and rustic, cozy, and dimly lit.

House specialties: *Fishmarket:* baby octopus mesquite grilled; Caribbean red snapper; Don's platter (grilled swordfish, pan-blackened catfish, and broiled Lake Superior whitefish). *Tavern:* New England clam chowder; peel–eat shrimp; Snug Harbor mussels; blackened tuna salad; lobster pasta; eggplant parmigiana.

Other recommendations: *Fishmarket:* sautéed fresh Florida diver scallops; steaks and chops (12-ounce New York strip, 20-ounce porterhouse, lamb rack). *Tavern:* fish and chips, ocean perch, tempura shrimp, jambalaya, fajitas.

Summary & comments: Don's Fishmarket has been a dependable, comfortable North Shore seafood restaurant for over 20 years. Executive chef Domingo Chavez offers a mix of low-fat preparations with vinaigrettes, as well as some with butter and cream sauces. Look for seasonal seafood promotions, such as summer Thrill of the Grill, a Crabfest, and an Autumn Lobsterfest. The tavern features special deals (e.g., shrimp and oysters, 40 cents each, Tuesday, 2–11 P.M.).

Elaine and Ina's

Zone 3   Near North
448 East Ontario Street
(312) 337-6700

New American
★★★½
Inexpensive/Moderate

Quality 89   Value B

Reservations:	Accepted for parties of 5 or more
When to go:	Any time
Entree range:	8–15.75
Payment:	Major credit cards
Service rating:	★★★★½
Friendliness rating:	★★★★½
Parking:	Validated in same building; enter 441 East Erie
Bar:	Wine and beer
Wine selection:	About 33; international, mostly Californian; several by the glass, $4.50–7.50; bottles, $18–50
Dress:	Casual
Disabled access:	Yes
Customers:	Mix of professionals, tourists, locals, suburbanites
Breakfast:	Served all day
Lunch:	Monday–Saturday, 11 A.M.–2 P.M.
Dinner:	Monday–Friday, 7 A.M.–9 P.M.; Saturday, 8 A.M.–9 P.M.; Sunday, 8 A.M.–3 P.M.

Atmosphere/setting: The atrium has seating for those desiring quick meals. Lovely, spacious dining room overlooks the sidewalk cafe.

House specialties: Breakfast: granola; Ina's pancakes; vegetable hash with two poached eggs. Lunch/dinner: medley of three grains salad with Moroccan couscous; cheese-filled ravioli; grilled chicken breast. Dinner: fish of the day. Desserts: Key lime pie; strawberry and blueberry shortcake; plum tart.

Other recommendations: Breakfast: Elaine's pasta frittata (also lunch and dinner); French toast with fresh fruit. Lunch: gazpacho; curried chicken salad; pasta of the day (also dinner). Dinner: shrimp bistro-style; pan-seared salmon. Desserts: chocolate truffle tart; angel food cake with chocolate frosting.

Entertainment & amenities: Espresso bar; pastry shop; sidewalk cafe where you can see Navy Pier and its Ferris wheel and fireworks.

Summary & comments: This is the reincarnation of the former five-year-old Ina's Kitchen & Elaine's Patio, a smaller location known for great breakfasts. Partners Ina Pinkney and Elaine Farrell moved here in spring 1997, and it's been bustling ever since. They bake everything except the bread. These women have their hearts in their business—everything is finely tuned.

El Dinamico Dallas

Zone 1   North Side
1545 West Howard Street
(773) 465-3320

Caribbean
★★½
Inexpensive
Quality 79   Value B

Reservations:	Accepted but not necessary
When to go:	Any time
Entree range:	$3.95–16; dinner buffet weekend evenings, $9.95
Payment:	Major credit cards
Service rating:	★★½
Friendliness rating:	★★★★
Parking:	Street
Bar:	None
Wine selection:	BYOB; corkage fee is only 50 cents per glass
Dress:	Casual
Disabled access:	Yes
Customers:	Locals, ethnics, students
Open:	Monday, Wednesday–Saturday, noon–10 P.M.; Sunday, 5–9 P.M.

Atmosphere / setting: Down-home, colorful, plant-filled storefront reminiscent of the Caribbean. Very casual.

House specialties: Spicy jerk pork or chicken; curried chicken; chilindron de chivo (goat meat stewed in beer and wine); lambi (conch in Creole tomato-wine sauce). Desserts made by co-owner Armonize Dallas include sweet potato pie, carrot cake, and chocolate caramel cake. Homemade tropical juices, such as papaya, orange banana, or passion fruit.

Other recommendations: Curried goat; black bean soup; Armonize tamales; fried plantains and congri (rice and beans); banana bread. The dinner buffet includes many hot and cold items, some of them changing; some standards are curried chicken, spaghetti with ground turkey, rum pound cake, and fruit punch.

Summary & comments: This long-lived Caribbean cafe is owned by the energetic husband-and-wife team, chef Erick and Armonize Dallas. It offers a slice of Caribbean island culture and well-prepared Jamaican, Cuban, and Haitian dishes that reflect the owners' heritage. The service is friendly and relaxed, and the menu is just as laid back; some items require translations and descriptions, so feel free to ask. Homemade bread comes with dinner, and banana bread can be ordered as dessert. Bring your own wine, or try their delightful array of tropical juices. They also make shakes. Catering is available.

Eli's, THE PLACE FOR STEAK

Zone 3   Near North
215 East Chicago Avenue
(312) 642-1393

Steak
★★★½
Moderate/Expensive

Quality 88   Value C

Reservations:	Accepted
When to go:	Early or late for both lunch and dinner
Entree range:	$17.50–32
Payment:	All major credit cards
Service rating:	★★★½
Friendliness rating:	★★★★
Parking:	$5 with validation at garage next door
Bar:	Full service
Wine selection:	Mostly American, some French and Italian;
	$16–260 per bottle, most in the $20–52 range
Dress:	Casual
Disabled access:	Yes
Customers:	Mixed, businesspeople (lunch), tourists, locals
Lunch:	Monday–Friday, 11 A.M.–2:30 P.M.
Dinner:	Sunday–Thursday, 4–10:30 P.M., Friday and Saturday,
	4–11 P.M.

Atmosphere/setting: Photo gallery of celebrities who have dined here;
comfortable carpeted dining room; a charming enclosed sidewalk cafe.

House specialties: Complimentary iced relishes, chopped liver, and breads;
Eli's special New York sirloin steak; Eli's house salad; Eli's Famous Garbage Salad
(garden vegetables served over mixed salad greens tossed in Eli's dressing)

Other recommendations: Soup of the day: good creamy tomato-based
seafood chowder; Eli's famous potato pancakes; Eli's chicken and matzo ball soup;
Eli's Caesar salad; calf's liver Eli. Eli's cheesecake (usually about a dozen varieties). Eli's
bakery also makes carrot cake, apple tart, and "Midnight Sensation" chocolate cake.

Summary & comments: You'll never forget where you are dining, since Eli's
name is reinforced throughout the menu. The special New York sirloin steak with
crushed black peppercorns was delicious and properly prepared to a medium-rare,
as ordered. The salmon fillet pesto proved that they cook fish well here, too.
Although Eli's is expensive, at least you get relishes, chopped liver, delicious bread,
and a potato included in the entree price, unlike some steak houses.

El Tipico

Zone 1   North Side
1836 West Foster Avenue
(773) 878-0839

Zone 11   Northern Suburbs
3341 Dempster Avenue, Skokie
(847) 676-4070; fax (847) 676-4079

Mexican	
★★½	
Inexpensive	
Quality 79	Value B

Reservations:	Recommended for weekends
When to go:	Weekdays
Entree range:	$5–13
Payment:	All major credit cards
Service rating:	★★★
Friendliness rating:	★★★★
Parking:	Yes
Bar:	Full service; Mexican beers and margaritas
Wine selection:	Limited; mostly American
Dress:	Casual
Disabled access:	Yes
Customers:	Mixed, young professionals, families, business-people
Lunch/Dinner:	Sunday–Thursday, 11 A.M.–midnight; Friday and Saturday, 11–2 A.M.

Atmosphere/setting: Intimate, charming, colorful, with some authentic artifacts; quiet overall. Nonsmoking dining rooms. Outdoor garden.

House specialties: Appetizer combo: shrimp fajitas (also chicken and beef), steak tacos, pollo en mole, burrito ranchero; steak a la pequeña. Huge portions.

Other recommendations: Traditional Mexican dishes (e.g., enchiladas) and good flan.

Entertainment & amenities: Occasional weekend trio.

Summary & comments: Very comfortable and pleasant neighborhood restaurant serving good, fresh south-of-the-border fare and huge portions at reasonable prices. Attractive setting and caring management, plus the good value aspect, make it a place for repeat visits.

154

Emilio's Meson Sabika
Tapas Bar Restaurant

Zone 8   Southern Suburbs
1025 Aurora Avenue, Naperville
(630) 983-3000; fax (630) 983-0715

Spanish/Tapas
★★★★
Moderate
Quality 93   Value C

Reservations:	Accepted; after 6 P.M. Friday and Saturday, limited to 6 or more
When to go:	Weekdays
Entree range:	$9.95–13.95; tapas, $2–12
Payment:	Major credit cards
Service rating:	★★★½
Friendliness rating:	★★★★
Parking:	Lot
Bar:	Full service; the spirits are Spanish
Wine selection:	Largely Spanish; extensive; from $15 a bottle; special list offers about 13 by the glass, $3.50–5; 2 sangrías; many sherries
Dress:	Casual to formal
Disabled access:	Yes
Customers:	Diverse
Lunch/Dinner:	Monday–Thursday, 11:30 A.M.–10 P.M.; Friday, 11:30 A.M.–11 P.M.
Dinner:	Saturday, 5–11 P.M.; Sunday, 4–10 P.M.

Atmosphere/setting: In the elegant 1847 Willoway Manor mansion, with six dining rooms, extended patio, and outside bar. Murals, hand-painted Spanish ceramics, mosaics, and lace curtains create a distinct authentic flair.

House specialties: Patatas con aïoli (cold potato salad); ostras a la pimienta (grilled fresh oysters); sautéed escargot paella a la Valenciana; sofrito de vieras con pasta (sautéed chopped tomato with scallops and pasta); flan de cafe; caramelized bread pudding.

Other recommendations: Thin roast veal slices, sun-dried tomatoes with raspberry vinaigrette; gambas al ajillo (grilled shrimp); daily special of imported white asparagus spears with a yellow tomato relish (in season); cazuela (earthenware stew pot) de pulpo (marinated octopus); citrus rice pudding; chocolate terrine with fresh raspberry sauce.

Entertainment & amenities: Flamenco guitarist and dancer Friday evening.

Summary & comments: The menu here is similar to Emilio's first tapas bar in Hillside. The food and service have improved over the years. Special event dinners and wine tastings are educational. An extraordinary restaurant, done in Emilio's great style.

Emilio's Tapas Bar Restaurant

Zone 1   North Side
444 West Fullerton Avenue
(773) 327-5100

Spanish/Tapas
★★★★
Moderate

Quality 91   Value C

Reservations:	Accepted Monday–Thursday and Saturday
When to go:	Weekdays
Entree range:	$13–14; tapas, $2–12
Payment:	VISA, MC, AMEX
Service rating:	★★★½
Friendliness rating:	★★★★
Parking:	Lot
Bar:	Full service
Wine selection:	Mostly Spanish; sherries and sangría; $15 and up
Dress:	Casual
Disabled access:	Yes
Customers:	Diverse
Lunch/Dinner:	Monday–Thursday, 11:30 A.M.–10 P.M.; Friday and Saturday, 11:30 A.M.–11 P.M.
Dinner:	Sunday, 4–9 P.M.

Atmosphere/setting: Colorful ceramic decor complements the setting, which has the feel of Andalusia, the Spanish province from which Emilio hails.

House specialties: Paella de mariscos (seafood); patatas con aïoli (potato salad); tortilla española (a Spanish omelet); salpicon de Burgos (marinated shrimp, scallops, and monkfish); pan con tomate, jamón, y queso (tomato bread topped with serrano ham and manchego cheese); ensalada de verduras templadas (grilled seasonal vegetables); gambas a la plancha (grilled shrimp brochette); pincho de pollo al mojo picon (grilled and marinated chicken brochette); datiles con bacon (dates wrapped in bacon).

Other recommendations: Empanada de cordero con curri (puff pastry filled with lamb, chorizo, and curry); cazuela de judias con almejas (casserole of lima beans, Manila clams, and shallots); mejillones al ajillo (black mussels); lomo de cerdo al ajillo (pork tenderloin medallions with Spanish potatoes).

Entertainment & amenities: Flamenco on occasion.

Summary & comments: Known as the King of Tapas, Emilio Gervilla brought the Spanish tapas concept to Chicago over a decade ago. Since then he's expanded to several locations; this one is the latest. Emilio is from Granada, knows his cuisine well, and is a hands-on restaurateur. An authentic trip to Spain.

EMPEROR'S CHOICE

Zone 5   South Loop
2238 South Wentworth Avenue,
  Chinatown
(312) 225-8800

Chinese
★★★½
Inexpensive/Moderate

Quality 88   Value B

Reservations:	Recommended on weekends
When to go:	Weekdays are less busy
Entree range:	Lunch, $5.95–9.95; dinner, $6.95–19.95
Payment:	VISA, MC, AMEX, D
Service rating:	★★★★
Friendliness rating:	★★★★
Parking:	Validated parking in Chinatown lot
Bar:	Full service
Wine selection:	Limited; several by the glass
Dress:	Casual
Disabled access:	Yes
Customers:	Family, locals, tourists
Lunch:	Monday–Friday, 11:45 A.M.–3 P.M.
Lunch/Dinner:	Monday–Saturday, 11:45–1 A.M.; Sunday, 11:45 A.M.–midnight; kitchen closes half an hour before dining room

Atmosphere/setting: Intimate storefront with tablecloths and walls decorated with framed prints of the most famous emperors of the ten dynasties. The focal point of this cozy restaurant is a robe worn by a Ching dynasty emperor.

House specialties: Seafood dishes such as Maine lobster baked with ginger and onion; pea pod sprouts with crabmeat sauce; Empress's beef (marinated tenderloin) sole two ways.

Other recommendations: Scallops and shrimp with walnuts; shrimp and chicken in bird's nest; pot stickers; Emperor's egg rolls; Peking duck (with one-day notice).

Summary & comments: One of the best restaurants in Chinatown and one of the most creative for seafood dishes. Quality ingredients, careful cooking, and attentive service have made this place popular for years, and it continues to get high reviews from critics. The food is served on beautiful china in a regal fashion, and happily, the prices are not royal. This is one of the best values for excellent Chinese cuisine.

Entre Nous

	French
Zone 4 The Loop	★★★★
Fairmont Hotel,	Moderate/Expensive
200 North Columbus Drive	
(312) 565-7997	Quality 90 Value C

Reservations:	Highly recommended
When to go:	Early evenings
Entree range:	Dinner, $19–34
Payment:	All major credit cards
Service rating:	★★★★½
Friendliness rating:	★★★★★
Parking:	Hotel garage, validated; valet, $12
Bar:	Full service
Wine selection:	Award-winning, extensive, international
Dress:	Moderately upscale
Disabled access:	Yes
Customers:	Mostly locals, a few tourists
Dinner:	Monday–Saturday, 5:30–10:30 P.M.

Atmosphere/setting: Elegant, plush, and sophisticated. Large table with flowers and display of some dishes is the central focus of dining room; one wall is a wine library.

House specialties: Specialties change daily. Dinner appetizer: pan-fried Chesapeake crab cakes (with sautéed arugula and lobster sauce). Dinner entrees: pot-au-feu of grouper and prawns with root vegetables and basil; roast rack of Sonoma lamb with mustard-herb crust and rosemary lentils. Weekly table d'hôte four-course dinner menu, $29; $44 with wine.

Other recommendations: Lobster bisque; applewood-smoked chicken breast with caraway cabbage and fire-roasted chestnuts. Dessert tray holds several light, layered pastries; almond cheesecake; chocolate raspberry torte.

Entertainment & amenities: Jazz in the Metropole; ask about dinner-jazz package.

Summary & comments: Entre Nous (between us) is an intimate French phrase and charming name for this romantic hotel dining room. The creative cuisine has many innovative touches (the marrow melted over herbed tenderloin, for example). Note seasonal promotions and menus. The service is gracious and accommodating and, overall, dining here is distinctive.

Honors/awards: Wine collection has received the Award of Excellence from *Wine Spectator* for two consecutive years; four stars from *Mobil Travel Guide*.

ERWIN

Zone 1   North Side
2925 North Halsted Street
(773) 528-7200

New American/Midwestern
★★★★
Inexpensive/Moderate

Quality 94   Value B

Reservations:	Accepted
When to go:	Any time; early dinner is usually less busy
Entree range:	$7.95 (hamburger), $12.95–16.95
Payment:	AMEX, C, DC, MC,VISA
Service rating:	★★★★½
Friendliness rating:	★★★★½
Parking:	Valet
Bar:	Full service, including microbrewery beers
Wine selection:	International; 75% American, 25% mixed; several by the glass
Dress:	Casual and chic; business
Disabled access:	Completely
Customers:	Professionals, couples, families, locals
Brunch:	Sunday, 10.30 A.M.–2.30 P.M.
Dinner:	Tuesday–Thursday, 5:30–10 P.M.; Friday and Saturday, 5:30–11 P.M.; Sunday, 5–9:30 P.M.

Atmosphere/setting: Inviting, casual bistro. Whimsical border mural of city rooftops.

House specialties: Smoked trout in thin herbed pancake with salmon caviar; vegetable tart; tomato salad; whitefish; sautéed calf's liver; wood-grilled flank steak; caramel pot de crème; chocolate–sour cherry torte; seasonal fruit pie.

Other recommendations: Gazpacho with wood-grilled shrimp; seared rare tuna with salad, vegetables, and fried wontons; wood-grilled salmon or hamburger; vegetarian dish of roasted stuffed sweet pepper; pecan-maple tart à la mode; seasonal fruit sorbets.

Entertainment & amenities: Seasonal cooking classes; off-premises catering; private parties on Monday for dinner and daily for lunch.

Summary & comments: Owners chef Erwin and his wife, Cathy Drechsler, are seasoned restaurateurs; details matter. Chef Drechsler's cooking techniques have a French foundation, but the end result is American with assertive flavors. Erwin's menu is efficient; each dish is listed by its main ingredient. The savvy staff is educated in theoretical and practical topics of food, wine, and service.

Honors/awards: *Wine Spectator* Award of Excellence; *Wine Enthusiast* award for creativity and excellence; *Bon Appetit* Best New Restaurant 1994; chef Erwin is a member of Chef 2,000 (top 2,000 chefs in North America).

EVEREST

Zone 4   The Loop
440 South LaSalle Street (One Financial
    Place, 40th Floor)
(312) 663-8920

French
★★★★★
Expensive

Quality 98   Value C

Reservations:	Required
When to go:	Varies; call before you go
Entree range:	À la carte, $26.50–32.50; pretheater menu, $39; evening tasting menu, $69
Payment:	All major credit cards
Service rating:	★★★★★
Friendliness rating:	★★★★½
Parking:	Complimentary valet in building garage
Bar:	Full service
Wine selection:	Extensive award-winning list with 650 international wines, mostly French, Alsatian, and American; $39-plus per bottle; 10–12 selections by the glass
Dress:	Jacket and tie suggested; dressy
Disabled access:	Wheelchair accessible; call ahead for special accommodations
Customers:	Upscale; businesspeople, couples
Dinner:	Tuesday–Thursday, 5:30–8:30 P.M.; Friday and Saturday, 5:30–10 P.M. (open 7 days a week for private events)

Atmosphere/setting: Softly lit, romantic, simple elegance; flowers and candle-light; stunning western view of Chicago; tuxedo-clad waiters. Six private dining rooms for parties of eight or more, open daily for breakfast, lunch, and dinner (reservations must be made in advance).

House specialties: Smoked salmon served with warm oatmeal blinis (cold appetizer); creamless watercress soup with Louisiana crayfish (creaminess comes from milk and pureed potatoes and a bit of rice); marbre of cold bouillabaisse (a creative terrine idea with sea bass, clams, mussels); crispy soft-shell crab with red beet coulis and fava beans, wrapped in egg roll wrapper (unique summer item; the chef says the wrap hides the crab legs, which some people are squeamish about); roasted Maine lobster; one great special is veal simmered with vegetables, Alsatian kneple dumplings (flavors melt together with the succulent meat). Desserts by pastry chef Chad Gilchrist are phenomenal, and are recited by the waiter in cold and hot categories. Samples include: cold fantasy of chocolate (five

(continued)

items), including hazelnut mocha cake and cocoa honey ice cream in a chocolate tuile; composition of caramel, including ice cream, Napoleon of caramelized apple, and pecan tarte Tatin; warm Grand Marnier soufflé (20- to 25-minute wait); warm California peach strudel, peach ice cream, vanilla sauce.

Other recommendations: Appetizer: roasted New York state foie gras with roasted fingerling potato salad (warm, rich); double lamb consommé, mini–goat cheese ravioli; creamless navy bean soup; terrine of pheasant, partridge, and squab marbled with wild herbs and vegetables; confit of rabbit. Entrees: a special of Copper River salmon with onion crust, pinot noir sauce (in summer); saddle of Millbrook venison, wild huckleberries, Alaska Wassertriwella; ballotine of skate stuffed with mushrooms and wrapped around nonsour Alsatian sauerkraut in a light Riesling juniper berry sauce. Desserts: tropical sorbet with medley of exotic fruits, almond cookie nougat; warm apricot tarte Tatin with verbena ice cream; Napoleon of sautéed Bing cherries, kirsch ice cream, sour cherry sauce. Pretheater dinner menu with seatings at 5:30 P.M., $39; degustation menu, $69 per person.

Entertainment & amenities: The spectacular western view of Chicago.

Summary & comments: Mount Everest was climbed first by Sir Edmund Hillary, and chef Jean Joho has succeeded in making his Everest the pinnacle of French gastronomy in Chicago —in fact it's one of the country's premier restaurants. In partnership with Lettuce Entertain You Enterprises, Joho is a protégé of Paul Haeberlin of the acclaimed l'Auberge de L'Ill in Alsace, France. He began training at 13 as an apprentice; his education continued in French, Italian, and Swiss kitchens, and at age 23, he became sous-chef of a Michelin two-star restaurant with the command of a staff of 35. His French cuisine is masterful, with much use of his beloved Alsatian homeland's ingredients; each dish is a work of art to behold. Dining here is truly tops for food, service, and view of the city.

Honors / awards: Four-star reviews from the *Chicago Tribune*, the *Chicago Sun-Times*, *Chicago* magazine; featured in *Playboy* and *Esquire*; winner of Ivy Award and Gault Millau honors; chef-owner Jean Joho won the James Beard Award for Best Chef in Midwest and *Food and Wine* magazine's Top Chef of the Year Award; he's been inducted into *Nation's Restaurant News'* Fine Dining Hall of Fame and received the *Wine Spectator* Award of Excellence 1992.

Filippo's

Zone 1   North Side
2211 North Clybourn Avenue
(773) 528-2211

Italian
★★★
Inexpensive/Moderate

Quality 82   Value C

Reservations:	Recommended
When to go:	Any time
Entree range:	$6.95–16.95
Payment:	VISA, AMEX, MC
Service rating:	★★★½
Friendliness rating:	★★★★
Parking:	Street, theater lot; may have a valet soon
Bar:	Full service, including grappa selection
Wine selection:	Italian, 30-plus types; $16–55 a bottle; several by the glass
Dress:	Casual to dressy
Disabled access:	Yes
Customers:	Professionals, businesspeople, dates, families
Lunch:	Planning to serve lunch soon
Dinner:	Monday–Thursday, 5–11 P.M.; Friday and Saturday, 5 P.M.–midnight; Sunday, 5–10 P.M.

Atmosphere/setting: Intimate storefront with gold-hued walls and old-world Italian touches, such as pictures of cherubs and an antique copper cappuccino machine. Tables are covered with mix-and-match tablecloths handmade by one owner's mother.

House specialties: Homemade ravioli annarella (ricotta and spinach in cream sauce with Parmigiano); daily fish (swordfish steak with Mediterranean sauce of lemon, olive oil, basil, rosemary, and garlic); veal scaloppine in sage sauce with mushroom and mozzarella. Desserts: flourless chocolate espresso cake, chocolate hazelnut torte, zuccotto.

Other recommendations: Calamari fritti; antipasto vegetariano (assorted grilled veggies); fettuccine Giorgione (light tomato sauce, sautéed chicken breast, broccoli, and blue cheese).

Summary & comments: The owners have great pride in their homey place. The atmosphere is warm and inviting—customers are personally greeted at each table. The menu includes the chef's refined interpretations of dishes his mother cooked for everyday meals.

162

Flat Top Grill

Zone 3   Near North
319 West North Avenue
(312) 787-7676

Zone 11   Northern Suburbs
707 Church Street, Evanston
(847) 570-0100

Zone 2   North Central/O'Hare
1000 West Washington
(312) 829-4800

American Stir-fry

★★★

Inexpensive

Quality 85   Value B

Reservations:	Not accepted
When to go:	Earlier in the week
Entree range:	$9.95 for dinner; $6.95 for lunch; $4.95 for children (11 years old and under) on weekends, free Monday–Thursday evenings
Payment:	MC, VISA, D, DC, CB
Service rating:	★★★½ (partly self-serve)
Friendliness rating:	★★★★½
Parking:	*Chicago:* car valet, $5; bicycle and rollerblade valet, $2.50; *Evanston:* car valet, $4; city garage
Bar:	Full service; Asian beers; signature drinks like Tricky Vicky Punch and Singapore Slings
Wine selection:	A small selection of American, including Kendall Jackson chardonnay and Buena Vista sauvignon blanc; from $3.95–5.95 a glass and $15–29 a bottle; reserve list available.
Dress:	Casual
Disabled access:	Yes
Customers:	Urban professionals, locals, theatergoers, students
Lunch:	*Chicago:* Saturday and Sunday, 11:30 A.M.–3 P.M.; *Evanston:* Monday–Sunday, 11:30 A.M.–3 P.M.
Dinner:	*Chicago:* Sunday–Thursday, 5–10 P.M.; Friday and Saturday, 5–11 P.M.; *Evanston:* Monday–Thursday, 5–9:30 P.M.; Friday and Saturday, 5–10:30 P.M.; Sunday, 4–9 P.M.

Atmosphere/setting: A casual, bustling atmosphere with an open kitchen featuring the flat-top grill in the front window. Overwhelming blackboard menus hang on the walls. There are both raised and lowered mahogany wood tables and

(continued)

chairs and cushioned booths; wood-paneled ceiling; soft lighting; and loud rock/pop music in the background.

House specialties: Flat Top Grill Sauce is a citrus- and soy-based sauce that mixes well with the other sauces and combinations of vegetables and meats; David's recipe (two ladles of Flat Top Grill Sauce, one ladle of oyster sauce, one ladle of ginger water, one ladle of plum sauce, fresh garlic to taste, raw egg [optional] as a binder, one ladle of red chili paste) is great with seafood, salad, noodles, mu shoo, chicken, or rice on the side; fresh fruit sundae with orange-ginger sauce drizzled over peach ice cream and fresh raspberries and black raspberries (or whatever fruits are in season), topped with a sprig of mint; chocolate storm, a rich chocolate brownie with French vanilla ice cream; mango juice; and mocha java coffee.

Other recommendations: Mu shoo (stir-fry variation); vegetable broth (stir-fry variation); salad (stir-fry variation); organic mixed greens with cucumber dressing and cinnamon apple crisp.

Summary & comments: This create-your-own stir-fry restaurant has the comforts of a full-service restaurant. Customers create their own stir-fry meals by choosing from a food line that offers a bountiful selection of more than 70 fresh organic vegetables, spices, rice, noodles, meats, poultry, and seafoods complemented with a choice of 20 Asian sauces. Customers simply drop off their filled bowls at the end of the line and relax while it is cooked on the restaurant's custom flat-top grill and returned promptly to their tables. Guests are not limited to stir-fry. They can also create soup, salad, and moo shoo with a little help from the chefs. If you are overwhelmed by all the stir-fry ingredients offered, the large blackboard menu and helpful servers offer suggestions about what combinations of sauces and ingredients make a great stir-fry meal.

More than one-third of the stir-fry selection is showcase organically grown, locally distributed vegetables, including organically grown bok choy, mushrooms, broccoli, corn, and red onions. While chicken and beef remain a staple, the fresh food bar offers a daily rotation of meats and seafood, including shrimp, squid, turkey, lamb, and pork. The Flat Top Grill recently began offering monthly exotic meats (such as buffalo, ostrich, and alligator). This is the only restaurant of its type that we know of offering these upscale ingredients. Carryout available during business hours.

foodlife

Zone 3   Near North
835 North Michigan Avenue,
   Water Tower Place
(312) 335-3663

American
★★★
Inexpensive
Quality 82   Value C

Reservations:	Not accepted
When to go:	Avoid peak lunchtime and rush-hour business
Entree range:	$4.50–8
Payment:	All major credit cards
Service rating:	★★★ (largely self-serve)
Friendliness rating:	★★★★
Parking:	Water Tower underground garage
Bar:	Wine, beer, and sangría only
Wine selection:	Wine by the glass only
Dress:	Casual
Disabled access:	Yes
Customers:	Professionals, shoppers, tourists, families, couples
Open:	*Juice, espresso, and Corner Bakery:* Monday–Saturday, 7:45 A.M.–10 P.M.; Sunday, 7:45 A.M.–9 P.M.; *all other kiosks:* Monday–Saturday, 11 A.M.–10 P.M.; Sunday, 11 A.M.–9 P.M.

Atmosphere/setting: Attractive food court. Environment-friendly atmosphere. Large variety of food stations; all food is displayed in an appealing manner.

House specialties: Thirteen food stations: juice bar, grains, burgers, Mexican, greens, pizza, pasta, hot stuffs (stuffed potatoes), rotisserie chicken, stir-fry, desserts, sacred grounds (espresso, candy, cakes, cookies), and the Corner Bakery. Mediterranean rice dishes; grilled, marinated vegetables; "enlightened" Caesar; vegetarian pizza; pot stickers; rotisserie chicken; pies and cookies.

Other recommendations: Cold and hot bean salads; health burgers; salsa bar; stir-fry; yogurt-fruit shakes and power drinks.

Summary & comments: This is one of the most innovative food concepts by Rich Melman of Lettuce Entertain You Enterprises, who explains, "We have a social life, a business life, a family life, and a love life. Now there is an environment dedicated to your food life. It's about choices." The freshest ingredients are used without preservatives. Customers are given a sensor card to use at each station; it tracks the meal cost, and the total is tallied at the cashier station. Convenient and fast. A new adjacent foodlife market offers freshly prepared foods for carryout (phone (312) 335-3663).

Francesco's Hole in the Wall

	Italian
	★★★
	Inexpensive/Moderate

Zone 11   Northern Suburbs
254 Skokie Boulevard, Northbrook
(847) 272-0155

Quality 83   Value B

Reservations:	Not accepted
When to go:	Early, just after 5 P.M.
Entree range:	$12 average
Payment:	Cash only
Service rating:	★★★½
Friendliness rating:	★★★★
Parking:	Lot
Bar:	Limited; liquor provided on request
Wine selection:	Fairly extensive; all Italian; several by the glass
Dress:	Casual
Disabled access:	No
Customers:	Diverse, from locals to celebrities
Lunch:	Monday, Wednesday–Friday, 11:30 A.M.–2:15 P.M.
Dinner:	Monday, Wednesday, and Thursday, 5–9:15 P.M.; Saturday, 5–10:15 P.M.; Sunday, 4–8:45 P.M.

Atmosphere/setting: Rural Italian; unfinished wooden floor; blackboard menu. Nonsmoking. Small and intimate, but larger than the original.

House specialties: Chicken and veal Vesuvio; fettuccine with shrimp, scallops, broccoli, tomato, and Asiago; porcini ravioli; osso buco; risotto pichi-pachi (Italian rice with sautéed spinach and tomato sauce). The special house salad is like a tossed antipasto with greens, pepperoni, cheese, and roasted peppers.

Other recommendations: Spidini (homemade bread rolled around mozzarella and tomato); thin pizza; bruschetta; lemon-roasted chicken, broccoli, and red peppers. Unusual dessert: chocolate cannoli with chocolate ricotta, studded with tiny chocolate chips.

Summary & comments: This small restaurant's comical name dates to pre-expansion, when a full house meant 21! The daily menu is written on the board, but certain specialties are frequently available. This is a casual, whimsical place with no pretense. Limos are often seen in the parking lot, a testimonial to the good food here. The well-heeled and celebrities mingle here with average diners. The owner opened an Italian bistro next door, and named it just that—Next Door, (847) 272-1491.

166

FROGGY'S FRENCH CAFE

Zone 11 Northern Suburbs	New French
306 Green Bay Road, Highwood	★★★
(847) 433-7080; fax (847) 433-6852	Moderate
	Quality 84 Value B

Reservations:	Accepted for 6 or more
When to go:	Monday–Wednesday, early and late
Entree range:	$11.95–18.95
Payment:	All major cards except AMEX
Service rating:	★★★★
Friendliness rating:	★★★★½
Parking:	Street, lot at library
Bar:	Yes
Wine selection:	About 100 selections; changes every 45 days; $13.95–150 a bottle; 3–4 selections by the glass, $4–5
Dress:	Chic casual
Disabled access:	Entrance, yes; rest rooms, no
Customers:	Locals, businesspeople, tourists, families, couples
Lunch:	Monday–Friday, 11:30 A.M.–2 P.M.
Dinner:	Monday–Thursday, 5–10 P.M.; Friday and Saturday, 5–11 P.M.

Atmosphere/setting: Casual and comfortable; low-key and a bit old-fashioned in decor. Frog theme is depicted in charming ways. Outdoor seating.

House specialties: Salads (e.g., Belgian endive salad, sweet onion confit); lobster with vanilla sauce; cassoulet of duck or tripe; broiled salmon in Provençal sauce; baked red snapper or striped bass with herbs. Menu changes every 90 days. Pastries: meringue with espresso; cappuccino mousse; custard with orange blossom caramel; during the Christmas season, bûche de Noël.

Other recommendations: Ostrich with raspberry vinaigrette; venison in pastry shell; a special of roast pheasant with chestnut puree and port wine sauce; rack of lamb; desserts (e.g., lemon mousse in pastry shell).

Entertainment/amenities: The Gourmet Frog, the owner's pastry shop three doors away; classes, including private lessons, offered.

Summary & comments: Chef Thierry Lefeuvre has consistently produced appealing French food at modest prices. He wanted to prove that French cuisine need not include costly ingredients and a high price tag, and he considers cost one of the challenges of cooking. With his keen marketing and kitchen skills, he's proven that dining in a French restaurant can be affordable.

FRONTERA GRILL

Zone 4   The Loop
445 North Clark Street
(312) 661-1434

Mexican
★★★★
Inexpensive

Quality 93   Value B

Reservations:	For parties of 5–10
When to go:	Midweek, early or late
Entree range:	$8–17
Payment:	All major credit cards
Service rating:	★★★½
Friendliness rating:	★★½
Parking:	Valet, $4
Bar:	Shares common bar with Topolobampo; good tequila and Mexican beer list
Wine selection:	Quite extensive; very international
Dress:	Casual
Disabled access:	Yes
Customers:	Locals, travelers, businesspeople, couples
Lunch:	Tuesday–Friday, 11:30 A.M.–2:30 P.M.
Dinner:	Tuesday–Thursday, 5:20–10 P.M.; Friday and Saturday, 5–11 P.M.

Atmosphere/setting: Casual and rustic; attractive Mexican folk art and artifacts; sidewalk cafe; recently expanded–bar moved next door.

House specialties: Menu changes every two weeks. Tacos al carbón; wood-grilled fish and meats, such as pork tenderloin marinated in red chili–apricot mole sauce and black tiger shrimp in green pumpkin seed mole. Good desserts, such as cooked plantains and special ice cream.

Other recommendations: Tortilla soup; jicama salad; pollo en crema poblana. Various types of chilies are used in sauces that range from mild and earthy to hot and spicy.

Summary & comments: The menu offers a great variety of some rarely known dishes. Owners Rick Bayless (chef) and wife Deanne (manager) co-authored a cookbook, *Authentic Mexican*; both the book and restaurant received good reviews. Service could be friendlier, especially at the entrance. You've probably never tasted Mexican cuisine like this.

Honors/awards: Numerous positive reviews, including *International Herald Tribune, New York Times.* Chef Rick Bayless won the 1995 Best Chef in America Award from the James Beard Foundation.

Gabriel's Restaurant

Zone 11 Northern Suburbs	French/Italian
310 Greenbay Road, Highwood	★★★★
(847) 433-0031; fax (847) 433-7499	Moderate/Expensive
	Quality 93 Value C

Reservations:	Recommended
When to go:	Busiest on weekends but also full during week
Entree range:	$17–29; 4-course degustation menu, $40
Payment:	All major credit cards
Service rating:	★★★★½
Friendliness rating:	★★★★½
Parking:	Street and behind restaurant
Bar:	Full service; also separate bar from dining area
Wine selection:	90 French, Italian, and Californian; $26–225 a bottle; $6 and up a glass
Dress:	Upscale casual, from chic shorts to business suits
Disabled access:	Yes
Customers:	Varied; couples, families, businesspeople, locals
Dinner:	Tuesday–Saturday, 5–10 P.M.

Atmosphere/setting: European bistro with mahogany trim; beautiful open kitchen with the chef-owner and several sous chefs in white toques; well-lit, alive, and active. When bustling, it can be noisy.

House specialties: Pastas such as the flavor-intense fettuccine with artichokes, sun-dried tomatoes, and crespelle with spinach and cheese roasted capon with prosciutto and mushrooms; papillote of bass (beautifully served with the top of the paper wrap peeled off, showing the bass and potatoes with green herbs around); tender veal saltimbocca.

Other recommendations: Risotto (e.g., with corn, spinach, Gorgonzola); roasted saddle of rabbit with rosemary sauce. Desserts like roasted pear with mascarpone cream and warm apple tart with caramel ice cream.

Summary & comments: Gabriel Viti was executive chef at Carlos' in nearby Highland Park after working with some of the best European chefs in France, Switzerland, and Italy. In May 1993, he opened his own place and designed it to be relaxed and comfortable, offering both Italian and French cooking at moderate prices. He avoids the luxury high-priced items, but uses his classic techniques on quality ingredients and produces some wonderful food, all served with style. Try the degustation meal, a surprise menu from the chef, which includes an appetizer, pasta, entree, and dessert.

Gateway Bar & Grill

Zone 1 North Side	Eclectic
7545 North Clark Street	★★★
(773) 262-5767; fax (773) 262-9515	Inexpensive/Moderate
	Quality 85 Value B

Reservations:	Accepted
When to go:	Weekdays; late Wednesday–Saturday for music
Entree range:	$7.95–16.95
Payment:	All major credit cards
Service rating:	★★★½
Friendliness rating:	★★★★½
Parking:	Ample free lots nearby
Bar:	Full service
Wine selection:	Primarily American; inexpensive to moderate
Dress:	Casual, no jacket required
Disabled access:	Yes
Customers:	Regulars, jazz and blues enthusiasts, fish and BBQ lovers
Lunch:	Tuesday–Saturday, 11:30 A.M.–2:30 P.M.
Dinner:	Tuesday–Thursday, 4:30–11 P.M.; Friday and Saturday, 4:30 P.M.–midnight; (open at 3:30 P.M. Tuesday–Saturday in winter); Sunday, 3:30–9:30 P.M.

Atmosphere/setting: Contemporary supper club; lovely wall mural in lounge of Lake Shore Drive and waterfront. Airy, bright decor in dining rooms.

House specialties: Shrimp de Jonghe; oysters Rockefeller; tilapia broiled Grecian-style; grilled salmon with smoked apple broth; Grecian-style broiled Lake Superior whitefish; Cajun vegetarian penne; BBQ ribs; Grand Marnier custard crème brûlée; black bottom pie.

Other recommendations: Wood-grilled octopus; catfish with Thai shrimp gumbo; fajitas; London broil; barbecued pulled pork; Key lime pie.

Entertainment & amenities: Live jazz, blues, and easy-listening music in lounge: Wednesday–Saturday, starting at 9 P.M. Wednesday is Cajun night, with New Orleans food (music starts earlier). Occasional music on Sunday.

Summary & comments: Formerly My Place For?, it changed its name to Gateway Bar & Grill because of the large Gateway Plaza Shopping Center development in the area (indicating the gateway from Evanston to Chicago). Changes include redecorating, menu refocusing, and hiring a new executive chef, Nick Furlan, who has added some new dishes. Ownership, headed by Steve Dorizas, is the same. The management wisely adjusts the menu for current dining needs.

Geja's Cafe

Zone 1   North Side
340 West Armitage Avenue
(733) 281-9101

Fondue	
★★★½	
Expensive	
Quality 90	Value B

Reservations: Accepted Sunday–Thursday; on Friday and Sat-
                          urday first seating at 5 P.M.
When to go: Weeknights, early in evening
Entree range: $20–30
Payment: Major credit cards
Service rating: ★★★★
Friendliness rating: ★★★★½
Parking: Valet, $5
Bar: Full service
Wine selection: 250 international selections; 30 by the glass
Dress: Upscale casual to formal
Disabled access: Several stairs down from sidewalk; no access
Customers: Couples, professionals of all ages, wine lovers
Dinner: Monday–Thursday, 5–10:30 P.M.; Friday,
                          5 P.M.–midnight; Saturday, 5 P.M.–12:30 A.M.;
                          Sunday, 4:30–10 P.M.

Atmosphere/setting: Intimate and charming, with secluded booths and
tables; wine bottle decor; dimly lit and romantic.

House specialties: Classic cheese fondue; seafood (a personal favorite),
chicken, steak, and combo fondues; chocolate fondue served with fruit and cake.

Other recommendations: Sausage and cheese platter with salad.

Entertainment & amenities: Nightly flamenco and classical guitarist.

Summary & comments: Walk down a few steps into a romantic oasis and
enter a sensual culinary experience that was created over three decades ago by
visionary and wine lover John Davis. Fondue is a communal way of dining, and it's
alive and thriving at Geja's. Restaurant holds an annual amateur wine contest and
various wine promotions and winemaker dinners. Order à la carte or a complete
dinner, which includes cheese fondue, entree fondue, salad, and chocolate fondue.
Each person can order his or her own entree and wine separately. For a taste of
Switzerland, try the classic cheese fondue of Gruyère and kirschwasser, with bread
and crisp apple wedges for dipping. Flaming chocolate fondue is flambéed with
orange liqueur and served with fruit and pound cake for dipping.

Honors/awards: Voted Most Romantic Restaurant many times by *Chicago*
magazine and other publications.

Gibson's Steakhouse

Zone 3   Near North
1028 North Rush Street
(312) 266-8999

Steak	
★★★★½	
Moderate/Very Expensive	
Quality 94	Value C

Reservations:	Recommended
When to go:	Crowded most evenings; go early
Entree range:	$11–48; colossal surf and turf, $85
Payment:	All major credit cards
Service rating:	★★★★½
Friendliness rating:	★★★★½
Parking:	Valet
Bar:	Full service; the signature drink is the Gibson (large martini)
Wine selection:	International; mostly Californian and French
Dress:	Business, dressy; tuxedos are not unusual
Disabled access:	Yes
Customers:	Diverse, masculine group; mostly locals ages 20–60; local and international celebrities
Dinner:	Monday–Saturday, 5 P.M.–midnight; Sunday, 4 P.M.–midnight; bar remains open every day, noon–12:30 A.M.

Atmosphere/setting: 1940s clubby wooden art deco; looks old (but not worn) with antiques and dated photos; comfortable.

House specialties: Steaks are prime aged. Bone-in sirloin (also known as Kansas City strip); Chicago cut (huge rib-eye steak with fat trimmed); snow and stone crab claws appetizer.

Other recommendations: Lobster tail; planked whitefish; chargrilled swordfish; one and one-quarter-pound baked potatoes; carrot cake.

Entertainment & amenities: Live piano every evening; lively bar.

Summary & comments: Recognized by steak aficionados as one of the city's top places for prime cuts, with prices to match. All the quality steak houses are expensive, so this one is competitive with the herd. Food is elegantly served by polite waiters in attractive, comfortable surroundings.

Golden Ox

Zone 1   North Side
1578 North Clybourn Avenue
(312) 664-0780

German/American
★★★★
Moderate
Quality 90   Value C

Reservations:	Recommended
When to go:	Any time
Entree range:	$11.50–25
Payment:	All major credit cards
Service rating:	★★★
Friendliness rating:	★★★½
Parking:	Free valet
Bar:	Full service
Wine selection:	Substantial international list; French, Spanish, German, domestics
Dress:	Casual to formal
Disabled access:	Yes
Customers:	Diverse, locals, travelers, couples, businesspeople, families
Lunch/Dinner:	Monday–Saturday, 11 A.M.–11 P.M.; Sunday, 3–9 P.M.

Atmosphere/setting. Magnificent and very comfortable. Intricate decoration with shiny brown shellacked walls, paintings, murals depicting classics, cuckoo clocks, ornate beer steins, dirndl-clad waitresses. Looks like an ancient castle or museum.

House specialties: Bavarian-style bratwurst; smoked Thuringer; potato pancakes; Wiener Schnitzel; sauerbraten; paprika rahm schnitzel; crisp roasted half-duckling; fresh seafood (e.g., imported Dover sole, broiled walleyed pike). Entrees are served with choice of spaetzle, potato, or butter noodles.

Other recommendations: Hasenpfeffer (in season—imported rabbit, marinated and stewed); sausage plate; fresh chopped chicken liver; oysters à la Golden Ox; kalte kartoffel (cold potato) suppe; tortes.

Entertainment & amenities: Zither player on Saturday evenings; strolling musician on Friday evenings. Browsing through the spectacularly decorated rooms.

Summary & comments: Pricier than most German restaurants, but Golden Ox has a fuller traditional German menu—well prepared—and an exquisite atmosphere. Quality has been maintained over the years, but service can be slow and occasionally uninformed about wine. Overall, friendly and accommodating.

Honors/awards: *Food Industry News* award for Best German Restaurant.

GORDON

Zone 4 The Loop	New American
500 North Clark Street	★★★★½
(312) 467-9780	Expensive
	Quality 94 Value C

Reservations:	Recommended
When to go:	Destination dining; special occasions
Entree range:	$19–28
Payment:	All major credit cards
Service rating:	★★★★
Friendliness rating:	★★★★
Parking:	Valet, street, and nearby lot
Bar:	Full service; specializes in single-malt Scotches
Wine selection:	American, French; many by the glass and half bottle; $7–12 a glass
Dress:	Jackets requested, tie optional; business attire; dressier in evenings
Disabled access:	Yes
Customers:	Businesspeople, celebrities, socialites, couples
Lunch:	Tuesday–Friday, 11:30 A.M.–2 P.M.
Dinner:	Sunday–Thursday, 5:30–8:30 P.M.; Friday and Saturday, 5:30–11:30 P.M.

Atmosphere/setting: Attractive bar entry. Eclectic and ornate; slightly surreal contemporary art with colorful, amusing avant garde murals and flowers.

House specialties: Menu changes seasonally, but some dishes remain. Signature Gordon artichoke fritter with béarnaise; sautéed foie gras with braised beef brisket; smoked salmon Napoleon; butterscotch-ginger brûlée with shortbread.

Other recommendations: Roasted rack of lamb; grilled duck breast; creative salads. Gianduja mousse with coconut sorbet; chilled Bing cherry soup.

Entertainment & amenities: Mellow jazz and dancing weekend nights.

Summary & comments: Gordon Sinclair's flamboyant style, high standards, and occasional promotional events make this a rather eccentric place of quality. Executive chef Don Yamauchi aims to continue the restaurant's renowned "highly creative approach" to dining. Sinclair offers only half-portions of entrees; for those who want more of a good dish, double portions are available at double the price, minus $2. Sinclair's own farm-grown produce appears on the menu sometimes. Celebrators who call ahead can see their names on the menu.

Honors/awards: *Mobil Travel Guide,* four stars; *Wine Spectator* Award of Excellence. Chef Yamauchi named one of *Food and Wine's* 10 Best Chefs in America, 1993 and nominated for Best Chef in Midwest by James Beard Foundation, 1992.

Green Dolphin Street

	Contemporary/Eclectic
Zone 1 North Side	★★★½
2200 North Ashland Avenue	Moderate/Expensive
(773) 395-0066	Quality 89 Value C

Reservations:	Accepted
When to go:	After 7 P.M. to hear jazz right after dinner
Entree range:	$13.50–25
Payment:	AMEX, VISA, DC, MC, D
Service rating:	★★★
Friendliness rating:	★★★½
Parking:	Valet
Bar:	Full service
Wine selection:	Large international list; mostly American and French with some Italian, Australian, German, and Austrian; about 26 by the glass
Dress:	Casual
Disabled access:	Yes
Customers:	Locals, suburbanites, professionals who enjoy jazz
Dinner:	Every day, 5:30–10 P.M.

Atmosphere/setting: What was once an eyesore junkyard has become a lovely, large jazz club with a spectacular outdoor garden on the river, stairs to the river's edge, and a landing dock. Simply decorated and comfortable.

House specialties: Pork rillettes with toasted bread and gherkins; Granny Smith apple salad with Belgian endive; roasted onion, leek, and potato soup. Roasted pork loin chop with molasses-barbecue sauce; porcini-crusted halibut; grilled venison with Yukon gold buttermilk puree; milk chocolate soufflé cake; banana croissant pudding; crème caramel with gingered peaches.

Other recommendations: Seafood stew in tomato crazy water; grilled ostrich in a shrimp bisque; carrot chowder; sautéed salmon with grilled portobello mushrooms, mushroom sauce and dill oil; fettuccine with spicy basil pesto; cassis cheesecake with mango and three sauces; strawberry-banana-coconut cream Napoleon.

Entertainment & amenities: Jazz club, Tuesday–Thursday, 8:30 P.M.; Friday and Saturday, 9:30 P.M. Stunning outdoor patio with a river dock.

Summary & comments: Chef Marshall Blair produces creative dishes with French, Asian, and Italian influences, along with regional American ingredients such as Iowa Maytag blue cheese or Vermont white cheddar. Some dishes are light and delicate, others are robust. Sometimes an ingredient listed on the menu doesn't appear in the dish. Be sure to call first about jazz performance times.

The Greenery

<table>
<tr><td></td><td>American</td></tr>
<tr><td>Zone 10   Northwest Suburbs</td><td>★★★½</td></tr>
<tr><td>117 North Avenue, Barrington</td><td>Moderate/Expensive</td></tr>
<tr><td>(847) 381-9000; fax (847) 381-7659</td><td>Quality 88   Value C</td></tr>
</table>

Reservations:	Recommended
When to go:	Any time
Entree range:	$16–24
Payment:	All major credit cards
Service rating:	★★★★
Friendliness rating:	★★★★★
Parking:	Street
Bar:	Full service, including award-winning beer list
Wine selection:	Extensive, award-winning all-American list
Dress:	Casual but elegant
Disabled access:	Has 3 front stairs, but staff will help those in wheelchairs
Customers:	Diverse
Dinner:	Monday–Thursday, 5:30–9 P.M.; Friday and Saturday, 5:30–10 P.M.

Atmosphere/setting: Casually elegant. Housed in a wing of an 1850 schoolhouse. White linen-covered tables, fresh flowers.

House specialties: Seasonal menu; jumbo Gulf shrimp and grilled sausage; sauté of wild mushrooms; Maryland blue crab cakes with three-citrus sauce; barbecue pork tenderloin; sweet corn puree; blue cheese with potatoes; pesto-marinated Chilean sea bass with angel hair; blackened beef tenderloin with Cajun crab enchiladas and lobster. Apple pie with caramel.

Other recommendations: Grilled Missouri pheasant with leeks, roasted red peppers, and jalapeños; roasted South Carolina quail stuffed with caramelized garlic and mashed potatoes; hickory-grilled breast of turkey with sage-mustard marinade; southern Florida spicy chicken and sweet potato salad. Banana cream pie.

Entertainment & amenities: Jazz music.

Summary & comments: The menu here takes the diner on a regional tour of America with many state foods featured, including Wisconsin goat cheese and Missouri pheasant, and a sprinkling of Creole and other New Orleans touches. The added pleasure of dining at the Greenery is the charming historical building and peaceful setting. It's worth a drive from the city—unless there's a snowstorm.

Honors/awards: *Wine Spectator* Award of Excellence since 1988; three stars by the *Chicago Tribune*; four stars by *North Shore* magazine.

Hans' Bavarian Lodge

Zone 10 Northwest Suburbs	German/American
931 North Milwaukee Avenue, Wheeling	★★★
(847) 537-4141	Inexpensive/Moderate
	Quality 80 Value B

Reservations:	Recommended
When to go:	Weekdays
Entree range:	Lunch, $6.25–9.25; dinner, $13.95–18.95
Payment:	All major credit cards
Service rating:	★★★
Friendliness rating:	★★★½
Parking:	Lot
Bar:	Full service
Wine selection:	Limited German, Californian; by the glass (from $3) or bottle (from $13.95)
Dress:	Casual
Disabled access:	Yes, including rest rooms
Customers:	Locals; busloads come for Oktoberfest
Lunch/Dinner:	Tuesday–Thursday, 11:30 A.M.–11 P.M.; Friday and Saturday, noon–9 P.M., Sunday, noon–4 P.M.

Atmosphere/setting: Warm family atmosphere. Large with old world decor; quaint with stained-glass windows.

House specialties: Sauerbraten; beef roulade; veal creations (e.g., Wiener Schnitzel; mushroom schnitzel, natur schnitzel Berghoff); German pizza.

Other recommendations: Roast duck; chicken schnitzel; filet mignon; combinations; American items (e.g., crab cakes and stuffed mushrooms).

Entertainment & amenities: Friday, zither and piano player; Saturday and Sunday, strolling accordionist.

Summary & comments: This suburban restaurant is owned by a member of the famous Berghoff restaurant family and is hugely successful. They sure know how to throw a big Oktoberfest that continues for weeks, all under heated tents with many bands. People come in from all over the Midwest for it. Beer garden features beers from around the world while in season.

Honors/awards: Rated Number One German Restaurant by *North Shore* magazine.

HARRY CARAY'S

Zone 4   The Loop
33 West Kinzie Avenue
(773) 465-9269

American/Italian
★★★½
Moderate/Expensive

Quality 86   Value C

Reservations:	Lunch, recommended; dinner for 8 or more
When to go:	Any time
Entree range:	Lunch, $8–13; dinner, $12–29
Payment:	Major credit cards
Service rating:	★★★★
Friendliness rating:	★★★★
Parking:	Valet
Bar:	Full service; American and imported beers
Wine selection:	Extensive Italian, American; from $13 a bottle
Dress:	Casual; you'll see a good share of Cubs-wear
Disabled access:	Yes, including rest rooms
Customers:	Locals, businesspeople, baseball fans, couples
Lunch:	Monday–Friday, 11:30 A.M.–4 P.M.
Dinner:	Monday–Friday, 5–10 P.M.; Friday and Saturday, 5–11 P.M.; Sunday, 4–10 P.M.

Atmosphere/setting: Historic red brick building; memorabilia of the famous, late sportscaster; active bar and lounge; comfortable dining room. Private rooms upstairs. Bar is 60 feet, 6 inches long, the same distance from home plate to the pitcher's mound.

House specialties: Chef Abraham's calamari; steamed mussels; chicken Vesuvio (with all white meat for $3 extra); grilled 16-oz. New York sirloin steak.

Other recommendations: Harry's Italian salad; cheese ravioli; grilled fresh fish (marinated tuna, lightly crumbed with rosemary); trio of double lamb chops oreganato. Great carrot cake; small ice cream profiteroles with hot fudge and crème anglaise.

Entertainment & amenities: Memorabilia; gift shop.

Summary & comments: You can't miss this Chicago restaurant; the late Harry Caray's favorite exclamation, "Holy Cow!" is emblazoned on the outside. Named for the former Cubs announcer, Harry Caray's is a splendid dining experience. Caray loved Italian fare, so it's on the menu, from salads to pastas and chicken Vesuvio (a Chicago invention—not Italian). All the fish is fresh and cooked to perfection. Weekend lunchers might try the sandwich cart. The country cousin in Wheeling has separate management and some menu differences, but is otherwise similar. Good Italian desserts and wines.

178

HARRY CARAY'S (WHEELING)

American/Italian
★★★½
Moderate
Quality 85   Value C

Zone 10   Northwest Suburbs
933 North Milwaukee Avenue, Wheeling
(847) 537-CUBS

Reservations:	Recommended
When to go:	5–7 P.M. or after 9 P.M.
Entree range:	Lunch, $8–13; dinner, $12–29
Payment:	All major credit cards
Service rating:	★★★★
Friendliness rating:	★★★★
Parking:	Nearby lot; complimentary parking, Monday–Saturday
Bar:	Full service
Wine selection:	Italian and American; several by the glass
Dress:	Casual to dressy
Disabled access:	Yes
Customers:	Diverse, locals, businesspeople, baseball fans, families
Lunch:	Monday–Friday, 11 A.M.–4 P.M.
Dinner:	Monday–Thurday, 4–10 P.M.; Friday and Saturday, 4–11 P.M.; Sunday, 4–9 P.M.

Atmosphere/setting: Cubs memorabilia; fun but loud at times; comfortable dining room. One room is nonsmoking. Lovely outdoor deck.

House specialties: Harry's bruschetta with marinated tomatoes; toasted ravioli (meat or cheese); chicken Vesuvio; Italian salmon; filet mignon; sirloin steak; Harry's Italian salad; variety of pastas with choice of sauces; capellini Aurora (creamy plum sauce). Tiramisu for dessert.

Other recommendations: Chicken Marsala; linguine Baraise, BBQ baby-back ribs, osso buco (veal shank cooked with risotto and bordelaise sauce, garnished with julienned vegetables); fresh fish. Desserts: carrot cake and raspberry cheesecake.

Summary & comments: This second Harry Caray's, named for the late Cubs announcer, might have separate management and some differences in the menu and atmosphere, but it's a kindred spirit to its city cousin. It closes a bit earlier. Fans miss the well-known veteran sportscaster's appearances at both locations.

Hatsuhana

Zone 3 Near North	Japanese
160 East Ontario Street	★★½
(312) 280-8808	Inexpensive/Moderate
	Quality 76 Value C

Reservations:	Recommended
When to go:	Early for lunch and before 7 P.M. for dinner
Entree range:	$11–18; Hatsuhana special, complete dinner, $30
Payment:	All major credit cards except DC
Service rating:	★★★
Friendliness rating:	★★★
Parking:	Public lot nearby
Bar:	Full service, including Japanese beer
Wine selection:	Mostly Japanese; cold sake, some hot; limited Californian
Dress:	Casual, business
Disabled access:	Yes, including rest rooms
Customers:	Locals, mostly Americans
Lunch:	Monday–Friday, 11:45 A.M.–2 P.M.
Dinner:	Monday–Friday, 5:30–10 P.M.; Saturday, 5–10 P.M.

Atmosphere/setting: Designed to be a classic Japanese sushi bar with tables off to the side for those who prefer not to sit at the sushi bar. Simple, contemporary look. Often busy at lunch and certain dinner times.

House specialties: American combination sushi and chef's choice sushi. This is the best reason for coming here. Picture menus assist in ordering.

Other recommendations: Tempura and teriyaki dinners, which include soup, rice, and dessert. Some items available à la carte.

Entertainment & amenities: Sitting at the sushi bar to watch the chefs' skilled hands quickly cut fish fillets into sashimi. Order as you eat for more interaction and fun.

Summary & comments: Long-standing Gold Coast place with a loyal following as well as some newcomers and tourists. Pricey compared to neighborhood sushi houses, but quality and variety are usually very good. Sushi bar items are the highlight; some Japanese dishes are inconsistent, as is the service.

HEAVEN ON SEVEN

Zone 4   The Loop
111 North Wabash Avenue
(312) 263-6443

Cajun/Creole
★★★½
Inexpensive

Quality 86   Value B

Reservations: Not accepted
When to go: Breakfast, 7 A.M.; lunch, 11:30 A.M.; before the
                         lines or after lunchtime
Entree range: $3.50–9.95
Payment: Cash only
Service rating: ★★★½
Friendliness rating: ★★★★
Parking: Garage
Bar: None
Wine selection: Californian, Chilean, French, Italian; $15–75 a
                         bottle, $4.50–6.50 a glass
Dress: Casual
Disabled access: Yes
Customers: Diverse; businesspeople, professionals, shoppers
Breakfast/Lunch: Monday–Friday, 8.30 A.M.–5 P.M.; Saturday,
                         10 A.M.–3 P.M.
Dinner: Every third Friday of the month, 5:30–9:30 P.M.;
                         and Fat Tuesday with a live New Orleans jazz
                         band

Atmosphere/setting: Upbeat; brown tables, each with several bottles of hot sauce. Wooden floor, red plantation plants, New Orleans art.

House specialties: Southern fried-chicken salad; soft-shell po'boys; pasta shrimp angry, pasta shrimp voodoo; crayfish tamales; jambalaya; Louisiana soul.

Other recommendations: Crab cakes; chicken-fried steak; rabbit with mushroom étouffée.

Summary & comments: Funky place on the seventh floor of the Garland building in the Loop, which began as the Garland Restaurant and Coffee Shop. The Bannos family–owned place still serves regular breakfast, but it has made its reputation on the great Creole and Cajun fare (including the Cajun and Creole breakfast) every bit as delicious as in Louisiana. Long lines at lunch move quickly. Those who love food with a burn will have a field day trying the various hot sauces on the table. After a meal here, you'll think you've gone to Cajun heaven. A new, larger location is open at 600 North Michigan Avenue, (312) 280-7774.

Honors/awards: Recommended by *Newsweek, National Geographic,* and local publications.

181

HOANG MAI

Zone 1   North Side
5020 North Sheridan Road
(773) 561-3700

Vietnamese/Chinese	★★★½
Inexpensive
Quality 89   Value A

Reservations:	Accepted, but usually not necessary on weekdays
When to go:	Any time
Entree range:	$3.95–8.95
Payment:	VISA, MC
Service rating:	★★★
Friendliness rating:	★★★★½
Parking:	Street
Bar:	None
Wine selection:	BYOB
Dress:	Casual
Disabled access:	Yes, including rest rooms
Customers:	Locals, professionals, ethnics, families, singles
Open:	Tuesday–Thursday, 10 A.M.–10 P.M.; Friday, 10 A.M.–11 P.M.; Saturday, 9:30 A.M.–11 P.M.; Sunday, 9:30 A.M.–10 P.M.; breakfast items available all day

Atmosphere/setting: Attractive, clean storefront seating up to 100; simple decor with Asian wall hangings and plants. Warm and rather intimate.

House specialties: Fresh spring rolls; Vietnamese crêpes (filled with shrimp-pork-vegetable mixture); fried catfish with ginger sauce; lemongrass shrimp; camp-fired beef; seafood in bird's nest. Roast quail is a special worth asking for.

Other recommendations: Hoang Mai special soup with shrimp, pork, mushroom, and vegetables; crab rangoon; shrimp wrapped in sugar cane with vegetables and vermicelli; eel in coconut milk curry; steamed rice noodles, grilled beef, and lemongrass; exotic chicken stir-fried with vegetables and spicy plum sauce; crispy noodle with combo topping.

Summary & comments: This simple, welcoming restaurant is family owned; the wife and mother, Mai, is the chef. Her husband assists occasionally and so do her sons. Care pervades here from the fine, cooked-to-order food to the attentive service. The extensive menu lists 183 items—awesome! On several visits over the years, every item has been delectable. Thai coffee is a nice finish. Available for private parties. Since you can bring your own wine or beer and the prices are friendly, this gem is a real bargain.

Home Bakery

Zone 2   North Central/O'Hare
2931 North Milwaukee Avenue
(773) 252-3708

Polish/European	
★★½	
Inexpensive	
Quality 77	Value B

Reservations: Recommended
When to go: Any time
Entree range: $5–10
Payment: VISA, MC, D
Service rating: ★★½
Friendliness rating: ★★★½
Parking: Street; can be somewhat difficult
Bar: Beer, wine, vodka, cognac, and limited mixed
                       drinks
Wine selection: About 10 selections; $12–15 a bottle; $3 by the
                       glass
Dress: Casual; dressier on the weekend
Disabled access: Yes
Customers: International; couples, businesspeople, families,
                       locals, out-of-towners
Open: Monday–Saturday, 8 A.M.–9 P.M.; Sunday,
                       9 A.M.–9 P.M.

Atmosphere/setting: Space includes shop, deli, bakery, and 100-seat restaurant.
Semiromantic, medium lighting; gallery of paintings on the wall.

House specialties: Soups: chicken noodle, white borscht. Roast duck with
rice, peppers, and mushrooms; Wiener Schnitzel; beef Stroganoff; Polish hunter's
stew (bigos); Hungarian goulash; pierogi (dumplings stuffed with choice of
cheese, potato, meat, blueberry, or strawberry filling).

Other recommendations: Polish plate; Swiss steak; large, crispy potato pancakes
(some of the best); chicken Kiev; variety of herring; barley sausage. Soups of the day,
such as tomato soup and potato soup on Wednesday. Polish pastries and torte.

Summary & comments: Food is simple, honest, well seasoned, and very
home-style. Menu is varied enough for a variety of tastes. Breakfast items include
omelets, waffles, and cereal. Lunch includes sandwiches and an à la carte special.
Dinner can be à la carte or, for $1 more, complete with potato, rice or dumplings,
vegetables, choice of Polish salad, soup, and dessert. This is one of the few places
in the city where you can have a full dinner for about $5—amazing.

HONG MIN RESTAURANT

Zone 5   South Loop
221 West Cermak Road, Chinatown
(312) 842-5026

Zone 8   Southern Suburbs
8048 West 111th Street, Palos Hills
(708) 599-8488

> Chinese/Dim Sum
> ★★★
> Inexpensive/Moderate
>
> Quality 85   Value B

Reservations:	Only accepted for 6 or more
When to go:	Weekdays; weekends 11 A.M.–3 P.M. and 6–8 P.M. are busiest
Entree range:	$6.95–19.95 (1 item $21)
Payment:	*Chicago:* VISA, MC; *Palos Hills:* MC, AMEX
Service rating:	★★
Friendliness rating:	★★½
Parking:	*Chicago:* 2-hour free parking at community lot on Cermak and Wentworth with validation; *Palos Hills:* 60-car lot
Bar:	*Chicago:* BYOB; *Palos Hills:* full service
Wine selection:	*Chicago:* international; *Palos Hills:* mostly domestic
Dress:	Casual
Disabled access:	*Chicago:* no; *Palos Hills:* yes
Customers:	Locals, ethnics, professionals, tourists
Lunch/Dinner:	*Chicago:* Every day, 10–2 A.M.; *Palos Hills:* Every day, 11:30 A.M.–10 P.M.

Atmosphere/setting: *Chicago:* casual storefront with booths and tables. *Palos Hills:* casual, American, booths and tables.

House specialties: Seafood (e.g., fish with black bean sauce; steamed sole; butterfly scallops); dim sum; special hot pot dishes.

Other recommendations: Special menu with over 75 special Chinese dishes (e.g., bird's nest soup; duck of West Lake with barbecue pork and vegetables; kung pao chicken with roasted peanuts and hot sauce).

Summary & comments: Chef-owner William Tam created a very ambitious menu, including some items the Chinese love, such as duck feet with black mushrooms, and some mundane chop suey and egg foo yong items. Virtually every category holds some culinary treats.

House of Blues

Zone 3 Near North	American/Southern
329 North Dearborn Street	★★★★
(312) 527-2583	Inexpensive/Moderate
	Quality 90 Value B

Reservations:	Recommended
When to go:	Any time; Sunday gospel brunch (if you want hand-clapping, uplifting entertainment)
Entree range:	$8.50–12.95
Payment:	All major credit cards
Service rating:	★★★½
Friendliness rating:	★★★½
Parking:	Valet
Bar:	Full service; imported, domestic beers
Wine selection:	*Restaurant:* mostly domestic; *Foundation Room:* international
Dress:	Casual
Disabled access:	Yes
Customers:	Varied; those who enjoy blues, country, jazz, gospel, and southern fare
Open:	Every day, 11:30–1 or 1:30 A.M. (depending on entertainment)

Atmosphere/setting: Spectacular (even bathrooms); large Delta folk art collection. Three dining rooms: Chicago Room, Delta Room, B.B. Blues Bar.

House specialties: Mississippi cat bites (catfish); shrimp rémoulade; New Orleans–style chicken and sausage gumbo; étouffée (fresh crawfish and Gulf shrimp with rich, medium-spiced sauce); jambalaya.

Other recommendations: Crawfish cheesecake appetizer; Memphis barbecue chicken; mesquite-grilled veggie sandwich; sides of cornbread with maple butter and turnip greens; pecan tasty with ice cream. Gospel brunch (eggs, sausage, jambalaya, bread pudding), which is so popular there are now three seatings (10 A.M., 12:15 P.M., and 2:30 P.M.).

Summary & comments: The largest of the House of Blues (HOB) locations, this music sanctuary defies description and exudes soul. Founder Isaac Tigrett said this HOB opening (November 1996) was the most important one he'll ever do, since Chicago is the living home of the blues. This multimedia restaurant seats over 300, and the menu offers good southern specialties by executive chef Samuel McCord, who had the same post at HOB in New Orleans. HOB celebrates diversity and brotherhood and promotes racial and spiritual harmony. Just getting that message makes everyone feel accepted and respected.

Hubbard Street Grill

Zone 4   The Loop
351 West Hubbard Street
(312) 222-0770

New American	
★★★	
Inexpensive/Moderate	
Quality 81	Value C

Reservations:	Recommended
When to go:	Any time
Entree range:	Lunch, $6.95–15.95; dinner, $7.95–24.95
Payment:	VISA, MC, AMEX, D, DC
Service rating:	★★★½
Friendliness rating:	★★★★
Parking:	Valet for dinner
Bar:	Full service
Wine selection:	100 American; up to $35 a bottle; 9 by the glass, $3.95–4.95
Dress:	Chic casual
Disabled access:	Yes
Customers:	Mixed locals, couples
Lunch/Dinner:	Monday–Thursday, 11:30 A.M.–10 P.M.; Friday, 11:30 A.M.–11 P.M.
Dinner:	Saturday, 5–11 P.M.

Atmosphere/setting: Large loft space decorated in muted greens; recently remodeled banquet room. Open kitchen; chic and casual interior; art gallery.

House specialties: Dill-cured king salmon with Dijon glaze. Mixed grill with salmon fillet, shrimp skewer (the best of the trio), and skirt steak (slightly dry); award-winning barbecue ribs; grilled ahi tuna steak (was properly cooked); grilled Gulf shrimp with angel hair; herb-roasted half chicken. All entrees come with generous sides, such as roasted garlic-Romano mashed potatoes; wilted spinach with olive oil and lemon; and steamed broccoli.

Other recommendations: Boneless grilled chicken breast with goat cheese–pesto filling; Caesar salad; superb Grillroom salad; grilled calamari appetizer; Ketchapeño, the chef's creation—a ketchup-jalapeño blend.

Entertainment & amenities: Pianist Wednesday–Saturday evenings.

Summary & comments: This sophisticated but casual modern American grill opened in spring 1994; David Schy, who bought out his partner and is now chef-owner, is offering all his favorite dishes. Portions are large, so many appetizers can be shared. Cooking is hearty but light, using naturally reduced sauces and lively salsas. A couple of items were bland, such as the red chile–black bean couscous. The menu has something for just about any taste. Service is attentive, knowledgeable, and cordial.

INdiAN SUMMER

Zone 8   Southern Suburbs
6020 South Cass Avenue, Westmont
(630) 769-9662

Indian	
★★★★	
Inexpensive/Moderate	
Quality 94	Value C

Reservations:	Accepted for 4 or more, especially on weekends
When to go:	Any time
Entree range:	Lunch buffet, $7.95; menu, $7.95–19.95
Payment:	All major credit cards
Service rating:	★★★
Friendliness rating:	★★★★
Parking:	Free lot
Bar:	Full service; Indian beers; 20 single-malt Scotches
Wine selection:	International; from $16 a bottle and $4 a glass
Dress:	Casual
Disabled access:	Yes
Customers:	Businesspeople, groups for Indian banquets
Lunch:	Monday–Sunday, 11:30 A.M.–2:30 P.M.
Dinner:	Sunday–Thursday, 5–10 P.M.; Friday and Saturday, 5–11 P.M.

Atmosphere/setting: Lovely, elegant interior, saltwater fish tank with exotic blue fish. Monsoon Bar; Rainbow Dining Room; Peacock Boutique.

House specialties: Special appetizer: Bhajia (vegetables fried in chickpea batter); vegetable samosa (pastry filled with peas and potatoes); keema samosa (with ground lamb); panir pakora (cheese fried in chickpea batter); and chicken pakora. superior Murg Malai Tikka (marinated chicken); tandoor vegetable-nut–stuffed bell peppers; lamb biryani; onion kulcha (flat bread with onion filling); jumbo tandoori shrimp; tandoori chicken salad; baingan piaz masala (roasted eggplant sautéed with fresh tomatoes). Megan's mango melba; mango kulfi (egg-free ice cream); Rinku's leechie mix (a house surprise specialty).

Other recommendations: Mulligatawny soup; rack of lamb; tandoori mixed grill (lamb, chicken, and prawn); palak panir (cheese cubes with spinach, tomatoes, onions); lamb vindaloo (lamb and potato curry cooked in yogurt, tomatoes); traditional gulab jamun (dumplings of reduced milk in rose-flavored syrup).

Summary & comments: This friendly restaurant has elevated Indian cuisine to a higher level with dishes that are lighter than the usual traditional cooking. Spicing is moderate and can be turned up on request. Flavorful chutneys add a nice dimension. Kids' menu.

Iron Mike's Grille

Zone 3 Near North	Classic American Bistro
100 East Chestnut	★★★½
(312) 587-8989	Moderate/Expensive
	Quality 90 Value C

Reservations: Accepted
When to go: Any time
Entree range: $10.89–28.89
Payment: VISA, MC, D, DC
Service rating: ★★★★½
Friendliness rating: ★★★★½
Parking: Valet
Bar: Full service
Wine selection: International
Dress: Business casual
Disabled access: Yes
Customers: Football fans, Italian food lovers, professionals, couples, tourists
Open: Sunday–Thursday, 6:30 A.M.–11 P.M.; Friday and Saturday, 6:30 A.M.–midnight

Atmosphere/setting: Main floor includes a mahogany bar and handsome dining room with sports memorabilia. Upstairs cigar parlor; newly added End Zone, a sidewalk cafe.

House specialties: Ditka's favorite—pork chops with grilled pancetta; "Black & Blue" tuna puttanesca; duck cigar, a crêpe filled with braised duck, served on a wooden cigar box; Grabowski sausage cassoulet (grilled pheasant and duck sausage); Grille (house) salad.

Other recommendations: Midwesterner (French toast or pancakes, bacon or sausage, juice, and morning beverage); Training Meal (beef fillet, eggs, potatoes, juice, bread, and beverage); Fridge Burger (available lunch and dinner); angel hair with pesto and oven-dried tomatoes; linguine with shrimp, calamari, scallops, and mussels; crispy cayenne-crusted oysters with balsamic-jalapeño mayonnaise (a touch of New Orleans, reflecting Ditka's current job as Saints coach); Super Bowl salad (huge).

Summary & comments: Over 2,000 people, including many VIPs, attended the grand opening in February 1997, making big news everywhere. The prices end in numbers reflecting important years for Da Coach, such as a side dish priced at $3.20–4.20, symbolizing Super Bowl XX, when he coached the Bears to the world championship. New End Zone sidewalk cafe will be open daily, 11 A.M.–11 P.M., during the summer, weather permitting.

Jerome's Red Ginger

	Fusion
	★★★½
Zone 1 North Side	Inexpensive/Moderate
2450 North Clark	
(773) 327-2207	Quality 89 Value B

Reservations:	For parties of 7 or more; on the weekends
When to go:	Any time
Entree range:	$10.50–16.95; Sunday buffet, $14
Payment:	All major credit cards
Service rating:	★★★★
Friendliness rating:	★★★★½
Parking:	Free at Columbus Health Pavilion
Bar:	Full service; specialties: martinis and red ginger Bloody Mary
Wine selection:	Mostly American, French; $4–6 a glass and $15–39 a bottle
Dress:	Casual
Disabled access:	Rest rooms are accessible; staff will help guests up the few stairs
Customers:	Diverse; professionals, families, locals
Open:	Monday–Thursday, 11:30 A.M.–10 P.M.; Friday, 11:30 A.M.–11 P.M.; Saturday, 9:30 A.M.–11 P.M.; Sunday, 9:30 A.M.–10 P.M.

Atmosphere/setting: A red ginger theme pervades; lovely outdoor cafe; the dining room has an Art Deco look, a tin ceiling, attractive lighting.

House specialties: Vegetarian spinach wraps; mallard duck egg rolls; house salad; excellent sautéed Lake Superior whitefish in a fresh herb-sesame crust. Sumatra chocolate torte; Red Ginger carrot cake.

Other recommendations: Black mushroom risotto with scallions; traditional crab cakes; roast chicken; filet mignon with East Indian spices (a special); seared scallops over tomato-basil noodles; Jerome's eight-ounce beefburger; seared chicken strips, sprouts, scallions, and shredded romaine in a tomato wrap; and a homespun plum cobbler (a special).

Entertainment & amenities: Bakery is located in restaurant.

Summary & comments: In the space of the former Jerome's, Red Ginger debuted in October 1996. The new owner, Howard Wong, who had a restaurant in St. Louis and admits he loves dining in Paris, organized a professional crew. Our waiter was knowledgeable and accommodating, and co-chefs Sergio Hernandez and Chris Holderman created an enticing menu and produced superb food.

Jilly's Café

Zone 11   Northern Suburbs
2614 Green Bay Road, Evanston
(847) 869-7636

New American	
★★★½	
Inexpensive/Moderate	
Quality 85	Value B

Reservations:	Recommended
When to go:	Any time
Entree range:	$9–15
Payment:	VISA, MC, AMEX
Service rating:	★★★★
Friendliness rating:	★★★★½
Parking:	Street
Bar:	Wine and beer
Wine selection:	International; $15–72; many by the glass, $3.50–6
Dress:	Casual to elegant
Disabled access:	Yes
Customers:	North Shore clientele; businesspeople, couples
Brunch:	Sunday, 10:30 A.M.–2 P.M.
Lunch:	Tuesday–Friday, 11:30 A.M.–2 P.M.
Dinner:	Tuesday–Thursday, 5–9 P.M.; Friday and Saturday, 5–10 P.M.; Sunday, 5–8 P.M.

Atmosphere/setting: Charming, intimate setting—resembles cozy French country inn with white stucco and dark wood walls. Nonsmoking restaurant.

House specialties: Escargot with Gorgonzola cream and grilled polenta; daily focaccia; fresh fish, such as oven-roasted Chilean sea bass with sesame-seed crust and stir-fry angel-hair pasta in ginger tomato broth. Nicely balanced small menu with pastas, seafood, fowl, game, beef, and veal, such as the creative scaloppine with Maytag blue cheese. Pastries are handmade. Trio of desserts: strawberry crème brûlée (flavors change); ice cream and lemon sherbet with raspberry sauce; chocolate apricot cake with chocolate sauce.

Other recommendations: Special appetizer: toasted cheese ravioli with tomato sauce; vegetarian entree: eggplant Napoleon with sweet potato haystack and vegetable coulis; special lamb chops and mashed potato topped with mashed sweet potato; apricot-almond tart.

Summary & comments: A little gem in Evanston that's worth seeking out. The atmosphere is charming, and the service reflects the tastes of the attentive European owner, Eric, and his wife, Diane, who is the pastry chef. Many of the staff are French; service is attentive and friendly. Generally full-flavored, healthful cooking. Entrees come with soup or house salad and sorbet intermezzo. A great value.

Honors/awards: Two stars from *Mobil*.

Julio's Latin Cafe

Zone 10   Northwest Suburbs
99 South Rand Road, Lake Zurich
(847) 438-3484

Caribbean
★★★
Moderate
Quality 83   Value C

Reservations:	Recommended
When to go:	Any time
Entree range:	$11.95–18.95
Payment:	VISA, MC, AMEX, D, DC
Service rating:	★★★★
Friendliness rating:	★★★★
Parking:	Free lot
Bar:	Small bar; several types of margaritas
Wine selection:	American, Chilean, Argentinean, Spanish, and Californian
Dress:	Casual
Disabled access:	Yes
Customers:	Locals
Lunch:	Tuesday–Friday, 11:30 A.M.–3 P.M.
Dinner:	Monday–Thursday, 4:30–10 P.M.; Friday and Saturday, 4:30–10:30 P.M.; Sunday, 4–8:30 P.M.

Atmosphere/setting: Casual fine dining; cozy with South American touches.

House specialties: Pollo Caribe (skinless, boneless chicken sautéed, garnished with shrimp, and served with mango sauce); paella (seafood, chicken, and sausage over Spanish saffron rice); parrillada gaucho (grilled New York strip steak with chicken and turkey sausage, roast bell peppers, and fried bananas).

Other recommendations: Ceviche; shrimp avocado salad; Caribbean Cornish hen (semiboneless with sweet-sour tamarind sauce).

Entertainment & amenities: Live entertainment on weekends, 7:30–10:30 P.M. Classical and jazz guitarist from Brazil; Spanish and English singers. Mexican guitarist, Sunday, 5:30–8:30 P.M.

Summary & comments: This intimate spot has carved a niche for itself in the northwest suburban area. Discriminating diners enjoy the food and the friendly service anytime, and the bonus of live jazz on weekends doubles the pleasure. Recently expanded.

Kanval Palace

	Indian
Zone 1 North Side	★★½
2501 West Devon Avenue	Inexpensive
(773) 761-7270	
	Quality 76 Value B

Reservations:	Recommended
When to go:	Weekdays
Entree range:	$6.50–15.95
Payment:	All major credit cards
Service rating:	★★★
Friendliness rating:	★★★
Parking:	Street
Bar:	Full service, including Indian beer
Wine selection:	Mostly Californian; house by the glass, carafe, or half carafe
Dress:	Casual, business
Disabled access:	Yes, including rest rooms
Customers:	Locals, some Indians
Lunch:	Every day, 11:30 A.M.–3:30 P.M.
Dinner:	Sunday–Thursday, 5–10 P.M.; Friday and Saturday, 5–11 P.M.

Atmosphere/setting: Attractive, cozy, moderately elegant.

House specialties: Assorted appetizers including pakora (vegetable fritters); papadum (crisp lentil wafer); samosas (meat and vegetable patties). Chicken tikka (boneless tandoori chicken with butter-onion sauce); tandoori assorted grill (marinated chicken, lamb, and fish); charga chicken (whole bird marinated, deep fried, and garnished with dry mango powder and cilantro); murg (chicken) and/or lamb vindaloo, cooked with potatoes in tangy sauce.

Other recommendations: Bhuna gosht (boneless lamb cooked with tomatoes, onion, and bell peppers in a spicy gravy); Palace Royal biryani (basmati rice with saffron, cooked with lamb, chicken, shrimp, and nuts); pista kulfi (homemade ice cream).

Summary & comments: Straightforward traditional dishes with a well-balanced menu. On one occasion the biryani was on the dry side, and the meats appeared to be leftovers. Tandoor-cooked food fared better. Cooking tends to be Americanized and less spicy than traditional Indian cooking.

KARYN'S FRESH CORNER

Zone 1   North Side
3351 Lincoln Avenue
(773) 296-6990

Vegetarian/Natural	
★★★	
Inexpensive	
Quality 84	Value C

Reservations: Accepted
When to go: Any time
Entree range: $5.25–11
Payment: All major credit cards
Service rating: ★★½
Friendliness rating: ★★★½
Parking: Street
Bar: None; BYOB
Wine selection: None
Dress: Casual
Disabled access: Yes
Customers: Locals, psychics, musicians, professionals, families
Open: Monday–Friday, 11:30 A.M.–9 P.M.; Saturday and
                      Sunday, 10 A.M.–9 P.M.

Atmosphere/setting: Spacious, with a garden motif; ledges decorated with fresh flowers, sprouts, wheat grass, and herbs; attractive place mats on tables; ozonated and oxygenated air; and an open kitchen.

House specialties: Gazpacho; vegan Caesar salad; veggie burger in a pita; taco roll; wheatgrass juice; raw apple pie (raw apples, bananas, dates, cashew-and-almond butter, tahini, honey, cinnamon, and vanilla in a dehydrated pie shell).

Other recommendations: Raw zucchini "pasta" with pesto; Sicilian pizza (raw cured eggplant, fresh or sun-dried tomatoes, heavy garlic, select mushrooms on a creamy pesto sauce); banana delight (fresh bananas with a vibrant protein seed mixture, topped with a cashew sauce); and paradise pies of mango, blueberry, or the best fruit in season.

Entertainment & amenities: Nutrition classes and a detox program. Outdoor cafe and retail shop. Toys for kids. Dog biscuits and water for canines.

Summary & comments: Proprietor and nutritional counselor Karyn Calabrese advocates eating organic and uncooked foods and juices; all her dishes are vegan and most are not cooked. She believes these uncooked foods, known as raw living foods, leave all the vitamins, minerals, and enzymes available for the body's total use, thus helping the body to fend off sickness and the aging process. When Calabrese has to dehydrate some foods, nothing is heated over 105° Fahrenheit. For those who do enjoy a hot meal, Calabrese now offers some international cooked foods such as Spanish rice and meatless hot dogs.

Katsu Japanese Restaurant

	Japanese
Zone 1 North Side	★★★½
2651 West Peterson Avenue	Inexpensive/Moderate
(773) 784-3383	Quality 90 Value B

Reservations:	Recommended
When to go:	Early weekday evenings
Entree range:	$10–20
Payment:	VISA, MC, AMEX, DC, D
Service rating:	★★★★
Friendliness rating:	★★★★★
Parking:	Abundant on street; city lot nearby
Bar:	Full service
Wine selection:	Small; Californian and Japanese
Dress:	Casual
Disabled access:	Yes
Customers:	Japanese, locals, sushi lovers
Dinner:	Every day, 5–11 P.M.

Atmosphere/setting: Newly remodeled with a contemporary Japanese decor. Sushi bar and dining room with benches and tables.

House specialties: Katsumaki (avocado, crab stick, cucumber, and fresh tuna); sushi; authentic Japanese ramen noodles.

Other recommendations: Tempura; combination box; beef roll; grilled squid; gomae (steamed spinach with delicate sesame sauce); maki sushi (popeye roll, spinach roll, and salmon roll); combination dinners.

Summary & comments: A charming, quiet, little Japanese jewel in an inconspicuous northwest neighborhood. Japanese businessmen who work and live in the suburbs come here weekly or more for their sushi and home-style food fix, and they entertain clients here as well. Prices are right and encourage repeat visits. Some dishes served are only found in Japanese homes, not in restaurants. Husband-and-wife team excels in service and graciousness. Kampai! (Bottoms up!)

Honors/awards: Highest rating by Sherman Kaplan, dining critic at WBBM (CBS) Radio.

Kiki's Bistro

Zone 3   Near North
900 North Franklin Street
(312) 335-5454

French Bistro
★★★★
Inexpensive/Moderate

Quality 94   Value C

Reservations: Recommended
When to go: Any time
Entree range: Lunch, $8.50–12; dinner, $9.50–22
Payment: All major credit cards
Service rating: ★★★★
Friendliness rating: ★★★★
Parking: Free valet
Bar: Full service
Wine selection: 20 French and 15 American whites, over 30 reds,
                       $20–60; 8 champagnes, $35–100; 12 by the
                       glass, $4.50
Dress: Informal; no athletic wear
Disabled access: Yes, entrance and rest rooms
Customers: International; celebrities, businesspeople, families,
                       couples
Lunch: Monday–Friday, 11 A.M.–2 P.M.
Dinner: Monday–Thursday, 5–9:45 P.M.; Friday and Saturday,
                       5–10:45 P.M.

Atmosphere/setting: Resembles a French inn; lovely cottage-style wood-work and rustic decor; romantic and intimate; separate bar/lounge. Noise level can be high with a full house.

House specialties: Sautéed breast of duck; daily fish (Atlantic salmon, grilled grouper, or halibut); duck pâté with pistachio; mixed wild mushroom salad; tarte de Provence (ratatouille and goat cheese in a light pastry); steak au poivre with cognac cream sauce.

Other recommendations: Onion soup gratinée; poulet roti (marinated roast chicken with mashed potatoes); steak pommes frites; pizza du jour; seared quail; crème brûlée; croustade de poire (pear in pastry with caramel sauce); crème caramel; sautéed Bing cherries with goat cheese ice cream.

Summary & comments: Many of the French bistro standards—steak pommes frites, onion soup gratinée, and poulet roti—are standouts, prepared expertly by chef Michael Gregson. Owner Georges Cousances (Kiki), an experienced restaurateur, makes certain the place runs smoothly. Service, food, wine, and charming atmosphere combine to make this a quintessential bistro without the claustrophobic closeness of many others.

KINZIE STREET CHOPHOUSE

Zone 4 The Loop	Steak
400 North Wells Street, Chicago	★★★★
(312) 822-0191	Moderate
	Quality 91 Value B

Reservations:	Suggested
When to go:	4:30–6 P.M.
Entree range:	$8.95–27.95
Payment:	All major credit cards
Service rating:	★★★★½
Friendliness rating:	★★★★½
Parking:	Valet, Wednesday–Saturday
Bar:	Full service
Wine selection:	Italian, Spanish, Australian, Californian, and French; reserve lists; ports; several by the glass, $4.95–5.95
Dress:	Casual, business
Disabled access:	Yes
Customers:	Suburbanites to locals, professionals, executives, operagoers
Lunch/Dinner:	Monday–Saturday, 11 A.M.–10 P.M.

Atmosphere/setting: Dimly lit and welcoming with a masculine look: dark brown wild-grain oak paneling and oak floor; cozy banquettes; many private tables well spaced.

House specialties: Sesame-crusted yellowfin tuna; Australian lobster tail (mammoth!); 20-oz. porterhouse; Daily specials: live Maine lobsters.

Other recommendations: Garlic shrimp scampi; wild mushroom and goat cheese tart; cheddar-stuffed jalapeños; black bean soup; filet mignon; double-cut domestic lamb chops; surf and turf; crispy onions; baked scallion smashed potatoes (with pieces of skins); asparagus, hot with hollandaise.

Summary & comments: Excellent-quality steaks and seafood in generous portions. A fine, dependable place for a business meal. Attentive, savvy, good-humored staff with great pride in their work. Well-rehearsed waiters roll over a cart and show the plastic-wrapped raw products to assist you in ordering. Service is professional but never intimidating.

Kitty O'Shea's

Zone 5   South Loop
Chicago Hilton and Towers,
    720 South Michigan Avenue
(312) 922-4400

Irish Pub	
★★★	
Inexpensive	
Quality 81	Value B

Reservations:	No
When to go:	Evenings
Entree range:	$7.25–12.75
Payment:	All major credit cards
Service rating:	★★★
Friendliness rating:	★★★½
Parking:	Street and valet
Bar:	Full service, including Guinness, Harp; local microbrews
Wine selection:	American
Dress:	Casual
Disabled access:	Yes
Customers:	Locals, conventioneers
Open:	Every day, 11–1:30 A.M.

Atmosphere/setting: Dimly lit, Dublin-style pub with antiques, including the beer taps.

House specialties: Potato and leek soup; Irish lamb stew; shepherd's pie; Blarney Burger Deluxe with Irish cheese and O'Shea's fries; Biddy Mulligan's fish and chips.

Other recommendations: Dublin wings; Kitty's corned beef and cabbage; Brannigan's bread pudding.

Entertainment & amenities: Monday–Saturday, 9 P.M.–1 A.M., live Irish folk music.

Summary & comments: You can't get more Irish than Kitty O'Shea's. Not only is much of the interior imported from Ireland, so is the staff. Guinness and Harp are drawn from antique beer taps (try the layered black and tan), the food is simple pub fare, and the spirited entertainment (some big names) completes the picture. Kilkenny-born manager Eamonn Brady uses his impressive entertainment background to book the lively musical groups here. It's hand-clapping fun!

Klay Oven

Zone 4   The Loop
414 North Orleans Street
(312) 527-3999

	Indian
	★★★★
	Moderate
	Quality 94 Value B

Reservations:	Highly recommended
When to go:	Weekdays less crowded
Entree range:	$6.95–24.95
Payment:	Major credit cards
Service rating:	★★★½
Friendliness rating:	★★★★½
Parking:	Street and garage nearby
Bar:	Full service; Indian beer and a large single-malt Scotch collection
Wine selection:	Extensive; several nice choices by the glass; Omar Khayam sparkling wine from India
Dress:	Moderately casual to upscale
Disabled access:	Yes
Customers:	International; diverse; businesspeople (lunch)
Lunch:	Tuesday–Friday, 11:30 A.M.–2:30 P.M.; Saturday and Sunday, noon–3 P.M. (buffet)
Dinner:	Sunday–Thursday, 5:30–10 P.M.; Friday and Saturday, 5:30–10:30 P.M.

Atmosphere / setting: Upscale casual with light wood, white tablecloths; divided into intimate alcoves, many of which are perfect for private parties.

House specialties: Thali (traditional taster platter of nine items; vegetarian or nonvegetarian); nonvegetarian thali includes keema samosa (lamb in pastry), murg makhani (butter chicken curry), and raita (yogurt sauce). Tiger prawns marinated in spiced yogurt; marinated mahi mahi fillets.

Other recommendations: Tandoori mixed grill (boneless lamb, boneless chicken, and prawn, each marinated differently); rack of lamb; and ras malai, an exquisite dessert pudding of milk, honey, and pistachio.

Summary & comments: Klay Oven elevates Indian cuisine to a fine-dining experience, from the freshly cooked food to the nonsmoking, lovely setting and professional service. The centuries-old clay oven (tandoor) and the Indian wok (karahi) are virtually greaseless cooking methods. The nan bread takes 30 seconds to cook; shrimp takes only 4 seconds.

Honors / awards: *Chicago* magazine's Critic's Choice Top 25 Restaurants; *Food Industry Guide,* Award of Excellence, 1996–97.

KOREA GARDEN

Zone 8   Southern Suburbs
204 North Cass Avenue, Westmont
(630) 852-1900

Korean	
★★★½	
Inexpensive/Moderate	
Quality 88	Value B

Reservations:	Accepted only for 6 or more
When to go:	Any time
Entree range:	$8.95–15.95
Payment:	All major credit cards
Service rating:	★★★★
Friendliness rating:	★★★★½
Parking:	Street; free city lot across the street on Cass
Bar:	No mixed drinks, only liquor on the rocks and beer
Wine selection:	Very small; some by the glass
Dress:	Casual
Disabled Access:	Yes
Customers:	Mixed; about half Korean, half American
Lunch/Dinner:	Monday–Saturday, 11:30 A.M.–10 P.M. (discount lunch menu only available Monday–Friday, 11:30 A.M.–3 P.M.); Sunday, 2–10 P.M.

Atmosphere/setting: Clean, modern decor; serene music. Some tables have an authentic Korean wood charcoal grill (and a vent hood). Comfortable chairs.

House specialties: Goomandoo (pan-fried Korean dumplings); kim chi; bindaetok (Korean pancake made with mung bean flour with pork and vegetables); chapchae (a mixture of mushrooms, clear noodles, vegetables, and beef in a sweet, mild sauce); bulgogi (thin slices of marinated beef grilled at the table, served with the nontraditional moderately spicy miso sauce, doenjang, and lettuce leaves); saewoo gui (shrimp and marinated vegetables); bibimbop (stir-fried vegetables, bulgogi, and fried egg and rice); marinated calamari (listed as calamary) with mushrooms and vegetables; salmon charbroiled.

Other recommendations: Roasted seaweed; gahlbi (pork with rind marinated in hot sauce); Spanish mackerel; yellow corvina (light-fleshed Asian fish).

Summary & comments: Korea Garden touts its cuisine as "truly authentic Korean, no MSG . . . using corn oil and sesame oil." It offers a large amount of seafood for a Korean restaurant. You can grill your own meats and vegetables. Complimentary orange slices and hot corn tea are served at the end of the meal. One of the better Chicago-area restaurants for a fine Korean dining experience. Ingredients are fresh, sauces are richly flavored, and management is attentive.

Kuni's

	Japanese
Zone 11 Northern Suburbs	★★★★½
511 Main Street, Evanston	Inexpensive/Moderate
(847) 328-2004	
	Quality 96 Value C

Reservations:	Accepted only for 6 or more
When to go:	Any time
Entree range:	$10–18.50 and up
Payment:	VISA, MC, AMEX
Service rating:	★★★★
Friendliness rating:	★★★★
Parking:	Street
Bar:	Wine and beer, including Japanese beers
Wine selection:	Limited; more Japanese sake than American
Dress:	Casual
Disabled access:	No
Customers:	Locals, Northwestern students, sushi devotees
Lunch:	Monday, Wednesday–Saturday, 11:30 A.M.–1:45 P.M.
Dinner:	Monday, Wednesday–Sunday, 5–9:45 P.M.

Atmosphere/setting: Simple, clean decor. Lovely sushi bar with great fish display.

House specialties: Sushi and sashimi: pristinely fresh, top-quality, expertly sliced, and a great variety; try chef's favorites. Sunomono (sashimi salads): oyster, crab, and mixed; maki sushi of several types, such as tekkamaki (tuna and rice in seaweed wrap, sliced); omakase maki (tuna and avocado rolled inside-out with black seaweed center, rice outside); and spider maki (soft-shell crab and shredded mushrooms). A la carte items: excellent age dashi tofu (fried, with delicate sauce); oshitashi (steamed spinach and Japanese-style sauce); gyoza (fried/steamed meat dumplings); tairagai no butteryaki (scallops broiled in butter).

Other recommendations: Cooked food: tempura (shrimp and vegetables); soft-shell crab in season; chicken teriyaki; fish teriyaki; and sukiyaki (sliced beef and vegetables). Kuni's special includes tempura, sushi, or sashimi; a teriyaki dish; gomae; sunomono; bean soup, salads, steamed rice, and green tea.

Summary & comments: By far, in a class by itself when it comes to top-flight sushi and sashimi. Owner-chef Yuji Kunii is a master sushi expert. Our last waitress was extraordinarily well informed, patient, and efficient. International celebrities and other sushi enthusiasts stop here to indulge. Some connoisseurs say there are few other sushi bars as fine as this in the entire country!

La Bocca della Verità

<table>
<tr><td>Italian</td></tr>
<tr><td>★★★</td></tr>
<tr><td>Inexpensive/Moderate</td></tr>
<tr><td>Quality 84   Value B</td></tr>
</table>

Zone 1   North Side
4618 North Lincoln Avenue
(773) 784-6222

Reservations:	Suggested on Friday and Saturday
When to go:	Weekdays less busy
Entree range:	Pastas, $9.75–12.95; segundis, $12.75–19.95
Payment:	VISA, MC, AMEX, D
Service rating:	★★★★
Friendliness rating:	★★★★½
Parking:	Street
Bar:	Full service, including about 10 beers
Wine selection:	Fairly extensive; almost all Italian, a few French champagnes; about 12 by the glass, $4.25; bottles, $13–190
Dress:	Casual
Disabled access:	Yes
Customers:	Diverse, locals, students; all ages
Dinner:	Tuesday–Sunday, 5–11 P.M.

Atmosphere/setting: Cozy and loaded with European charm. Smoking and nonsmoking dining areas; new 50-seat party room.

House specialties: Menu changes every week. Antipasto misto; calamari affogati (marinara sauce, white wine); risotto asparagi with cream sauce; whole sea bass baked in salt (old recipe); whole sea bass prepared with fresh thyme, rosemary, olives, and white wine; whole Dover sole sautéed, then baked; pollo campagnola (chicken breast, roasted potatoes); grilled baby Mediterranean octopus.

Other recommendations: Shrimps and baby artichokes; carpaccio; insalata della casa; gnocchi al pomodoro (potato dumplings, tomato sauce, basil, Parmigiano); ravioli Anatra (ravioli filled with duck breast, sage, and shallot filling). Desserts are made in-house, including tiramisu and covilio (espresso gelato, amaretto cookie, Strega liqueur).

Summary & comments: Restaurant's name means "the mouth of the truth," and the owner, Cesare, has put up a whimsical mask with a moving mouth at the doorway. This comical practice stems from the old custom of having a hole in the city buildings in Italy, where people could denounce infidels and other trespassers. If people weren't truthful, their hands would be "bitten" when in the hole. Altogether, this place is delightful and homey; our waitress was caring and attentive. The place has grown a bit more sophisticated in the past two years. A hidden Italian gem.

LA CRÊPERIE

Zone 1   North Side
2845 North Clark Street
(773) 528-9050

French Cafe	
★★½	
Inexpensive	
Quality 80	Value A

Reservations:	Only for 6 or more; not accepted on holidays
When to go:	Any time; Thursday evenings for the music
Entree range:	$6.25–15
Payment:	All major credit cards
Service rating:	★★★½
Friendliness rating:	★★★★½
Parking:	Street or public garage across the street
Bar:	Full service, including French waters and ciders
Wine selection:	Mostly French; $15–29 a bottle; $3.25–5 a glass
Dress:	Casual
Disabled access:	Yes
Customers:	Some foreigners; families, locals, professionals, celebrities
Lunch:	Tuesday–Friday, 11:30 A.M.–3:30 P.M.
Brunch:	Saturday and Sunday, 11 A.M.–4 P.M.
Dinner:	Tuesday–Saturday, 5–11 P.M.; Sunday, 5–9:30 P.M.

Atmosphere/setting: A romantic, homey setting with a "lived in" look. In the evening the garden cafe is magical, lit with lanterns and tiny lights—it transports you to a French country garden.

House specialties: Crêpes Bretonnes (large buckwheat crêpes folded into squares) are the house specialty, including coq au vin, boeuf bourguignonne, and seafood and sauce crêpes. Also pâté, salade maison, onion soup gratinée. Dessert crêpes: chocolate crêpe and Grand Marnier crêpe.

Other recommendations: Spinach creme crêpe; chicken and mushroom crêpe; orange roughy; and bananas Sara. Brunch: egg crêpe; cream cheese and chive omelet; and crêpe Florentine.

Entertainment & amenities: A strolling accordionist, Thursdays 8–11 P.M.

Summary & comments: La Crêperie features buckwheat crêpes like those from Brittany, the homeland of chef-owner Germain Roignant. La Crêperie celebrated its 25th anniversary in 1997 and still makes all the crêpes by hand. The dinner that includes a cup of soup du jour or salade maison, one entree crêpe, and one dessert crêpe costs just $14—a bargain. A seafood entree crêpe dinner is only $15. La Crêperie's prepackaged crêpes are sold in supermarkets.

La Strada

Zone 4   The Loop
155 North Michigan Avenue at
Randolph Street
(312) 565-2200

Italian	
★★★½	
Moderate/Expensive	
Quality 87	Value C

Reservations:	Accepted; especially for lunch
When to go:	Any time; can be busy at lunch
Entree range:	Lunch, $10–15; dinner, $20–30
Payment:	All major credit cards
Service rating:	★★★★½
Friendliness rating:	★★★★½
Parking:	Lunch, street or garage; dinner, valet
Bar:	Full line of all spirits, grappas, cognacs, ports, beers, and cordials
Wine selection:	Over 200 selections; several by the glass
Dress:	Business, semiformal; no shorts
Disabled access:	Glass elevator; rest rooms not handicap accessible
Customers:	Businesspeople, professionals, travelers, politicians
Lunch:	Monday–Friday, 11:30 A.M.–2:30 P.M.
Dinner:	Monday–Thursday, 4–10 P.M.; Friday, 4–11 P.M.; Saturday, 5–11 P.M.

Atmosphere/setting: Crystal chandeliers, elegant tabletops, large booths and spacious tables for privacy; Renaissance frescos; recently renovated.

House specialties: Mussels posillipo (in tomato-wine sauce); insalata della casa. Prime Provimi veal chops (three preparations); lobster fra diavolo (spicy with clams, mussels, and linguine); angel hair with prosciutto and mushrooms.

Other recommendations: New Zealand lamb chops (three preparations); veal scaloppine (two preparations); fettuccine with porcini. Tiramisu; Venetian bombe; and zabaglione.

Entertainment & amenities: Live piano entertainment nightly in the piano bar.

Summary & comments: This downtown Michigan Avenue restaurant is one of the few places that emphasizes Northern Italian cuisine. The menu is very ambitious. Food is served in sumptuously comfortable, private surroundings with attentive service. The restaurant's adjacent casual eatery is J. Randolph's Bar & Grill, open Monday–Saturday, phone (312) 565-2203.

Honors/awards: *Travel Holiday* for 12 years; one of two Illinois restaurants selected to receive the DiRoNA Award in 1997; three-star Mobil Award; *Chicago Sun-Times,* three stars.

LAWRY'S THE PRIME RIB

Zone 3   Near North
100 East Ontario Street
(312) 787-5000

Prime Rib	
★★★★	
Moderate	
Quality 90	Value B

Reservations:	Highly recommended
When to go:	Weekday lunch or dinner
Entree range:	Lunch, $5.95–10.95; dinner, $18.95–25.95
Payment:	All major credit cards
Service rating:	★★★★
Friendliness rating:	★★★★
Parking:	Valet during dinner, $5.75
Bar:	Full service
Wine selection:	Very good; mostly American; several by the glass
Dress:	Lunch, business; dinner, dressy-casual to dressy
Disabled access:	No
Customers:	Businesspeople, conventioneers, families, couples
Lunch:	Monday–Friday, 11:30 A.M.–2 P.M.
Dinner:	Monday–Thursday, 5–11 P.M.; Friday and Saturday, 5 P.M.–midnight; Sunday, 3–10 P.M.

Atmosphere/setting: Housed in the stately, elegant century-old McCormick family mansion on the Gold Coast. The original Lawry's opened in 1938 in Beverly Hills, California.

House specialties: Roast prime ribs of beef (the reason for coming here), available in four cuts: California (smaller), English (thinner slices), Lawry (traditional, generous), and Chicago (extra-thick with rib bone). Original spinning bowl salad; Yorkshire pudding. Mashed potatoes and whipped cream horseradish come with prime rib; Lawry's baked potato is almost a meal itself—share it.

Other recommendations: Lunch: prime rib; turkey, pastrami, corned beef sandwiches; Cobb salad; English trifle. Dinner: fish special; creamed spinach.

Summary & comments: The restaurant is committed to the finest prime, dry-aged beef and other quality ingredients prepared to perfection. Wine list includes Lawry's private selection and two featured wines. Attention to detail and service is impressive. The "ale and sandwich bar" offers an affordable, casual lunch in a majestic mansion. Since Jackie Shen was appointed executive chef (formerly of Jackie's), diners can continue to enjoy her signature dessert: chocolate bag filled with white chocolate mousse, strawberries, and kiwi, with raspberry sauce.

Honors/awards: *North Shore* magazine, Best Prime Rib; much good press over the years.

Le Colonial

Zone 1   North Side
937 North Rush Street
(312) 255-0088

French/Vietnamese
★★★½
Moderate

Quality 88   Value C

Reservations:	Recommended
When to go:	Avoid peak mealtimes without a reservation
Entree range:	$12.50–19
Payment:	VISA, MC, AMEX, DC
Service rating:	★★★★
Friendliness rating:	★★★★
Parking:	Valet, $6
Bar:	Full service
Wine selection:	French and American, $18–225; several by the glass, $5–16
Dress:	Business casual
Disabled access:	Yes, also rest rooms
Customers:	Chic professionals, businesspeople, couples (weekends)
Lunch:	Monday–Saturday, noon–2:30 P.M.
Dinner:	Monday–Friday, 5–11 P.M.; Saturday, 5 P.M.–midnight; Sunday, 5–10 P.M.

Atmosphere / setting: The interior design was inspired by the film *Indochine,* and it offers patrons a choice of two atmospheres: the bar and tranquil dining room downstairs; and the romantic lounge upstairs with a terrace. The decor transports diners to the 1920s era of French-colonial Southeast Asia—potted palms, fans whirring, louvered shutters, and rattan furniture.

House specialties: Chao tom (grilled shrimp wrapped around sugarcane with angel hair); steamed dumplings with chicken and mushrooms; spicy beef salad with lemongrass; crisp-seared whole red snapper; sautéed jumbo shrimp with eggplant; banana tapioca pudding; tropical fruit sorbets.

Other recommendations: Pho (hearty oxtail soup); spring rolls; oven-roasted chicken; ginger-marinated roast duck; grilled eggplant; stir-fried rice with lemongrass, shrimp.

Summary & comments: You won't miss Le Colonial from Rush Street, since the dove gray vintage townhouse is clearly from another era and place. When you enter Chicago downtown's first French-Vietnamese, fine-dining restaurant, you get lost in an Asian time warp. Ceiling fans stir the banana trees and palms. Photos of life in Saigon during the 1920s dot the walls. Le Colonial has two siblings: one in Manhattan, the other in Los Angeles.

Le Français

Zone 10 Northwest Suburbs	**French**
269 South Milwaukee Avenue,	★★★★★
Wheeling	Expensive
(847) 541-7471	Quality 97 Value C

Reservations:	Strongly recommended, especially on weekends
When to go:	Weeknights
Entree range:	$27–30.50; 4-course dinner (by 6 P.M.), $35
Payment:	All major credit cards except DC
Service rating:	★★★★★
Friendliness rating:	★★★★½
Parking:	Free valet
Bar:	Full service
Wine selection:	A grand "bible" with 40–50 pages; $30–5,000 a bottle; by the glass: lunch, $5.25–6; dinner, $7
Dress:	Jacket required, tie preferred
Disabled access:	Yes
Customers:	Couples, businesspeople, celebrators
Lunch:	Tuesday–Friday, 11:30 A.M.–2 P.M.
Dinner:	Tuesday–Friday, 5–9 P.M.; Saturday and Sunday, only two seatings, 6 and 9:15 P.M.

Atmosphere/setting: Exquisite, opulent, country-style interior; quiet, romantic, elegant, and full of flowers.

House specialties: Marinated tuna, smoked salmon, fennel salad. Seafood trilogy: lobster cannelloni, sautéed sea scallops, soft-shell crab. Dessert soufflés: chocolate, Grand Marnier, raspberry, lemon; flan; white chocolate mousse.

Other recommendations: Artichoke terrine with tomato coulis; pâté d'escargot with wild mushrooms; game and farm plate with roasted squab and stuffed rabbit loin; lemon tarte; hot symphony of chocolate.

Summary & comments: At this famous temple of gastronomy, a customer is given a complimentary appetizer *before* the menu, and at the finale, a sweet. Chef Roland Liccioni and wife and pastry chef, Mary Beth, leased this internationally famous temple of gastronomy from master chef Jean and manager-wife Doris Banchet several years ago. Liccioni's cooking is lighter with some Asian influences, reflecting his Vietnamese heritage. Lunch can be uninspired sometimes, but always executed perfectly; dinner is preferable. This exquisite restaurant put Wheeling on the culinary map.

Honors/awards: AAA five diamonds; five stars, *Mobil Travel Guide; Wine Spectator* Grand Award last five years; listed in *Tradition Et Qualité* and *Relais Et Chateaux* guides.

Le Titi de Paris

Zone 10   Northwest Suburbs
1015 West Dundee Road,
   Arlington Heights
(847) 506-0222

New French
★★★★½
Moderate/Expensive

Quality 97   Value C

Reservations:	Strongly recommended
When to go:	Weeknights
Entree range:	$19.75–28
Payment:	All major credit cards
Service rating:	★★★★★
Friendliness rating:	★★★★½
Parking:	Free lot
Bar:	None
Wine selection:	Over 650, French, American; $18 and up; 7 by the glass, from $5
Dress:	Jacket preferred; dressy, business
Disabled access:	Yes, entrance and rest rooms
Customers:	Mostly couples, some families; businesspeople (lunch), celebrators
Lunch:	Tuesday–Friday, 11:30 A.M.–2:30 P.M.
Dinner:	Tuesday–Thursday, 5:30–9:30 P.M.; Friday, 5:30–10 P.M.; Saturday, 5–10:30 P.M.

Atmosphere/setting: Gracious, romantic, comfortable elegance—filled with flowers. A high level of service without stuffiness.

House specialties: Sampler of hot and cold foie gras on toasted brioche; terrine of vegetable mousse; lobster bisque; assortment of pâtés. Norwegian salmon; roasted rack of lamb and confit of duck; daily specials. Napoleon; chocolate symphony; pyramid of pear with chocolate, Kahlúa mousse; opera pastry.

Other recommendations: Nut-crusted wild striped bass; panache of quail filled with spinach mousse, sweetbreads and veal loin; nouveau seafood cassoulet. Fresh fruit tart; manjari (bittersweet chocolate and passion fruit); circus fantasy.

Entertainment & amenities: Maître d' plays guitar and sings; wine and regional dinners. Bastille Day celebration.

Summary & comments: Owner-chef Pierre Pollin is one of the finest French chefs in the area and certainly one of the most easygoing, which may be why his employees stay a long time. He offers the traditional regional dishes of bouillabaisse and cassoulet Tuesday–Friday, January–March. This place has never been pretentious—just warm and inviting.

Honors/awards: DiRoNA Award, 1994.

Le Vichyssois

Zone 10 Northwest Suburbs	French
220 West Route 120, Lakemoor	★★★★½
(815) 385-8221	Moderate
	Quality 95 Value B

Reservations:	Suggested
When to go:	Wednesday or Thursday evenings, early Friday or Saturday evenings
Entree range:	$14.95–29.95
Payment:	VISA, MC, DC
Service rating:	★★★★½
Friendliness rating:	★★★★½
Parking:	Lot
Bar:	Full service
Wine selection:	100 French and American, $18–132; 15 by the glass, $4–8
Dress:	Moderately casual, neat
Disabled access:	Yes
Customers:	Young and old, couples, businesspeople
Dinner:	Wednesday and Thursday, 5:30–9 P.M.; Friday and Saturday, 5:30–10 P.M.; Sunday, 4:30 P.M.–9 P.M. (closing time = last reservation)

Atmosphere/setting: Authentic French country inn style with lovely table settings and a display of oil paintings for sale. Comfortable and cozy.

House specialties: Seafood and desserts are the chef's forte. House salad included with entree. Start with the vichyssoise (hot or cold). Other soups: shiitake mushroom and asparagus, morel, or crayfish. House pâtés: duck, quail, rillette. Escargots and mushroom gâteau; warm salmon crêpes and salmon caviar; Dover sole with vermouth sauce; roast duck in sherry wine-vinegar sauce; veal loin medallions; salmon en croûte in champagne sauce.

Other recommendations: Warm terrine of pike, salmon, and crayfish; French green beans, morels, mesclun, goat cheese, and walnut oil dressing; roasted rack of lamb with tarragon sauce; tournedos bordelaise; lobster à la nage. Three-course Country Bistro Menu, $21.50 (not served on Saturday).

Summary & comments: The first taste of chef Bernard Cretier's creations justifies the 50-mile trip northwest of Chicago. Cretier says, "I am free-spirited and didn't want a partner; I found this place—the price was right, the location was not. I hoped Chicagoans would make the trip." They did, and they've been making the pilgrimage since he and his partner and wife, Priscilla, opened in Lakemoor in 1976. The menu is seasonal with creative daily specials.

L'Olive Cafe

Zone 1   North Side
3915 North Sheridan Road
(773) 472-2400

Moroccan/Mediterranean
★★★½
Inexpensive

Quality 91   Value A

Reservations:	Recommended for 5 or more
When to go:	Any time
Entree range:	$10.95–15.95
Payment:	VISA, MC, DC, D
Service rating:	★★★
Friendliness rating:	★★★★½
Parking:	Street
Bar:	None
Wine selection:	BYOB, $1.50 a person corkage fee; limited selection at nearby shop
Dress:	Casual
Disabled access:	Yes, except rest room
Customers:	Locals, Moroccans, French, politicians
Dinner:	Tuesday–Sunday, 5–11 P.M.

Atmosphere/setting: Intimate and homey former diner. Decorated with ceiling fans, mirrors, wall border murals, colorful rugs, Moroccan tagines (conical clay vessels), and mix-matched chairs.

House specialties: Bastilla (traditional flaky pigeon pie), here with chicken, almonds; merguez (spicy Moroccan lamb sausage); warm fig salad; couscous (vegetarian with saffron, calamari, grilled chicken breast, lamb, royal; tagines (oven-braised dishes cooked in conical clay pots), with lamb or chicken; specials.

Other recommendations: Goat cheese hummus; Moroccan olives; zaalouk (roasted eggplant); shrimp peel peel with spinach and chickpeas; sautéed fresh sardines stuffed with roasted peppers and tomatoes; Moroccan combination salad. Warm, flaky apple tart with caramel sauce; proverbial Moroccan mint tea.

Summary & comments: L'Olive (pronounced "low-leave" in French) is aptly named, since the olive is a key Mediterranean ingredient and paramount to Morocco, the North African homeland of chef-owner Mohamed Ben Mchabcheb. His French cuisine training and passion for his native cuisine show in his exquisite versions of bastilla, couscous, and tagines. It's fun to share several appetizers. Chef does catering, private parties, and carryout. Excellent value.

Honors/awards: Rated among top ten restaurants in Chicago by WBBM; three stars from *Chicago Tribune;* features in several publications, including the *Chicago Sun-Times.*

Lulu's

Zone 11 Northern Suburbs	Pan-Asian
626 Davis Street, Evanston	★★½
(847) 869-4343	Inexpensive
	Quality 80 Value B

Reservations:	Not accepted
When to go:	Afternoon
Entree range:	$5.75–6.95
Payment:	VISA, MC, AMEX
Service rating:	★★★
Friendliness rating:	★★½
Parking:	Street, city lot
Bar:	Limited selection of beer and wine
Wine selection:	Limited, mostly white wines; several by the glass
Dress:	Very casual; T-shirts okay because that's what the staff wears
Disabled access:	Yes
Customers:	Locals, Northwestern University students, Chicago food lovers
Lunch/Dinner:	Monday–Thursday, 11:30 A.M.–10 P.M.; Friday and Saturday, 11:30 A.M.–11 P.M.; Sunday, 11:30 A.M.–9 P.M.

Atmosphere/setting: Bright; open kitchen; nonsmoking restaurant.

House specialties: Japanese, Chinese, and Vietnamese noodles served in styles from soups to salads to stir-fry; many vegetarian versions. From "Small Eats" section of menu: dim sum; vegetable spring rolls; gyoza filled with pork and scallions; blue mussels in spicy chile-garlic broth; crispy fried sesame ball with mochi rice around sweet bean paste. From "Big Eats" section: Japanese udon noodle soup with chicken, mushrooms, and bamboo shoots; spicy barbecue pork and thin Chinese egg noodles stir-fried.

Other recommendations: Charcoal-grilled steak salad with mixed greens and fresh vegetables; jumbo shrimp and mixed veggies with Thai panang coconut curry and rice.

Summary & comments: Chef Daniel Kelch opened this casual spot in Evanston with his wife and partner, Laura Van Dorf. The dishes are alive with flavor and served in a no-frills environment for very reasonable prices. It was an instant success, and the people keep returning. They've opened their second location in Hyde Park, another university community.

210

Lutnia Continental Cafe

Zone 2 North Central/O'Hare	Polish
5532 West Belmont Avenue	★★★½
(312) 282-5335	Inexpensive/Moderate
	Quality 87 Value C

Reservations:	Recommended
When to go:	Any time
Entree range:	$8.95–20
Payment:	Major credit cards
Service rating:	★★★★
Friendliness rating:	★★★★
Parking:	City garage
Bar:	Full service, including Polish vodka
Wine selection:	International, including Hungarian
Dress:	Casual and dressy, depending on occasion
Disabled access:	Yes
Customers:	Locals, some Europeans, businesspeople, couples
Lunch/Dinner:	Saturday and Sunday, 1–11 P.M.
Dinner:	Tuesday–Friday, 5–11 P.M.

Atmosphere/setting: Elegant and romantic: candelabras, red carpet, and musical instruments and paintings on walls; white tablecloths with fresh roses and candles.

House specialties: Duck breast flambé in orange sauce; Stroganoff tenderloin flambé served in pastry shell; stuffed boneless quail with cranberry sauce. Besides flambéed dishes, there is tableside service of certain salads, such as Caesar (for two). Traditional Polish dishes all get high marks: potato pancakes, pierogi (stuffed dumplings), and bigos (hunter's stew).

Other recommendations: Mushrooms stuffed with escargots and scallops; white borscht (tart, with sour cream and sausage); cucumber salad; spinach salad. Apple cake and flambéed blintzes; Polish old-fashioned coffee with honey liqueur.

Entertainment & amenities: Live piano nightly (romantic music).

Summary & comments: Gracious Polish couple, Chris and Evana Ruban, are owners; the recipes served here are Chris's. Dinner includes an appetizer, bread, soup, and a vegetable. The upscale food is very good, served on fine china by an attentive staff with European flair.

Honors/awards: *North Shore* magazine, Best Eastern European Restaurant.

Machu Picchu

Zone 1   North Side
5427 North Clark Street
(773) 769-0455

Peruvian	
★★	
Inexpensive	
Quality 74	Value B

Reservations:	Recommended on weekends and for large groups
When to go:	Any time
Entree range:	$6.95; for a 3-course dinner, $14.95
Payment:	VISA, MC
Service rating:	★★½
Friendliness rating:	★★★½
Parking:	Street
Bar:	BYOB
Wine selection:	BYOB
Dress:	Casual
Disabled access:	Yes
Customers:	Diverse; neighborhood residents, some ethnics
Dinner:	Tuesday–Saturday, 5:30 P.M.–? (whenever things simmer down)

Atmosphere/setting: Ethnic artifacts, including llama figurines; lovely Peruvian rugs on the walls; and posters of Machu Picchu, the famous ruins in Peru.

House specialties: Escabèche; papa rellena (stuffed potato); steak cucho (beef marinated in anticucho sauce).

Other recommendations: Shrimp soup with corn and soft dumplings; ocopa de camarones (octopus and shrimp); langosta (small spiny lobster) pâté; pork in peanut sauce; Peruvian flan.

Summary & comments: Owner Moises Asturrizaga introduced Peruvian cooking to Chicago more than 27 years ago at Piqueo. Today, he is cooking and managing the front of the house at this restaurant, which is intimate and charming. Service can be slow at times. Overall, the appetizers are better than the main courses. For example, the duck was a bit overcooked and chewy. The flan and Peruvian coffee are great, and you can't beat the prix-fixe dinner bargain. Bring your own wine or beer.

Maggiano's Little Italy

Zone 4   The Loop
516 North Clark Street
(312) 644-7700

Zone 8   Southern Suburbs
Route 83 at 22nd Street, Oak Brook Center, Oak Brook
(708) 368-0300

Zone 11   Northern Suburbs
175 Old Orchard, Skokie
(847) 933-9555

Italian	
★★★	
Moderate	
Quality 81	Value C

Reservations:	*Chicago and Skokie:* accepted; *Oak Brook:* for 6 or more
When to go:	Any time; weekends busiest
Entree range:	*Chicago:* $8.50–26.95; *Oak Brook:* $12–22; *Skokie:* $10–25
Payment:	Major credit cards
Service rating:	★★★
Friendliness rating:	★★★½
Parking:	*Chicago:* valet $4; *Oak Brook:* mall lot, valet $3.50; *Skokie:* mall lot
Bar:	Full service
Wine selection:	Italian; small by-the-glass selection
Dress:	Casual
Disabled access:	Yes; call first
Customers:	Mixed
Lunch:	*Chicago:* Monday–Saturday, 11:30 A.M.–2 P.M.
Dinner:	*Chicago:* Monday–Thursday, 5–10 P.M.; Friday, 5–11 P.M.; Saturday, 2–11 P.M.; Sunday, noon–10 P.M.
Lunch/Dinner:	*Oak Brook:* Monday–Thursday, 11:15 A.M.–10 P.M.; Friday and Saturday, 11:15 A.M.–11 P.M.; Sunday, noon–9 P.M. *Skokie:* Monday–Thursday, 11:15 A.M.–10 P.M.; Friday and Saturday, 11:15 A.M.–11 P.M.; Sunday, noon–10 P.M.

Atmosphere/setting: Re-creation of a New York City prewar "Little Italy" dinner house; simple decor in large dining room. The three locations are similar in style.

(continued)

Maggiano's Little Italy   *(continued)*

House specialties: Grand portions of classic Italian-style pasta, chicken, veal, and steaks; country-style rigatoni; whole roast chicken with rosemary and garlic.

Other recommendations: *Chicago:* garlic shrimp with shells; apple crostada. *Oak Brook:* angel hair al'arrabbiata; escarole with white beans and sausage. *Skokie:* roasted shells with vegetables; Maggiano salmon; chicken Parmesan; tiramisu.

Entertainment & amenities: Each has an outdoor cafe for summer dining with full menu available.

Summary & comments: The Maggiano's Little Italy concept of traditional Italian cuisine with generous portions was so successful that the restaurant expanded to several other locations, including Schaumburg (phone (847) 240-5600). Downtown, you enter the restaurant through the Corner Bakery, which provides the great variety of breads and some of the desserts served. The 190-seat restaurant has old-Italian charm and hearty food, and it encourages sharing by offering half- or small orders of many items. Family dinners are served for parties of eight or more. In the Chicago location, the salmon oreganato was very undercooked, but everything else was perfectly prepared and robustly seasoned. Call other locations for specifics. Menus are basically the same with the exception of several specialties. Private party facilities can handle large groups.

Mama Desta's Red Sea Ethiopian Restaurant

Zone 1   North Side
3216 North Clark Street
(773) 935-7561

Ethiopian	
★★★	
Inexpensive	
Quality 86	Value B

Reservations:	Recommended for 4 or more
When to go:	Weekdays after 7 P.M.
Entree range:	$6–8.50
Payment:	Major credit cards
Service rating:	★★★★
Friendliness rating:	★★★★
Parking:	Public lots nearby
Bar:	Full service
Wine selection:	Mixed; mostly African and American
Dress:	Casual
Disabled access:	Yes
Customers:	Diverse; locals, internationals, usually 20–30 somethings
Lunch:	Friday–Sunday, 11:30 A.M.–3 P.M.
Dinner:	Monday–Thursday, 3–11 P.M.; Friday–Sunday, 3 P.M.–midnight

Atmosphere/setting: Two cozy, candlelit rooms. Diners can sit at tables and in booths in one room, or at mesobes (large woven baskets that serve as tables; no chairs) in another.

House specialties: Lentil-vegetable soup; vegetable dishes: yemisir wat (spiced green lentils, pureed); kosta (chard cooked with onions, garlic, coriander, green peppers); gomen (green vegetables sautéed with garlic, cumin, green peppers); doro wat (chicken simmered in spicy berbere sauce); doro tibs (boneless chicken sautéed with onions, green pepper, tomato, and awaze, a mixture of spices and herbs with a red pepper base). Zizil wat (beef simmered in berbere); yasa tibs (mildly spicy boneless fish—great sautéed catfish). Red Sea cream (pudding).

Other recommendations: Yebeg tibs (lamb cubes sautéed with peppers, onions, spices, berbere sauce); Tej (an Ethiopian wine) is good with piquant food.

Summary & comments: The saucy dishes are hearty, wholesome, and colorful, and are served family style on classic injera, a tart sourdough pancake-like bread. To eat Ethiopian style, pick up one type of food with a piece of torn injera and eat them together. Ethiopians do not use knives and forks. The bread is both a plate and spoon.

Honors/awards: *Chicago Tribune*, three stars.

Mandar Inn

Zone 5   South Loop
2249 South Wentworth Avenue,
    Chinatown
(312) 842-4014

Chinese	
★★★½	
Inexpensive/Moderate	
Quality 88 Value C	

Reservations:	Accepted; recommended for weekends
When to go:	Any time
Entree range:	$6.50–28
Payment:	VISA, MC, AMEX, DC
Service rating:	★★★★
Friendliness rating:	★★★★★
Parking:	Community Chinatown lot offers 2 hours free with validation
Bar:	Full service
Wine selection:	Mostly Californian, some French, Asian; inexpensive; 8 by the glass
Dress:	Casual, some dressy
Disabled access:	No
Customers:	Locals, families, tourists; mix of Asians and non-Asians
Open:	Sunday–Thursday, 11:30 A.M.–9:30 P.M.; Friday and Saturday, 11:30 A.M.–10:30 P.M.

Atmosphere/setting: Recently redecorated in shades of rose and maroon with comfortable green banquettes. Linen napkins and artistic touches.

House specialties: Flaming appetizers (for two), including shrimp toast, egg roll, ribs, and barbecue pork; kwoh-te (pot stickers); empress chicken; Szechuan green beans (great texture and flavor); Szechuan eggplant; lobster and scallops volcano (dramatically served on a sizzling-hot platter).

Other recommendations: Orange chicken; moo shu pork; Peking duck (one day's advance notice required; compared to most other places, it's a bargain); beef in a nest.

Summary & comments: You can get more than Mandarin cuisine at this respected Chinatown restaurant. Szechuan, Hunan, and Cantonese cuisines are also offered on the extensive menu. If you're dining with a group, consider the fixed-price Mandar dinners listed for parties of two to eight; the larger the group, the more dishes can be sampled. Owner Sharolyn Jay develops the recipes and oversees the operation, and her daughter assists with the front of the house. Their graciousness prevails, and customers feel very welcome.

Honors/awards: Three stars from *Mobil Travel Guide*.

216

MANGO

Zone 3   Near North
712 North Clark
(312) 337-5440

American Bistro
★★★½
Inexpensive/Moderate

Quality 90   Value B

Reservations:	Yes
When to go:	Early, around 5 P.M., or late, after 8 P.M.
Entree range:	$9–17
Payment:	Major credit cards
Service rating:	★★★★½
Friendliness rating:	★★★★½
Parking:	Lot next door
Bar:	Full service
Wine selection:	Fairly extensive; about 13 by the glass; affordable
Dress:	Casual, chic, business
Disabled access:	Yes
Customers:	Business by day, a blend of all kinds by night
Lunch:	Monday–Friday, 11:30 A.M.–2 P.M.
Dinner:	Monday–Friday, 5–11 P.M.; Saturday, 5 P.M.–midnight; Sunday, 4–9 P.M.

Atmosphere/setting: Two dining rooms: an open, airy room on the main level and one in an intimate wine cellar with tile and brick. Smoke-free.

House specialties: Mediterranean fish soup; risotto with asparagus; duck prosciutto; chicken and walnut tart; freshwater shrimp wrapped in potato; tower of smoked salmon; Chiappetti's lamb shank; roasted pork chop with northern beans and sweet mustard sauce.

Other recommendations: Goat cheese brick; tomato cucumber salad; Amish-raised chicken with garlic potatoes and lemon-rosemary sauce. Wright's flourless chocolate cake; banana-chocolate mousse cake; honey-glazed pear in phyllo crust with frozen passion fruit parfait.

Summary & comments: Chef Steven Chiappetti's family owns Chiappetti Lamb Packing, so it's not surprising the finest quality of lamb is found on his menu and that he prepares it expertly. But fish and poultry don't take a backseat here, and neither do vegetarian items. An enjoyable dining experience without the guilt of breaking the budget. Chiappetti and his partner George Guggeis recently opened Grapes at 733 North Wells (phone (312) 943-4500) and Rhapsody at the new Symphony Center, 65 East Adams (phone (312) 786-9911).

Honors/awards: In 1996, Chiappetti was the only American chef to compete in the Bocuse d'Or, an international chef cook-off; he ranked in the top ten. In 1997, he was the only Chicago nominee for the James Beard Rising Star Chef of the Year.

Mantuano Mediterranean Table

	Mediterranean
	★★★★
Zone 3 Near North	Inexpensive/Moderate
455 City Front Plaza, NBC Tower	Quality 91 Value C
(312) 832-2600	

Reservations:	Recommended
When to go:	Any time; off-meal times for light fare and wine
Entree range:	$13.95–26.95
Payment:	All major credit cards except D
Service rating:	★★★★
Friendliness rating:	★★★★½
Parking:	Valet
Bar:	Full service
Wine selection:	Fairly extensive, especially Mediterranean; wine tastings; many by the glass
Dress:	Moderately casual, business
Disabled access:	Yes
Customers:	Couples, young professionals, tourists, families
Lunch:	Monday–Friday, 11:30 A.M.–2 P.M.
Dinner:	Monday–Saturday, 5–11 P.M.; Sunday, 5–9 P.M.

Atmosphere/setting: Spacious hallway with several cafe tables leads to a colorful retail market. Two artistic dining rooms available for private parties; the bar room with a view is more bustling than the romantic inner room.

House specialties: Flaming ouzo shrimp; grilled portobello with manchego, marinated tomatoes; Casbah platter; rotisserie half-chicken; Portuguese seafood Cataplana (shrimp, lobster, clams, mussels, calamari, octopus); Moroccan vegetable tagine; double-cut Greek lamb chops; gnocchi with mushrooms and Romano; double-decker garlic mushroom pizza. Flourless chocolate cake; gelatos and sorbets.

Other recommendations: Greektown grilled calamari and octopus; real San Daniele prosciutto; Mediterranean Caesar. Large herbaceous seafood ravioli with asparagus and cremini (special); baccalà alla Calabrese (southern Italian–style cod); brick oven–roasted salmon. Warm raisin and cinnamon bread pudding with walnut gelato and caramel sauce.

Entertainment & amenities: Retail market; views of Chicago's architecture.

Summary & comments: Chef Tony Mantuano and his wife, Cathy, who organizes the wine list, outgrew their location at Tuttaposto on North Franklin Street and moved downtown in spring 1997 in a joint venture with Taste America Restaurants, Inc. Although lamb is the meat of the Mediterranean, there is more beef on this menu. The chef adds unique creative touches.

Maple Tree Inn

Zone 8   Southern Suburbs
13301 South Western Avenue
(708) 388-3461

Cajun/Creole	
★★★½	
Inexpensive/Moderate	
Quality 88 Value B	

Reservations: For large groups
When to go: Any time; usually busier on weekends
Entree range: $10–19
Payment: VISA, MC, D
Service rating: ★★★
Friendliness rating: ★★★½
Parking: Street
Bar: Full service, including Southern Comfort, New
                       Orleans punch, and Dixie Jazz Light; 27 beers
                       on draft, all craft-brewed; reasonably priced
Wine selection: International; by the glass or bottle; affordable
Dress: Casual
Disabled access: Yes
Customers: Mixed
Dinner: Tuesday–Saturday, 5–10 P.M.

Atmosphere/setting: This second location resembles an old New Orleans building with a covered outdoor verandah. Three dining rooms (a full-length alligator and large flying frog hang from the ceiling of one room); two bars; a fun atmosphere.

House specialties: Alligator and oyster gumbo; hickory-buttered barbecued shrimp; Dixie stuffed pork chop; Creole jambalaya; pork chop with sun-dried sweet cherries and bourbon glaze; chocolate mud mousse in a pastry shell.

Other recommendations: Seafood okra gumbo; oyster assortment (Bienville, Rockefeller, deviled); jumbo blackened scallops; New Orleans boiled dinners (crawfish, shrimp, or blue crab); crawfish A-2-Fay; Miz Ruby's shrimp Creole (available occasionally); bread puddin' with Rebel Yell bourbon sauce.

Summary & comments: You don't find many places with alligator both on the menu and hanging from the ceiling. Maple Tree Inn is settled in its new location with a fun atmosphere; it has been serving Cajun/Creole cuisine in this general area for many years. There are blackened items, a big seafood platter, lots of sides, bread boats, and po' boys, in addition to a good selection of entrees. The whimsical menu is one of the most complete of its type. Former location was like a big house with a lovely outdoor patio under a maple tree—thus the restaurant name. Maple Tree Inn has lost its real tree, but it has become the tree of Cajun/Creole life in this area and is one of the best restaurants on the South Side.

Mei-Shung Chinese Restaurant

	Chinese/Taiwanese
	★★★½
Zone 1 North Side	Inexpensive
5511 North Broadway	Quality 87 Value B
(773) 728-5778	

Reservations:	Suggested on weekend evenings
When to go:	Any time; weekdays less busy
Entree range:	Lunch, $6.95–10.95; dinner, $6.95–14.95
Payment:	VISA, MC, AMEX, DC
Service rating:	★★★★
Friendliness rating:	★★★★★
Parking:	Street and church lot
Bar:	BYOB
Wine selection:	BYOB
Dress:	Casual
Disabled access:	Yes
Customers:	Diverse; locals, ethnics
Lunch:	Tuesday–Friday, 11:30 A.M.–3 P.M.; Saturday and Sunday, noon–3 P.M.
Dinner:	Tuesday–Thursday, 3–10 P.M.; Friday and Saturday, 3–11 P.M.; Sunday, 3–9:30 P.M.

Atmosphere/setting: Elegantly decorated storefront; lovely plants and flowers add warmth and color. Comfortable, white tablecloth atmosphere.

House specialties: Taiwanese menu: Mei-Shung scallops; prawn with spiced salt; pineapple with shrimp; steamed bean curd roll (ugly but very good); delicious chicken shreds salad; sliced chicken with sweet basil. Regular menu: pot stickers; three in a nest (chicken, shrimp, and scallops with vegetables); two color shrimp. Complimentary chocolate fortune cookies and jasmine tea.

Other recommendations: Taiwanese menu: dry-cooked string beans; red-cooked beef noodles; stir-fried crab. Regular menu: moo shu pork; Mongolian chicken; pressed duck; Peking duck (order 24 hours in advance; one of the best prices for this specialty at $19.95).

Summary & comments: A Chinese jewel on the mid-North Side, Mei-Shung has an ambitious menu of mostly Mandarin, but also Hunan, Szechuan, and Cantonese cuisine and an entire Taiwanese menu. Everything is expertly prepared and nicely served. Many creative items are not seen elsewhere. Staff and couple who own the restaurant are delightful and maintain fine quality here.

Honors/awards: Voted one of the 15 best restaurants in Chicago by *Chicago* magazine.

220

MIA FRANCESCA

Zone 1   North Side
3311 North Clark Street
(773) 281-3310

Italian	
★★★	
Inexpensive/Moderate	
Quality 82	Value B

Reservations: First-come, first-served basis
When to go: 5–5:15 P.M. or after 9 P.M.
Entree range: $7–14
Payment: VISA, MC
Service rating: ★★★
Friendliness rating: ★★★
Parking: Valet
Bar: Full service
Wine selection: Fairly extensive; all Italian; good by the glass
Dress: Casual, chic
Disabled access: Yes, including rest rooms
Customers: Yuppies, young local couples, groups
Dinner: Sunday–Thursday, 5–10 P.M.; Friday and Saturday,
                     5–11 P.M.

Atmosphere/setting: Simple interior; ceiling fans; paper-covered white tablecloths. It's well lit and noisy—the opposite of romantic. Outdoor garden.

House specialties: Pollo a la Romano; mussels and spicy pomodoro. Menu changes daily; robust thin-crust pizzas are made in individual serving size.

Other recommendations: Lusty al dente pastas such as spicy penne alla verdure (sautéed wild mushrooms, cherry tomatoes, vegetables, garlic); fish dishes such as salmon and calamari (both sautéed with roasted peppers, capers, lemon, garlic).

Summary & comments: Very popular with young professionals who enjoy noisy, crowded places. Although not for everyone, this place serves excellent food with full flavors, and the prices are reasonable for the quality. Chef-owner Scott Harris created a magical blend of robust Italian cooking, generous portions, affordable prices, and a handwritten (photocopied) daily menu at Mia Francesca on Clark Street in Chicago, and then he repeated the concept at two suburban locations: La Sorella di Francesca (18 West Jefferson Street, Naperville, phone (630) 961-2706), and Francesca's North (Northbrook Shopping Plaza, 1145 Church, Northbrook, phone (847) 559-0260). Harris opened a similar trattoria together with Joe and Ann Doppes—Francesca's on Taylor (1400 West Taylor, phone (312) 829-2828).

Honors/awards: Voted Best Italian Restaurant by the *Chicago Sun-Times.*

MichAEl JordAN's RestAURANT

Zone 3   Near North
500 North LaSalle Street
(312) 644-DUNK

<table>
<tr><td>American</td></tr>
<tr><td>★★★½</td></tr>
<tr><td>Inexpensive/Moderate</td></tr>
<tr><td>Quality 85   Value C</td></tr>
</table>

Reservations:	Lunch only
When to go:	1–3 P.M. and 5–7 P.M.
Entree range:	Lunch, $7.25–13.99; dinner, $8.99–35.99
Payment:	Major credit cards
Service rating:	★★★
Friendliness rating:	★★★½
Parking:	Valet or self-park across the street
Bar:	Full service with separate food menu
Wine selection:	3 dozen selections; mostly Californian; 14 by the glass
Dress:	Casual, sporty, dressy
Disabled access:	Yes
Customers:	Execs and staff, sports fans, couples, families
Lunch:	Every day, 11:30 A.M.–3 P.M.
Dinner:	Every day, 5–11 P.M.

Atmosphere/setting: Three-level site including a first-floor sports bar with video wall; a second-floor dining room with glass-enclosed private dining room for Jordan; and top-floor banquet facilities. Sporty, casual, and comfortable.

House specialties: MJ's crab-and-shrimp cake; barbecued rib sampler; cheddar cornbread; Caesar salad; fresh fish of the day; fried farm-raised catfish; Michael's barbecue chicken; MJ's pregame meal (23-ounce New York strip); rotisserie pork chop; grilled chicken breast; banana pudding (creamy, rather bland).

Other recommendations: New England clam chowder; Juanita's macaroni and cheese (rather bland). Hickory-smoked ribs; the hamburger (10-ounce); bowtie pasta with grilled chicken. Desserts vary.

Entertainment & amenities: Watching for Michael; souvenir shop.

Summary & comments: This place is jumping during the playoffs. Some of Michael's favorite foods and recipes from his wife, Juanita, are on the menu. Outdoor cafe serves bar menu items. The place is frequented by Bulls and fans, and it can be crowded at times. Food has improved, but the latest menu change includes mashed potatoes or fries with too many of the main courses; there are many other starch choices. It's still a challenge to get through to a human on the automated phone service, which has a recording of Michael calling your menu options.

Honors/awards: *Fitness* magazine three-star rating.

Mirabell Restaurant

Zone 2   North Central/O'Hare
3454 West Addison Avenue
(773) 463-1962

German/American
★★★½
Inexpensive/Moderate

Quality 88   Value B

Reservations:	Recommended Friday and Saturday
When to go:	Weekdays
Entree range:	$9.95–17.95
Payment:	All major credit cards
Service rating:	★★★★
Friendliness rating:	★★★★½
Parking:	K-Mart lot across the street is free
Bar:	Full service; schnapps and imported beers
Wine selection:	Fairly extensive; mostly German, several by the glass; affordable
Dress:	Casual
Disabled access:	Yes, including rest rooms
Customers:	Local and suburban
Lunch:	Monday–Saturday, 11:30 A.M.–3 P.M.
Dinner:	Monday–Thursday, 5–10 P.M.; Friday and Saturday, 5–10 P.M.

Atmosphere/setting: Charming German motif. Nonsmoking room behind the bar has spectacular murals; garden room has display of Hummel figurines (now a banquet room).

House specialties: Wiener schnitzel, any type; Kalbsteak Mirabell (sautéed veal); wiener roastbraten (New York sirloin steak); old-world classics (e.g., sauerbraten; Bavarian-style braised beef, dumplings).

Other recommendations: Veal fricassee; steaks (pepper steak, New York sirloin tips); Hungarian chicken paprikash; seafood platter; goulash soup; Hungarian goulash. Most entrees come with spaetzle or noodles and a vegetable.

Summary & comments: This establishment, tucked away in a neighborhood, has an old-world exterior with a colorful garden. Anita and chef Werner Heil, the owners, are attentive and caring, and their pride and joy in their work shows. They offer a large selection of ethnic specialties and several American selections. Prices here are in between the bargain Berghoff and the top-shelf Golden Ox. Mirabell seems to be even better today (their rating has gone up), although little has changed on the menu, including the reasonable prices.

Honors/awards: Only German restaurant listed in *Ochsner Pocket Guide to Finest Restaurants in the World.*

223

The Mity Nice Grill

Zone 3 Near North	American
835 North Michigan Avenue,	★★★½
Water Tower Place, Mezzanine	Inexpensive/Moderate
(312) 335-4745	Quality 86 Value C

Reservations: Recommended
When to go: Any time
Entree range: Lunch, $11–13; dinner, $13–18
Payment: All major credit cards
Service rating: ★★★½
Friendliness rating: ★★★★½
Parking: Water Tower underground garage (discount after
                       5 P.M.)
Bar: Full service
Wine selection: Good selection; several by the glass
Dress: Casual
Disabled access: Yes
Customers: Professionals, business, couples, families, shoppers,
                       tourists
Lunch/Dinner: Monday–Saturday, 11 A.M.–10 P.M.; Sunday,
                       11 A.M.–9 P.M.

Atmosphere/setting: Casual, neighborhood-style spot downtown. Classic
bar for people-watching. A 1940s-style decor with a 1990s grill.

House specialties: Grilled flatbreads; turkey steak; chicken, fish, and special
roasts of the day; steaks; abundant salads; pastas; great homemade crumble-topped
apple pie.

Other recommendations: Minute Chicken Terri D., a loyal customer's
favorite dish named for her; weekly specials based on seafood (in season), such as
Copper River salmon.

Summary & comments: Rich Melman, founder of Lettuce Entertain You
Enterprises, says, "Today, more than ever, we need to be nice to each other. That's
why I decided to call it Mity Nice Grill." It's a great concept for a restaurant in
our stressful world. The staff is mity nice here, and so is the food.

224

Mongolian Barbeque

Zone 1   North Side
3330 North Clark
(773) 325-2300
Zone 8   Southern Suburbs
221 South Washington, Naperville
(630) 428-0300

Asian grill
★★★
Inexpensive
Quality 85   Value B

Reservations:	Recommended for parties of 6 or more
When to go:	Avoid the peak hours between 7:30 and 9 P.M.
Entree range:	Lunch, $6.95; one-bowl stir-fry with one trip to soup and salad bar, $8.95; all-you-can-conquer Mongolian feast, $9.95 (lunch) or $11.95 (dinner). Children ages 12 and under, $4.95
Payment:	AMEX, D, MC, VISA
Service rating:	★★★½ (largely self-serve)
Friendliness rating:	★★★★½
Parking:	*North Side:* Public lot or street; *Naperville:* street and nearby free municipal lot
Bar:	Full service, including 6 taps, microbrewed and international beers
Wine selection:	Mostly American, some Italian; several by the glass, $3.95 and up
Dress:	Very casual
Disabled access:	Yes
Customers:	*North Side:* largely young professionals; *Naperville:* locals, families, older couples, young couples on dates
Open:	*North Side:* Monday–Thursday, 11:30 A.M.–10 P.M.; Friday and Saturday, 11:30 A.M.–11:30 P.M.; Sunday, noon–10 P.M. *Naperville:* Monday–Thursday, 11 A.M.–10:30 P.M.; Friday and Saturday, 11 A.M.–11:30 P.M.; Sunday, noon–10 P.M. Carryout available.

Atmosphere/setting: The spacious Naperville interior has contemporary and upbeat decor, but diners get a peek at the Mongolian culture and lifestyle of the past; there is a huge mural of a Mongolian village and a large *yurt,* a replica of a traditional Mongolian mud home, suspended over the six-foot grill. North Side location is smaller and seems more crowded but is basically similar. Not a relaxed or romantic setting.

(continued)

House specialties: Diners create their own stir-fry dishes by selecting from a variety of fresh meats, seafoods, vegetables, sauces, spices, and oils. They then take their creations to the grill where the cooks prepare the stir-fry. The restaurant's advice is to use only one meat at a time, at least two ladles of sauce, and one ladle of oil. Be careful not to overdo it with the spices. Reeses peanut-butter pie; Oreo cream pie (special).

Other recommendations: Cream of broccoli soup (daily special); salad from salad bar with garlic or blue cheese dressings. Snickers bar pie; caramel-apple cobbler.

Entertainment & amenities: Watching the grillers; hearing them clang the bell when they get a tip in the bowl.

Summary & comments: Mongolian Barbeque is very popular with the young crowd who like noise, entertainment, action, and interactive dining, especially because it's affordable. It's a fun date. Favorite recipes from customers might appear on the recipe cards displayed at the beginning of the ingredient bar. Those with big appetites can return to the salad and ingredient bars as many times as they wish. The service here is friendly and accommodating. The ingredients are fresh, the variety will please most people, and the sauces and oils are well defined and flavorful. The company's press-release description, "eatertainment in an atmosphere of controlled chaos," is apt.

MONTPARNASSE

	New French
	★★★★½
	Moderate/Expensive
	Quality 95 Value C

Zone 8   Southern Suburbs
200 East 5th Avenue, Naperville
(630) 961-8203

Reservations:	Recommended for lunch and dinner
When to go:	Weeknights
Entree range:	Lunch, $8–15; dinner, $23–33
Payment:	All major credit cards
Service rating:	★★★★½
Friendliness rating:	★★★★½
Parking:	Free lot
Bar:	None
Wine selection:	200 French and Californian, $18–100 a bottle; 8 by the glass, $3.50–7; great variety
Dress:	Jacket required, tie preferred
Disabled access:	Yes, entrance and rest rooms
Customers:	Mixed; couples, businesspeople, locals
Lunch:	Monday–Friday, 11:30 A.M.–2 P.M.
Dinner:	Monday–Saturday, 6–9:30 P.M.

Atmosphere/setting: Not the usual fine-dining French restaurant look; a rehabilitated factory boiler room with brick walls, soft lighting, and casual elegance.

House specialties: Galette of crab meat; grilled quail salad; sautéed John Dory (in season); pan-roasted Atlantic salmon; grilled breast of Canadian pheasant; crème brûlée; lemon custard tart; ice creams and sorbets; macaronade of chocolate; mango and cashew tart.

Other recommendations: Roasted forelle pear and Roquefort salad; cassoulet of shrimp, corn, chanterelles, bacon; ramekin d'escargots Chablisienne; French onion soup gratinée; roasted rack of lamb carved tableside; grilled noisette of venison on foie gras; hot apple tart, vanilla ice cream; bittersweet chocolate terrine, vanilla ice cream; charlotte of peaches, hazelnuts, and raspberries.

Summary & comments: Jean-Paul Eskenazi, an alum of Le Français, opened this fine-dining French restaurant in 1988 before the area's population explosion. New executive chef Rosen do Santillanes (Franco) continues the style here in preparing creative, contemporary French cooking with substantial daily specials. Fifth Avenue Bistro upstairs has a more casual menu that's available downstairs for lunch. This is one of the best restaurants in the southwestern suburbs.

Honors/awards: DiRoNA Award 1993; *Fox Valley Villages 60504,* five stars.

Morton's of Chicago

	Steak
	★★★★
	Expensive
	Quality 93 Value C

Zone 3   Near North
1050 North State Street
(312) 266-4820

Zone 8   Southern Suburbs
One Westbrook Corporate Center,
   22nd Street and Wolf Road, Westchester
(708) 562-7000

Zone 2   North Central/O'Hare
9525 West Bryn Mawr Avenue, Rosemont
(847) 678-5155

Reservations:	Suggested
When to go:	Any time
Entree range:	$17–30
Payment:	All major credit cards
Service rating:	★★★★½
Friendliness rating:	★★★★½
Parking:	*Rosemont and Westchester:* free; call downtown location for details
Bar:	Full service; 40 varieties of martini
Wine selection:	Extensive, international; about 12 by the glass, from $5.50; bottles, from $22 but most $30–80
Dress:	Jacket preferred, tie optional; dressy casual
Disabled access:	Yes, for all locations
Customers:	Locals, businesspeople, couples, travelers; downtown, also celebrities
Lunch:	*Westchester:* Monday–Friday, 11:30 A.M.–2:30 P.M.
Dinner:	Monday–Saturday, 5:30–11 P.M.; Sunday, 5–10 P.M.

Atmosphere/setting: Comfortable and well appointed with a club atmosphere. Suburban places are quieter and more intimate; downtown is bigger and more crowded.

House specialties: 24-ounce porterhouse, also available as a 3-pound double; whole baked Maine lobster; farm-raised salmon; black bean soup; steamed asparagus with hollandaise.

Other recommendations: Sicilian veal chop; domestic rib lamb chops; Cockenoe oysters on the half shell; Caesar salad; sautéed fresh spinach and mushrooms; baked Idaho potato; Godiva hot chocolate cake; soufflé for two—chocolate, Grand Marnier, or lemon.

(continued)

MORTON'S of CHICAGO   *(continued)*

Entertainment & amenities: Watching the show-and-tell performance by the waiters with the display cart of huge cuts of steaks, chops, live lobsters, and other raw ingredients.

Summary & comments: Many steak connoisseurs stake their claim in Morton's as their favorite place for porterhouse or certain other cuts. The management maintains high quality, and the kitchen prepares the meat properly to order. The diner pays dearly for both. The $29 steak gets only a garnish; everything else must be ordered à la carte, as is the case in many steak restaurants. Clockwork service makes everything move along at a great pace. Needs are anticipated by the professional servers. A great place for business entertaining.

Honors/awards: *Restaurant Business* magazine ranks it among the top 50 growth restaurant chains in the United States.

MRS. PARK'S TAVERN

Zone 3 Near North	Inventive American
198 East Delaware Place	★★★½
(312) 280-8882	Inexpensive/Moderate
	Quality 89 Value C

Reservations:	Recommended
When to go:	Any time, but weekends are busier
Entree range:	$13–28.50
Payment:	All major credit cards
Service rating:	★★★★
Friendliness rating:	★★★½
Parking:	Valet
Bar:	Full service
Wine selection:	Extensive, international; about 250 full-bottle wines, starting at $18; 15–18 half-bottles, starting at $7; several by the glass, starting at $5.25
Dress:	Casual
Disabled access:	Yes
Customers:	Gold Coast residents, tourists, and celebrities, including Julia Roberts and Dennis Rodman
Breakfast:	Every day, 7–10:30 A.M.
Lunch/Dinner:	Every day, 11:30–2 A.M.

Atmosphere/setting: Unique, fascinating interior; the tavern's flag motif is enhanced with a full-wall American flag mural, a monumental folk-art American flag sculpture suspended in one of the dining rooms, a star-studded back bar, and a bounty of whimsical American folk art that makes for interesting browsing when customers take a break from eating.

House specialties: Spice-glazed crab cakes; barbecued chicken and jack cheese dumplings; Phil's Gold Coast chips with goat cheese fondue; tuna won ton, deep fried; pastrami salmon on rye bagel; ditali with tomato, basil, and parmesan; roasted chile-rubbed half chicken; chili-oil whipped potatoes; mushroom hash; Mrs. Park's crème brûlée.

Other recommendations: Duck liver pâté; spinach salad with ratatouille and goat cheese parfait; Grace Ann's cheddar cheese meat loaf. Warm java pudding; peanut-butter crunch; tempting house-made ice creams and sorbets.

Summary & comments: The mix of informal ambiance, appealing American bistro menu, and professional service at moderate prices make Mrs. Park's Tavern ideal for casual dining. Restaurant's savvy wine list and well-informed servers allow diners to match appropriate wines with their orders. Some excellent wine promotions are held here.

Mykonos

	Greek
Zone 11 Northern Suburbs	★★★½
8660 Golf Road, Niles	Inexpensive/Moderate
(847) 296-6777	Quality 92 Value B

Reservations:	Recommended for 4 or more
When to go:	Weekdays; avoid weekend evenings
Entree range:	$6–15
Payment:	Major credit cards except DC
Service rating:	★★★★½
Friendliness rating:	★★★★½
Parking:	Valet in own lot
Bar:	Full service
Wine selection:	Mostly Greek, with about 24 selections; several ordinary Californian
Dress:	Casual
Disabled access:	Yes, including rest rooms
Customers:	Diverse; Greek Americans
Lunch/Dinner:	Sunday–Thursday, 11 A.M.–11 P.M.; Friday and Saturday, 11 A.M.–midnight

Atmosphere/setting: Decorated in blue and white; charming interior resembles a cafe on the picturesque "white" island it's named for. Also a beautiful outdoor cafe.

House specialties: Broiled Florida red snapper, Greek-style with lemon juice and oregano (filleted by server on request); shrimp saganaki ala Mykonos (baked with tomato sauce, onions, peppers, and feta); tender spring lamb with artichokes in egg-lemon sauce; individual giouvetsi ala Mykonos (baked lamb with pasta and cheese); chicken breast ala Dimitri (sautéed in white wine, lemon, and spices); avgolemono soup; baby octopus vinaigrette. Baklava, rice pudding, and crema caramele. Specials.

Other recommendations: Homemade loukaniko (Greek sausage with orange peel); souvlaki (shish kebab of marinated pork tenderloin); broiled lamb chops; house-made gyros with yogurt sauce; light, custardy galaktoboureko and nougatina desserts.

Summary & comments: This suburban restaurant is far more serene than the lively spots in Greektown, and the cooking is distinctive. Owner-chef Dimitri has a penchant for seafood, which is exemplified in his appealing preparations of fresh fish and his never-fail treatment for tender baby octopus. He cares about all the details, so his restaurant is well managed. Dining here is always uplifting.

N. N. SMOKEHOUSE

Zone 1   North Side
1465–1467 West Irving Park Road
(773) TNT-4700

Barbecue/Filipino
★★★
Inexpensive/Moderate
Quality 82   Value B

Reservations:	Not accepted
When to go:	Any time; busy during mealtimes
Entree range:	$5.85–14.95
Payment:	Major credit cards
Service rating:	★★★½
Friendliness rating:	★★★★½
Parking:	Street, lot in back
Bar:	BYOB
Wine selection:	None
Dress:	Casual
Disabled access:	Yes
Customers:	Young professionals, locals, suburbanites
Lunch/Dinner:	Tuesday–Thursday, 11:30 A.M.–10 P.M.; Friday, 11:30 A.M.–11 P.M.; Saturday, noon–11 P.M.; Sunday, noon –9 P.M.

Atmosphere/setting: Comfortable, very casual place with hand-painted mural. Blues background music and black-and-white photos of blues musicians.

House specialties: Award-winning, tender barbecue-smoked ribs; pulled Memphis pork; barbecue half-chicken dinner; house platter from the smoker (beef brisket, ribs, pulled pork, and turkey); pancit noodles (Filipino), either vegetarian or meat.

Other recommendations: Spicy seafood jambalaya; famous Mediterranean Salad (grilled breast of chicken on romaine with feta, chopped tomatoes, and Dijon dressing); Mississippi catfish sandwich (steaks); Mother Mildred's velvety sweet potato pie; pecan pie.

Summary & comments: The barbecue sauce is a 100-plus-year-old recipe, according to owner Larry Tucker, who runs this bustling restaurant and a great catering business with his wife, Nida. His father lived for several years in the Philippines, Nida's homeland—thus the Filipino touches. Tucker is expanding N. N. Smokehouse and is renovating the space next door at press time. He recently installed a new kitchen. Several VIPs, including a famous judge who married the couple in October 1996, frequent this place for their barbecue fix.

Honors/awards: Won Illinois State Fair Number One Pork Ribs, August 1997.

NHU HOA CAFE

Zone 1   North Side
1020 West Argyle
(773) 878-0618

Vietnamese and Laotian
★★★½
Inexpensive/Moderate
Quality 89   Value B

Reservations: Yes
When to go: Wednesday and Thursday are less busy
Entree range: $6.95–18.95
Payment: All major credit cards
Service rating: ★★½
Friendliness rating: ★★★
Parking: Street or lot 3 blocks away
Bar: Limited selection of mixed drinks and beers
Wine selection: Very small, domestic; from $2.75 a glass and $14 a
                         bottle
Dress: Casual
Disabled access: Yes
Customers: Ethnically diverse; locals, businesspeople, families
Lunch/Dinner: Every day, 11:30 A.M.–10 P.M.

Atmosphere/setting: Two lion statues at the front door are believed to protect guests who enter. Vietnamese videos are shown in the back room.

House specialties: Banh xeo (Vietnamese pancakes with bean sprouts, pork, shrimp); banh cuon cha lua (steamed rice paper rolled with ground pork); com ga xao xa ot (steamed rice with spicy chicken); goi cuon (shrimp, pork, and vegetables rolled in rice paper); tom cuon chien (Vietnamese shrimp rolls); goi tom thit (a mixed vegetable salad with shrimp and pork); ca kho to (catfish simmered in a clay pot); ga xao xa ot (stir-fried chicken with lemongrass); keng som kung (Laotian tangy soup with shrimp, tomatoes, mushrooms, and lemongrass); Laotian garlic shrimp stir-fried with cucumber and broccoli; hot and sour shrimp stir-fried with ginger, garlic, onions, peppers, and steamed broccoli; vit tay cam (stewed roast duck and quail egg); tamarind duck (boneless roast duck stir-fried with mixed vegetables).

Other recommendations: Pho tai (beef with rice noodle soup); bun thit heo nuong cha gio (rice noodles with grilled pork and egg roll); com bi suon cha (steamed rice with grilled pork chops, minced pork pie, and egg); mi xao tom (crispy fried or soft egg noodles with shrimp and vegetables); hu tieu xao tom thit (pan-fried rice noodles with shrimp and barbecue pork); cha gio (egg rolls); sup mang cua (crab meat asparagus soup); ca hong chien nuoc mam toi ot (crispy,

(continued)

233

fried whole red snapper); bo xao xa ot (stir-fried beef with lemongrass); satay (choice of chicken, beef, or pork marinated in Laotian herbs served with peanut sauce and cucumber salad); papaya salad; spicy seafood stir-fried with bamboo shoot, red and green peppers, and peanuts in a red curry sauce; som varn (stir-fried tomatoes, onions, cucumbers, red and green peppers, and pineapple in a delicious sweet-and-sour sauce); Laos noodles (stir-fried noodles with shrimp, chicken, egg, green onions, and bean sprouts topped with ground peanut and chilies); Laos special fried rice with onions, tomatoes, bean sprouts, and cucumber topped with egg, served with your choice of beef, chicken, pork, shrimp, squid, mussels, or mixed seafood; and vegetable rainbow (stir-fried assorted vegetables in a light brown sauce).

Entertainment & amenities: One dining room is equipped with a video projector that plays Vietnamese music videos and concerts.

Summary & comments: The lengthy menu has over 206 items, with a nice variety of Vietnamese and Laotian dishes. Something for everyone. At press time, the owner was planning to open a Cambodian/Laotian/Vietnamese restaurant, Indochine.

Honors/awards: Positive reviews from local newspapers, including the *Chicago Tribune* and the *Chicago Sun-Times*.

Nick's FishMARKET

Zone 4   The Loop
One First National Plaza, Monroe Street
    at Dearborn Street
(312) 621-0200

Zone 2   North Central/O'Hare
10275 West Higgins Road, O'Hare International Center, Rosemont
(708) 298-8200

	Seafood
	★★★★
	Moderate/Expensive
	Quality 95 Value D

Reservations:	Recommended
When to go:	Weekdays
Entree range:	$14–46.50
Payment:	All major credit cards
Service rating:	★★★★½
Friendliness rating:	★★★★½
Parking:	Lot (Rosemont)
Bar:	Full service
Wine selection:	International; several by the glass; priccy
Dress:	Jacket suggested; collared shirt or sweater required
Disabled access:	Yes
Customers:	Largely businesspeople, professionals, couples
Lunch:	*Downtown:* Monday–Friday, 11:30 A.M.–3 P.M.
Dinner:	*Downtown:* Monday–Thursday, 5:30–11 P.M.; Friday and Saturday, 5:30 P.M.–midnight; *Rosemont:* Sunday–Thursday, 6–10 P.M.; Friday and Saturday, 6–11 P.M.

Atmosphere/setting: Lovely aquariums and plush, club-like setting; tuxedoed waiters. Interior redesign and relocation across the plaza planned for 1998.

House specialties: Grilled or sautéed Hawaiian or other fresh fish; abalone; classic house salad with tiny shrimp; black and blue ahi served ultra rare and cold.

Other recommendations: Lobster bisque; Atlantic swordfish with soy mustard; Maine lobster; teriyaki fish preparations; steaks; chops; pastas.

Entertainment & amenities: Live music at both locations; call for specifics.

Summary & comments: Top-quality seafood restaurant with pristinely fresh catches. Well-known owner-founder Nick Nicholas owns several restaurants. Service is proficient and gracious, geared to expense-account business clientele. Steer toward simple preparations, since some of the more complex treatments don't enhance the delicate fresh seafood.

OCEANIQUE

Zone 11   Northern Suburbs
505 Main Street, Evanston
(847) 864-3435

French/American
★★★½
Moderate/Expensive

Quality 88   Value C

Reservations:	Recommended for weekdays, required for Saturday
When to go:	Avoid weekends; 6:30–8:30 P.M.
Entree range:	$13.95–28.95
Payment:	All major credit cards
Service rating:	★★★½
Friendliness rating:	★★★★
Parking:	Metered street
Bar:	Full service, including Bombay martinis
Wine selection:	Award-winning wine and reserve wine lists; 500 whites and reds, about 100 reserves; 10 by the glass, $5.75–12; bottles, $24–900; reserve bottles, $85–900
Dress:	Dressy casual, no jacket or tie required
Disabled access:	Yes, entrance and rest room
Customers:	North Shore locals, couples, professors from Northwestern University
Dinner:	Monday–Thursday, 5:30–9:30 P.M.; Friday and Saturday, 5:30–10 P.M.

Atmosphere/setting: Spanish-style building; quaint French decor, tile floor from the 1900s, white tablecloths, mahogany chairs. Two separate dining rooms.

House specialties: Roasted beet salad served warm with grilled scallops and tarragon; bouillabaisse Oceanique with salmon, bass, shrimp, squid, mussels, clams, and aïoli; summer squash, mushrooms, tomatoes, basil, garlic, and cream; skate sauté. Seasonal fish changes daily. Pastries, ice cream, sorbets.

Other recommendations: Chilled Maine lobster; farfalle pasta tossed with grilled eggplant; sautéed Lake Superior whitefish; roast Australian rack of lamb; pan-roasted sirloin of beef.

Summary & comments: The name says it for this chef-owned restaurant—French seafood. Local ingredients are used, and there are many Italian, Spanish, and Asian influences in the cooking. New rest rooms and air-conditioning system; 99 percent smoke-free; smokers must make reservations and specify that they're smokers. Chef Mark Grosz is a Jean Banchet disciple and demonstrates his fine training and talent here.

Honors/awards: *Wine Spectator* Award of Excellence, 1994–96.

P. S. Bangkok

Zone 1   North Side
3345 North Clark Street
(312) 871-7777

Thai
★★★
Inexpensive

Quality 84   Value A

Reservations:	Recommended on weekends
When to go:	Any time, but especially Sunday brunch
Entree range:	$5.95–9.95; market price for some dishes
Payment:	VISA, MC, AMEX, D, DC
Service rating:	★★★½
Friendliness rating:	★★★½
Parking:	Street
Bar:	Beer and wine only
Wine selection:	Fairly extensive list of 30 types
Dress:	Casual
Disabled access:	Yes, except no ramps; several steps
Customers:	Locals, couples, some families, ethnics
Brunch:	Sunday, 11:30 A.M.–4 P.M.
Lunch/Dinner:	Sunday–Thursday, 11:30 A.M.–10 P.M.; Friday and Saturday, 11:30 A.M.– 11:30 P.M.

Atmosphere/setting: Large, ornately decorated room filled with plants, Thai antiques, art, and other artifacts. A large Thai musical instrument, a lanat, is displayed on the windowsill, and there is an unobtrusive Buddhist shrine. The Thai garden party room has a waterfall, pond, and private bar.

House specialties: Banana blossom salad (with shrimp, chicken, peanuts, roasted garlic, and coconut); steamed fish with fresh Thai herbs; stuffed Pacific langoustine.

Other recommendations: Love Me Tender duck over crispy rice noodles with Thai sauce; lotus blossom curry with seafood; Thai-style chicken cashew. From the special menu: buttercup squash–curry patty (appetizer); Siamese red curry noodle; house-made Thai cantaloupe cake.

Summary & comments: The authentic menu lists 115 items plus many specials, and it is as ambitious and elaborate as the cooking. Pay attention to dishes listing hot chilies or having "fiery" in the title; they may be incendiary, although some are described as mild. The restaurant honors requests for substitutions. If you are a die-hard Thai-food fan, go to the Sunday brunch, which features more than 100 vegetarian, seafood, and meat dishes. Service is courteous and efficient. Catering, takeout, and delivery are available.

Palm Restaurant

Zone 4 The Loop	Steak/Seafood
Swissôtel Chicago,	★★★½
323 East Wacker Drive	Moderate/Expensive
(312) 616-1000	Quality 87 Value C

Reservations:	Recommended
When to go:	Any time; busy at peak lunch and dinner hours
Entree range:	Lunch, $8–14; dinner, $18–36
Payment:	VISA, MC, AMEX, DC
Service rating:	★★★★½
Friendliness rating:	★★★★½
Parking:	Valet, $7; nearby lot
Bar:	Full service; handsome bar area
Wine selection:	Fairly extensive; 92 by the bottle, $21–210; 12 by the glass
Dress:	Casual to dressy
Disabled access:	Yes
Customers:	Diverse; locals, tourists, celebrities
Lunch/Dinner:	Every day, 11:30 A.M.–11 P.M.

Atmosphere/setting: The new, spacious setting offers some dining areas with lakefront views. The Wall of Fame features caricatures of VIPs. Great views of Navy Pier from the second level. Outdoor patio dining in summer.

House specialties: Jumbo Nova Scotia lobsters, three pounds and more; steaks: prime-aged New York sirloin, steak à la Stone, filet mignon, porterhouse, prime rib; Gigi salad; good selection of sides; lobster club, a towering layered bun sandwich of lobster salad. Excellent desserts: Key lime pie, chocolate pecan pie.

Other recommendations: Linguine with red or white clam sauce; pasta of the day; veal in various styles; salads. Daily lunch specials. They are best known for New York cheesecake (which, unfortunately, was once served still slightly frozen); deep-dish apple cobbler.

Entertainment & amenities: Perusing the "Wall of Fame."

Summary & comments: The luxurious Swissôtel Chicago became the new site of the Palm in fall 1996 after a 14-month hiatus. Formerly at the Mayfair Regent Hotel for 15 years, the restaurant was forced to move when the hotel was sold. With a more beautiful setting overlooking the lakefront and almost double the space, the new Palm has retained its menu and veteran staff. Known for its spirited service, this restaurant is also fun and entertaining because of the caricatures on the walls and characters at the tables. Other locations include Los Angeles, Houston, Atlanta, Boston, and Mexico City.

PAMPANGA RESTAURANT

Zone 1   North Side
6407 North Caldwell Avenue
(773) 763-1781

Filipino
★★½
Inexpensive
Quality 77   Value B

Reservations:	Recommended
When to go:	4–7 P.M.
Entree range:	$5.95–9.95
Payment:	VISA, MC
Service rating:	★★★
Friendliness rating:	★★★★
Parking:	Street in front; parking also in back of restaurant
Bar:	BYOB
Wine selection:	BYOB
Dress:	Casual
Disabled access:	Yes
Customers:	Mixed; locals, Filipinos, couples, businesspeople
Lunch/Dinner:	Monday, 3–8:30 P.M.; Wednesday–Sunday, 11:30 A.M.–8:30 P.M.

Atmosphere/setting: Colorful, tropical decor. Charming artifacts from the Philippines, including wood carvings and paintings; intimate.

House specialties: Lumpia frito (traditional egg roll); lumpianitas (bite-size spring rolls); ukoy (fritters of shredded vegetables topped with shrimp); pancit bihon guisado (rice noodles stir-fried with vegetables and with—or without—pork, fish ball, sausage, and shrimp); Pampanga's fried rice; tocino (Pampanga's homemade, cured, sliced pork).

Other recommendations: Pork or chicken adobo; beef or goat kalderetang. Wonderful dessert (not on menu) is a coconut rice-flour cake baked in a banana leaf. Calamansi (Filipino lemonade—very refreshing); Filipino tea is oolong, brewed with toasted rice.

Summary & comments: Pampanga is a province near Manila in the near-north section of the Philippine Islands. The owner started this restaurant in 1977, and it's evident there's a lot of family caring and a loyal clientele. Although Tagalag is the national language, Filipinos speak Spanish since the islands were under Spanish rule for about 500 years. There's Spanish influence in the cuisine, but many items are distinctively Filipino, utilizing tropical fruits and vegetables, seafood, and pork. One of the few places serving Filipino food.

PANE CALDO

Zone 3　Near North	Northern Italian
72 East Walton Street	★★★½
(312) 649-0055	Moderate/Very Expensive
	Quality 89　Value D

Reservations:	Recommended
When to go:	Lunch or early dinner, 5–6 P.M.
Entree range:	$9.50–19.95
Payment:	VISA, MC, AMEX
Service rating:	★★★★
Friendliness rating:	★★★★
Parking:	Valet; reduced rate parking at 100 East Walton
Bar:	Full service; grappas and sambuca selections
Wine selection:	Extensive; 25 by the glass; mostly Italian; riserva list
Dress:	Upscale casual
Disabled access:	Yes
Customers:	Businesspeople, couples, shoppers, tourists
Lunch:	Every day, 11:30 A.M.–2:30 P.M.
Dinner:	Sunday–Thursday, 5–10 P.M.; Friday and Saturday, 5–11 P.M.

Atmosphere/setting: Intimate trattoria-style setting. Sophisticated, soft lighting; original paintings; attractive floral arrangements.

House specialties: Antipasti: grilled calamari with scampi in aromatic oil; mille foglie di pollo (layers of chicken, prosciutto, collard greens, and mozzarella). Tortelloni di zucchini al Parmigiano; ravioli stuffed with lobster in creamy saffron sauce.

Other recommendations: Antipasti: duck and chicken dumplings with hyssope sauce. Primi: porcini mushroom risotto. Secondi: roasted baby lamb chops with sweet garlic and mustard-rosemary sauce; roasted veal chop stuffed with Gorgonzola, with changing sauces (a special). Daily specials, with four appetizers and six fishes (e.g., seared salmon with asparagus and cauliflower fricasee in mustard grain sauce).

Entertainment & amenities: On-premises bakery.

Summary & comments: Pane Caldo, "warm bread" in Italian, is an appropriate name since there's an ample supply from the bakery. Delicious focaccia and rosemary bread are standouts. Additional bonuses include an intermezzo apple-Armagnac sorbetto and chocolate truffles and sweets at the finish. Owner Antoine Cedicci uses edible wild herbs in the cooking. Chef Maurice Bonhomme produces at least six vegetarian items using organic ingredients. The pâtisserie offers a "dolci" menu with about two dozen temptations (e.g., peach tarte Tatin and choco-misu).

Honors/awards: Voted most authentic Italian cuisine by *Chicago* magazine, 1994.

PAPAGUS GREEK TAVERNA

Zone 3   Near North
Embassy Suites Hotel,
    620 North State Street
(312) 642-8450

Zone 6   South Central/Midway
270 Oakbrook Center, Oakbrook
(630) 472-9800

Greek	
★★★½	
Moderate	
Quality 90	Value C

Reservations:	Recommended
When to go:	Any time for mezedes (little plates); lunch or dinner
Entree range:	$7–25
Payment:	Major credit cards
Service rating:	★★★★
Friendliness rating:	★★★½
Parking:	Valet, $6 for 3 hours; validated parking in Embassy Suites underground lot, Monday–Friday; free mall lot at Oakbrook
Bar:	Full service
Wine selection:	Expansive; mostly Greek
Dress:	Casual to dressy
Disabled access:	Yes
Customers:	Mixed; locals, travelers, businesspeople
Lunch/Dinner:	Monday–Thursday, 11:30 A.M.–10 P.M.; Friday, 11:30 A.M.–midnight; Saturday, noon–midnight; Sunday, noon–10 P.M.

Atmosphere/setting: Comfortable, rustic, old world–style taverna.

House specialties: Mezedes (appetizers) are the centerpiece here: taramosalata (cod or lobster roe salad); spanikopita (spinach pie); saganaki (flambéed cheese); grilled garlic-marinated shrimp. Main courses: Greek roast chicken; spicy lamb and beef meatballs; braised lamb with orzo.

Other recommendations: Roasted eggplant spread; marinated chargrilled octopus; olive bread salad; char-grilled skewer of swordfish.

Summary & comments: Some of the best light renditions of traditional Greek cuisine, served in a colorful, rustic setting. Chef uses creative license on many items. This may not be in Greektown, but it has brought a good taste of Greece to the downtown area. Even the earlier skeptics have conceded that this place knows its stuff. Greek family-style feast is available.

Honors/awards: *Chicago Tribune,* Best Greek Restaurant in Chicago.

Pappagallo's

Zone 11   Northern Suburbs
246 Greenbay Road, Highwood
(847) 432-6663

Italian/American
★★★
Inexpensive/Moderate
Quality 84   Value B

Reservations: Recommended
When to go: During the week
Entree range: $9.95–20.95
Payment: All major credit cards
Service rating: ★★★½
Friendliness rating: ★★★½
Parking: Lot
Bar: Full service
Wine selection: Extensive; mostly Italian
Dress: Casual
Disabled access: Yes
Customers: Locals, businesspeople, couples
Lunch: Monday–Friday, 11 A.M.–3 P.M.
Dinner: Monday–Thursday, 4–10 P.M.; Friday and Saturday,
                      4–11 P.M.; Sunday, 4–9 P.M.

Atmosphere/setting: Bright and cozy; green and white tablecloths; canopied front porch for al fresco summer dining.

House specialties: Mama Lena's tortellacci (with three cheeses and spinach—great al forno); award-winning artichoke fritters; veal Pappagallo (scaloppine sautéed with lemon, butter, artichokes, and asparagus); grilled Norwegian salmon; grilled calamari; steak al forno; grilled swordfish; pollo Maria (a "heart smart" item of angel hair pasta with grilled chicken). Chocolate dream dessert; camparama dessert (almond cookie with amaretto, hazelnut whipped cream, and a chocolate shell).

Other recommendations: Bruschetta alla Pappagallo; fried calamari; grilled baby lamb chops; linguine alla Pappagallo (sautéed shrimp and scallops with sun-dried tomatoes, Italian mushrooms tossed with pesto, and black and white linguine); spicy chicken Vesuvio; grilled eggplant topped with marinara sauce ("heart smart"). Spumoni; tiramisu.

Summary & comments: Formerly Bertucci's, the family name. The restaurant, seven years old in 1997, has otherwise remained the same—known for its steak and seafood with Italian specialties. They now offer home catering, according to manager Bruce Bertucci, who is usually around to greet guests.

242

Park Avenue Cafe

Zone 3   Near North
199 East Walton Place
(312) 944-4414

New American
★★★★½
Moderate/Expensive

Quality 94   Value C

Reservations:	Recommended
When to go:	Avoid peak mealtimes without a reservation
Entree range:	$19.50–28.50; tasting menu, $52
Payment:	AMEX, VISA, MC, D, DC
Service rating:	★★★★½
Friendliness rating:	★★★★½
Parking:	Valet
Bar:	Full service
Wine selection:	Ambitious list, mostly American; $18–392 a bottle; extensive list of ports, single-malts, and cognacs
Dress:	Casual; no T-shirts or cutoffs
Disabled access:	Yes
Customers:	Locals, travelers, professionals, couples, singles
Brunch:	Sunday, 10:30 A.M.–2 P.M.
Dinner:	Monday–Saturday, 5–11 P.M.; Sunday, 5–10 P.M.

Atmosphere/setting: Country contemporary design; open kitchen; bake shop; warm lighting. Two private dining rooms are available.

House specialties: Menu changes daily according to seasonal ingredients. Examples include chef David Burke's (Park Avenue Cafe, New York) trademarked Swordfish Chop (a fillet cleverly molded around a chop bone); his trademarked pastrami salmon; salmon tartare and house-smoked salmon; hand-rolled cavatelli with wild mushrooms; seared scallops with oxtail stew; grilled loin of lamb, Gorgonzola ravioli, and lamb sausage. The unique Chocolate Cube is a fun toylike dessert.

Other recommendations: Chestnut soup with smoked goose confit; bouillabaisse with snapper, shrimp, and littleneck clams. Napoleon of pears with goat cheese ice cream.

Summary & comments: Chef John Hogan, formerly of Kiki's Bistro, made a smooth transition to American bistro fare. The restaurant, along with Mrs. Park's Tavern downstairs (see profile), has frequent wine promotions to showcase its extensive list. This restaurant introduced the first American dim sum brunch, with more than 50 tasting portions of the restaurant's specialties as well as Asian items.

Honors/awards: AAA, four diamonds; *Chicago Tribune,* three stars; John Hogan is member of Chef 2,000 (top 2,000 chefs in North America).

PARS COVE

	Persian
Zone 1 North Side	★★★½
435 West Diversey Parkway	Inexpensive
(773) 549-1515	Quality 89 Value B

Reservations:	Recommended
When to go:	Any time
Entree range:	$5.95–9.95
Payment:	All major credit cards
Service rating:	★★★½
Friendliness rating:	★★★★½
Parking:	Limited parking behind restaurant; street and nearby garage
Bar:	Full service
Wine selection:	International; several by the glass
Dress:	Varied; can range from casual to formal
Disabled access:	No, but willing to help; 4 steps down
Customers:	Diverse; businesspeople, ethnics, couples
Open:	Monday–Thursday, 4–11 P.M.; Friday, 4 P.M.–midnight; Saturday, 11 A.M.–midnight; Sunday, 11 A.M.–11 P.M.

Atmosphere/setting: The decor is attractive and cozy, especially the front nonsmoking room. Nice Persian decorative touches; dimly lit and romantic.

House specialties: Chicken fessenjan, a very popular Persian dish of chicken breast simmered with pomegranate and walnut sauce; charbroiled kebabs of lamb, beef, or filet mignon; variety of seasonal fresh fish, including salmon, whitefish, swordfish, trout, and red snapper. Seafood degustation for two or more, $12.95 each, includes appetizers, baked shrimp, scallops, lobster, fish with vegetables, couscous, and rice. Vegetarian specialties such as veggie Mediterranean and veggie fessenjan.

Other recommendations: Appetizers, including baba gannoujh, dolmeh, tabbouleh, and herb yogurt served with Persian bread. Lentil soup; Pars salad. Zolobia, a fried Persian dessert with yogurt and honey.

Summary & comments: This place has a following. The fish and seafood have always been its strengths, but chicken, meat, and vegetarian items are equally savory and somewhat exotic. Persian cooking uses lots of herbs, citrus marinades, and pomegranate juice, so sauces tend to be fragrant and slightly sweet-tart. Most entrees come with fluffy Persian rice pilaf. Portions are generous, and service is gracious.

Honors/awards: *Chicago Tribune* and *Chicago* magazine, four stars.

THE PARTHENON

Zone 4 The Loop	Greek
314 South Halsted Street, Greektown	★★★★
(312) 726-2407	Inexpensive/Moderate
	Quality 95 Value B

Reservations: Recommended
When to go: Weekdays usually less busy
Entree range: $6–10
Payment: Major credit cards
Service rating: ★★★★½
Friendliness rating: ★★★★★
Parking: Free valet
Bar: Full service
Wine selection: Extensive, mostly Greek; house wines by the
                           glass, carafe, bottle
Dress: Casual
Disabled access: Wheelchair access, rest rooms
Customers: Greek Americans, diverse Americans, a cross-section
                           of the universe
Lunch/Dinner: Sunday–Friday, 11–1 A.M.; Saturday, 11–2 A.M.

Atmosphere/setting: Barbecuing lamb on a spit; enter through the original bar area. New, chic, contemporary bar was recently added next door. Several comfortable dining rooms, all with lovely murals; lively Greek setting with waiters' shouts of "Oopa!" as they flambé saganaki. Tables are well spaced for privacy.

House specialties: Flaming saganaki (kasseri used instead of the saltier kefalotiri) and succulent housemade gyros (pronounced "yee-ros")—both introduced to Chicago here. Great assortment of mezedes (substantial appetizers), such as spinach-feta pies, braised octopus, and tzatziki; a special assortment platter for two or more, $10.95 a person. Entrees: meatballs à la Smyrna (Tuesday and Wednesday); Greek-style broiled whole red snapper or sea bass, filleted tableside if desired; top-quality lamb prepared in various ways: rotisserie roasted, extra thick prime chops, broiled to order, fork-tender lamb with artichokes avgolemono; tigania (pork tenderloin chunks marinated in wine sauce); Athenian broiled chicken; and chicken breast spanaki (stuffed with spinach and feta).

Other recommendations: Kotopitakia appetizer (chicken and vegetable phyllo pie); dolmades (rice- or meat-stuffed vine leaves); broiled octopus; vegetarian moussaka; lamb sweetbreads; shrimp flambée; Aegean platter (panfried

(continued)

scallops, codfish, baby squid, and smelt, with skordalia—garlic potato dip). Galaktoboureko; baklava; yogurt with honey and walnuts; rice pudding.

Summary & comments: The Parthenon is the oldest restaurant in Greektown (30 years in July 1998) and has remained tops for the most comprehensive menu, consistent quality of food, and gracious service. The name carries a deep responsibility for excellence, and the Liakouras family never takes that lightly. Chris Liakouras, who started this restaurant with his brother Bill, now runs it with his daughter, Joanna, who is a partner along with chef Sotiris Stasinos. New dishes are always being added, and there are daily dinner specials. The family-style dinner ($13.95) is large and complete. Many items are à la carte; most mezedes are offered in two sizes. This concept is ideally suited to the Greeks' cultural sense of filoxenia (hospitality). Kali orexi! (Good appetite!)

Honors/awards: Great press over the years, including the *Chicago Sun-Times,* the *Chicago Tribune, Chicago* magazine, and the *Los Angeles Times.*

PASTEUR

Zone 1   North Side
5525 North Broadway
(773) 878-1061

Vietnamese	
★★★★	
Inexpensive/Moderate	
Quality 92	Value B

Reservations:	Accepted
When to go:	Early dinner
Entree range:	$8.95–13.50; market price
Payment:	All major credit cards
Service rating:	★★★
Friendliness rating:	★★★
Parking:	Street; church lot across street
Bar:	Full service
Wine selection:	Limited; affordable; bottles, $18–69; by the glass, $4–5.50
Dress:	Casual
Disabled access:	Yes
Customers:	Mixed
Open:	Monday–Thursday, 11:30 A.M.–10 P.M.; Friday and Saturday, noon–11 P.M.; Sunday, noon–10 P.M.

Atmosphere/setting: Spectacular split-level interior; large palm trees, ceiling fans. Beautiful private dining room upstairs and charming, cozy bar area. Sidewalk cafe.

House specialties: Appetizers: goi cuon (spring roll of shrimp, vegetables, noodles); banh tom co ngu (traditional Hanoi dish of shrimp, yams, and bananas, lightly fried); pho (Hanoi soup specialty: aromatic beef broth over rice noodles and beef strips). Entrees: tom sa-te (sautéed jumbo shrimp); ga kho gung (clay pot chicken); scallop kao me (with sesame seeds, grilled). Mango mousse cake.

Other recommendations: Appetizers: bo tai chanh (spicy charbroiled beef strips); chao tom (shrimp paste wrapped around fresh sugarcane, grilled). Entrees: bo cuon la lot (grilled beef rolls stuffed with chicken and shrimp); bo luc lac (sautéed marinated beef chunks); ca-ry ga (Saigon specialty of delicate curry broth with chicken slices).

Summary & comments: Pasteur has been reborn in a new location, and is a truly upscale Vietnamese fine-dining establishment at affordable prices. Ingredients mingle well in various specialties here, and there is a profusion of fresh herbs. It's more fun to dine with three or four for a better sampling. Pasteur also offers full-blown services for banquets, catering, carryout, and delivery. It's definitely a destination Vietnamese dining experience.

Pastiche

Zone 1   North Side
4343 North Clarendon Street
(773) 296-4999

Global/Eclectic	
★★★½	
Inexpensive/Moderate	
Quality 87 Value B	

Reservations: Accepted
When to go: Any time
Entree range: $9.95–15.95
Payment: All major credit cards
Service rating: ★★★★
Friendliness rating: ★★★★½
Parking: Available upon request
Bar: Full service, including international beers
Wine selection: About 50 international, $15–39; 12 by the glass
Dress: Casual
Disabled access: Yes; private elevators
Customers: Diverse; all ages
Brunch: Sunday, 10:30 A.M.–2:30 P.M.
Dinner: Tuesday–Thursday, 5–10 P.M.; Friday and Saturday,
                     5–11 P.M.; Sunday, 5–9 P.M.

Atmosphere/setting: Private elevator delivers guests to the lounge over-looking the roof-deck and outdoor terrace. Artistic blend of styles and colors; comfortable and friendly.

House specialties: Starters: Yin Yang soup (two soups—one mild, one spicy—swirled in a bowl); hot red pepper salad (goat cheese–filled half pepper); vegetarian southwest "handrolls" (tortillas filled with black beans, avocado, toma-toes—a special); plantain polenta (a fusion of Caribbean and Italian cuisines—a special). Fish du jour offered three ways: poached in mushroom broth, baked with Pernod and sage, or coated with coconut; spicy Jamaican jerk chicken; portobello steak with baked apple slices. Daily flan.

Other recommendations: Conch fritters; grilled fillet of yellowfin tuna (special); cardamom chicken (special); grilled-to-order beef tenderloin stuffed with Gorgonzola. Desserts change: Key lime pie; Yin-Yang crème brûlée; sweet potato pie (seasonal).

Summary & comments: The colorful decor, international wine list, and menu with a global reach reflect the definition of *pastiche,* "an artful harmony of unrelated items brought together as one." Chef Patti Davids Mockus's unique talent is to select favorite foods from various countries, blend them together, and present them artistically. The large selection of tapas encourages spontaneity in ordering and sharing. Affordable prices.

248

Pazzo's Cucina Italiana

Zone 2   North Central/O'Hare
8725 West Higgins Road
(773) 714-0077
Zone 8   Southern Suburbs
Three Westbrook Corporate Center,
    22nd and Wolf Road, Westchester
(708) 531-1112 or (708) 531-TOGO

New Italian
★★½
Inexpensive/Moderate

Quality 79   Value B

Reservations:	Accepted
When to go:	Off-peak times
Entree range:	Most items around $10
Payment:	VISA, MC, AMEX, DC
Service rating:	★★★
Friendliness rating:	★★★★★
Parking:	Building lots, street, free garage
Bar:	Full service
Wine selection:	Extensive; bottles of Pazzo's Chianti on tables, $3.75 a glass
Dress:	Casual
Disabled access:	Yes
Customers:	Businesspeople, locals, families
Lunch/Dinner:	Monday–Thursday, 11 A.M.–10 P.M.; Friday, 11 A.M.–11 P.M.; Saturday, 4:30–11 P.M.

Atmosphere/setting: Contemporary, casual, and spacious; open kitchen. Private rooms are available for parties.

House specialties: Brick-oven pizza; Pazzo's Caesar; insalatina di gamberetti (with marinated shrimp); polenta cup filled with basil pesto and ragôut of vegetables; fresh pastas: zebra panzottini (striped pasta filled with ricotta and spinach); mushroom-filled tortelloni; pollo rigatoni (square rigatoni with chicken). Veal chop Milanese; Pazzo's strip steak; Pollo della Casa. Chocolate-raspberry cake; tiramisu; gelato.

Other recommendations: Oriental lime-chicken salad; Mediterranean salad.

Summary & comments: Fun and delicious Italian cuisine, colorful presentations, generous portions, low prices, and friendly staff—these are the buzzwords that spell success for this California based chain (other locations around the country are known as Milano's Italian Kitchen). It's not surprising that this place wins over first-time customers. Bonus at the new Westchester location: live entertainment by singing servers.

Honors/awards: *Chicago Sun-Times'* Top Three Caesar Salads in the City award.

Pegasus Restaurant and Taverna

Zone 4   The Loop
130 South Halsted Street, Greektown
(312) 226-3377

	Greek
	★★★
	Inexpensive/Moderate
	Quality 83 Value C

Reservations:	Recommended
When to go:	Weekdays; Friday and Saturday are busy
Entree range:	$5.75–19.75
Payment:	Major credit cards
Service rating:	★★★★
Friendliness rating:	★★★★
Parking:	Valet
Bar:	Full service
Wine selection:	Mostly Greek (about 98 percent)
Dress:	Casual
Disabled access:	Yes, including rest rooms
Customers:	Diverse; internationals, tourists, and locals
Lunch/Dinner:	Monday–Thursday, 11 A.M.–midnight; Friday, 11–1 A.M.; Saturday, noon–1 A.M.; Sunday, noon–midnight

Atmosphere/setting: Bright with Mediterranean colors and murals of Mykonos. Summer roof garden. Dramatic view of the Chicago skyline from rooftop.

House specialties: Shrimp Alexander; broiled lamb chops; whole red snapper; Athenian-style chicken; beef tash kebab (in wine-tomato sauce); briami (cooked fresh vegetables); traditional Greek dishes such as pastitsio (baked macaroni and meat with béchamel).

Other recommendations: Grilled marinated baby octopus; Alexander's salad; swordfish kebab. Special walnut-raisin cake; creamy rice pudding.

Entertainment & amenities: Lovely roof garden.

Summary & comments: The menu is a blend of authentic and original home-style dishes from several regions, prepared in a light, healthy way. A mezedes (small course) menu was created for the roof garden, which is especially pleasant on a warm summer evening.

PIEROGI INN

Zone 2   North Central/O'Hare
5318 West Lawrence Avenue
(773) 736-4815

Polish
★★½
Inexpensive
Quality 79   Value B

Reservations:	Recommended for large parties
When to go:	Any time
Entree range:	$4.95–9.95
Payment:	Cash and personal checks; no credit cards
Service rating:	★★★
Friendliness rating:	★★★★½
Parking:	Street
Bar:	None
Wine selection:	BYOB
Dress:	Casual
Disabled access:	Yes, including rest rooms
Customers:	Polish Americans, including radio celebrities; other locals
Lunch/Dinner:	Every day, 10 A.M.–10 P.M.

Atmosphere/setting: Original storefront has a comfortable setting with a carryout counter; adjacent dining room is divided into alcoves, decorated with traditional Polish colorful paper cuttings, wooden birds, and costumed figurines.

House specialties: Pierogi (dumplings filled with the traditional mushrooms, cabbage, potato, and cheese, with creative items such as shrimp, whitefish, strawberries, and other seasonal fruits); great soups, especially mushroom, barley, and barszcz with uszka (red beet soup with wild mushroom dumplings).

Other recommendations: Roast duck; chicken or beef goulash; veal cutlet with sauerkraut; golabki (stuffed cabbage rolls); uszka with tomato-mushroom sauce; nalesniki (cheese blintzes).

Summary & comments: Pierogi Inn began as a small storefront with a large carryout business, and it soon expanded to the space next door so there could be a dining room. Although it remains simple with a blackboard menu, it has loads of charm; it's popular because the Polish cooking is authentic and flavorful, and it's a good value. Chef Richard Anton's mother, Alexandra, is usually in the kitchen and makes all the delicious pierogis—the main attraction here. Catering and carryout. Smacznego!

Honors/awards: Silver Platter, 1994–96.

PRAIRIE

	Midwestern
Zone 5 South Loop	★★★★½
500 South Dearborn Street	Moderate/Expensive
(312) 663-1143	Quality 95 Value C

Reservations:	Recommended
When to go:	Monday is the slowest, but any time is fine
Entree range:	Lunch, $9.75–18.25; dinner à la carte, $16–27
Payment:	All major credit cards
Service rating:	★★★★
Friendliness rating:	★★★★½
Parking:	Valet ($5 day, $8 evening)
Bar:	Full service
Wine selection:	Mostly Californian; some smaller bottles available
Dress:	Summer, casual to formal; winter, business and dressy (optional)
Disabled access:	Yes, including rest rooms
Customers:	Businesspeople, theatergoers, couples, Bears fans
Breakfast:	Monday–Friday, 6:30–10 A.M.; Saturday and Sunday, 7–10 A.M.
Brunch:	Saturday and Sunday, 11 A.M.–2 P.M.
Lunch:	Monday–Friday, 11:30 A.M.–2 P.M.; Saturday, 11 A.M.–2 P.M.
Dinner:	Monday–Saturday, 5–10 P.M.; Sunday, 5–9 P.M.

Atmosphere/setting: Striking split-level space with tall windows and honey-colored oak cathedral ceiling. Fine example of Prairie School architecture.

House specialties: Heartland products in seasonal preparations. Some examples: Sauté of wild mushrooms in sweet potato basket with roasted corn and charred red pepper sauces—beautiful presentation; baby coho salmon with bacon, leeks, and black walnuts; seared duck breast with roasted cherry sauce; roasted lamb with country apple sausage; Lake Superior whitefish with roasted pepper relish; strawberry-rhubarb tart with apple-cinnamon ice cream (in spring).

Other recommendations: Baby lettuces in raspberry dressing with warm goat cheese; corn chowder; Asiago and artichoke fondue with roasted vegetables.

Summary & comments: Chef Stephen Langlois opened this restaurant after combing old heartland cookbooks and unearthing recipes from farm cooks, then imaginatively incorporating such seasonal ingredients as edible flowers into stunningly visual creations. It's refined, contemporary dining with historical roots. The only Chicago restaurant devoted exclusively to midwestern cuisine.

Honors/awards: DiRoNA Award, 1996–97.

The Primavera Ristorante

Zone 4 The Loop	Italian
200 North Columbus Drive,	★★★½
Fairmont Hotel	Inexpensive/Moderate
(312) 565-6655	Quality 88 Value C

Reservations:	Recommended
When to go:	Any time
Entree range:	$11–22; cover charge $1.50 a person
Payment:	All major credit cards except DC
Service rating:	★★★
Friendliness rating:	★★★★
Parking:	Valet
Bar:	Full service; the Primavera Bar is well known for its signature drink of a yard or half-yard of beer served tableside; it also features a microbrewed beer each month and a wall-size television screen
Wine selection:	Mostly Italian, Californian, French; nice choices by the glass
Dress:	Semicasual; dressier when people are celebrating
Disabled access:	Yes
Customers:	Families and celebrators; couples; tourists, professionals, conventioneers, celebrities, music lovers
Breakfast:	Monday–Sunday, 6–11:30 A.M.
Lunch:	Monday–Sunday, 11:30 A.M.–2 P.M.
Dinner:	Monday–Friday, 5:30–10:30 P.M.; Saturday, 5:30–11 P.M.; Sunday, 5:30–10 P.M.

Atmosphere/setting: The ambiance of an Italian country trattoria is enhanced with a glorious floral display, cozy banquettes, and wall-size frescos. Female servers wear colorful peasant dresses and male servers wear red bandanas and black coats, giving a theatrical flair.

House specialties: Appetizers: antipasto della casa (chef's selection of assorted specialties); prosciutto, mozzarella, pomodori secchi (prosciutto di Parma, fresh mozzarella, sun-dried tomatoes, dates); calamari fritti con limone (fried squid with lemon); insalata romana (Italian Caesar salad). Entrees: rigatoni con pollo e basilico (rigatoni tossed with grilled breast of chicken, mushrooms, Gorgonzola); ravioli ai quattro formaggi con funghi (four-cheese and shiitake ravioli baked with tomato and basil cream sauce); linguine ai frutti di mare (linguine, shrimp, scallops, calamari, clams, and mussels); lasagna di spinaci e vegetali (spinach lasagna with fresh seasonal

(continued)

vegetables, Asiago, mascarpone, and ricotta); Branzino dell adriatico (sautéed striped bass with fresh clams, mussels, and calamari on angel hair). Desserts: chocolate mousse cake is the complimentary birthday cake; award-winning tiramisu; cannoli alla Primavera (filled with white and dark chocolate mousse); and caffe di amaretto (cappuccino, amaretto, and fresh whipped cream).

Other recommendations: Appetizers: polenta con vegetali e salsa di funghi (soft polenta, grilled vegetables, wild mushroom sauce, and goat cheese); fresh seafood risotto; seasonal vegetable risotto; porcini mushroom risotto; spaghetti con funghi e gamberi (with wild mushrooms and shrimp); petti di pollo Vesuvio (sautéed breast of chicken); scaloppine di vitello della casa (veal scaloppine sautéed with shiitake mushrooms and fresh baby artichokes); castolette di agnello alla grigalia (roast rack of lamb). Desserts: amaretto crème brûlée; torta di ricotta (ricotta, roasted pine nut, and citron tart); torta di cioccolato al zabaione (rich chocolate mousse cake); and espresso affogato (espresso, vanilla gelato, and sambuca).

Entertainment & amenities: Every evening for dinner, the "Primavera Singers" perform favorite songs from operas, operettas, and musical comedies in between taking orders and delivering meals. Some of their resumes boast leading roles in productions by the Chicago Lyric Opera, New York City Opera, Chicago Symphony Orchestra, and San Francisco's Opera Merola Program.

Summary & comments: Music and dining are two of life's greatest pleasures, and they come together beautifully at Primavera Ristorante. Diners can pick up a playbill here to read about the performers, who are also the servers. The wait staff is very cheerful, and it's evident they love their jobs as performers, too. Chef Giovanni De Nigris enhances his cooking with his commitment to freshness, simplicity, taste, consistency, and presentation. In fact, he often visits with the guests and will go out of his way to prepare a dish per a guest's request.

There might be an occasional lag in the service, but Primavera can be forgiven minor flaws considering the dual roles of the servers. Dinner at Primavera is one of the best ways to celebrate a birthday, anniversary, or any day you want a musical lift. For a birthday, all the singers gather around, serve the cake with a candle, and sing the Happy Birthday song (lyrics by Eric Barnes, copyrighted) to the Hallelujah chorus—spectacular!

Honors/awards: Silver Platter Award, 1995 and 1996. *Food Industry News* magazine honored Chef Giovanni De Nigris as one of its 1995 Top Five Italian Chefs and honored the Primavera Ristorante with its Top Five Italian Restaurants awards in Chicago.

PRINTER'S ROW

Zone 5   South Loop
550 South Dearborn Street
(312) 461-0780

New American
★★★★½
Moderate
Quality 95   Value B

Reservations: Recommended
When to go: Any time; weekdays usually less busy
Entree range: Lunch, $8.50–12.95; dinner, $13.95–21.95
Payment: VISA, MC, AMEX, D
Service rating: ★★★★½
Friendliness rating: ★★★★
Parking: Street or lots nearby
Bar: Full service
Wine selection: Big American list; many by the glass, bottle, or
                      half-bottle
Dress: Casual
Disabled access: Yes
Customers: Locals, businesspeople, travelers, suburbanites
Lunch: Monday–Friday, 11:30 A.M.–2:30 P.M.
Dinner: Monday–Thursday, 5–10 P.M.; Friday and Saturday,
                      5–11 P.M.

Atmosphere/setting: In the historic Printers Row area, this establishment is both sophisticated and comfortable. Great private party location.

House specialties: Grilled duck breast; weekly menu features a shellfish or wild and farm-raised fish and a venison item (e.g., venison chop with a sun-dried blueberry–grappa sauce). Tuna seared with Chinese molasses, cucumber, and chile vinaigrette is an example of the Asian influence here. Vegetable paella, mildly spicy with saffron rice, satisfies any Spanish cravings.

Other recommendations: Grilled salmon with prosciutto-pasta cake; roasted custom-cut pork chop; various ice creams; coffee crème brûlée (flavors change); pear tart with lemon ice cream.

Summary & comments: Chef-owner Michael Foley opened this restaurant about 20 years ago when the Printers Row area was not yet renovated. This pioneer soon received recognition for his innovative American cooking, which is committed to healthful preparations based on fresh, local products and is influenced by his travels. Menus change weekly and focus on servicing daily diners through à la carte items. This remains one of Chicago's best dining experiences. Can accommodate private functions from 15 to 120.

Honors/awards: *Travel Holiday* magazine Good Dining Award, 1992–94; *Wine Spectator*'s Award of Excellence, 1988–93; DiRoNA Award, 1993.

The Pump Room

Zone 3 Near North
Omni Ambassador East Hotel,
1301 North State Parkway
(312) 266-0360

	American/Continental
	★★★★
	Expensive
	Quality 92 Value C

Reservations: Recommended
When to go: Friday or Saturday evenings
Entree range: Breakfast, $6–12; lunch, $9–15; dinner, $20–40
Payment: All major credit cards
Service rating: ★★★★½
Friendliness rating: ★★★★½
Parking: Valet, $11; nearby self-park garage
Bar: Full service; cognacs, sherries, single-malts, ports
Wine selection: Extensive, international, from $20; 8 by the glass
Dress: Lunch, business; dinner, dressy (jacket after 4:30 P.M.)
Disabled access: No
Customers: Professionals over 30, celebrities, couples
Breakfast: Monday–Saturday, 6:30–11 A.M.
Brunch: Sunday, 11:15 A.M.–2:30 P.M.
Lunch: Monday–Friday, 11:30 A.M.–2:30 P.M.
Dinner: Monday–Thursday, 6–9:45 P.M.; Friday and Saturday,
                         6–11 P.M.; Sunday, 5–10 P.M.

Atmosphere/setting: Formal, elegant, stunning split-level dining room with bar/lounge and gallery of celebrity photos. Mahogany-toned room lavishly appointed with crystal chandeliers, floral arrangements, and sheer ceiling drapes with tiny lights. This atmosphere and the restaurant's history still cast a spell.

House specialties: Aged prime rib of beef; roast duck; chicken Vivien Leigh (pecan-crusted with sage, cherry sauce); oven-roasted halibut stuffed with crab, herb rice; roasted rack of lamb; Pump Room and Caesar salads; baked Alaska.

Other recommendations: Pump Room pâté with herb toast points and whole-grain mustard; escargot wrapped in spinach; Norwegian smoked salmon with grilled brioche; à la carte creamed spinach and garlic-and-horseradish whipped red potatoes; frozen banana soufflé.

Entertainment & amenities: Live music and dancing nightly in lounge.

Summary & comments: Booth One is a legend made famous by this Chicago landmark, a premier celebrity gathering place since the late 1930s. Complimentary hors d'oeuvre buffet in the lounge during weekday cocktail hours. Special place for business meals, celebrity sightings, and romantic dinners.

Honors/awards: AAA, four diamonds; *Chicago Tribune,* Best Brunch.

R. J. Grunts

Zone 1   North Side
2056 Lincoln Park West
(773) 929-5363

American
★★★
Inexpensive
Quality 82   Value A

Reservations: For 6 or more
When to go: Any time a craving hits
Entree range: $7.95–15.95
Payment: Major credit cards
Service rating: ★★★
Friendliness rating: ★★★½
Parking: Street
Bar: Full service; imported, domestic, on-tap brews
Wine selection: Mostly lower-priced domestic; very limited; 6 by
                         the glass or half-carafe; 4 by the bottle
Dress: Blue-jean casual
Disabled access: Yes; call first
Customers: Mixed; families, singles, couples, all ages
Brunch: Sunday, 10 A.M.–2:30 P.M.; $10.95 buffet or order
                         from the menu
Open: Monday–Thursday, 11:30 A.M.–10 P.M.; Friday and
                         Saturday, 11:30 A.M.–11 P.M.; Sunday, 3–10 P.M.

Atmosphere/setting: Casual; stucco walls showcase original comical art, including a tribute to the waitresses. Centerpiece salad bar provides colorful decor.

House specialties: Signature salad bar with 40-plus items, including pre-pared salads and fresh fruit; oversized cheeseburgers or other options, including the turkey burger; award-winning vegetarian chili and steak Terry Yaki-Witch (sandwich); baby-back ribs; R. J.'s chop stake (as spelled on menu).

Other recommendations: Vegetarian items in every menu category except "Flashbacks," and even that might have a veggie quiche of the day.

Summary & comments: This first Lettuce Entertain You creation is still alive and well and basically unchanged after 27 years. This place recognizes the importance of choices and offers a varied menu. In recent years, it expanded the menu with vegetarian offerings in each category. This funky place launched the original salad bar in 1971; most entrees include the salad bar—a real deal. Odd placement of some salad bar items (such as chocolate mousse next to chopped chicken liver) results in occasional surprises in the mouth. Even the beverages—fresh-squeezed juices, herbal teas, giant malts and shakes, and espresso—follow the motto of catering to our variable tastes.

Red Tomato

Zone 1   North Side
3417 North Southport Avenue
(773) 472-5300

Italian
★★★
Inexpensive
Quality 84   Value B

Reservations:	Accepted Friday and Saturday, but limited
When to go:	Early evenings any day
Entree range:	$8.95–15
Payment:	All major credit cards
Service rating:	★★★
Friendliness rating:	★★★★
Parking:	Street
Bar:	Full service
Wine selection:	Extensive, mostly Italian; $20–125; several by the glass, $3.50–4.50
Dress:	Casual
Disabled access:	Yes, including rest rooms
Customers:	Locals, professionals, couples, business
Lunch/Dinner:	Monday–Thursday, 11 A.M.–9:30 P.M.; Friday and Saturday, 11:30 A.M.–10:30 P.M.; Sunday, 1–9 P.M.

Atmosphere/setting: Colorful exterior; near El tracks in a Northwest Side neighborhood. Two sections—one is casual and the other is semiformal; also outdoor dining section.

House specialties: Scaloppini al Red Tomato (medallions of veal over fresh tomato sauce topped with buffalo mozzarella); lasagnas; pizza ochri; pizzette Red Tomato (artichoke, tomato, capers, onion, and pepper).

Other recommendations: Fresh fish specialties (e.g., salmone al vapore—fillet steamed and served over Chianti sauce); involtini di melenzane (grilled eggplant rolled with spinach and ricotta, topped with Bel Paese cheese and roasted peppers); beef and veal items.

Summary & comments: The chef-owner Joe Divenere is dedicated to creating dishes and adding his mark to regional recipes. Meet him and you'll witness how much he loves his work. The restaurant grew out of the original pizza place next door, and the pizzette is quite good. This is one Italian place without a pasta emphasis; it's refreshing to see many alternatives. It can be bustling on weekends.

Relish

	American
Zone 1 North Side	★★★½
2044 North Halsted Street	Inexpensive/Moderate
(773) 868-9034	Quality 86 Value C

Reservations:	Accepted
When to go:	Dinner
Entree range:	$9.50–16.50; on Sunday all entrees are $7
Payment:	VISA, MC, AMEX, DC, CB
Service rating:	★★½
Friendliness rating:	★★★
Parking:	Street
Bar:	Full service
Wine selection:	All American; 45 sold by the glass, $4.50–8.50; bottles, $15–65
Dress:	Chic casual
Disabled access:	Yes
Customers:	Locals, professionals, couples, businesspeople
Dinner:	Tuesday–Thursday, 5–10 P.M.; Friday and Saturday, 5–11 P.M.; Sunday, 4:30–9 P.M.

Atmosphere/setting: Intimate with colorful, contemporary art. A recent massive expansion included quadrupling the bar, moving the kitchen upstairs, and making more private space. Two private dining rooms now: one seats 10–12, the other seats 32. New lighting and decor gives a warmer feel. A balcony offers seating for seven more tables. Intimate garden is available for summer al fresco dining.

House specialties: Potato and goat cheese terrine; shrimp roll with spicy, fermented cabbage in ponzu sauce; salmon wrapped in leek with cod and corn cake; barbecued tuna steak and crisp Tabasco onions. Award-winning dessert, "chocolate orgasm."

Other recommendations: Wild mushrooms roasted in a paper bag with roasted garlic and shallots with porcini powder; spicy Portuguese chicken sausage and charred bread pudding; Maryland lump crab cake. Peach, bourbon, and cherry bread pudding.

Summary & comments: Charming place with an easy-to-miss entryway from the street. The hidden garden is lovely for outdoor summer dining. The main dining room is smoke-free. Chef Ron Blazek's cooking is forward in flavor and very creative in the combination of ingredients and preparation methods; his presentations are attractive and often whimsical. Several reports have told of great lapses in service, but there's good reason to hope that is being improved.

REZA'S

Zone 1   North Side
5255 North Clark Street
(773) 561-1898

Zone 3   Near North
432 West Ontario Street
(312) 664-4500

Persian/Vegetarian	
★★★½	
Inexpensive/Moderate	
Quality 89	Value C

Reservations:	Recommended Thursday, Friday, and weekends
When to go:	Avoid end of week and weekends
Entree range:	$6.95–14.95
Payment:	VISA, MC, AMEX, DC, D
Service rating:	★★★½
Friendliness rating:	★★★★½
Parking:	*Downtown:* valet; *Clark Street:* free lot
Bar:	Full service
Wine selection:	Extensive; international; fairly priced; several by the glass
Dress:	Moderately casual
Disabled access:	Yes, including rest rooms; elevators
Customers:	*Downtown:* more business; *Clark Street:* more locals
Lunch/Dinner:	Every day, 11 A.M.–midnight

Atmosphere/setting: Clark Street location is modern Persian; attractive and comfortable. Downtown location is site of a former brewery; spacious room with exposed brick walls.

House specialties: Vegetarian samplers and Persian-style seafood dishes; eggplant steak appetizer (thick eggplant slice broiled in herbed sauce of onion, garlic, and tomatoes); grilled mushrooms (trio of skewered charbroiled mushrooms with tart marinade); Reza's salad (mixed lettuce with radish, tomato, black olives, feta, green pepper, and croutons); kebabs: lamb and chicken combo; shrimp and fillet with veggies.

Other recommendations: Dolmeh felfel (stuffed green pepper), baba gannoujh, tabbouleh, hummus; Reza's special chicken; duck breast with sweet-and-sour pomegranate sauce and walnuts; marinated charbroiled quail.

Entertainment & amenities: Clark Street: Wednesday, guitar; other weeknights, piano. Call first. Downtown: nightly music and a free shuttle bus for lunch.

Summary & comments: The original Reza's has expanded several times and does brisk business. The huge, newer place is in the former Sieben's Brewery, which was later Berghoff Brewery and Restaurant. A great place for casual business lunches and vegetarian specialties. Knowledgeable and accommodating servers.

Riva

Zone 3 Near North	Seafood/Steak/Pasta
Navy Pier, 700 East Grand Avenue	★★★½
(312) 644-7482	Moderate/Expensive
	Quality 90 Value C

Reservations:	Recommended
When to go:	Avoid peak mealtimes without a reservation
Entree range:	Lunch, average $14; dinner, $10.95–24.95
Payment:	Major credit cards
Service rating:	★★★½
Friendliness rating:	★★★½
Parking:	Sheltered valet parking, $7
Bar:	Full service
Wine selection:	Lengthy international list; reserve list; good selection by the glass
Dress:	Casual to dressy
Disabled access:	Yes, elevator available
Customers:	Tourists, locals, celebrities, politicians
Lunch/Dinner:	Sunday–Thursday, 11 A.M.–10:30 P.M.; Friday and Saturday, 11 A.M.–11:30 P.M.

Atmosphere/setting: Beautiful restaurant offering a fantastic view of Navy Pier, Monroe Harbor, and Chicago's downtown skyline. Spacious main dining room with exposed brick walls, brass chandeliers and ceiling fans, and a lobster tank in center; colorful decor; 40-foot-long display kitchen; welcoming bar area; three private dining rooms.

House specialties: Crab cakes with jalapeño tartar sauce and radicchio cole slaw; baby spinach salad; fillet mignon of tuna marinated, grilled, and served over horseradish mashed potatoes in roasted shallot sauce. Grandmother's Cake (lemon custard tart with almonds, pine nuts, and confectioners' sugar).

Other recommendations: Swordfish and other seafood; chocolate truffle torte; atomic cake (three layers of banana, vanilla chiffon, and chocolate chiffon cakes with fruit and custards, whipped cream filling); Italian sorbets.

Summary & comments: President and Mrs. Clinton were here, and there's a photo to prove it. The city's politicians and other dignitaries have visited, as well, and there has been a steady flow of locals and tourists since the grand opening in 1995. "Riva" is Italian for "shoreline," and restaurateur Phil Stefani's newest place is aptly named. While some have reported uncaring service here, other experiences have been favorable. Definitely a destination restaurant. Riva Cafe, on the first floor downstairs, is more informal and serves light fare; it opens onto an outdoor dining area in warm weather.

261

Rodiys

Zone 4   The Loop
222 South Halsted Street, Greektown
(312) 454-0800

Greek	
★★★	
Inexpensive/Moderate	
Quality 89	Value B

Reservations:	Recommended
When to go:	Weekdays; avoid busy weekends
Entree range:	$6.95–15.50; market price
Payment:	VISA, MC, AMEX
Service rating:	★★★★½
Friendliness rating:	★★★★½
Parking:	Lot across the street
Bar:	Full service
Wine selection:	Mostly Greek (about 16; 3 by the glass); 3 American
Dress:	Casual
Disabled access:	Wheelchair access, including rest rooms
Customers:	Diverse; some Greeks, mostly Americans
Lunch/Dinner:	Sunday–Friday, 11–1 A.M.; Saturday, 11–2 A.M.

Atmosphere/setting: Attractive two-room space balances classical and modern impressions; open feeling from high ceilings and mirrors in the south room. Relaxed.

House specialties: Rodiys special platter mixes hot spinach-cheese pie with cold items (e.g., taramasalata, cheeses, octopus salad); broiled octopus appetizer; broiled fresh red snapper. Lamb dishes such as unusual village-style cutlets (minichops pan-fried and then flambéed with green peppers, onions, garlic, and tomato); braised lamb in tomato sauce; roast lamb; broiled lamb chops.

Other recommendations: Whole fried squid; horta (boiled dandelions); large dolmades with beef and rice; broiled whitefish. Rice pudding; nougatina.

Summary & comments: The slightly spicier, home-style traditional cooking here gives this 24-plus-year-old place its large Greek following, especially after church on Sunday. Half of the menu is in Greek, which testifies to the clientele. This place and the Parthenon tend to be where most of the Greeks like to dine.

Rosebud Cafe

Zone 5   South Loop
1500 West Taylor Street
(312) 942-1117

	Italian
	★★★
	Inexpensive/Moderate
	Quality 83 Value C

Reservations:	Highly recommended
When to go:	Before 7 P.M. and after 9 P.M.
Entree range:	Pastas, $10.95–15.95; chicken, $14.95; veal, $29.95
Payment:	All major credit cards
Service rating:	★★½
Friendliness rating:	★★★
Parking:	Lot, valet
Bar:	Full service
Wine selection:	Extensive; international; some outstanding Italian choices
Dress:	Upscale casual; no jacket required
Disabled access:	Yes, including rest rooms
Customers:	Locals, internationals, tourists
Lunch:	Monday–Friday, 11 A.M.–3 P.M.
Dinner:	Monday–Friday, 5–11 P.M.; Saturday, 5–11:30 P.M.; Sunday, 4–9:30 P.M.

Atmosphere/setting: Loud, crowded, very "in Chicago." New second floor where 120 can be seated for private dining.

House specialties: Calamari and mussels in either light red wine or white wine broth; chicken Vesuvio; pappardelle (square noodles) marinara; baked cavatelli; special pasta such as tortiglioni arrabbiata (spirals in spicy red sauce).

Other recommendations: Roasted red peppers; veal Parmigiana; lemon ice; cannoli.

Summary & comments: This Taylor Street mecca of fine, traditional Italian cooking is a true trattoria; service is friendly and knowledgeable, the portions are too generous, and the place is often packed. Waits are common even with reservations. It has been widely recognized by the press, and it has maintained a steady customer flow for 23 years, which is admirable. Not a place to go for a quiet business dinner or romantic evening. Offshoots of this restaurant are on Rush Street and other locations, and newest additions to the family are La Rosetta (70 West Madison) and Rosebud in Naperville.

RUSSIAN TEA TIME

Zone 4   The Loop
77 East Adams Street
(312) 360-0000

Russian
★★★★
Moderate

Quality 93   Value C

Reservations:	Highly recommended
When to go:	Quieter from 2 to 5 P.M.
Entree range:	$10–26
Payment:	Major credit cards
Service rating:	★★★★
Friendliness rating:	★★★★½
Parking:	Lots nearby
Bar:	Full service, including Russian vodkas and caviar
Wine selection:	Two dozen selections; several by the glass
Dress:	Casual to moderately upscale and dressy
Disabled access:	Yes; menus available in braille
Customers:	Russian Americans, symphony and opera crowd, many from television and radio stations nearby
Lunch/Dinner:	Sunday and Monday, 11 A.M.–9 P.M.; Tuesday–Thursday, 11 A.M.–11 P.M.; Friday and Saturday, 11 A.M.–midnight

Atmosphere/setting: Cozy, old-world atmosphere with a great deal of woodwork, Russian urns, pots, and tablecloths; well-spaced booths and tables.

House specialties: Blini with top-quality Russian caviar; borscht; goriachaya zakuska (appetizer platter for two-plus); wild game; jumbo stuffed mushrooms with spinach, onion, and cheese; hot farmer's cheese blintzes.

Other recommendations: Kulebiaka (meat pie) filled with ground beef, cabbage, and onions; blinchiki (crêpes—the beef stroganoff are great; also salmon and cheese); roast pheasant "Erevan";Tashkent carrot salad (named for hometown of owners; à la carte or with entrees); chicken croquettes; hearty apricot-plum strudel (thick-crusted Russian version); Russian tea (blend of three, including black currant).

Summary & comments: This exquisite cafe received rave reviews within the first several months of opening in fall 1993. The Chicago Symphony bought the building that originally contained the cafe, so it moved here. The conductor, former conductor, symphonygoers, and operagoers all dine here before or after events. The cafe also expanded its vegetarian options recently; the *Chicago Sun-Times* has named Russian Tea Time as one of the city's top ten vegetarian-friendly spots.

Honors/awards: *Vegetarian Journal's* Ten Best Restaurants in North America.

264

Ruth's Chris Steakhouse

Zone 4   The Loop
431 North Dearborn Street
(312) 321-2725

Steak	
★★★★	
Moderate/Expensive	
Quality 93	Value B

Reservations: Recommended
When to go: Avoid peak times, 6–8 P.M. weekends
Entree range: $10–27
Payment: All major credit cards
Service rating: ★★★½
Friendliness rating: ★★★★
Parking: Free valet
Bar: Full service
Wine selection: International; heavy Californian bent; several by
                    the glass
Dress: Casual to dressy
Disabled access: Yes
Customers: Very local
Lunch/Dinner: Monday–Friday, 11:30 A.M.–11 P.M.; Saturday,
                    4:30–11 P.M.

Atmosphere/setting: Clubby; plaid carpet; lots of sports memorabilia.

House specialties: All prime cuts here: New York strip steak, 16–18 ounces; 20-ounce T-bone; petite fillet of beef tenderloin (8 ounce); provimi veal chop. Veal sweetbreads; barbecued shrimp Orleans; three classic sauces offered with entrees and sides.

Other recommendations: Fish of the day; live Maine lobster; porterhouse for two; Prince Edward's mashed potatoes with garlic; turtle soup served with sherry; gumbo Louisiane; bread pudding with Jack Daniels whiskey sauce; pecan pie.

Summary & comments: This New Orleans franchise spot arrived on the Chicago dining scene several years ago and is very successful. It was the number one Ruth's Chris Steakhouse worldwide in 1996 for the greatest number of steaks sold. The menu pays tribute to its roots with several New Orleans touches. Steaks sizzle appealingly because they get a coating of butter. Juices are sealed into steaks on a 1,800° F grill. One of a fast-growing chain with a good reputation.

THE SALOON

Zone 3   Near North
200 East Chestnut Street
(312) 280-5454

Steak	
★★★½	
Moderate/Expensive	
Quality 89	Value C

Reservations:	Accepted
When to go:	Before 8 P.M.
Entree range:	$9.95–26.95
Payment:	VISA, MC, AMEX, D, DC, CB
Service rating:	★★★★
Friendliness rating:	★★★★
Parking:	Doorman parks cars; no valet
Bar:	Full service
Wine selection:	Extensive; large Meritage and Californian list
Dress:	Casual to jacket-and-tie dressy
Disabled access:	Yes
Customers:	Businesspeople, theatergoers, tourists
Lunch/Dinner:	Monday–Saturday, 11 A.M.–11 P.M.
Dinner:	Sunday, noon–10 P.M.

Atmosphere/setting: Enter through the handsome bar with a two-tone wood floor. Dining room has a warm, comfortable atmosphere; tiny candle lamps give soft lighting.

House specialties: Smoked 16-ounce pork chop; 48-ounce porterhouse steak; 18-ounce Kansas bone-in strip; 14-ounce filet mignon; surf and turf; potato-crusted fish of the day (e.g., walleyed pike); beefsteak tomato and onion with blue cheese; crispy calamari.

Other recommendations: Appetizer sampler plate (cheddar cheese–stuffed jalapeños, house smoked barbecue chicken skewers, and blackened scallops); buffalo mozzarella salad; shrimp cocktail; wood-grilled lobster tail; tuna tartare; baked jumbo asparagus; garbage salad. Desserts: banana steak, fresh fruit cobbler, Key lime tart, and crème brûlée.

Summary & comments: The Saloon was opened on the Gold Coast in 1991 by the Restaurant Development Group, which also owns Kinzie Street Chophouse. The two places have some similarities but more differences. A signature item here is the potato-crusted fish; the concept is great and usually works well, although one time the walleyed pike lacked seasoning and its crust was slightly greasy—the only minor flaw. To his credit, our well-schooled waiter noticed that the steak we ordered as medium-rare arrived more medium, and he whisked it back for another. Order several items and share, if possible. Save room for dessert.

¡Salpicón!, A Taste of Mexico

Zone 3 Near North	Mexican
1252 North Wells	★★★½
(312) 988-7811	Inexpensive/Moderate
	Quality 85 Value C

Reservations: Recommended
When to go: Dinner; less crowded weekdays
Entree range: $12.95–22.95
Payment: All major credit cards
Service rating: ★★★★½
Friendliness rating: ★★★★★
Parking: Street or nearby garages
Bar: Full service; super- and ultra-premium tequilas;
                        tequila flights (¾ ounce of 4); ¡Salpicón! Mar-
                        garita; Mexican and microbrew beers
Wine selection: Extensive; several by the glass, $6–13.50; bottles,
                        $21–295; reserve list
Dress: Casual
Disabled access: Yes
Customers: Locals, professionals, theater and opera crowd
Brunch: Sunday, 11 A.M.–2:30 P.M.
Dinner: Wednesday–Monday, 5 P.M.; set-price early menu
                        before 6:30 P.M.

Atmosphere/setting: Brightly painted storefront; colorful art by renowned Mexican artist Alejandro Romero. Recently expanded to include a dining area behind the bar.

House specialties: Jalapeños rellenos de queso capeados (jalapeños stuffed with Chihuahua cheese, dipped in a light egg batter, sautéed); Chiapas-style tamale with chicken and a sweet-seasoned pork picadillo with a classic mole poblano; ceviche (fresh fish marinated in lime juice with onions, tomatoes, fresh chilies, herbs); ensalada de espinaca con queso de cabra (fresh spinach salad with goat cheese, toasted sesame seeds, and caramelized red onions in a spicy chipotle-honey dressing); codornices en salsa de chile ancho con miel (garlic-marinated and grilled Manchester Farm quail served in a sauce of ancho chilies, garlic, caramelized onions, and honey with cilantro, potato, and queso anejo cakes); flan de caramelo (classic egg custard with a rich caramel sauce); arroz con leche (traditional rice pudding); pastel tres leches (light orange-flavored cake soaked in a trio of milks, served with fresh fruit sauce).

(continued)

Other recommendations: Tostaditas de Tinga (crispy small tortillas mounded with shredded pork and chorizo in a roasted tomato-chipotle sauce); jaibas al mojo de ajo (summer special: Chesapeake Bay soft-shell crabs sautéed); and cinnamon crêpes stuffed with mango and fresh raspberries under a house-made goat's milk caramel (special).

Summary & comments: Salpicón translates as a "splash," and owners Vincent and Priscila Satkoff truly bring a splash of Mexico to Chicago with their Old Town restaurant. The name is also a typical Mexican dish of shredded beef or chicken served at room temperature, and also a very spicy salsa from the Yucatán. Mexican-born chef Priscilla Satkoff's expert culinary skills and passion for food were inspired and developed by her grandmother and mother, who were gourmet cooks but didn't know it; they made everything from scratch. She moved to Chicago when she and Vince married in 1986. They opened ¡Salpicón! in fall 1994. Vince is the manager and planned the award-winning wine list. Satkoff's menu features authentic dishes that reflect Mexico's different regions and her creative and contemporary interpretation of Mexican cuisine. Only high-quality seafood and meats are used, and plate presentations are just as festive as the restaurant interior. All salsas and sauces are prepared fresh daily and everything is homemade, including tortillas (here usually a smaller size) and totopos (chips). The service staff is exceptionally friendly and well informed. Dining here is fun and educational.

Honors/awards: *Wine Spectator* Award of Excellence, 1996; three stars from both the *Chicago Tribune* and the *Chicago Sun-Times*. *Chicago* magazine named it one of the top ten new restaurants of 1995.

Santorini

Zone 4 The Loop	Greek
800 West Adams Street, Greektown	★★★
(312) 829-8820	Inexpensive/Moderate
	Quality 89 Value C

Reservations:	Recommended
When to go:	Weekdays
Entree range:	$8–16
Payment:	Major credit cards except DC
Service rating:	★★★★
Friendliness rating:	★★★★
Parking:	Free valet
Bar:	Full service
Wine selection:	International: Greek, American, French, Italian
Dress:	Varies from casual to formal
Disabled access:	Yes, including rest rooms
Customers:	Diverse; about one-third Greeks
Lunch/Dinner:	Sunday–Thursday, 11 A.M.–midnight; Friday and Saturday, 11–1 A.M.

Atmosphere/setting: Cozy with fireplace in room's center. Lovely authentic interior decorated with plates and baskets; art depicts the hilly island, Santorini.

House specialties: Seafood is the showcase: charcoal-grilled octopus; shrimp ala Santorini; charcoal-grilled swordfish steak with Santorini sauce; bacalao and garlic sauce; broiled red snapper fillet (unique here, instead of whole fish); shrimp Tourkolimano (butterflied jumbos baked in tomato and feta sauce); baked fish ala spetsiota; Santorini salad; sokolatina (semisweet chocolate mousse cake) with "Santorini" written over each slice.

Other recommendations: Appetizer spreads such as eggplant, fish roe, and spicy feta; tzatziki (cucumber-yogurt dip); chicken ala Santorini; lamb scharas (thin slices charcoal grilled and prepared the original Greek way); seafood platter (shellfish and fish); homemade yogurt with honey and nuts; nougatina (rich crème and nut cake).

Summary & comments: This fairly recent addition to Greektown is upscale and refined, and probably the most expensive. Many inexpensive items are on the menu, but there is an absence of the traditional dishes, which tend to be less costly. Daily specials are creative and enticing; some are repeated several times weekly, such as the lamb stamnas (crêpe filled with lamb, vegetables, cheeses, and pine nuts). Service is attentive and knowledgeable.

Sayat Nova

Zone 10   Northwest Suburbs
20 West Golf Road, Des Plaines
(847) 296-1776

Armenian	
★★★½	
Inexpensive/Moderate	
Quality 88	Value C

Reservations:	Recommended on weekends
When to go:	Weekdays
Entree range:	$10.50–15
Payment:	All major credit cards
Service rating:	★★★★
Friendliness rating:	★★★★½
Parking:	Lot
Bar:	Full service
Wine selection:	Limited (about 22); mostly American; 3 by the glass
Dress:	Casual, some dressy
Disabled access:	Yes
Customers:	Internationals, businesspeople, couples, families
Lunch:	Tuesday–Friday, 11:30 A.M.–2 P.M.
Dinner:	Tuesday–Thursday, Sunday, 4–10 P.M.; Friday and Saturday, 4–11 P.M.

Atmosphere/setting: Middle Eastern decor accented with tile inserts in wall alcoves. Very romantic and cozy; comfortable private booths; dimly lit.

House specialties: Spinach boereg (pastry); baba gannoujh; yalanji sarma (rice and pine nut–stuffed grape leaves); hummus and tahini with toasted pita bread; tabbouleh; jajic (minted yogurt and cucumber dip); Boghossian combination: lamb chop, lamb and chicken shish kebab, lula kebab (ground beef and lamb), rice pilaf, and broiled green pepper and tomato—a nice sampler.

Other recommendations: Various lamb specialties, including sautéed lamb and chops; shrimp kebab. Cheese and pear strudel, paklava (more delicious than they look); cheesecake with raspberry sauce—not Armenian, but a good light version; Armenian coffee.

Summary & comments: Sayat Nova is well established in this northwest suburb and has a steady clientele. It's reliable and a rarity for serving authentic Armenian cuisine. The gracious hospitality extended by this family-owned business, now into the second generation, invites return visits. One of the nicest places for a romantic evening or quiet business dinner. A member of the same family owns another Sayat Nova on Ohio in Chicago; the menu is similar, although the restaurants have separate management.

Seasons Restaurant

	American
Zone 3 Near North	★★★★★
Four Seasons Hotel,	Moderate/Expensive
120 East Delaware Place at Michigan Avenue	Quality 99 Value C
(312) 280-8800, ext. 2134	

Reservations:	Recommended
When to go:	Any time
Entree range:	$26–42; 5-course tasting menu, $56 or $84 with matching wines
Payment:	VISA, MC, AMEX, DC, D
Service rating:	★★★★★
Friendliness rating:	★★★★★
Parking:	Valet or self-parking on Rush or Walton Streets with covered access to hotel's 7th-floor lobby
Bar:	Full service
Wine selection:	320 selections; domestic and imported, including Californian sparkling wines and French champagnes; many fine selections by the glass
Dress:	Jacket required for men; upscale casual; dressy
Disabled access:	Yes
Customers:	Travelers, businesspeople, locals
Breakfast:	*Seasons Restaurant:* Monday–Saturday, 6:30–10:30 A.M.; Sunday, 6:30–10 A.M. *Seasons Cafe:* Sunday–Thursday, 8–11:30 A.M.; Friday and Saturday, 8 A.M.–12:30 P.M.
Brunch:	Sunday, 10:30 A.M.–1:30 P.M.
Lunch:	Monday–Saturday, 11:30 A.M.–2 P.M.
Dinner:	Every day, 6–10 P.M.

Atmosphere/setting: Opulent carpeted dining room with drapes, crystal sconces, and white tablecloths; lovely floral arrangements; elegant; artwork; nice view from tables near windows. Adjacent cafe is swank with a more casual approach.

House specialties: Menu changes each season, thus the name; daily specials and chef's tasting menu add more options. Some examples: maple-glazed quail and seared Hudson Valley foie gras salad, gingered rhubarb compote; grilled portobello mushroom, baby artichoke and asparagus terrine, a palette of infused oils, 50-year-old balsamico; Maine lobster and potato tower, applewood-smoked bacon, osetra caviar; organic field greens, Fourme d'Montbrisson cheese, air-dried strawberries,

(continued)

and 25-year-old balsamico; roasted Maui onion soup, smoked duck raviolini, aged Madeira; farm-raised striped sea bass, ragôut of peanut fingerlings, morels, and fava beans; superb honey-thyme glazed grain-fed guinea hen, corn polenta cake, spaghetti squash, wild blackberry vinegar (sauce a bit sweet but delicious overall); grilled organic veal chop, lemon-artichoke ragôut, crispy garlic potato cake. Desserts such as Eighth Wonder of the World (milk chocolate pyramid, caramelized bananas, coconut sorbet); exotic fruit and champagne soup, passion fruit sorbet in Florentine tuile; warm chocolate cappuccino cake, Tahitian vanilla bean ice cream, caramel pecan sauce; warm fig and blueberry compote.

Other recommendations: Lunch: Maine lobster salad with southwestern flavors; seared ahi tuna salad; steamed Atlantic salmon fillet on cucumber semolina; beef vinaigrette; scaloppine of chicken on fennel-potato pancake with spring morel–port wine sauce; grilled prime minute steak, Dijon mustard béarnaise, and shoestring fries. Dinner: roast Casco cod fillet with smoked cod-scallop hash; Seasons' vegetarian menu; roasted free-range chicken and pearl barley–sweet corn pilaf; prime rib-eye steak, rustic onion baked potato; Atlantic salmon fillet braised in chardonnay with fennel-herb risotto and shallot-wine reduction. Desserts: white chocolate marjolaine; orange-Drambuie ice cream with wild honey–cabernet sauce.

Entertainment & amenities: Jazz from the adjacent Seasons Lounge Friday and Saturday evenings can be heard in the dining room.

Summary & comments: Seasons specializes in innovative American cuisine made from fresh—often unusual—regional ingredients served in a simple style. Executive chef Mark Baker, who is from Boston, loves working with New England seafood, and it shows. He completely changes the menu the first day of spring, summer, and autumn, and changes it partially midwinter to utilize the freshest local products. Seasons has worked with the Department of Agriculture in several states to hand pick the highest-caliber regional suppliers. The restaurant also offers alternative cuisine that is low in calories, cholesterol, sodium, and fat (indicated by a star) and features vegetarian items (indicated by a vegetable icon). Baker's cooking overall avoids rich sauces; his stunning creations evolve with richness of flavor from prime ingredients cooked together and from reductions and vinaigrettes. Something new here is a tasting of Georg Weidemann's exquisite flavored apéritif wine vinegars from Switzerland, poured from a beautiful service into special hand-blown thimble glasses on long, thin stems. The vinegars are not harsh, and the chestnut and honey gold leaf are terrific. One of the most splendid hotel dining rooms anywhere. Try Seasons Cafe for lighter fare (any meal) at lower prices.

Honors/awards: Three and one-half stars from *Chicago* magazine; three stars from *Chicago Tribune*; named one of Chicago's eight top restaurants, *Wine Spectator*, 1997; recently recognized by *Food and Wine* and *Forbes* magazines.

Shaw's Crab House and Shaw's Blue Crab Lounge & Oyster Bar

Zone 4 The Loop	Seafood
21 East Hubbard Street	★★★★½
(312) 527-2722	Moderate
	Quality 95 Value C

Reservations:	*Main dining room*: suggested; *Blue Crab Lounge*: not accepted
When to go:	Any time
Entree range:	$12.95–18.95; Blue Crab Lounge a bit cheaper
Payment:	All major credit cards
Service rating:	★★★★
Friendliness rating:	★★★★
Parking:	Valet, $5
Bar:	Full service
Wine selection:	Largely Californian; seafood-friendly; good selection by the glass
Dress:	Casual to dressy
Disabled access:	Wheelchair accessible; call first
Customers:	Businesspeople, travelers, couples, singles
Lunch:	*Main dining room:* Monday–Friday, 11:30 A.M.–2 P.M.
Lunch/Dinner:	*Blue Crab Lounge:* Monday–Thursday, 11:30 A.M.–10 P.M.; Friday, 11:30 A.M.–11 P.M.; Saturday, 5–11 P.M.
Dinner:	*Main dining room:* Monday–Thursday, 5:30–10 P.M.; Friday and Saturday, 5–11 P.M.; Sunday, 5–10 P.M.

Atmosphere/setting: Two restaurants in one, with the main dining room and the Blue Crab Lounge (essentially a raw bar) serving the full menu.

House specialties: Shaw's crab cakes (my favorite); a great variety of oysters; blue crab fingers; baked clams casino; smoked salmon; spicy shrimp; griddled garlic shrimp; Shaw's seafood platter; whole Maine lobster; daily specials; sautéed Virginia striped bass; grilled Gulf swordfish. Blue Crab Lounge combo. Key lime pie; crème brûlée; pecan pie; cheesecake.

Other recommendations: Lobster bisque; seasonal specialties such as Maryland soft-shell crabs; chicken and prime beef. Chocolate hazelnut torte; fruit cobblers.

(continued)

Shaw's Crab House and Shaw's Blue Crab Lounge & Oyster Bar   (continued)

Entertainment & amenities: Lounge, jazz or blues, Tuesday and Thursday, 7–10 P.M.

Summary & comments: Pristinely fresh products, a variety of preparations, an extensive list of seafood-friendly wines, and knowledgeable service make Shaw's one of the best seafood places around. An on-staff seafood buyer constantly monitors products and storage temperatures. Promotions keep the crowds coming. Overall, simple preparations fare better than the more elaborate dishes. The bread basket items are addictive.

Shaw's Seafood Grill

	Seafood
Zone 11 Northern Suburbs	★★★
660 West Lake Cook Road, Deerfield	Moderate
(847) 948-1020	Quality 80 Value C

Reservations:	Suggested
When to go:	Any time
Entree range:	$10.95–32.95
Payment:	All major credit cards
Service rating:	★★★
Friendliness rating:	★★★
Parking:	Lot
Bar:	Full service
Wine selection:	Most selected for seafood; largely Californian, several international; good by the glass selection, from $4.25; about 10 featured wines
Dress:	Casual or business
Disabled access:	Wheelchair accessible, call first
Customers:	Mostly businesspeople, travelers, couples, singles
Lunch:	Monday–Friday, 11:30 A.M.–2:30 P.M.
Dinner:	Early evening menu, Sunday–Friday, 5–6 P.M.; Monday–Thursday, 5–9:30 P.M.; Friday and Saturday, 5–10:30 P.M.; Sunday, 4:30–9 P.M.

Atmosphere/setting: Resembles a 1940s East Coast seafood house with seating for 260 now after a remodeling. A live lobster tank has been added.

House specialties: Maryland-style crab cakes; New England clam chowder; Shaw's Caesar salad; assorted grilled fishes; grilled seafood salad; regional oyster specials; grilled flatbread with various toppings (as an appetizer for dinner or as a main course for early dinner and lunch); Lake Superior whitefish, garlic crusted. Key lime pie, crème brûlée, and pecan pie.

Other recommendations: Seasonal specialties such as Maryland soft-shell crabs, grilled Copper River king salmon (available only two or three weeks each summer), grilled Pacific halibut. Daily desserts: sorbet, cheesecake, and cobbler.

Summary & comments: Although similar to Shaw's Crab House in Chicago, this place, which started two years later in 1986, has some menu differences and is fashioned more like Blue Crab Lounge in the city. The same care is given to pristinely fresh products prepared in a variety of ways. With knowledgeable service and a good, seafood-friendly wine list and casual atmosphere, this is one of the best seafood restaurants in the suburbs. Look for seafood promotions such as the August Lobster Fest.

Sher-A-Punjab

Zone 1   North Side
2510 West Devon Avenue
(312) 973-4000

Indian	
★★★	
Inexpensive	
Quality 82	Value B

Reservations: Recommended
When to go: Any time
Entree range: $8–11.75; lunch buffet, $5.95; dinner buffet, $7.95
Payment: VISA, MC, D, DC, CB
Service rating: ★★
Friendliness rating: ★★★½
Parking: Two city lots nearby
Bar: None, BYOB
Wine selection: None
Dress: Moderately casual
Disabled access: Yes
Customers: Diverse, many ethnic families
Lunch/Dinner: Every day, 11 A.M.–11 P.M.

Atmosphere/setting: Clean and modern with pink tablecloths, plastic covers, candles, and plants.

House specialties: Saag panir (homemade cheese cooked in spiced spinach); dal (spiced lentil dip); mixed vegetable curry; chicken tandoori (not on buffet); delicate chicken biryani; lamb curry.

Other recommendations: Butter chicken; bharvan kulcha (stuffed bread); panir jalfrazie (cheese cubes sautéed with vegetables and spices); eggplant bhartha cooked in spicy yogurt.

Summary & comments: The extensive buffet here is a nice way of sampling the menu, except for certain items such as the tandoori specialties, which must be made to order. The buffet is replenished frequently and includes two breads. Spiced tea settles all. Service can have lapses. The proprietor also owns Bundoo Khan, a Pakistani restaurant on the same block. This restaurant is small, casual, and cozy, and it's also a very good value.

Shilla

Zone 1   North Side
5930 North Lincoln Avenue
(773) 275-5930

Korean/Japanese
★★★½
Moderate

Quality 86   Value C

Reservations:	Recommended, especially weekends
When to go:	Any time; Thursday and weekends busier
Entree range:	$7.95–28.95
Payment:	VISA, MC, AMEX, D
Service rating:	★★★
Friendliness rating:	★★★
Parking:	Free lot
Bar:	Full service; Asian brands, such as the Korean beers OB, Cass, and Nex
Wine selection:	International; house wine by the glass; sake and sweet plum wine; Korean soju
Dress:	Casual
Disabled access:	Yes
Customers:	Koreans, families, businesspeople
Open:	Every day, 11–2 A.M.; lunch buffet, 11 A.M.–3:30 P.M.; dinner buffet with 50 items and unlimited sushi, 5:30–10 P.M.

Atmosphere/setting: Large and upscale; an attractive 50-seat main dining hall with 7 rooms surrounding it. Smaller private dining rooms, some with grills in tables, are popular with businesspeople.

House specialties: Chap chae (pan-fried shredded pork, vegetables); mung bean noodles; nakji bogeum (stir-fried octopus, vegetables); kalbi (broiled short ribs); doenchang jige (spicy beef, vegetable, rice, and bean paste casserole—the bean paste takes six months to ferment); Korean barbecue, meats and chicken grilled at the table—wrap them in lettuce with bean paste; shik hae (off the menu), a punch drink of honeyed cinnamon broth with sweet rice and pine nuts.

Other recommendations: Pajun (scallion pancake with chopped octopus); buffets.

Summary & comments: Experience this place with several people if possible; it's fun to share specialties. The Korean menu is the least exotic Asian cuisine for the American palate, since it's based on grilled meats and barbecue-style sauces. A flotilla of side dishes is served with dinner. Dessert comes with dinners.

Honors/awards: 1996 Silver Platter; 1996 first-place winner, *Hard Kort* magazine.

Siam Cafe

Zone 1   North Side
4712 North Sheridan Road
(773) 769-6602

Thai	
★★★	
Inexpensive	
Quality 84	Value A

Reservations:	Accepted
When to go:	Any time; evenings and lunchtime can be busy
Entree range:	$4.75–8
Payment:	VISA, MC, AMEX, DC
Service rating:	★★★½
Friendliness rating:	★★★½
Parking:	Street
Bar:	Beer and wine
Wine selection:	American
Dress:	Casual
Disabled access:	Yes
Customers:	Locals
Lunch/Dinner:	Wednesday–Monday, 11:30 A.M.–9 P.M.

Atmosphere/setting: Attractively decorated with Thai furnishings; dressier than many Thai places.

House specialties: Hot and spicy seafood soup (one version is just shrimp; another is beef and chicken); spring rolls; mee krob (crispy rice noodle, fried tofu, shrimp, and sweet-and-sour sauce); yum nam tok (beef-onion salad with hot-and-sour sauce); pad thai (rice noodles, peanuts, bean sprouts, egg sauce); curry fried rice with choice of meat or shrimp.

Other recommendations: Kai yang (marinated charcoal chicken); kra tiem prik Thai (chicken, beef, or pork with garlic) without rice; red snapper with ginger or hot sauce.

Summary & comments: Large menu with many good choices for rock-bottom prices. Hot items on the menu are starred, and one column of dishes is called "original hot and spicy." Some of the ingredients include red and green curry paste, red chili sauce, jalapeño pepper, and red-hot spicy sauce! These are for the veteran hot food lovers—novices beware. There are numerous intriguing rice dishes and variations without rice.

The Signature Room
at the 95th

Zone 3   Near North
875 North Michigan Avenue, atop the
   John Hancock Center
(312) 787-9596

New American
★★★★
Moderate/Expensive

Quality 90   Value C

Reservations:	Recommended
When to go:	Any time
Entree range:	$19–29; Sunday brunch buffet, $25
Payment:	VISA, MC, AMEX, DC
Service rating:	★★★★½
Friendliness rating:	★★★★½
Parking:	Self-park garage
Bar:	Full service
Wine selection:	Award-winning, all-American with 155 choices; most moderately priced, from $25–250 a bottle; several good selections by the glass
Dress:	Chic casual, business; dinner, jackets suggested
Disabled access:	Yes
Customers:	Locals, businesspeople, couples, tourists
Brunch:	Sunday, 10:30 A.M.–2 P.M.
Lunch:	Monday–Friday, 11 A.M.–2 P.M.; buffet, $6.95
Dinner:	Sunday–Saturday, 5–10 P.M.

Atmosphere/setting: The view from the 95th floor of the John Hancock Center is spectacular on a clear day, a majestic backdrop for dining. Elegant, contemporary, sleek interior; a bright-hued mural depicts Chicago scenes.

House specialties: Honey-and-ginger-glazed salmon with napa cabbage, shiitake mushroom, and daikon salad; sautéed linguine with shrimp and bay scallops; various ice creams.

Other recommendations: Roasted portobello mushroom glazed with goat cheese, sun-dried tomatoes, and black olives, with basil pesto; chilled Gulf shrimp with avocado-tomato salsa and gazpacho sauce; fruit tart with chocolate layer on pastry.

Entertainment & amenities: Live music Saturday night and Sunday.

Summary & comments: Healthful, contemporary American cuisine based on organically grown produce and chemical-free ingredients. The greatest 360-degree panoramic view of Chicago and its lakefront is from this restaurant. The management donates 10 percent of profits to a chosen charity each month.

Honors/awards: *Wine Spectator* Grand Award; DiRoNA Top Ten; Restaurant of the Year by Food and Beverage Equipment Executives, 1996.

Skadarlija

Zone 1   North Side
4024 North Kedzie Avenue
(773) 463-5600

Serbian/Continental
★★★
Moderate
Quality 84   Value B

Reservations:	Accepted
When to go:	Dinner
Entree range:	$10.95–15.95
Payment:	AMEX
Service rating:	★★★★½
Friendliness rating:	★★★★½
Parking:	Street
Bar:	Full service, including slivovitz (plum brandy)
Wine selection:	Limited; Californian and Serbian
Dress:	Casual, but no shorts; dressy, depending on time
Disabled access:	Yes
Customers:	Locals, ethnics, families, couples
Open:	Wednesday–Friday, Sunday, 6 P.M.–2 A.M.; Saturday, 6 P.M.–3 A.M.

Atmosphere/setting: Restaurant has two levels of seating, an outdoor terrace, a bar area, and a dance floor. Dimly lit, comfortable dining room; seats about 100.

House specialties: Ajvar (spread of green and red sweet peppers); kjamak (fermented milk spread); Serbian cold plate (sausage, cheese, olives, and peppers); special appetizer of batter-fried, cheese-stuffed sweet peppers; raznici (shish kebab); tender Wiener Schnitzel; roast veal.

Other recommendations: Cheese strudel appetizer; cevapcici (national specialty of ground veal and beef, sometimes cheese-filled); gypsy plate (for two); karadjordjeva (veal steak wrapped around Bulgarian cheese, lightly breaded and baked). Palacinke (crêpes with preserves, chocolate, walnuts) and apple strudel. Serbian tea (flambéed slivovitz).

Entertainment & amenities: Live gypsy music every night. Serbian and Russian musicians. Owner Zvonko Klancnika plays accordion and synthesizer.

Summary & comments: Skadarlija is a well-known street in Belgrade frequented by musicians, artists, and writers; paintings of this street are on the walls. Traditional Serbian fare is prepared well and served in gracious style set by owners Nina and Zvonko Klancnika. There's a preponderance of meat in this cuisine, especially pork and veal, but a couple of fish items are offered. The atmosphere is warm and friendly, and authentic ethnic entertainment enlivens the evening.

Soul Kitchen

Zone 2   North Central
1576 North Milwaukee Avenue
(773)342-9742

Southern Regional American ★★★
Inexpensive/Moderate
Quality 84   Value C

Reservations: No
When to go: Avoid peak dinner hours (7:30–9 P.M.)
Entree range: $11–19; prix-fixe early dinner, $21.50–26, including
                        wine or cocktail
Payment: VISA, MC, AMEX
Service rating: ★★★
Friendliness rating: ★★★
Parking: Valet available
Bar: Full service; specialty cocktails such as Soul Martini,
                        Dixie Margarita, and the Barry White
Wine selection: International; $18–125 a bottle; $3.50–6.50 a glass
Dress: Casual
Disabled access: Yes
Customers: Diverse; all ages; some restaurant owners
Brunch: Sunday, 10 A.M.–2 P.M.
Dinner: Sunday–Thursday, 5–10:30 P.M.; Friday and Saturday,
                        5–11:30 P.M.

Atmosphere/setting: Vibrant and colorful decor: orange chairs; multicolored tiles; murals depicting city scenes; faux cheetah and reptile skin tablecloths.

House specialties: Coconut shrimp; pecan-coated catfish; shrimp and grits with tasso ham; two berry buckle (blackberry and raspberry buckle with lemon ice cream); ice creams and sorbets; and truffles (Frangelico, Kahlúa, or Bailey's).

Other recommendations: Wasabi-grilled calamari with Asian slaw; smoked free-range chicken; fire and spice lamb; toasted coconut flan.

Entertainment & amenities: Energetic soul and funk background music.

Summary & comments: Soul Kitchen's motto is "Loud food, spicy music." This funky Wicker Park neighborhood restaurant on the border of Bucktown features eclectic flavors of the South, including soul food, along with infusions of Caribbean, Latin American, and occasional Asian touches. Chefs Monique King and Michael Clark have created a constantly evolving menu, and they see their kitchen as a culinary playground. The assertive cooking and soulful music make this one of Chicago's cutting-edge and dynamic eateries.

Honors/awards: *Bon Appetit*, Best New Chicago Restaurant, October 1996; *Chicago* magazine, Pick of the Week, February 1996.

SPAGO

Zone 3   Near North
520 North Dearborn at Grand Avenue
(312) 527-3700

American	★★★★½
Moderate/Expensive	
Quality 94	Value B

Reservations:	Required
When to go:	Avoid peak mealtimes unless you have a reservation
Entree range:	Lunch, $12.50–18.75; dinner, $15.50–25.50
Payment:	VISA, MC, AMEX, CB, Optima, D, DC
Service rating:	★★★★½
Friendliness rating:	★★★★½
Parking:	Valet, $6
Bar:	Full service
Wine selection:	Mostly American, European; good selection by the glass; a bit pricey
Dress:	Jacket and tie preferred; dressy, business
Disabled access:	Yes
Customers:	Locals and travelers, mixed couples, families
Lunch:	Monday–Friday, 11:30 A.M.–2 P.M.
Dinner:	Sunday–Thursday, 5–10:30 P.M.; Friday and Saturday, 5–11 P.M.

Atmosphere/setting: This $5 million plus, 20,000-square-foot multilevel space in River North was designed by Adam D. Tihany of New York. The sophisticated nonsmoking dining room is decorated with patterned carpet and upholstery and subdued colors and lighting. The curved staircase leads to the second-floor club room bar and lounge with a fireplace and leather couches and chairs. The top level has three private party rooms with views of the skyline. Robert Rauschenberg paintings hang here, plus local artists' works.

House specialties: Menu changes seasonally. Pizzas baked in wood-burning ovens; fresh pastas; mesquite-grilled fish and meats; Spago house-made charcuterie plate; stir-fried spicy lamb with garlic, chile, cilantro, and ginger-sesame glaze; tuna tatki with marinated seaweed and cucumber salad; leek and artichoke ravioli with sautéed black bass and garlic-porcini sauce. Granny Smith apple tart with cinnamon ice cream; chocolate tart with vanilla ice cream and orange glaze.

Other recommendations: Sautéed foie gras with sweet potato chips and apple chutney; Maine scallops with pad thai noodles and spicy coconut sauce; roasted Cantonese duck with star anise, grapefruit, and a sesame bun; almond

(continued)

butter-crunch tart (lacking crunch) with maple-walnut ice cream.

Summary & comments: After several delays, Spago finally opened in fall 1996 and immediately received a lot of media attention. Chicagoans are glad that this Spago has been tailored to them. Austrian-born chef Wolfgang Puck, who is credited with recreating California cuisine with his Spago on Sunset Strip (opened 1982), said in a private interview that all his restaurants are like children; each is individual. He loves Chicago and is very pleased to be here. Wolfgang's brother Klaus and wife Amanda, with degrees from the Cornell School of Hotel Administration, are cogeneral managers. Managing partner Tom Kaplan has spent the past 14 years involved with Spago restaurants in Los Angeles, Tokyo, Las Vegas, and Mexico City. Executive chef François Kwaku-Dongo headed the kitchen at Spago in West Hollywood for five years before coming here to serve American cuisine with European and Asian influences and many midwestern ingredients. Puck gives his executive chef a lot of flexibility, and the food has been innovative and flavorful on all visits. Some of the signature dishes have been transplanted, but there are many new items in the repertoire. The grill and bar area have a separate menu.

Spago Grill

Zone 3   Near North
520 North Dearborn
(312) 527-3700

American
★★★★
Moderate/Expensive
Quality 94   Value B

Reservations:	Accepted
When to go:	Early dinner less crowded
Entree range:	$15.50–27
Payment:	VISA, MC, AMEX, CB, O, D, DC
Service rating:	★★★★
Friendliness rating:	★★★★
Parking:	Valet
Bar:	Full service
Wine selection:	American and European; several by the glass; a bit pricey
Dress:	Casual
Disabled access:	Yes
Customers:	Mixed; mostly businesspeople at lunch; evenings, families, professionals, couples, tourists, locals
Lunch/Dinner:	Sunday–Thursday, 11:30 A.M.–11 P.M.; Friday and Saturday, 11:30 A.M.–midnight

Atmosphere/setting: Spago and Spago Grill are housed together. To the left of the entrance is the cafe and bar area with its own menu. Open kitchen.

House specialties: Menu changes with what's seasonally available. Famous pizzas and calzones baked in wood-burning ovens; homemade pastas, such as François' angel hair pasta with tomato, basil, and garlic; mesquite-grilled fish and meats. Desserts may sometimes be the same as those offered in the dining room, such as Granny Smith apple tart with cinnamon ice cream. Others might be vanilla crème brûlée and tiramisu parfait.

Other recommendations: Pizza with duck sausage, shiitakes; oven-roasted Sonoma lamb with garlic potato puree and nicoise olive jus; roasted vegetable sandwich. Blonde brownie sundae; ice creams, sorbets, cookies.

Entertainment & amenities: Club room bar on second floor; retail shop.

Summary & comments: Austrian-born, superstar chef Wolfgang Puck shows his innovative culinary stuff here in Chicago at his Spago Grill as well as in his more sophisticated dining room, Spago. Executive chef François Kwaku-Dongo's American cuisine has European and Asian influences and a healthy portion of midwestern ingredients. The cooking is boldly flavored, a trademark of Wolf's. Children are welcome here at the grill, and booster seats and highchairs are provided; early reservations are suggested.

284

Spiaggia

Zone 3   Near North
980 North Michigan Avenue
(312) 280-2750

Italian	
★★★★½	
Moderate/Expensive	
Quality 95	Value C

Reservations:	Recommended
When to go:	Any time
Entree range:	$8.95–29.95; per person total, $50–60
Payment:	All major credit cards
Service rating:	★★★★
Friendliness rating:	★★★½
Parking:	Valet, underground city facility on Walton
Bar:	Full service
Wine selection:	Extensive; Italian; $25–125 a bottle
Dress:	Business, some semiformal and formal
Disabled access:	Yes
Customers:	Locals; national, international, business travelers; suburbanites, celebrities, and politicians
Lunch:	Monday–Saturday, 11:30 A.M.–2 P.M.
Dinner:	Monday–Thursday, 5:30–9:30 P.M.; Friday and Saturday, 5:30–10:30 P.M.; Sunday, 5:30–9 P.M.

Atmosphere/setting: Contemporary, rather formal dining setting over-looking Lake Michigan and Oak Street Beach.

House specialties: Stracci con ragu di funghi (rags of fresh pasta with wild mushrooms); ricotta ravioli filled with sweet Tuscan pecorino cheese; seafood risotto; wood-roasted veal chop, smoked pancetta; fillet of salmon with asparagus, basil, and white wine sauce; wood-roasted guinea hen with Savoy cabbage.

Other recommendations: Thin-crust gourmet pizzas; mascarpone torte; ice creams.

Entertainment & amenities: Piano every evening at 6 P.M.

Summary & comments: This very chic restaurant has had ups and downs. Under the talented direction of chef Paul Bartolotta, the food has been elevated to a new level. He's rescued it from the earlier experimental and creative Italian fare and brought it back to regional roots. The sometimes inconsistent, reserved service appears to have improved as well. Cafe Spiaggia next door offers excellent light fare for lower prices (see profile).

Honors/awards: Chef Paul Bartolotta received a James Beard Award, 1994; *Chicago* magazine's Critics Choice Award; Insegna del Ristorante Italiano del Mundo (for overseas Italian restaurants showing superior culinary achievement), June 1997.

SPRUCE

Zone 3 Near North	New American
238 East Ontario	★★★★½
(312) 642-3757	Inexpensive/Moderate
	Quality 94 Value B

Reservations:	Recommended
When to go:	Early or late, Monday through Thursday
Entree range:	$17–24
Payment:	MC, VISA, AMEX, DC, D
Service rating:	★★★★½
Friendliness rating:	★★★★★
Parking:	Valet, dinner; self-park
Bar:	Full service, but no seating
Wine selection:	Extensive; small American wineries; French and Italian; $25–100 a bottle; $6–8 a glass
Dress:	Business casual to dressy
Disabled access:	Yes
Customers:	Businesspeople, downtown shoppers, travelers
Lunch:	Monday–Friday, 11:30 A.M.–2 P.M.
Dinner:	Monday–Thursday, 5:30–10 P.M.; Friday and Saturday, 5:30–11 P.M.

Atmosphere/setting: Minimalist-style large dining room with hardwood floors, fresh flowers, warm lighting, original art. Private room (up to 45 guests).

House specialties: Menu changes to reflect seasonal availability. Prix-fixe lunch specials with dishes such as cream of broccoli cumin soup and chicken salad focaccia sandwich. Other examples: seared diver scallops and salt cod torte; winter greens with Auricchio grana cheese crisp; caramelized three-citrus torte.

Other recommendations: Herbed rabbit "chops" on crisp risotto cake with baba gannoujh (somewhat spicy). For dessert, seasonal offerings such as brioche bread pudding with roasted mango and Tahitian vanilla bean ice cream; chocolate banana mousse cake with rose hip and wildflower-honey sorbet; caramel, gianduja, and malted parfait pyramid.

Summary & comments: This is one of the most exciting, new fine-dining restaurants in downtown Chicago for the sheer pleasure of the food. Chef Keith Luce, with White House credentials (Bill Clinton's term), is in his late twenties and looks younger, but he's covered a lot of culinary ground in his career. The food is innovative, flavorful, and made from great ingredients, such as heirloom tomatoes, veggie chips, and top Wisconsin cheeses.

Honors/awards: *North Shore* magazine, Number One Readers' Favorite, 1997; AAA, four diamonds, 1994–1996; *Esquire*, Best New Restaurant, 1996.

Stanley's Kitchen & Tap

Zone 1 North Side	Southern
1970 North Lincoln Avenue	★★½
(312) 642-0007	Inexpensive
	Quality 79 Value A

Reservations:	For 8 or more
When to go:	Any time
Entree range:	$5.95–8.95
Payment:	All major credit cards
Service rating:	★★★
Friendliness rating:	★★★★
Parking:	Street, lot nearby
Bar:	Full service; over 120 kinds of American bourbon and whiskey
Wine selection:	All American; everything available by the glass
Dress:	Casual
Disabled access:	Yes
Customers:	Locals, couples, families, some businesspeople
Dinner:	Monday–Friday, 5 P.M.–2 A.M.; Saturday, noon–3 A.M.; Sunday, noon–2 A.M.

Atmosphere/setting: Entryway through 100-seat saloon with 32-foot mahogany bar. Very homey; wooden porch where you can play checkers, chess, dominoes, or backgammon in rocking chairs; 80-seat dining room resembles a stage set depicting a 1940s family kitchen. Downstairs dining room recently renovated.

House specialties: Kentucky-fried tomatoes; blackened catfish, tender and coated with Cajun seasonings; Stan's vegetarian lasagna; chicken-fried steak made with pounded sirloin, preferred over the usual cube steak; creamy chicken short-cake (on sourdough biscuits); mashed potatoes and macaroni and cheese.

Other recommendations: Fried catfish strips, blackened or buffalo-style; black bean chicken chili (thick with chicken); jalapeño Jack sticks. Suppers are served with side dish of choice. Exceptional side dishes: southern spaghetti (tossed) and wet fries (with gravy). Nightly specials such as shrimp Creole. Apple pie with cinnamon ice cream; bread pudding with warm vanilla sauce.

Entertainment & amenities: Playing games on the porch.

Summary & comments: This fun restaurant offers what our fast-paced lives make us yearn for—comforting food in a nurturing atmosphere. This is a home away from home and as close to Mom's cooking as you can get. The food is simple and good, served in generous portions in a caring environment, and the bargain prices add to the comfort factor.

St. Germain Restaurant/ Bakery Cafe

Zone 3   Near North
1210 North State Parkway
(312) 266-9900

French Bakery Cafe
★★★½
Inexpensive/Moderate

Quality 88   Value C

Reservations:	Not necessary, weekdays; suggested, weekends
When to go:	Any time; less busy 3–5 P.M.
Entree range:	Lunch, $7–13; dinner, $9.50–19
Payment:	All major credit cards
Service rating:	★★★½
Friendliness rating:	★★★½
Parking:	3 hours validated in lot across the street
Bar:	Full service
Wine selection:	French and Californian; several by the glass
Dress:	Casual
Disabled access:	Yes
Customers:	Locals, French, tourists
Open:	Monday–Thursday, 8 A.M.–10 P.M.; Friday and Saturday, 8 A.M.–11 P.M.; Sunday, 8 A.M.–9 P.M.

Atmosphere/setting: Charming; très Parisienne in style. Beautiful bakery with displayed breads and pastries. One section similar to a French outdoor cafe. Dimly lit bar room in rear.

House specialties: Change weekly. Some top choices include namesake pizza with mixed bell peppers, mushrooms, asparagus, and mozzarella; escargot de Bourgogne; grilled double breast of chicken; rib-eye steak grille; salmon grille; breads and pastries (e.g., fruit tarts). Choice of bread as well as french fries, rice, St. Germain potatoes, or fresh vegetables with meal.

Other recommendations: Soup du jour; crêpe du jour (crêpes Bretonnes such as spinach and cheese); grilled goat cheese sandwich; croque monsieur (French bistro classic of ham and melted Swiss cheese on toasted pain de mie).

Entertainment & amenities: Pianist on Saturday.

Summary & comments: A nice vicarious escape to France—the setting transports you, whether you carry out baked goods, have a snack, or enjoy an entire meal. Sandwiches can be made with your choice of bread or croissant. This is a relaxing place for Francophiles.

STIR CRAZY

Zone 9   Western Suburbs
105 Oakbrook Center, Oakbrook
(630)575-0155

Pan-Asian	
★★★½	
Inexpensive	
Quality 88 Value B	

Reservations:	For 8 or more weekdays
When to go:	Weekdays and Sunday evenings less busy
Entree range:	Small, $6.45–9.45 (lunch); large, $7.95–11.95
Payment:	AMEX, D, DC, MC, VISA
Service rating:	★★★½ (partly self-serve)
Friendliness rating:	★★★★½
Parking:	Free mall lot
Bar:	Full-service; wide variety of specialty drinks
Wine selection:	Japanese, American; $3.50–4.50 a glass; $15–19 a bottle
Dress:	Casual
Disabled access:	Complete
Customers:	Mixed; locals, businesspeople, families, couples
Lunch/Dinner:	Monday–Thursday, 11 A.M.–10 P.M.; Friday and Saturday, 11 A.M.–11 P.M.; Sunday, noon–10 P.M.

Atmosphere/setting: The name suggests casualness and whimsy, and the vibrant, contemporary decor echoes that tone. Colorful market bar; display kitchen.

House specialties: The create-your-own stir-fry has over 20 fresh vegetables; chicken, beef, pork, shrimp, salmon, and other seafood, which are topped off with three ladles of one of the eleven distinctive sauces and one ladle of a spice. White or brown rice and noodles; banana won tons with white chocolate; vanilla ice cream and caramel sauce; lemon-ginger sorbet.

Other recommendations: The "big and crazy platter" (imperial rolls, fried chicken and vegetable egg rolls, chicken satay, plum chicken); pineapple curried fried rice; wok-prepared garlic chicken and spicy kung pao chicken; Shanghai noodles and Vietnamese pho soup; Asian tiramisu; fruit-topped cheesecake.

Summary & comments: Stir Crazy Cafe has a special dual menu that gives customers the option to create their own stir-fry or choose from prepared dishes on the menu. This differentiates it from others in the "cook-your-own" Asian restaurant flock. This Oakbrook prototype embraces Asian cuisines, including Chinese, Japanese, Thai, and Vietnamese. The servers assist in recommending sauces. Then you're on your own to create your bowl full of ingredients.

SZECHWAN EAST

Zone 4   The Loop
300 East Ohio Street
(312) 255-9200

	Chinese
	★★★★
	Moderate
	Quality 92 Value C

Reservations: Recommended
When to go: Any time
Entree range: $7.95–31.95; average $11–14
Payment: All major credit cards
Service rating: ★★★★
Friendliness rating: ★★★★★
Parking: Validated garage
Bar: Full service; Mandarin cocktails, imported beers
Wine selection: About 24 international, several Asian choices
                          (2 served in jars); mostly affordable; upscale list
Dress: Casual, but most wear business attire
Disabled access: Yes, except rest rooms are down a set of stairs
Customers: Largely businesspeople, conventiongoers, tourists
Brunch: Sunday champagne buffet, 11:30 A.M.–2 P.M.
Lunch/Dinner: Sunday–Thursday, 11:30 A.M.–10:30 P.M.; Friday,
                          11:30 A.M.–11 P.M.; Saturday, noon–11 P.M.; lunch
                          buffet, Monday–Saturday, 11:30 A.M.–2 P.M., $8.95

Atmosphere/setting: Attractive, spacious dining rooms and niches; bar/lounge; lovely Chinese decor. New sidewalk cafe.

House specialties: Fire pot satay beef; Szechuan noodle salad. Black bean salmon (fillets); steamed fish fillet with rice and wine–ginger–black bean sauce; Mongolian-style veal. Vegetable dishes: Szechuan string beans; festival of mushrooms; steamed vegetable delight with tofu and garlic dipping sauce. "Gourmet menu" item: three jewels in a nest (scallops, escargot, filet mignon chunks). Chef's specialties: new Hwa Shee Jeer Surprise (chicken and escargot with mushrooms, vegetables); Governor's Chicken, a best-seller. Expanded lunch/brunch buffet.

Other recommendations: Assorted hot appetizers; hot and sour soup; Taiwanese escargot rice (healthier than fried rice); moo shu crêpes; Rich Chinese crêpes with dates, banana in flaming rum, or light almond tofu.

Summary & comments: This has long been one of the top Chinese restaurants because of the comprehensive menu, excellent cooking, and attentive service from the friendly staff. To celebrate Szechwan House's 13th anniversary, owner Alfred Hsiu added several new menu items. Wonderful banquets. You'll never be bored dining here regularly. Carryout and dinner delivery available.

SZECHWAN RESTAURANT

Chinese
★★★
Inexpensive/Moderate

Quality 83   Value C

Zone 3   Near North
625 North Michigan Avenue
(312) 482-9898

Reservations:	Recommended
When to go:	Any time
Entree range:	$6.95–19.95
Payment:	All major credit cards
Service rating:	★★★½
Friendliness rating:	★★★½
Parking:	Discount parking available
Bar:	Full service
Wine selection:	Mostly Californian, French; some Chinese; $14–26 a bottle; several by the glass, $4.50
Dress:	Casual
Disabled access:	Yes
Customers:	Diverse
Lunch/Dinner:	Every day, 11:30 A.M.–10:30 P.M.

Atmosphere/setting: Modern Chinese; spacious, handsome, comfortable interior; one level below sidewalk level.

House specialties: Dim sum available all day (e.g., steamed shrimp dumplings, vegetarian dumplings, pot stickers, shrimp toast, stuffed bean-curd rolls). Stuffed crab claws (Hunan appetizer); imperial honey ham (with lotus seeds in sweet laurel bloom flower sauce); empress sizzling lamb with leek; crispy chicken.

Other recommendations: Roast Peking duck (available with no advance notice); chrysanthemum fish sweet and sour; lobster with ginger and tomato sauce; peacock pork; stuffed banana with red bean paste (for two).

Summary & comments: This is one of the only places to get dim sum downtown and perhaps the only Chinese restaurant serving it all day long. Make a meal from the dim sum special menu, or start with dumplings and select one of the many unusual entrees. It's even possible to order Peking duck at the last moment here, unlike most other places, which request a day's advance notice. Hot and spicy dishes are starred.

TALLGRASS

Zone 8   Southern Suburbs
1006 South State Street, Lockport
(815) 838-5566

New French	
★★★★★	
Very Expensive	
Quality 98	Value C

Reservations:	Necessary
When to go:	Dinner
Entree range:	$45 (4-course) or $55 (5-course) prix-fixe menu
Payment:	Personal checks (local), MC, V
Service rating:	★★★★★
Friendliness rating:	★★★★
Parking:	Street
Bar:	Full service
Wine selection:	Fairly priced; several by the glass
Dress:	Upscale casual to dressy; jackets required for men
Disabled access:	Partially accessible; not bathrooms
Customers:	Diverse; upscale, sophisticated diners
Dinner:	Wednesday–Sunday, 6–9 P.M.

Atmosphere / setting: Victorian, eclectic setting in a historic building. Downstairs dining room: copper-hued lavolier walls and ceilings; the chef's Aubrey Beardsley–inspired paintings. Smoke-free; smoking permitted in hallway.

House specialties: Appetizer trio of crab cake, lobster lasagna, shrimp timbale; crispy brie with oyster mushrooms, mixed greens; potato sandwich of duck breast; foie gras and coddled eggs; mint-crusted spring lamb loin; walnut-sorrel pesto–coated rack of lamb; grilled Atlantic salmon and jumbo prawn; soufflé of Belgian dark chocolate and cherry puree. Signature dessert: Tallgrass chocolate and raspberry tower with two sauces.

Other recommendations: Asparagus pierogis on wild mushroom duxelle; lobster, mango, basil salad, and Parmesan tile; coconut-crusted sea scallops with pineapple risotto, curry beurre blanc; chèvre and baby watercress with walnut oil; veal sweetbreads Provençal; savoury of poached pear, spiced nuts, blue cheese; lemon mousse between almond wafer cookies with raspberries, almond cream.

Summary & comments: Co-owners J. Thomas Alves and chef Robert Burcenski embellished this 1895 Victorian building in the charming town of Lockport. Chef Burcenski masterfully mixes his special culinary techniques and quality ingredients to create deliciously unique, beautifully presented dishes. Portions are ample. Salads are listed and served after the main course. Service here is first class. One of the greatest dining experiences in the Chicago area.

Honors / awards: DiRoNA; *Conde Nast*, four diamond award; *Wine Spectator* Award; one of five Best of the Year restaurants, *Chicago* magazine.

Tango Sur

Zone 1 North Side	Argentinian
3763 North Southport	★★½
(773) 477-5466	Inexpensive/Moderate
	Quality 78 Value B

Reservations: For 6 or more
When to go: Monday, Tuesday, Wednesday, or Sunday
Entree range: $7.90–16
Payment: MC, VISA
Service rating: ★★★
Friendliness rating: ★★★★
Parking: Street
Bar: None; BYOB
Wine selection: None
Dress: Casual
Disabled access: Yes
Customers: Professionals, theatergoers, locals, suburbanites,
                        Argentinians, Peruvians, Colombians
Dinner: Monday–Thursday, 5–10.30 P.M.; Friday and Saturday,
                        5–11:30 P.M.; Sunday, noon–11 P.M.

Atmosphere/setting: Simple storefront colorfully decorated.

House specialties: Matambre (Argentine specialty of veal rolled and
cooked with vegetables , served cold); empanadas stuffed with beef, chicken, ham,
and ricotta cheese, or just spinach and ricotta cheese; pastas with Argentinian
tomato sauce; noqui (potato dumplings topped with beef stew); parillada (barbecue) featuring a variety of meats; traditional flan with Argentine caramel.

Other recommendations: Entradas: berenjena en escabeche (marinated sliced
eggplant); bife de chorizo (grilled boneless strip steak); suprema ala napolitana
(chicken breast breaded, topped with baked ham, mozzarella, tomato sauce); entrana
(grilled outer skirt); vacio (grilled flap meat). Postres: pionono (Argentine pound
cake rolled, filled with caramel).

Entertainment & amenities: Last Wednesday of every month, live folk or
tango music and all-you-can-eat nocquis for $7.50.

Summary & comments: This new restaurant's timely arrival is in step with
Argentina's higher profile, due mainly to the growing popularity of the tango
(highlighted in the successful "Tango Forever" performance), and the recent
release of the Alan Parker–directed *Evita.* Although the dance is sultry, this place
is not; it serves straightforward Argentinian fare with lively native music that is
often too loud for the small room. The staff is friendly, and the recommended
items are quite good. This is a beef-oriented cuisine, and servings are large.

TANIA'S

Zone 2   North Central/O'Hare
2659 North Milwaukee Avenue
(773) 235-7120

Cuban/Spanish
★★★½
Moderate

Quality 86   Value B

Reservations:	Accepted
When to go:	Any time
Entree range:	$11.95–21.95
Payment:	Major credit cards
Service rating:	★★★★
Friendliness rating:	★★★★
Parking:	Free valet, dinner only
Bar:	Full service
Wine selection:	Exceptional list; Spanish, French, Chilean, Californian
Dress:	Well-dressed business and casual; dancing attire late at night
Disabled access:	Yes
Customers:	Local; popular with the Cuban community; couples
Open:	Sunday–Friday, 11–4 A.M.; Saturday, 11–5 A.M.

Atmosphere/setting: Spacious, beautiful interior resembles a courtyard complete with a fountain filled with flowers—very romantic. Big bar area with dance floor. Upstairs dining area offers a view of the courtyard.

House specialties: Cuban black bean soup; croquetas de jamón; Estoril shrimp in sherry-garlic sauce; Cuban-style seafood paella served per person here (more liquid than Spanish version), requires almost one hour; red snapper Caribbean-style; shrimp in Creole sauce; lechon asado (Cuban roast pork slices cooked with yucca).

Other recommendations: Empanadillas vegetarianas (foldovers with ricotta and spinach); palomilla steak cut Cuban-style. Great guava flan; three milks cake. Caribbean coffee is an enjoyable production to watch, done tableside; when the waiter flambées the rum and cinnamon, sparks fly.

Entertainment & amenities: Wednesday–Sunday, 10:30 P.M.–4 A.M., live 12-piece band plays Cuban and Caribbean music.

Summary & comments: Menu is devoted mostly to Cuban specialties, which have a strong Spanish influence. Some Mexican and Puerto Rican dishes, as well. Very gracious service with flair. Menu changes twice a year, but certain signature items remain. Although the music can be loud, the overall cultural dining and dancing experience is fun.

Thai Borrahn

Zone 3   Near North
16 East Huron Street
(312) 440-6003

Thai
★★★★
Inexpensive/Moderate

Quality 90   Value B

Reservations:	Lunch, for large groups; dinner, recommended
When to go:	Any time
Entree range:	$6.25–18
Payment:	VISA, MC, AMEX, DC
Service rating:	★★★★
Friendliness rating:	★★★★½
Parking:	Street
Bar:	Full service; Singha, the popular Thai beer
Wine selection:	Limited international; Japanese sake, plum wine; mostly American; 11 by the glass; affordable
Dress:	Business casual to dressy
Disabled access:	No; restaurant on second floor—no elevator
Customers:	Local
Open:	Monday–Thursday, 11 A.M.–10 P.M.; Friday, 11 A.M.–10:30 P.M.; Saturday, 4–10:30 P.M.; Sunday, 4–10 P.M.

Atmosphere/setting: "Borrahn" in Thai means "ancient times," and this restaurant's attractive decor with some antiques underscores this theme. Classically patterned blue and white china, and authentic footed rice bowls.

House specialties: The famous pad thai (thin rice noodles, sweet turnip, bean sprouts, tofu, and egg stir-fried in sweet-sour tamarind sauce with a choice of meat or vegetables); tom yum chicken (hot and sour soup with lemongrass, cilantro, lime, chile, mint); on request, Thai Borrahn jan ront (sesame beef in a hot plate with oyster sauce, vegetables).

Other recommendations: Borrahn spring roll (avocado, cream cheese, and more); seaweed spring roll; house garden salad with mild curry peanut sauce; pad talay (seafood combination with vegetables, basil, ginger); catfish red curry.

Summary & comments: This upscale downtown restaurant offers affordable gourmet Thai cuisine from Bangkok, with some regional specialties as well. In its new home on the second floor of an East Huron building, Thai Borrahn continues its tradition of authentic recipes from chef Ratana's family. There's a seafood focus to the newly expanded, varied menu and several vegetarian items and options. The food is artfully presented and decorated with fruit and vegetable carvings, a signature trait on which Thai chefs pride themselves.

302 WEST

Zone 9   Western Suburbs
302 West State Street, Geneva
(630) 232-9302

Reservations:	Recommended
When to go:	Any time
Entree range:	$21–25 (perhaps slightly higher)
Payment:	VISA, MC, AMEX, DC, CB, D
Service rating:	★★★½
Friendliness rating:	★★★★
Parking:	Street
Bar:	Full service; premium labels
Wine selection:	Extensive American; unique styles; French champagnes; several $18–30, but most more expensive; many by the glass
Dress:	Casual; no dress code, but most guests are chic
Disabled access:	Yes
Customers:	Businesspeople, couples, wine lovers
Dinner:	Tuesday–Thursday, 6–9 P.M.; Friday and Saturday, 6–10 P.M.

Atmosphere/setting: Elegant, spacious restaurant on the second level of a historic bank building. High ceilings and 30-foot palladium windows. Relaxed fine dining; never intimidating.

House specialties: Menu changes daily. Examples: appetizers of roasted beefsteak tomato stuffed with goat cheese on angel hair; grilled, sliced southern-style barbecue rabbit tenderloin with corn pancakes; spicy Louisiana turtle gumbo; lightly smoked swordfish "tubetti" filled with tomato, cantaloupe, and pine nuts. Entrees: grilled Hawaiian moonfish steak; grilled, tequila-honey-lime marinated half free-range chicken on spiced red beans; roasted sablefish fillet in smoked salmon cream; excellent hickory-roasted pork loin. Desserts: homemade mascarpone ice cream with dark mocha sauce; malted-milk chocolate mousse cake; peach-almond ice cream cake; pear-vanilla sorbet; granita of wildly fruity Barbera wine.

Other recommendations: Appetizer of grilled jumbo sea scallops tossed with baby lettuces and chardonnay vinaigrette. Entrees: fresh Canadian walleye fillet sautéed; grilled buffalo rib-eye steak with horseradish mashed potatoes; roasted, sliced pork tenderloin with Cajun gravy and southern-style "goober

(continued)

peas." Desserts: fresh mission figs marinated in sweet Muscat wine with mascarpone cheese; Key lime cheesecake.

Entertainment & amenities: Regularly scheduled piano, harp, and vocal music.

Summary & comments: The daily menu is a single page, whereas the wine list is 13 pages (not counting the extensive list of ports, sherries, and Madeiras and an additional list of wines by the glass). Truly a wine-oriented restaurant, and the list is well worth scrutinizing before ordering, since this is a chance to try some very unusual selections. If you're waiting for a table at the upstairs bar, sip an apéritif wine and peruse the menu and wine list, which takes a bit of reading. Chef-owner Joel Findlay's personality definitely shines through his menu and wine lists. His wife, co-owner Catherine Findlay, warmly greets guests and oversees the front of the house. An ambitious dessert list with about 20 daily specials—some quite sweet, especially those with caramel sauce or brown sugar.

Honors/awards: *Wine Spectator* Award of Excellence; Best Seafood Chef Award from Illinois Seafood Association; DiRoNA.

Topolobampo

Zone 4   The Loop
445 North Clark Street
(312) 661-1434

Mexican
★★★★½
Moderate

Quality 95   Value C

Reservations:	Call a day before
When to go:	Tuesday, Wednesday, or Thursday
Entree range:	$14–25
Payment:	All major credit cards
Service rating:	★★★½
Friendliness rating:	★★½
Parking:	Valet, $5; street, public lots
Bar:	Shares common bar with Frontera Grill; good tequila and Mexican beer list
Wine selection:	Quite extensive; very international
Dress:	Formal, upscale
Disabled access:	Yes
Customers:	Locals and travelers, businesspeople, couples
Lunch:	Tuesday–Friday, 11:30 A.M.–2 P.M.; Saturday, 10:30 A.M.–2:30 P.M.
Dinner:	Tuesday–Thursday, 5:30–9:30 P.M.; Friday and Saturday, 5:30–10:30 P.M.

Atmosphere/setting: More formal and elegant than adjacent Frontera Grill; comfortable; handsomely appointed with native art. Recently expanded.

House specialties: Menu changes every two weeks. Cooking is refined at Topolobampo. Appetizer sampler might offer crispy, smoky-flavored pork carnitas, cactus salad, and more. Fish gets unusual treatment. A sampler plate might include chicken enchiladas; duck, cheese, and pepper quesadilla; tostada of cactus salad and black beans; lemon tart.

Other recommendations: Sopa Azteca with chicken breast, avocado, and cheese; cod empanadas; tamale of fresh masa with pheasant; roasted capon breast stuffed with squash blossoms and wild greens; various chocolate desserts.

Summary & comments: A great variety of some rarely known dishes. Owners Rick Bayless (chef) and wife Deanne (manager) co-authored a cookbook, *Authentic Mexican*; both the book and restaurant received good reviews. Service has become friendlier, especially at the entrance. Topolobampo is one of the best Mexican restaurants in the country; you've probably never tasted Mexican cuisine quite like this.

Honors/awards: Positive reviews from *International Herald Tribune*, *New York Times*. Chef Bayless won 1995 Best Chef in America Award from James Beard Foundation.

Toulouse on the Park

Zone 1   North Side
2140 North Lincoln Park West
(773) 665-9071

Light French-American	
★★★★½	
Moderate	
Quality 94	Value B

Reservations: Recommended
When to go: Any time with reservation
Entree range: $15.50–22; some specials $24.95
Payment: VISA, MC, AMEX, DC
Service rating: ★★★★½
Friendliness rating: ★★★★
Parking: Valet
Bar: Full service; outstanding cognac selection
Wine selection: More than 50 American, French, Italian; 8 half-
                       bottles; 7 by the glass, $5–6.50
Dress: Chic informal; fashionable casual; business attire
Disabled access: Yes
Customers: Upscale; businesspeople, romantic couples
Dinner: Monday–Thursday, 5–10:30 P.M.; Friday and Saturday,
                       5–11:30 P.M.
Bar: Monday–Thursday, 8 P.M.–1 A.M.; Friday,
                       6 P.M.–1 A.M.; Saturday, 6 P.M.–2 A.M.

Atmosphere/setting: The stunning interior is a shimmering jewel box, decorated and furnished in opulent Louis XV style. Mirrors reflect the hand-painted
ceiling and walls. The Toulouse Cognac Bar across the hall is romantic and plush,
and it's home to a large portrait of the namesake artist, Henri de Toulouse-Lautrec.

House specialties: Menus change seasonally. Appetizers: grilled portobello
mushroom with Romaine and concassé; sautéed sea scallops. Soup, fish, and game
du jour specials. From the menu: grilled salmon; noisette of sautéed veal; roasted
rack of lamb; roasted duck breast.

Other recommendations: House pâtés; sautéed chicken breast. Daily
desserts are presented with spun sugar decorations that are almost as spectacular as
the interior. Try raspberry and passion-fruit mousse; Napoleon (chocolate and
vanilla on raspberry ice cream); and chef's trio: petit fondant, petit brûlée, and
orange ice cream.

Summary & comments: This is one of the best fine dining restaurants in
the city, especially because it is surprisingly affordable for the fine French cuisine
in opulent surroundings. Chef Thomas Cicero meets the challenge of creating
menus with delicious, upscale dishes. Dining here is a sumptuous bargain.

Trattoria Gianni

Zone 1   North Side
1711 North Halsted Street
(312) 266-1976

Italian
★★★★
Inexpensive/Moderate
Quality 91   Value C

Reservations:	Requested
When to go:	After-theater crowd leaves at 7:30 P.M.
Entree range:	Pastas, $8.95–12.95; entrees, $10.95–16.95
Payment:	VISA, MC, AMEX, DC, CB
Service rating:	★★★★
Friendliness rating:	★★★★★
Parking:	Valet in front of restaurant
Bar:	Full service; all Italian beers
Wine selection:	All Italian regional wines; thoughtful list; several excellent choices by the glass
Dress:	Chic casual
Disabled access:	Yes
Customers:	Appeals to all ages, including families
Brunch:	Sunday, noon–3 P.M., Italian buffet brunch
Lunch:	Tuesday–Friday, 11:30 A.M.–2:30 P.M.
Dinner:	Tuesday–Thursday, 5–11 P.M.; Friday and Saturday, 5–11:30 P.M.; Sunday, 4–10 P.M.

Atmosphere/setting: Typical authentic Italian trattoria setting—warm, friendly, and bright. Recently expanded.

House specialties: Antipasti: portobello alla griglia (summer item: whole mushroom marinated in olive oil, garlic, rosemary, and balsamic vinegar, then grilled); polpo (grilled octopus); calamari vino blanco; insalata Variopinta (summer item: mixed baby lettuces, sliced apple and pear, arugula, caramelized pine nuts, goat cheese, Gorgonzola); rigatoni Nocerina (sun-dried tomatoes, mushrooms, olive oil, garlic, and basil in cream sauce); conchili del mercante (crumbled Italian sausage, mushrooms, fresh tomato sauce, scamorza cheese, peas); spaghetti Portofino (scallops, scampi, cherry tomatoes); vitello alla Gianni (scaloppine sautéed in brandy sauce with mushrooms, cherry tomatoes, artichoke hearts); pollo Toscana (boneless chicken breast marinated with fresh herbs); salmone al vino bianco (fillet of fresh Norwegian salmon grilled first, then sautéed); lombata (veal chop) Vesuvio. Desserts: housemade cannoli; tartufo; mandarino (sorbet inside frozen orange shell); tiramisu.

Other recommendations: Insalata alla Lipare (mixture of lentils and grilled and marinated calamari on a bed of arugula with chopped plum tomatoes)—not

(continued)

300

on the menu; gamberi alla Napolitana (mussels in marinara sauce and grilled vegetables); costolette d'agnello alla griglia (summer item: lamb chops marinated, grilled, and served with sautéed escarole and grilled potatoes); tonno alla griglia (summer item: fresh grilled tuna steak topped with cold sauce of chopped plum tomatoes, celery, green olives, green onion, olive oil, balsamic vinegar, with grilled vegetables); saltimbocca al sorrentina (tender veal scaloppine topped with prosciutto and mozzarella, sautéed with white wine and tomatoes).

Entertainment & amenities: Special wine dinners and other promotions.

Summary & comments: Chef Gianni Delisi established this, his first restaurant, in 1988, fulfilling his dream. When he first arrived here from Italy, he learned English and worked at the Italian Village and then at Trattoria Roma. He has woven into this place everything he considered important, including true Italian cuisine featuring family recipes. Some items are Delisi family creations, retained from his family's restaurant in Italy. The restaurant is comfortable and caring, and it offers some high-quality, innovative cooking at fair prices. This is one of the best trattorias around without the high noise level and crowds of some "in" spots. It's possible to have a relaxed dinner here even on a busy night. Buon appetito!

TRATTORIA PARMA

Zone 3   Near North
400 North Clark Street
(312) 245-9933

Italian	
★★★½	
Inexpensive/Moderate	
Quality 89 Value B	

Reservations:	Recommended
When to go:	Less busy before 6 P.M.
Entree range:	$7.95–16
Payment:	Major credit cards except D
Service rating:	★★★★
Friendliness rating:	★★★★½
Parking:	Limited street (lunch); valet (dinner), $6
Bar:	Full service
Wine selection:	Largely Italian, from $5 a glass and $20 a bottle
Dress:	Casual
Disabled access:	Yes
Customers:	Diverse; professionals, families, locals, tourists
Lunch:	Monday–Friday, 11:30 A.M.–2 P.M. Carryout menu, 11 A.M.–2 P.M., 2 hours notice requested; delivery ends at 2 P.M.
Dinner:	Monday–Thursday, 5:30–10 P.M.; Friday and Saturday, 5:30–11 P.M.; Sunday, 5–9 P.M.; carryout available

Atmosphere/setting: Rustic and comfortable ambiance of an Italian country home; wood chairs and floors, weathered green shutters, and lace cafe curtains. The beautiful large bar with a frescoed ceiling is from the 1930s.

House specialties: Antipasti parma (prosciutto di Parma with olives, giardiniera, and Parmigiano-Reggiano); eggplant parmigiana; rigatoni stuffed with chicken, wild mushrooms, ricotta; grilled shrimp and calamari; sautéed veal chops Milanese; panna cotta with raspberry sauce; chocolate cake topped with caramelized bananas.

Other recommendations: Fried calamari; tagliatelle Bolognese; penne carbonara; farfalle with vegetables, goat cheese; cannoli with ricotta cream filling and pistachios.

Summary & comments: This new Trattoria Parma, named for the gastronomic center of Italy (home of Parmigiano cheese), was launched in June 1997. This reincarnation of the former Mare, in the same location, is more casual with a completely new decor and authentic, Italian trattoria-simple dishes. Chef Paul LoDuca felt the River North area needed a friendly trattoria for a gathering spot. It has the right appearance and food combinations to make it successful.

TRIO

Zone 11   Northern Suburbs
1625 Hinman Avenue, Evanston
(847) 733-8746

Fusion
★★★★★
Expensive/Very Expensive

Quality 98   Value C

Reservations:	Highly recommended; accepted up to 3 months in advance
When to go:	Tuesday–Thursday
Entree range:	$17–30, some higher; 8- to 10-course degustation, $75; vegetarian version, $65
Payment:	VISA, MC, AMEX, D, DC
Service rating:	★★★★★
Friendliness rating:	★★★★★
Parking:	Valet, $5
Bar:	Full service; international beers; extensive single-malt Scotches; infused grappas
Wine selection:	Very extensive; international; many smaller wineries' quality vintage wines; good range of style and price, from $30 a bottle; 10–12 by the glass; wine flight tastings (e.g., 4 half-glasses); willing to open almost any bottle to serve a glass; reserve list; sommelier to assist
Dress:	Jackets suggested; dressy overall
Disabled access:	Yes; need assistance up 2 steps for rest rooms
Customers:	All types, all ages, except children (a few); business-people, couples, sophisticated food lovers
Lunch:	Friday, seating noon–1 P.M.; 4-course prix fixe ($26)
Dinner:	Tuesday–Thursday, 5:30–9:30 P.M.; Friday and Saturday, 5:30–10:30 P.M.; Sunday, 5–9 P.M.

Atmosphere/setting: Housed in The Homestead, a hotel designed in the Williamsburg Inn style. Country estate–type living room is a waiting lounge. Comfortable, warm main dining room and a brighter, more intimate porch room overlooking a garden. A subtle, rustic courtyard decor. The kitchen, with one table in an alcove, is a bit more than half of the 3,500 square feet of restaurant space.

House specialties: Appetizers: porcini "cappuccino" with Parmesan tuile; wild mushroom and Parmesan risotto; mirrored mosaic (fish changes: one example

(continued)

was great ginger-cured gravlax, Pacific oyster, and Szechuan tuna sashimi); domestic caviar service on a painter's palette; seared Hudson Valley foie gras (used lavishly here) with mango, or with roasted Granny Smith apple, black lentils, vanilla, and sake-infused veal reduction. Main courses: potato-crusted Columbia River sturgeon, Mt. Walden smoked trout, and lobster bordelaise; pomegranate-glazed pheasant breast, caramelized salsify, and Swiss chard in a bittersweet tangerine sauce. Specials such as lobster bisque; grilled veal chop and crispy sweetbreads with three-bean ragout, escarole, and pearl onions. Desserts: lemon tart Nico with white pepper ice cream, blackberry compote, dried apricots, and golden raisins; the Great Pumpkin Crème Caramel; and Valrhona chocolate bliss.

Other recommendations: Circle Ranch buffalo carpaccio, tempura tiger shrimp, and horseradish aïoli; hazelnut-and-herb-crusted rack of lamb with foie gras hummus, ratatouille; the Vegetarian is a daily celebration of seasonal market vegetables and grains; crème brûlée. Buy a box of Trio's truffles to take home.

Summary & comments: By far, one of the finest, most spectacular restaurants to open here in some time; it made culinary waves immediately after opening in October 1993. Shawn McClain, sous chef, was promoted to executive chef when the original "trio" split in November 1995. Henry Adaniya remains sole owner. Current pastry chef Della Gossett creates desserts as delicious as they are beautiful. The cooking is built on the trio of cuisines: classic French and Italian foundations with Asian influences. The finished dishes are avant garde. McClain's style is more delicate and subtle than his predecessor's; in one instance, a wonderful pomegranate-glazed pheasant breast was a bit short on sauce. Stunning presentations—some whimsical—are arranged on unusual surfaces such as marble, granite, and mirrors. A complimentary sorbet arrives as an intermezzo during dinner. An entire dinner parade of such spectacular menu items is definitely culinary theater. There are those who prefer the subtleties of dining and consider this theatrical display a bit ostentatious. However, there's no disagreement on the culinary expertise here and the passion and energy exhibited on every level. Informed servers anticipate diners' needs but are never doting. The joy of cooking here has rejuvenated even the most jaded, worldly diner. The degustation menu is a great spontaneous tasting opportunity. Kitchen table must be reserved weeks in advance.

Honors/awards: *Chicago Tribune* and *Chicago Sun-Times,* four stars, 1996; *Gourmet* magazine rated it among the nation's top restaurants, 1996; *North Shore* magazine, Top 30 in the City, 1996.

Tucci Milan

<table>
<tr><td></td><td>Italian</td></tr>
<tr><td>Zone 4 The Loop</td><td>★★★</td></tr>
<tr><td>6 West Hubbard Street</td><td>Inexpensive/Moderate</td></tr>
<tr><td>(312) 222-0044</td><td>Quality 82 Value C</td></tr>
</table>

Reservations:	Recommended
When to go:	Any time
Entree range:	Lunch, $9–13; dinner, $14–23
Payment:	Major credit cards
Service rating:	★★★
Friendliness rating:	★★★½
Parking:	Valet after 5 P.M.
Bar:	Full service
Wine selection:	Italian, American; about 25 nice selections at good value; about 12 by the glass
Dress:	Casual
Disabled access:	Yes
Customers:	Mixed; businesspeople, couples
Lunch/Dinner:	Monday–Thursday, 11:30 A.M.–10 P.M., Friday, 11:30 A.M.–11 P.M.; Saturday, noon–11 P.M.; Sunday, 5–10 P.M.

Atmosphere/setting: Vibrant interior features open kitchen with wood-burning oven, high ceilings, and colorful contemporary paintings; attractive, sophisticated bar; Offers accommodations for semiprivate parties.

House specialties: Daily rotisserie items featuring seasonal game such as half-duck with balsamic coriander glaze, red Swiss chard, grappa-soaked cherries, and polenta; ravioli del giorno; mezzaluna alla salsiccia (half-moon ravioli stuffed with Italian sausage; bruschetta; Margherita pizza (fresh tomato, pesto sauce, mozzarella, provolone, basil (mushrooms an option); pollo salute (grilled chicken breast stuffed with spinach and lowfat mozzarella).

Other recommendations: Daily antipasti platter; Roma salad (avocado, hearts of palm, Roma plum tomatoes); lasagne agli spinaci; salmone alla griglia (grilled Atlantic salmon, Rumesco sauce, crostini, caramelized leeks); herb-roasted chicken; caramelized shallot mashed potatoes; the sensuous chocolate budino.

Summary & comments: Earthy wood-burning aromas entice guests upon entering this rustic, cosmopolitan atmosphere. This Milanese cuisine is lively and hearty, centered around wood grilling and fresh antipasti and pastas. The recently expanded menu features creative pizzas, robust salads, and rotisserie game and chicken. Desserts are made in-house and include seasonal specialties and popular Milanese items. Fair prices for wine and food are an added bonus.

Tufano's (Vernon Park Tap)

Zone 5   South Loop
1073 West Vernon Park Place
(312) 733-3393

Italian	
★★½	
Inexpensive/Moderate	
Quality 76	Value B

Reservations:	Not accepted; walk-ins wait about half an hour on weekends
When to go:	Weekdays
Entree range:	$6–12
Payment:	Cash, personal checks (local); no credit cards
Service rating:	★★★
Friendliness rating:	★★★★
Parking:	Valet
Bar:	Full service
Wine selection:	Limited, mostly Italian
Dress:	Moderately casual
Disabled access:	Limited; ladies' rest room is handicap accessible
Customers:	Diverse
Lunch/Dinner:	Tuesday–Thursday, 11 A.M.–10 P.M.; Friday, 11 A.M.–11 P.M.
Dinner:	Saturday, 5–11 P.M.; Sunday, 3–9 P.M.

Atmosphere/setting: Casual and cozy.

House specialties: Lemon chicken; eggplant Parmigiana; Tufano special salad.

Other recommendations: Other pasta dishes (e.g., lasagna; mussels with angel hair, your choice of red or white sauce; tortellini Alfredo); veal Marsala.

Summary & comments: Also known as Vernon Park Tap, this is a cornerstone of the old Taylor Street Italian neighborhood, founded by the Tufano family over 60 years ago. It's hidden among a row of older buildings, and the restaurant is behind a bar room. This is no-frills decor with blackboards listing the daily selections. The menu offers choices of red or white sauce, charges a bit extra for meatballs or sausage, and has the old traditional Friday fish specials. The place is a time warp, and that's why it's especially fun. Chef Joey Di Buono turns out respectable versions of the old-guard Italian fare in large servings. Everyone who eats here seems to walk out happy.

TUSCANY

	Italian
Zone 5 South Loop	★★★
1014 West Taylor Street	Moderate
(312) 829-1990	Quality 84 Value C

Reservations:	Recommended; walk-ins wait about half an hour on weekdays, 1–2 hours on weekends
When to go:	Any time
Entree range:	$15–30; average dinner of appetizer, entree, and dessert is $30
Payment:	All major credit cards except DC
Service rating:	★★★
Friendliness rating:	★★★½
Parking:	Valet
Bar:	Full service
Wine selection:	American and Italian
Dress:	Moderately casual
Disabled access:	Yes
Customers:	Local, diverse
Lunch:	Monday–Friday, 11 A.M.–3:30 P.M.
Dinner:	Monday–Thursday, 5–11 P.M.; Friday and Saturday, 5 P.M.–midnight; Sunday, 2–9:30 P.M.

Atmosphere/setting: Cozy Italian decor with green and white tablecloths.

House specialties: Eleven dinner specials such as macaroni cippriani (freshly made square noodles with light cream-tomato sauce); rotisserie chicken; stuffed veal chop (a special now). All items are deftly prepared rustic-style.

Other recommendations: Mainstream antipasto and pastas with good sauces.

Summary & comments: One of the newest restaurants in Little Italy on Taylor Street. Owned by restaurateur Phil Stefani, this location has an open kitchen with a wood-burning oven and grill to produce typical Tuscan fare. Very popular and bustling. He owns several restaurants, including Stefani's Tuscany in Oak Brook and Riva on Navy Pier (see profile).

Honors/awards: 1993 Silver Platter Award.

Twisted Lizard

Zone 1   North Side
1964 North Sheffield Avenue
(773) 929-1414

Southwestern/Mexican
★★★½
Inexpensive
Quality 87   Value B

Reservations:	Not accepted
When to go:	Less crowded before 7 P.M. and after 10 P.M.
Entree range:	$6.75–12.75
Payment:	VISA, MC, AMEX, DC
Service rating:	★★★½
Friendliness rating:	★★★★½
Parking:	Street
Bar:	Full service; 8 types of margaritas; good selection of beers, including Mexican
Wine selection:	Small list: Spanish, Chilean, Mexican, Californian
Dress:	Casual
Disabled access:	Yes, call first
Customers:	Diverse; many young professionals
Brunch:	Sunday, 11 A.M.–3 P.M.
Lunch/Dinner:	Sunday–Wednesday, 11:30 A.M.–10 P.M.; Thursday, 11:30 A.M.–11 P.M.; Friday and Saturday, 11:30 A.M.–midnight

Atmosphere/setting: Cozy, subterranean cantina with bar. Rustic white cedar furniture; copper-top bar; colorful, wooden lizards; collection of dolls strung across the walls.

House specialties: Seafood queso fundido (sautéed shrimp and scallops baked and broiled with Chihuahua cheese, served with homemade flour and corn tortillas); barbecue chicken wings sprinkled with sesame seeds; flautas (three crispy corn tortillas rolled with choice of chicken or beef, topped with guacamole, sour cream, and Anejo cheese); Key lime pie; flan; good coffee.

Other recommendations: Enchiladas (three corn tortillas filled and baked with choice of meats, topped with choice of sauce and Chihuahua cheese); barbecue chicken breasts; fajitas (sizzling peppers, onions, and tomatoes with beef, chicken, or seafood with guacamole, pico de gallo, sour cream, rice, and beans).

Summary & comments: This is one of the best places for flavorful, top-flight southwestern and Mexican food, prepared by Mexican-born co-owner and chef Sergio Sanchez. The kitchen is so small that daily deliveries are essential, ensuring freshness. The interior is charming—although some people can't accept the lizard motif and are turned off by the name. Thriving catering business and carryout.

Un Grand Café

Zone 1 North Side	French Bistro
2300 North Lincoln Park West	★★★★
(773) 348-8886	Moderate
	Quality 92 Value C

Reservations:	Recommended
When to go:	Early weeknights; late weekends
Entree range:	Appetizers, $3.50–7.95; entrees, $12.95–21.95
Payment:	All major credit cards
Service rating:	★★★★
Friendliness rating:	★★★
Parking:	Valet, $6
Bar:	Full service; cocktail lounge for customers
Wine selection:	50 selections, French and American; $10–35 a bottle; 5 by the glass, $4–7; excellent sommelier will assist
Dress:	Casual
Disabled access:	Wheelchair accessible; call ahead
Customers:	Casual crowd, locals, media, city people; low-key after opera and art gallery crowd
Dinner:	Monday–Thursday, 6–10:30 P.M.; Friday and Saturday, 6–11:30 P.M.; Sunday, 5–9:30 P.M.

Atmosphere/setting: Continental flair and unique style in an elegant, renovated old hotel with high ceilings and French doors. Feels like a bistro on the West Bank of Paris; chic; intimate outdoor garden; view of Lincoln Park Conservatory and gardens; seats 120.

House specialties: Onion soup, crock-baked with croutons and Gruyère; steak frites; herb-roasted Amish chicken; sautéed Hawaiian black bass with potato puree and roasted tomato-saffron jus; sautéed red snapper with roasted root vegetables.

Other recommendations: Duck leg confit with lentils; seafood risotto with mussels, shrimp, scallops, and fish; potato–goat cheese salad with watercress.

Entertainment & amenities: Taking in the stately architecture and charming atmosphere, including the Lincoln Park Conservatory across the street.

Summary & comments: The grand architecture, classic Gallic bistro cuisine, and very competent service here combine to make this restaurant live up to its name. The cooking is directed by Lettuce Entertain You Enterprises managing partner, Gabino Sotelino, who hired Kenneth Harris as executive chef in 1996. Expect some innovative dishes amid the culinary anchors.

Honors/awards: Gold Cup Award.

Uncle Tannous

Zone 1   North Side
2626 North Halsted Street
(773) 929-1333

Lebanese	
★★★	
Inexpensive/Moderate	
Quality 84 Value B	

Reservations:	Recommended
When to go:	Weekends for action; weekdays for a quieter meal
Entree range:	$8–15
Payment:	All major credit cards
Service rating:	★★★★
Friendliness rating:	★★★★½
Parking:	Valet
Bar:	Full service
Wine selection:	Fairly extensive; several excellent choices by the glass
Dress:	Moderately casual to business
Disabled access:	Yes, including rest rooms
Customers:	Local, North Shore, celebrities
Lunch/Dinner:	Tuesday–Sunday, noon–11 P.M.
Dinner:	Monday, 5–10:30 P.M.

Atmosphere/setting: Exotic and romantic, with tin ceiling, alcoves, upper level, ceiling fans; photos of Danny Thomas (who would bring big parties here) and actor Hans Conreid, who played Uncle Tannous on the Danny Thomas Show. Old photos of stars.

House specialties: Lamb chops; kafta kebabs; broiled red snapper Uncle Tannous. Vast array of appetizers and vegetarian plates: falafel, hummus with tahini, baba gannoujh-mtabal, grape leaf rolls, chunky eggplant imam bayeldi, and kibbeh muklieh (superb chopped meat and cracked wheat balls stuffed with spiced meat and pine nuts).

Other recommendations: Mediterranean meze (sampler) for two. Dessert of the day; baklava; Turkish coffee.

Entertainment & amenities: Belly dancing on Saturday, 7:30–9:30 P.M. Perusing the photos on the walls.

Summary & comments: Dependable over the years for maintaining good quality in Lebanese cooking and service. Owner Joseph Skaff is visible most of the time and cares about details. Complimentary relish tray precedes dinner. A great cafe atmosphere for a business dinner (except Saturday) and for a casual evening of enjoyment. Catering for all occasions.

Uncle Tutunji's

Zone 3   Near North
615 North Wells Street
(312) 587-0721

	Middle Eastern
	★★★
	Inexpensive
	Quality 85 Value B

Reservations:	Recommended for weekends
When to go:	Any time
Entree range:	$5.50–11.95
Payment:	All major credit cards
Service rating:	★★½
Friendliness rating:	★★★★
Parking:	2 hours free; facilities on Erie and Wells, and Franklin and Ohio
Bar:	Full service
Wine selection:	Limited; mostly Californian; $16–28 a bottle; only 3 by the glass
Dress:	Casual
Disabled access:	Yes, including rest rooms
Customers:	95 percent locals, some Middle Easterners; travelers, businesspeople, couples
Lunch/Dinner:	Monday–Thursday, 11 A.M.–9 P.M.; Friday and Saturday, 11 A.M.–10:30 P.M.

Atmosphere/setting: Beautiful Assyrian murals depicting ancient Assyrian life, design circa 800 B.C.; two dining rooms with white tablecloths covered with paper.

House specialties: Dolmeh (stuffed grape leaves with meat or vegetables); kibbeh (fried cracked wheat and meat mixture); tabbouleh (cracked wheat salad); baba gannoujh (eggplant-tahini dip); Tutunji platter: shawerma (gyros), kifta kebab, lamb kebab, and chicken.

Other recommendations: Vegetarian entrees, including a combo plate; couscous (meat or vegetarian).

Summary & comments: This downtown gem is still one of the best Middle Eastern restaurants around for its charming atmosphere, array of skillfully prepared dishes, and friendly staff. Formerly Ishtar Inn, the restaurant was renamed when a new owner took over. On the last visit, lamb kebabs were tough and the service had rough edges. The cuisine is very meat-and-vegetable oriented—no fish. All the dishes sampled were robustly well flavored and fresh; entrees come with salad, rice, and pita bread. The bargain prices are unheard of downtown—a real find!

Va Pensiero

Zone 11   Northern Suburbs
Margarita European Inn,
    1566 Oak Avenue, Evanston
(847) 475-7779

Italian
★★★★½
Moderate

Quality 96   Value C

Reservations:	Recommended
When to go:	Any time
Entree range:	$15.50–21.95; trattoria menu (early and late), 4-course dinner, $22
Payment:	VISA, MC, AMEX, D, DC
Service rating:	★★★★½
Friendliness rating:	★★★★★
Parking:	Valet, Monday–Saturday evening
Bar:	Full service, including grappas
Wine selection:	Recently expanded cellar inventory of more than 100 selections; all-Italian regional list; $18–148; excellent selections; about 12 by the glass, $5–8.50
Dress:	Moderately casual, business, dressy
Disabled access:	Yes
Customers:	Mostly upscale North Shore Italian food lovers; city businesspeople, couples
Lunch:	Monday–Friday, 11:30 A.M.–2:30 P.M.
Dinner:	Monday–Thursday, 5:30–9 P.M.; Friday and Saturday, 5:30–10 P.M.

Atmosphere/setting: Housed in the historic Margarita European Inn. Very Romanesque portico. Dining room has a Tivoli Garden look with plasterlike reliefs, peach-hued walls, candelabras, and white tablecloths. More casual cafe, the Verdi Room, open weekends. In spring 1997, quaint outdoor terraced roof garden was added.

House specialties: Antipasti: sautéed shrimp on crispy onion risotto cake, topped with pistachio pesto; insalata di calamari (warm); great house salad. Entrees: signature fazzoletti imbottiti (delicate white wine pasta filled with ricotta-spinach blend, with Parmesan and roasted tomato sauces); chicken breast stuffed with fontina cheese and prosciutto; crespelle al formaggio caprino (thin parsley crepes rolled with creamy mild goat cheese, baked and topped with ragôut of wild mushrooms, cannellini beans, red wine, spinach); roasted Atlantic salmon with a mustard-mascarpone glaze. Desserts: budino al cioccolato (sensuous warm

(continued)

bittersweet chocolate cake with a creamy center, served with an almond milk sauce); silky cappuccino custard; their version of tiramisu (rich butter cake soaked in espresso and liqueurs, layered with whipped mascarpone).

Other recommendations: Homemade pastas (e.g., parsley ravioli stuffed with slow-roasted butternut squash and ricotta cheese); pan-browned veal tenderloin medallions; slow-roasted lamb shank. Desserts: rhubarb ice cream (in season); spumoni (trio of flavors of gelatti).

Summary & comments: Va Pensiero means "think freely" in Italian, and is the name of the composition a chorus sings in the opera Nabucco. It's an appropriate name for this restaurant, and the staff is living up to it. Chef-owner Peggy Ryan's refined, earthy cooking sings out in harmony now with her new chef, Jeff Muldrow, who was Ryan's sous chef in the early days of Va Pensiero and then executive chef at Vinci and Avanzare. His skills and her overall culinary vision combine with a new, energetic management staff to inject more vibrancy into this fine North Suburban Italian restaurant. The quiet, rather formal dining room has lightened its image; the men managers now wear attractive white shirts instead of jackets. The restaurant is more active with special events, as listed in their newsletter; they hold regional dinners every second Tuesday of the month; dinners featuring certain wines; holiday dinners; and festivals (in May they hold a Po River Festival, the best of Northern Italy, and a spring artichoke festival). Chef Ryan has conducted cooking classes, which have been repeated on popular demand. People often ask her how a chef named Ryan can cook Italian so well. Her instincts in combining Italian flavors and textures have been on target in all the dishes sampled on several occasions. The upscale setting in the vintage building is charming—a soothing environment with good jazz background music for enjoying fine Italian cuisine and regional wines.

Honors/awards: *Wine Enthusiast* magazine 1996 Restaurant Award (for excellence in service, storage, and wine list creativity); 1995–96 Silver Platter Award: Number One Favorite Italian Restaurant (voted by Chicagoland Restaurateurs); 1996 Silver Platter Award: Peggy Ryan voted Top Five Favorite Chefs.

Via Veneto

Zone 1   North Side
3449 West Peterson Avenue
(773) 267-0888

New Italian
★★★½
Inexpensive

Quality 85   Value B

Reservations:	Recommended weekends
When to go:	Any time; weekdays less busy
Entree range:	$6.95–14.95
Payment:	Major credit cards
Service rating:	★★★½
Friendliness rating:	★★★½
Parking:	Street, small lot in rear
Bar:	Full service
Wine selection:	Mostly Italian, Californian, French; many affordable at $16 a bottle; Riserva and champagne, $52 a bottle; several by the glass
Dress:	Casual, business
Disabled access:	Yes, including rest rooms
Customers:	Diverse; locals, businesspeople, couples
Open:	Monday–Friday, 11:30 A.M.–10 P.M.; Saturday, 11:30 A.M.–11 P.M.; Sunday, 3–11 P.M.

Atmosphere/setting: Cozy, bright, rather elegant with white tablecloths; Italian-style with display case of food; a sit-down bar and sidewalk cafe.

House specialties: Antipasto: melenzane stuzzicante (eggplant with tomato, garlic, olive oil, and mozzarella); shrimp sautéed with garlic and oil; grilled octopus with balsamic vinegar. Pastas: pumpkin ravioli in tomato–goat cheese sauce; penne Bolognese with rich meat sauce. Fish of the day; vegetarian dishes made from home-grown vegetables.

Other recommendations: Stuffed calamari; risotto with porcini mushrooms or four cheeses; the namesake chicken breast with mushrooms in white wine; tiramisu.

Summary & comments: Several years ago this was a hidden gem on the Northwest Side; it has since grown in popularity. Chef-owner Tony Barbanente's penchant for healthy, light dishes results in fresh, cooked-to-order items. The care shows both in the attentive cooking and accommodating service. An excellent value off the beaten restaurant path. Barbanente has opened La Donna Nord, serving regional northern Italian cuisine (1001 West Golf Road, Hoffman Estates, 60195, (847) 843-8620), and La Donna, serving Roman cooking (5146 North Clark Street, Chicago, 60640, (773) 561-9400).

Viceroy of India

Zone 1 North Side	Indian
2520 West Devon Avenue	★★★
(773) 743-4100	Inexpensive/Moderate
Zone 9 Western Suburbs	Quality 84 Value B
19 West 555 West Roosevelt Road,	
Lombard	
(630) 627-4411	

Reservations:	Recommended
When to go:	Any time; weekends are busy
Entree range:	$6–13; lunch buffet, $6.95
Payment:	Major credit cards
Service rating:	★★★
Friendliness rating:	★★★
Parking:	Street, lots nearby
Bar:	Full service plus 3 Indian beers
Wine selection:	Limited
Dress:	Casual
Disabled access:	Yes
Customers:	Locals, ethnics, tourists
Lunch:	Every day, noon–3:30 P.M.; buffet available
Dinner:	Sunday–Thursday, 5–10 P.M.; Friday and Saturday, 5–10:30 P.M.

Atmosphere/setting: Formal, large dining room; dim lights and breezy sitar music; part of the wall is carved to resemble the intricate Mughal art often seen in ancient Indian Muslim architecture. Separate carryout and casual dining room; large private party room.

House specialties: Chicken tandoori is deliciously juicy; butter chicken is rich and creamy; light peas pulao (with fried long-grain rice) has the perfect taste balance with spicy bhuna gost (lamb cubes, tomato-onion gravy) and tender shish kebab (lamb).

Other recommendations: Chutneys are heartier than most; appetizers such as the steam cheese pakora (steam cheese fritters in graham flour batter) and samosa (flour patties stuffed with delicately spiced potatoes and peas) are light, golden, and crisp; onion kulcha (bread stuffed with onion, dry mango, spices); kulfi, an Indian-style pistachio-and-saffron ice cream; the mango lassi (an icy yogurt-mango drink).

Summary & comments: This is one of the nicest Indian restaurants on famed Devon Avenue, which has a string of Indian shops, cafes, and restaurants. Banquet facility for up to 400 people; restaurant can seat up to 150.

VIVERE (ITALIAN VILLAGE)

Zone 4   The Loop
71 West Monroe Street
(312) 332-4040

Italian	
★★★★½	
Moderate	
Quality 95	Value C

Reservations:	Recommended
When to go:	Any time
Entree range:	Lunch, $8.75–12.75; dinner, $11.50–22.50
Payment:	Major credit cards
Service rating:	★★★★★
Friendliness rating:	★★★★★
Parking:	Valet, $6
Bar:	Full service
Wine selection:	Extensive, well balanced; mostly Italian; award-winning 950-selection reserve list
Dress:	Chic casual, dressy, business
Disabled access:	Yes
Customers:	Businesspeople, couples, operagoers, theatergoers
Lunch:	Monday–Friday, 11:30 A.M.–2:30 P.M.
Dinner:	Monday–Thursday, 5–10 P.M.; Friday and Saturday, 5–11 P.M.

Atmosphere/setting: Award-winning decor is unique "modern Italian baroque," a blend of a medieval castle with futuristic fantasy. Intimate mezzanine area.

House specialties: Tortine di funghi misti (garlic-infused mushrooms in cream sauce); carpaccio, fava beans, spinach soufflé; roasted butternut squash–filled pasta; braided lobster-filled tomato pasta; duck breast with zucchini puree, crisp leeks, celery root, red wine–balsamic vinegar sauce; veal tenderloin in porcini-pancetta-gin cream sauce with vegetables; seafood of the day (Atlantic salmon in artichoke tomato sauce).

Other recommendations: Pheasant-filled pasta; eggless pasta with four-cheese filling; daily risotto; oak-grilled lamb chops. Mango sorbetti; gelatti; chocolate truffle cake creation; panna cotta (timbale of sweet cream, caramel sauce, nougat).

Summary & comments: Vivere means "to live" in Italian, and indeed, this is the way to do it Italian-style. Vivere is part of a triad of restaurants that make up the Italian Village: Vivere is on the main floor; the Village, upstairs; and Cantina Enoteca (seafood), downstairs. Two generations of the Capitanini family operate this village. Chef Marcelo Gallegos prepares exciting contemporary, regional Italian food. The wine lists are dazzling and the prices overall spell good value.

Honors/awards: *Wine Spectator* Grand Award since 1984; *Interiors* magazine award, 1991; tied for second as *Wine Spectator*'s Best Italian Restaurant in U.S., 1997.

WALKER Bros. ORIGINAL PANCAKE HOUSE

American	
★★★	
Inexpensive	
Quality 88	Value B

Zone 11   Northern Suburbs
153 Greenbay Road, Wilmette
(847) 251-6000

Zone 10   Northwest Suburbs
1615 Waukegan Road, Glenview
(847) 724-0220

Zone 10   Northwest Suburbs
825 Dundee Road, Arlington Heights
(847) 392-6600

Reservations:	Not accepted
When to go:	Breakfast, brunch
Entree range:	$3.75–6.50
Payment:	VISA, MC, D
Service rating:	★★½
Friendliness rating:	★★★
Parking:	Free lot
Bar:	None
Wine selection:	None
Dress:	Casual
Disabled access:	Yes
Customers:	Locals, families
Open:	Sunday–Thursday, 7 A.M.–10 P.M. (10:30 P.M. in Wilmette); Friday and Saturday, 7 A.M.–11 P.M.

Atmosphere/setting: Comfortable and casual with stained-glass decor. The original place in Wilmette was the set for the film *Ordinary People.*

House specialties: Huge baked German pancake—the apple version is great; puffy omelet; French crêpes with strawberries and cheese.

Other recommendations: Waffles; spinach crêpes; corned beef hash.

Summary & comments: This is an old standby in several Chicago-area locations. The newest outlets are in Highland Park (with an expanded menu serving soups, salads, and sandwiches) and Lincolnshire (also serving salads and sandwiches). The quality of food exceeds the sometimes uneven service. A great family place for breakfast or brunch, and a fine place for a light supper—or late snack after a movie.

Widow Newton's Tavern

Zone 3   Near North
Navy Pier, 700 East Grand Avenue
(312) 595-5500

American Pub
★★★
Moderate
Quality 85   Value C

Reservations:	Recommended
When to go:	Any time, but be sure to have a reservation
Entree range:	$8.95–17.95
Payment:	All major credit cards
Service rating:	★★★★
Friendliness rating:	★★★★
Parking:	Valet, evenings; garage, daytime
Bar:	Full service; imported and domestic beers, including Widow Newton's Tavern's own brew for $4 a pint; they specialize in microbrews
Wine selection:	American, $16–40 a bottle; by the glass, $4–5.50
Dress:	Casual
Disabled access:	Yes
Customers:	Tourists and locals; all ages
Open:	Sunday–Thursday, 11 A.M.–10 P.M.; Friday and Saturday, 11 A.M.–11 P.M.

Atmosphere/setting: Lovely view of Navy Pier entrance and bridge; library/pub/church mélange with astrological and spiritual elements; gift shop in a converted confessional.

House specialties: Spinach and artichoke dip served with crispy whole-wheat tortillas; grilled portobello with watercress and red onion salad; Louisiana pan-fried oysters with Asian jicama relish; marinated shrimp with cold jasmine rice; roast Atlantic salmon glazed with mustard dill and cider; warm brownie sundae topped with sliced almonds, mocha ice cream, and white chocolate sauce; peach and blueberry cobbler with cinnamon ice cream.

Other recommendations: Rotisserie Amish chicken; pan-seared Lake Superior whitefish with escarole and grilled tomato vinaigrette (although inconsistent); angel food cake; apple bundt cake.

Summary & comments: The name is derived from owner Cathy Newton becoming a widow suddenly on July 12, 1993, the day after she and her late husband approved this location for her next restaurant. Her surname evolved from the Old English, "new place." The rest is history, and the booklet, "An Epoch Tale," on every table, explains the rest regarding astrological and spiritual nuances. The food is pub fare and affordable.

Wild Onion

Zone 1   North Side
3500 North Lincoln Avenue
(773) 871-5555

American/Italian/French
★★★½
Inexpensive/Moderate

Quality 85   Value B

Reservations:	Accepted
When to go:	Any time
Entree range:	$9.95–17.95
Payment:	All major credit cards
Service rating:	★★★
Friendliness rating:	★★★½
Parking:	Street (ample)
Bar:	Full service
Wine selection:	American West coast, French, and Italian
Dress:	Casual
Disabled access:	Yes
Customers:	Locals, professionals, couples
Brunch:	Sunday, 10:30 A.M.–2:30 P.M.
Lunch:	Monday–Saturday, 11:30 A.M.–5 P.M.
Dinner:	Monday–Thursday, 5–10 P.M.; Friday and Saturday, 5–11 P.M.; Sunday, 3–8:30 P.M.

Atmosphere/setting: Loft-style building with high ceilings, exposed brick walls, hardwood floors, lovely outdoor patio dining area. Recently remodeled.

House specialties: Grilled shrimp; crab cakes; duck enchiladas with mole sauce; grilled chicken salad, peanut dressing; smoked chicken chili. Four vegetarian entrees at dinner, and patrons can request other dishes to be made without meat or seafood. New pasta items.

Other recommendations: Baked artichoke hearts with blue cheese; seafood dill angel hair with garlic-tarragon cream sauce; crème brûlée; flourless chocolate cake.

Summary & comments: Out of the way in an unlikely neighborhood, this place, named for Chicago (the Indian name for "wild onion"), has always been rather creative with its food. The chef has a penchant for artichokes, and the menu has been expanded with more Italian and French infusion. The food is well prepared, portions are ample, and the service and atmosphere are pleasant—and the bonus is the pricing. Well worth a visit.

Wildfire (Russell Bry's)

Zone 3   Near North
159 West Erie Street
(312) 787-9000

American
★★★
Inexpensive/Moderate

Quality 84   Value C

Reservations:	Recommended
When to go:	5–6:30 P.M. and 9:30–11 P.M.
Entree range:	$6.95–20.95
Payment:	All major credit cards
Service rating:	★★★
Friendliness rating:	★★★★
Parking:	Valet, $6; pull into garage next door to valet
Bar:	Full service; a dozen local microbrews; martinis; single-malt Scotches; small-batch whiskeys; and signature cocktails, such as Fired Up!
Wine selection:	Mostly Californian, a few Italian; several by the glass, $3.95 and up; bottles from $18
Dress:	Casual
Disabled access:	Yes
Customers:	Diverse; all ages, families, young urban professionals
Open:	Monday–Thursday, 5–10 P.M.; Friday and Saturday, 5–11 P.M.; Sunday, 4:30–9 P.M.

Atmosphere/setting: Rustic yet sophisticated; chestnut wood, lush carpeting, dim lighting; large bar area overlooks the dining room and open kitchen.

House specialties: Maine crab-and-shrimp cakes; house salad; woodland mushrooms oven-roasted pizza (shiitake, cremini, and portobello mushrooms with three cheeses); barbecued chicken house-smoked over maple and hickory; and oak-planked Pacific salmon.

Other recommendations: Wildfire chopped salad; smoked chicken oven-roasted pizza; double-cut pork rib chop; and roasted fish of the day.

Entertainment & amenities: Special promotions; winemakers' dinners.

Summary & comments: Talented chef-proprietor Russell Bry prepares simple, hearty-flavored American cuisine in the oldest tradition of cooking—over a natural wood fire in an open wood grill, wood-fire oven, or on the rotisserie. The grill's amazing 1000° F heat seals in flavors and obviously cooks food very quickly. Sounds like a hot kitchen job! Diners can see Bry's unique roasting and smoking methods first hand through the open kitchen near the dining room.

Honors/awards: Chef Russell Bry named 1997 Celebrated Chef by the National Pork Producers Council.

Woo Lae Oak

Zone 3 · Near North
30 West Hubbard Street
(312) 645-0051

	Korean
	★★★★
	Inexpensive
	Quality 94 Value C

Reservations:	Accepted
When to go:	Less crowded on weekdays
Entree range:	$8–16
Payment:	VISA, MC, DC
Service rating:	★★★★
Friendliness rating:	★★★★
Parking:	Free valet
Bar:	Full service; sake; small selection of beers, including Korean and Japanese
Wine selection:	Limited; mostly domestic and French
Dress:	Casual; many in business attire
Disabled access:	Yes
Customers:	Businesspeople
Open:	Every day, 11:30 A.M.–11 P.M.

Atmosphere/setting: Upscale decor with tables separated by frosted glass partitions and half walls of natural wood allowing for privacy. Ancient Korean pottery and classical music add to the elegance.

House specialties: Goo jul pan (Korean hors d'oeuvres of nine various ingredients wrapped in a pancake); mo doom jun (combination of pan-fried meatballs, shrimp fillet, fish fillet, and green peppers stuffed with ground beef, all coated with egg and flour); bul go ki (thin slices of marinated, grilled tender beef); kal bi (grilled boneless short rib cubes); jun gol (sukiyaki); buh sut jun gol (variety of mushrooms, thin slices of beef, and other vegetables; available without meat); dol sot bi bim bap (grilled, marinated strips of beef and vegetables topped with fried egg, hot paste sauce); su jung gua (sweet ginger-flavored drink).

Other recommendations: Se wu tui gim (deep fried battered shrimp and vegetables); dak gui (lightly marinated, grilled boneless sliced chicken); yeon aw gui (fresh broiled salmon); chap chae (vermicelli noodles and vegetables sauteed in specially seasoned sauce); sik hee (sweet rice-flavored Korean punch); guail (seasonal fresh fruits).

Summary & comments: Each table has a built-in gas grill so diners can cook their own food. All main courses are served with kim chee (pickled and spiced cabbage), as well as side dishes such as spinach and spicy daikon radish. Opened in March 1996, 50 years after the Jang family founded their first restaurant in Seoul, the Chicago venue of Woo Lae Oak is the eighth restaurant opened by Jin Keun Jang. His intention is to introduce Korean culture through high-quality food.

Yoshi's Cafe

Zone 1   North Side
3257 Halsted Street
(773) 248-6160

New French/Japanese
★★★★
Inexpensive/Moderate

Quality 94   Value B

Reservations:	Recommended
When to go:	Weekend nights are busiest
Entree range:	$6–18
Payment:	All major credit cards except DC
Service rating:	★★★★½
Friendliness rating:	★★★★½
Parking:	Valet, $6
Bar:	Full service; bar/lounge adjacent to dining room
Wine selection:	About 80, mostly American and French; $25 a bottle and up; 15 by the glass, $4.50–6
Dress:	Casual
Disabled access:	Yes
Customers:	Diverse, locals, visitors, Europeans, businesspeople
Dinner:	Tuesday–Thursday, 5–10:30 P.M.; Friday and Saturday, 5–11 P.M.; Sunday, 5–9:30 P.M.

Atmosphere/setting: Very romantic, airy dining room; white linen table-cloths and lots of silver; recently expanded to seat about 130 patrons.

House specialties: Seafood emphasis, with some occasional unusual items, such as domestic fugu (blowfish—domestic fugu is not poisonous). Items change due to availability. Tuna tartare with guacamole and toast; Japanese sushi and sashimi; salad of tomato, green beans, and cucumber with basil-infused oil vinaigrette; buckwheat pasta (soba) with Oriental vegetables; veal scaloppine with mushroom Calvados sauce. Specials such as grilled half-duck, boned, with fresh persimmon sauce. Dark chocolate pecan cake; velvety crème brûlée of the day; refreshing lemon tart; apple tart.

Other recommendations: Grilled seared tuna with red wine–garlic-honey sauce; tofu steak with shrimp and shiitakes; grilled beef tenderloin with zinfandel sauce; veal with curry port sauce; rotisserie of chicken.

Summary & comments: Yoshi Katsumura and his wife, Nobuko, have operated their Franco-Japanese fine-dining gem on Halsted for more than a decade. In 1995, they renovated and enlarged the dining room; they also revamped the menu and lowered prices dramatically. Yoshi's French food with Asian influences is still mostly superb in his subtle style and beautifully presented. The professional service remains unwavering, but the feeling is more casual.

Honors/awards: DiRoNA Award since 1992; *Chicago Tribune* and *Chicago Sun-Times,* three stars; *Gourmet,* America's Favorite Chicago Restaurant, 1996.

YVETTE

Zone 3   Near North
1206 North State Parkway
(312) 280-1700

	New French
	★★★½
	Inexpensive/Moderate
	Quality 85 Value C

Reservations:	Recommended
When to go:	Any time; weekdays less busy
Entree range:	$12–20
Payment:	VISA, MC, AMEX, DC
Service rating:	★★★½
Friendliness rating:	★★★★½
Parking:	City lot across the street (discounted)
Bar:	Full service
Wine selection:	American, French, Italian, $24–150 a bottle
Dress:	Informal, tastefully casual, some dressy
Disabled access:	Yes
Customers:	Upscale, largely professionals, couples; all ages
Brunch:	Saturday and Sunday, 11 A.M.–3 P.M.
Dinner:	Monday–Thursday, 4:30 P.M.–midnight;
	Friday and Saturday, 4:30 P.M.–1 A.M.;
	Sunday, 4:30–11 P.M.; 365 days a year

Atmosphere/setting: Sophisticated cabaret ambiance in cafe area up front, set to accommodate musicians; dining room in back is comfortable. Chic Gold Coast bistro with an al fresco sidewalk cafe during the warmer months.

House specialties: Eggplant Mediterranean; shrimp Provençal with tomato concassé; French onion soup au gratin; seared bay scallops with spinach and roasted tomatoes over fusilli and mushrooms; roasted fillet of lamb with rosemary couscous, grilled ratatouille; salmon Yvette, smoked to order and served over angel hair with vegetables and beurre blanc; signature chocolate oblivion.

Other recommendations: Fruit and cheese plate with glass of port; a daily selection of house-made desserts, such as lemon tart with raspberry sauce.

Entertainment & amenities: Every night, live music (jazz, cabaret) and dancing; no cover.

Summary & comments: Unique French bistro with a cabaret atmosphere. Owner Bob Djahanguiri's hallmark with all his restaurants is designing them himself and blending live music with good French food and ambiance. In addition to this, he owns Yvette Wintergarden and Toulouse on the Park (see profiles). Yvette is a very romantic place for a special occasion or any time you're yearning for a taste of France.

Yvette Wintergarden

Zone 4   The Loop
311 South Wacker Drive
(312) 408-1242

New French
★★★½
Inexpensive/Moderate

Quality 85   Value C

Reservations:	Recommended
When to go:	Any time; before theater or opera
Entree range:	$10.50–16
Payment:	VISA, MC, AMEX, DC
Service rating:	★★★★
Friendliness rating:	★★★★
Parking:	Adjacent lot, $5 after 5 P.M.
Bar:	Full service
Wine selection:	French, American, Italian; $15–350 a bottle; many $20–35; half-bottles around $8; 6 by the glass
Dress:	Informal, casual; dressier in the evening
Disabled access:	Yes
Customers:	Upscale, professionals, all ages
Lunch:	Monday–Friday, 11:30 A.M.–2 P.M.
Dinner:	Monday–Thursday, 5–9 P.M.; Friday and Saturday, 5–10:30 P.M.; complimentary hors d'oeuvres, Monday–Friday, 5:30–7 P.M.

Atmosphere/setting: Spectacular tropical atrium entrance; dining room is intimate and dimly lit; comfortable seating in one dining room designed to view live performances.

House specialties: Menu changes seasonally. Lobster and artichoke fritters; baked escargot (snails with blue cheese, garlic butter, and tomato concassé); sautéed striped sea bass.

Other recommendations: Seasonal terrine of the day; salade Niçoise; grilled tenderloin of pork with three-mustard sauce; fresh desserts of the day (tarts, mousse).

Entertainment & amenities: Monday–Saturday, live music; dance floor.

Summary & comments: The latest menu deviates from French cuisine to include Italian items such as beef carpaccio and chicken pesto, and a Cajun blackened fillet of fresh tuna. Some items are the same as, and many similar to, those at Yvette. Owner Bob Djahanguiri has a talent for creating romantic French bistros, restaurants, and cabarets with appropriate live music. This place developed after Yvette. It's larger and a great downtown spot for before the theater or opera, or for relaxing with dinner and dancing. Private parties for 10–1,500.

Zum Deutschen Eck
(The German Corner)

Zone 1   North Side
2924 North Southport Avenue
(312) 525-8121

Continental/German
★★★½
Inexpensive/Moderate

Quality 88   Value C

Reservations:	Recommended for weekends
When to go:	Early evenings, 4 P.M. on weekends
Entree range:	$13.95–17.95
Payment:	VISA, MC, AMEX, CB, DC, D
Service rating:	★★★½
Friendliness rating:	★★★½
Parking:	Ample free parking; 3 lighted lots
Bar:	Full service; seats 40 people
Wine selection:	Fairly extensive; American and German
Dress:	Casual
Disabled access:	Yes, wheelchair accessible
Customers:	From longtime, loyal Europeans to new neighbors
Lunch/Dinner:	Monday–Thursday, 11:30 A.M.–10:30 P.M.; Friday, 11:30 A.M.–midnight; Saturday, noon–midnight; Sunday, noon–10 P.M.

Atmosphere/setting: Bavarian chalet style with colorful bar, Zum's Lounge; two charming dining rooms; three banquet rooms. Warm and welcoming; super-clean.

House specialties: Liver dumpling soup; German schlachtplatte (Thuringer, knackwurst, Kasseler Rippchen/smoked pork loin). Various schnitzels: Wiener Schnitzel, Dijon, rahmschnitzel (with bacon), schnitzel à la Jäger (in red wine sauce). Giant pork shank with sauerkraut; sauerbraten (long-marinated beef); hasenpfeffer (marinated rabbit).

Other recommendations: Scallop strudel; herring salad; fresh seafood; half roast duckling. Apple strudel with ice cream; German chocolate cake; cherries jubilee.

Entertainment & amenities: Live entertainment Friday, Saturday, and Sunday; Hans Rager Duo, including accordion and synthesizer; sing-alongs.

Summary & comments: This place started in a slower era as a neighborhood corner bar. Founded and owned by the Wirth family since 1956, Zum Deutschen Eck has been transformed into a successful restaurant/banquet complex, and the live entertainment with sing-alongs (song sheets are given to guests) make weekends quite lively. Entrees come with dumplings, noodles, or potato as well as choice of appetizer and salad. Dining here, especially weekend evenings, is a slice of Bavaria sans Lufthansa Airlines.